WALT WHITMAN

THINKER AND ARTIST

By

ARTHUR E. BRIGGS

GREENWOOD PRESS, PUBLISHERS
NEW YORK   1968

CONTENTS

Part I

Part II

1

HAVE THE WHITMANITES BETRAYED HIM?

❖ ❖ ❖ ❖ ❖ ❖

"I charge you therefore reject those who
would expound me."
"I am untranslatable."

❖ ❖ ❖ ❖ ❖ ❖

I Became a Whitmanite.

QUITE CASUAL EXPERIENCES OFTEN INFLUENCE ONE DEEPLY.
The event of a brief moment—perhaps unnoticed or barely noticed at the time—may be the beginning point which
ties up with other events and thus obtains meaning far beyond its momentary consequence. First acquaintance with
Whitman was such an event for me.

I accompanied a classmate to the college library. He
withdrew a copy of *Leaves of Grass,* turned the pages to
the poem, *I Sing the Body Electric,* and we read it together.
But as I read on to "man-balls, man-root" I felt the kind
of disgust as when salacious suggestions were made to me
from passages of the Bible. I had not then gone far from
my early religious teaching and its prejudices.

Fifteen years or more later I read *Leaves of Grass* with
understanding and appreciation that it meant somewhat to
me for the interpretation of my own experiences.

Nearly fifteen years after that I met Oscar Lovell Triggs,
and we organized and held a Whitman dinner at the old

1

Men's City Club in Los Angeles. I was Chairman of the
meeting.

Almost every year since then an Annual Whitman Fellowship Celebration has been held in the City of the Angels.
After Triggs passed away, a few years later, Dr. G. P. Wiksel
from Boston kept the annual meeting going. The last with
him was at his West Adams home on the lawn. We missed
the celebration the next May 31st. Since then we have met
every year.

I Began to Doubt

A dozen years in the Whitman Fellowship aroused no
special interest, at least I took no pains, to learn much
about Whitman's life and character. I understood his book,
that seemed enough. But about 1941 I was stimulated to
acquire some scholarly knowledge about him. It is little
more than I have been hearing for some time in our Whitman circle as the common coin of the Whitman tradition.

I had long felt a discrepancy between the book and
the tradition and the scholarship. At least I had to have
an independent knowledge of my own about Whitman's
character and ideas, to resolve the doubts. So I set myself to
a more accurate study, and of that I now give my general
reflections, leaving to the body of this book the specific
data and detail of my findings.

The Key to Whitman.

The key to Whitman is his conception of personality.
It explains him. It enunciates his principles. It is what he
propounded consciously as the heart of his teaching. In the
following essay I present his major themes, because they
bring out more clearly that personality I have shown there
to be subordinated to or merged in his conception of the
democratic-individual personality of the average man.

But personality, though closer to man than any other
abstraction, is significant only as it interprets man. In my

own thought I have felt the need to treat personality as fundamental to the science of man, not as if personality were like the unseen atoms or simpler elements which compose man, but as the evident qualities by which we analyze the very composite and subtle nature of man.

And if I have read something of my own thought into Whitman which he did not too clearly think himself, it may be justified in this way: The value of our predecessors now is what they have started in us. If we can see more what they saw at least dimly, recalling their original impressions and insight may be the means for revivifying that thought in us. We have then a more direct sense of the human reality of it. For in our efforts at comprehensiveness and refinement of thought, we tend to become more and more abstract, and at length we may have lost quite the concrete essence of the thing.

Whitman's Poetic Expression of Philosophy.

Because poetry served just that function of concreteness for him, it was the genius of the man by his method and form of expression to have saved himself from the abstractions whch should clarify but more often becloud thinking, because they have departed so far from immediate experience. It should be the art of the poet to humanize. It should be, but often the poet too becomes lost in his symbols and is guilty as any of extreme abstractionism. Whitman succeeded better than most in any field of expression or art by keeping the larger reflections of men close to actual experience.

Some have denied him philosophic depth because of that. Rather I regard his achievement as unusually provocative of those themes which we deem philosophic. That he did not treat them in the way of systematic discussion of philosophic matters, but used the insight and medium of poetry, may start the professional philosopher's jealousy of others who invade his preserves. He may therefore deny

Whitman recognition as a philosopher. However, those philosophers who refuse to acquaint themselves with what is called literature probably betray just that abstractionism which taking total possession of them has given philosophers not without cause the reputation of being impractical persons. For it is preeminently in literature that writing has come nearest to the expression of immediate human experience. The popularity of the novel is mostly due to that fact.

But poetry is the art which may be the philosopher's nearest approach to concrete human expression of his peculiar themes. The poet's art heightens humanness by contacting those rarer experiences of the spiritual life of man which intrigue the philosopher. But it is a dangerous vocation for either poet or philosopher. In the intoxication of that experience one easily becomes the mystic or abstractionist.

Whitman's Involvment in the Cults.

I have endeavored to point out Whitman's triumph over that tendency which some of his would-be interpreters have attempted to involve him in. Therefore, I have been led to the task of redeeming or rescuing him from his mistaken biographers who may, nevertheless, have aided considerably in giving him vogue, but too often have been guilty of identifying him with their own special aberrations in some cult or other from which he really strove to free himself.

Whitman the religious mystic, of the cult of free love, of communistic addiction to comradeship, as a belated and bewildered democrat, of being the vagarious corrupter of youth who want to be poets—these are reputations from which Whitman has suffered, but which it must also be admitted, if we are to understand Whitman, something in him gave rise to. It is not enough therefore to refute the imputations of doctrines to Whitman, we must endeavor to ascertain his relations to them. This may not be the only way to expound his intrinsic humanism, but does aid greatly in appreciating it.

If my procedure does not overcome the unmerciful consideration of critics whom I challenge for the revision of their untoward opinions or to convict of their errors, yet I hope more for the reinvigoration of the Whitman Fellowship and to guide and inspire the many readers of Whitman who have never been indoctrinated in any of the Whitman cults.

At the same time it would be an injustice not to feel some reverence for the cultists who were responsible for recognition of Whitman when the orthodox would have obliterated him. But they have lived their day and must now retire before the truer conception of Whitman which their narrower fanatical viewponts denied them.

My Purposes.

Analysis of Whitman's ideas, which is part I of this book, may be aided by a preliminary consideration of the principal groups which comprise the Whitman Fellowship and probably to a considerable extent the number of his readers. The enumeration which follows is not intended to be exhaustive but roughly indicative of the reasons why interest in Whitman has been maintained and kept going.

We seek here to fill a void which we regard as existing despite the many works about Whitman. There are numerous biographers, and the publication of Canby's Whitman, which was published after the greater part of this study was made, provides a fairly satisfactory biography and criticism of the narratives told about Whitman. I seek to give a more intimate account of what may be called the Whitman Movement, of which the Whitman cults are only part. Not a history of the Whitman cults. Nor a story

of the success of Whitman; that has often been done. This
is not at all a narrative. It is an interpretation which takes
account of the contrariety of views about Whitman which
have had shape in the Whitman cults. It is far more important to get at the heart of Whitman than to thread the
vagaries of opinions about him. But the cults provide me
with starting points to be left soon behind in arrival at
Whitman's major conceptions which, as he protested, are
not to be confined by any cult or school.

Of course I have my own peculiar reasons for undertaking this study. I may be accused of forming another
cult, the ethical humanist cult of Whitman. But if so,
it is because I am convinced that personal humanism is
the best interpretation of Whitman. By his own statement Whitman's key word and idea is Personality. Personality is the great synthesis of the many-sidedness of his
character. Therefore I may be relieved of the charge of particularism by the fact that under the concept of personality
Whitman's humanism embraced so inclusive an assembly
of people as to give some encouragement to the several
particularisms that claim him as their own.

His Cultist Biographers.

Every great man who cares about his reputation with
posterity has reason to worry about his biographers. Hern-
don related that Lincoln was apprehensive about them.
For as he rated biographies they are mainly lies, tending
especially to glorify their subjects. Today the opposite
tendency is in vogue, and for more than a generation we
have had a flood of debunking biographies.

Whitman was not only anxious about his biographers.
He chose them. And was very fortunate at least in one of
his choices—John Burroughs. Whitman was in his way and
with his means as sedulous as the Pharaohs of Egypt to erect
a monument to his memory. He used a large part of his

small capital from savings in his later years to build a mausoleum for himself and at his death it was ready for his interment.

He labored as diligently to establish a Whitman legend. He craved and cultivated fame with as persistent activity as did ever any man. He seemed in his avidness for celebrity to have had his eye continually upon his lasting reputation. In Horace Traubel he found a lesser Boswell.

Whitman himself was responsible for the several Whitmanite cults which have such variant characters as in the singularities of them to give us in each a different Whitman. Therefore the Whitman factions tend to divide in sects such as characterize the Christian and Mohammedan religions. To understand and to discover the true Whitman it is as necessary to study these several offshoots of the Whitman tradition as it is to rediscover Socrates in the schools of Greek philosophy which sprang from him.

That is what I undertake briefly to do in this review of Whitman's biographers and the Whitman cults. I make a tentative classification of them. I name them: the Uranians, Cosmotheticians, Evolutionists, Socialists, and Humanists. That is quite an array. And I think one should feel astonishment that such variant and even opposite points of view should find themselves akin in the Whitman Fellowship.

It is necessary to understand the reasons for so wide and variant an interest in Whitman as is thus represented if we wish to understand Whitman himself or his work. It is also necessary to redeem Whitman from his friends in order to save him as he wished to be saved for the larger following to which he is entitled. We cannot escape the problem of interpreting Whitman. He knew the peril to himself of interpretation and biography, and in a notable poem protested against this being done to him. But no man who belongs to the ages can avoid it.

But also, if Whitman belongs to a wider circle than even the broad Whitman Fellowship, both they and his biographers must be taken into account.

The Uranians.

First, among the Whitmanites the Uranians are notable. This is the strangest and least reputable of the Whitman sects. Usually one will not readily discover from any of these sects a clear conception of its special traits, and I hope to be pardoned if I bring into light the secretive characteristics of each. In the case of the Uranians there is a complex and inconsistent origin of the cult and of its members. It is an attempt to fasten to some specific idea and practice the sex philosophy of Whitman.

Recently Malcolm Cowley in the New York Times and New Republic attempted to discover the clue to Whitman's character and writings as what in plainer language than his would be called homosexuality. In Whitman's lifetime this reputation was well started, and Whitman himself tried to stop or thwart it. One of his worst tormentors, John Addington Symonds, tried to force a confession from him, and Whitman made the matter worse near the end of his life by writing Symonds a letter in which he boasted he had six children.

It is on the basis of that letter that he may be claimed by one variety of Uranians. According to the Greek myth Uranus, the highest god of the sky, hated and cast off his children. Also that singular genius, Jean Jacques Rousseau, in his Confessions described himself as an upright citizen after Plato's ideal by virtue of having caused each of his children at birth to be taken to the foundling's home, thus losing their parental identity. He probably lied in that confession. But in these characters of the mythological Uranus, Rousseau, and the supposititious unfatherliness of Whitman, this Uranian cult can claim a distinguished ancestry for itself. In one member of our Los Angeles Fellowship I discern such an Uranian. Marriage he disdained and in his rather unconventional relationship with one woman he abandoned her and her child; in his next illicit relationship he insisted upon abortion, with the self-righteous declaration he would raise no children for "cannon fodder."

Whitman's biographers give some suspicious circumstances in his friendships with men which might, if we had more positive data, also mark him as a homosexual. In his *Song of Myself* there is a passage notably suggestive. Also in the poem, *Once I Passed,* upon which a New Orleans woman of mystery is projected by such romancers as Frances Winwar and Babette Deutsch, the significant fact is that as originally written it was a man instead of a woman. Possibly Whitman changed the sex character of that poem to get rid of its homosexual implications.

Whitman deliberately in the re-editing of his poems tried to portray the cosmic Whitman, not as any particular sexualite but as universal in his sexuality. An experience of my own illustrates the point. Quite a number of years ago I had correspondence with a woman in Alaska which was begun by her. She reminded me of meeting her at our annual celebration, which I did not recall. But she wrote in such a sprightly and interesting manner that I enjoyed the correspondence while it lasted. It was evident that she was seeking to intrigue me into romantic expressions which I carefully avoided. But at length she wearied of the effort and frankly expressed herself that she suspected me of being the universal type of lover that Whitman was, while she on the contrary desired particularization of love. Now my realistic sense could hardly admit of particularizing the sex relation with a woman in Alaska while I remained in Los Angeles. However, I once heard Upton Sinclair suggest that explicit sex intercourse could be had by telepathy although the participants were then separated from each other by distance half way around the world. One begins to perceive what sexual varietism becomes speculatively possible in a Whitman Fellowship.

But I have not yet finished with the speculations upon the subject of Whitman's sexuality. I think the best of the lot of extremists is probably represented by Edward Carpenter. The first notable recognition of Whitman came from the English, and Carpenter was one of that company who made a pilgrimage to America to visit Whitman. Carpenter in his *Love Coming of Age* and *The Intermediate Sex* and other books proclaimed the existence of a third sex which is neither man nor woman and to which he argued the greatest geniuses of mankind belong. Of course Carpenter included Whitman in that noble company.

Men or women Whitman seemed to treat them all alike excepting for the close fellowship he had with a few men, most of whom were surely not homosexuals. There is no definite proof that any of them were. Walt's brother George said he never knew of Walt having paid any attention to any woman. Whitman may have been too old and infirm to be swayed by the ardent advances of Anne Gilchrist who seems to have been the only woman who ever nearly intrigued him.

The bulk and stature of Whitman gave him a manly appearance and he liked that pose and made much of it. This is Cowley's Whitman II. But he was unique in his freedom of comradeship. He would hold hands and kiss men as well as women and children, quite contradictory of Cowley who says that this Whitman II "never appeared in public life."

The doctrines of Whitman about sex do not justify claiming him for only one mode of sexual relationship. Whitman believed in the equality of men and women and in free companionship between them. His is the very opposite of the primitive world and tradition of ages long which separated men and women by nearly impassable barriers of social division and taboo. These were abhorred by Whitman and he hated all pruderies and false conventions which interfere with the most intimate comradeship of men and women. This was the literary and personal Whitman known by Burroughs and Eldridge who knew him best. This is not Cowley's "secret" Whitman nor even Carpenter's noble conception, for neither expresses Whitman's ideal of comradeship. Havelock Ellis' authority should not be questioned:

> "However important inversion may be as a psychological key to Whitman's personality, it plays but a small part in Whitman's work, and for many who care for that work a negligible part."

The Evolutionists.

The evolutionism of Whitman got off to a better start because it had the best of interpreters and biographers in John Burroughs. Burroughs was a naturalist who lived close to nature, and that was the reason why he was readier to accept the kind of evolutionism Whitman believed in. For Whitman was not a mid-19th century evolutionist. He was not a materialist. His type of evolution was rather that of Goethe at the beginning of the century. It was human evolutionism. Burroughs sensed that and described it well. He aided undoubtedly a better Whitman tradition. But with most people names are far more important than ideas, and so by reason of identifying Whitman with the current evolutionism there is a considerable following of materialists in the Whitman Fellowship.

Burroughs was Whitman's most trusted biographer. The Burroughs biography indeed was in considerable part written by Whitman. Burroughs' better prose style is dominant in that biography and interpretation. To make more evident the difference between the Whitman-Burroughs evolutionism and the stock 19th century materialist evolutionism, we should add a further explanation. Whitman's evolution was humanist as the other was not. Most of the great 19th Century evolutionists took as much pleasure in underrating man as did the theologians whom they opposed. The materialists and the theologians had in common the minimizing of man. The materialists liked to show by their astronomic learning what an infinitesimal speck in the universe is man and of how little account he is in the scheme of things. On the other hand Whitman was extremely anthropomorphic. I, "Walt Whitman, a kosmos," he boldly announced.

The distinguished evolutionists of today hold views similar to Whitman's. For instance, Julian S. Huxley, the grandson of Thomas H. Huxley and one of the most outstanding biologists of our time, with more knowledge than had Burroughs and Whitman of Nature's ways and the terrestrial plan, says that man is unique and stands alone as the one living creature who has not run into a dead end of evolution but has it within him, as Whitman also believed, to go on in development. Man is himself a creator who improves on Nature's plan, and this scientific view supports Whitman's assertions about man which seemed so absurd to his contemporaries.

The Cosmotheticians.

Another phase of Whitman's viewpoints gave rise to the cosmotheticians. Among them was one of the authorized contemporary biographers of Whitman, Dr. Richard M. Bucke of Canada, a very capable and successful M.D. who treated psychopathological ailments. He is responsible for the phrase, "cosmic consciousness." The late Dr. G. P. Wiksel, a dentist of Los Angeles, was a firm believer in this cult. The tolerance of the Fellowship is superbly shown in the good humored way in which all listen to the aberrations of their fellow Whitmanites. Dr. Wiksel in his leadership never once suppressed his spiritualism and metaphysical notions. There he propagandized Oahpse as pertinaciously as he did Whitmanism.

However, there was in Whitman a tendency which gives some color to that occultism, especially if one fails to understand what Whitman meant by "a kosmos". Whitman was not intentionally cryptic or obscure. Anything is obscure to one who does not understand the language, who comes with preconceived notions or prejudices which pervert the meaning of the author.

Probably Whitman was considerably influenced by Dr. Bucke, not in the beginning, for Whitman was using the term "kosmos" long before he came in contact with Bucke. It was Bucke who seized upon the term and read a different meaning from Whitman's into it. Knowing that Whitman did not agree with his meaning, he charged that Whitman had departed from the true doctrine or had lost the faculty in his later life. But Whitman was troubled by mental ills which afflicted some members of his family and placed great confidence in Dr. Bucke's understanding of them.

My attention to Whitman's own case started in a conversation with Dr. Wiksel. I was looking with him at his collection of photographs of Whitman, and I remarked at one, "The man looks there like a person somewhat unbalanced in mind." He replied knowingly, "Quite so." And I believe there is quite a bit of evidence that Whitman cracked up some time soon after the New Orleans fiasco. The photograph I mention is the daguerreotype of 1854. My belief is that the *Leaves of Grass* is the product of getting hold of himself—getting entirely realistic—coming to himself—whole for the first time in his life up to then. That is, instead of going up in the air with the cosmotheticans he got down to earth with himself.

Although he presented the cosmic Walt Whitman in his poems of 1855, it was not until much later that his most spiritual qualities were developed. It was not until he was writing what Masters calls the greatest poems of his career, the *Passage to India* and *Chanting the Square Deific*. *Night on the Prairies* did precede his Civil War experiences. Also in the poem seeing the Christ in the face of the dead soldier lad was that tendency so characteristic of his latest poems. That later period of deepening religious consciousness is beyond the comprehension of most of the Uranians and evolutionists. There is mystic idealism in his more mature poems which gives his thought a depth and earnestness only nascent in the 1855 edition. I do not agree with those who think that Whitman's powers waned but rather that they increased after the Civil War period and that he continued to write masterful poetry till almost the very end of his life, though greatly diminished in quantity.

Nor do I agree with the interpreters who think that Whitman became an Hegelian and transliterated Hegel into his American rhapsody. There is nothing Hegelian in Whitman, despite his profession to that effect. Nor was Whitman "the last of the Transcendentalists". New England Transcendentalism flourished with Emerson and Alcott who understood little of what Kant and his German successors taught. And Whitman understood still less.

To have appreciation of Whitman's cosmic consciousness rather than Bucke's one must keep in mind Whitman's dominant humanism. It is not something transcending man which is Walt Whitman's kosmos; it is the immanent, indwelling cosmos of "I, Walt Whitman", which he celebrates. But before considering Whitman's humanism we should mention another group of persons who attach themselves to the Whitman Fellowship.

The Socialists.

This other group we may designate in the large as the Socialists. I include in them the Communists, however offensive this may be to both of those sectarians. For they are at the bottom and philosophically of the same general temper and opinions; as all Christians of whatever sect and however violently they disagree with each other have yet something in common, so do these.

What attaches the Socialists to the Whitman company? It was at the beginning chiefly Traubel, the Boswell of Whitman. As Canby suggests, Traubel desired to make Whitman appear a Socialist like himself. State Socialists and Bolsheviks have just as much right to appropriate Whitman as they have to represent themselves as liberals and democrats.

The Socialist is one who recognizes only society—the individual is merged in society. As the totalitarians express it, society is superior to the individual and he must always yield to it. That is not what Whitman believed and taught. He carefully distinguished the individual and the mass, the man from democracy. He saw clearly as the Socialists do not see how society may smother the man. On the other hand, he saw just as clearly, as extreme individualists and anarchists and pure idealists do not see, that men must stand together in a universal comradeship and that institutions matter and that government is necessary.

Whitman's Humanism:

But it is in Whitman's personalistic humanism that one will find the synthetic principle which harmonizes sex, science, religion, and government without sacrifice of man or men. And again one has to distinguish Whitman's personalism and humanism from the current varieties. For now that humanism has become popular there are as many different kinds of it as there are philosophies. Traditionalism rediscovers medieval, 16th century Renaissance, 18th century romantic, and 19th century evolutionist types of humanism and attempts to revive them as offset to the more genuine type of today which has better claim to scientific and uptodate philosophy than the older sorts.

Whitman took neither the metaphysics of materialism nor that of absolute idealism as his pattern for humanism, both of which subordinate man to suppositional forces above him—God, Nature, or Society. Whitman asserted the divinity of man as free from dependence upon God as from slavery of man to man. Against naturalistic determinism with its enslavement of the human spirit he asserted man's creative freedom. His humanism projected the self of man into the external world to make it subject to man's will. Whitman's humanism in contrast with the traditional varieties may be termed creative humanism, for it has faith in the special creative power of man.

But the term by which Whitman preferred his philosophy to be known was Personalism. After I developed my own theory of personality I discovered that most of its content had already been declared by Whitman. He understood personality in its true historical derivation. The stage in ancient times had discovered personality, the dramatis personae. The characters which come and go on the stage of life, the characters that change in each of us with the change of situation and circumstance, the characters that communicate us to our fellowmen. These representations of our inner selves reveal us to others at the same time that they form and expand our beings. Every man is in a sense the sum of his persons. He grows to maturity as his development of personality in its many facets takes hold of the fundamental substance of him and shapes it in the various manifestations which give specificity and character to him.

Whitman his Own Biographer.

Although essaying in a special sense to be another biographer of Whitman, instead of taking the course of previous biographies which turn Whitman aside to some particularistic form which he would have repudiated, I will take a safer course which Whitman could hardly have refuted, namely, of representing him in his own interpretation. I have studied the incidents of his life and tried to relate them to some phase of his poetry. I have analyzed the subject matter of his poems and brought together his expressions on the topics which according to his own statements he deemed vital. By that partially autobiographic method I let Whitman's thought speak for itself.

Thus, instead of denoting him as an Uranian, homosexual, or sexual pervert of any kind, I let him speak for himself. I follow his own effort to avoid sexual particularism and to become inclusive of all sex desires and tendencies which enhance comradeship and goodwill between the sexes and between man and man.

Instead of joining with the materialistic evolutionists I take Whitman's humanistic evolutionism which, in accord also with recent biology, discovers the unique significance of man in the evolutional scheme. In a better sense than Bergson's this is creative evolution. Man is the supreme creator, so far as we may know, in the universe. At least in that part of it known to us.

Instead of cosmic consciousness of the metaphysical variety I take Whitman's conception of the human cosmos. For all the universe may be reflected in man's consciousness of it as man projects himself into that universe perceived by him and draws it into himself. This gives man mastery in the universe in the measure that he gains control over it. Man's effort is to free himself from subservience to any forces beyond or over him.

As Whitman is distinguished from the orthodox cosmotheticans, whom he thought of as reducing him to nothing, so even more did he reject all varieties of totalitarianism, socialist and communist. He was thoroughly an American democrat of the Jefferson-Lincoln stamp, and in that respect close to Thoreau and Emerson.

In the chapters which follow I try to remain faithful
to Whitman's own version of his thought and philosophy.
There we will observe and criticize attempts to designate
him a pantheist, panpsychist, or to ally him with Hindu
passivism, New England transcendentalism, German idealism, Borden P. Bowne's personalism, as well as further
consideration of the Whitmanite cults we have already
mentioned.

Interpretation Rather than Biography Needed.

But this study is an interpretation and not a biography.
Probably the biographies are as nearly adequate as at this
time are needful for our purpose. For those who want a
very brief history of Whitman in the next chapter we
will sketch the main incidents of his life.

Those who want a sane and generally reliable biography
may find it in Canby's Whitman. It is not fanciful as
most of his biographies are. It carries no special theory
about Whitman. It does not, like Dr. Bucke, Professor
Allen, and some others try to metaphysicize him. It has
the good sense and judgment that characterize Burroughs'
writings. It relies chiefly on original sources about Whitman. It discards and gives reasons for rejecting the myths
about Whitman. It does not prettify him. It is compara-
tively free from romancing. It is not a philosophical interpretation of Whitman or anything more than a biography. Not even for an estimate of Whitman's literary
art does it suffice, although its author is a distinguished
literary critic. It does not pretend to be nor is it a profound book.

Whitman did not write a systematic interpretation of
himself as a personality which he professed to have as a
main objective, or of his book, or of his philosophy. But
he did speak a doctrine, and if that is worth while there
must be interpreters and systematizers of that doctrine.

Whitman's Aversion Must be Disregarded.

However much we may dislike as Whitman disliked them, every prophet is in need of expounders. Furthermore, they check each other off, and even in or because of the multiplicity of them comes clarity.

Whitman wanted himself inconsistently to live solely in his book. Nevertheless, he prompted biographies and interpretations, wholly or partially written by himself. If we respected his expressed feelings in the matter, no new biography and no further interpretation would be written of him. But in that case he would be a dated and neglected Whitman.

It has been the habit of his friendly biographers and critics to absolve themselves of the usual function of the critic, assuming that Whitman is beyond analysis, and they take his repugnance to biographical interpretation and his insistence that not even he could interpret himself, so why should any one else attempt to do so, as authority that it couldn't be done. By that escape they make a mist of Whitman.

He then becomes like Aristotle's God, so big that there is nothing left for him to be but a belly-gazing Buddha. Thus they abandon him to his detractors. But there is some justification for Whitman's attitude: Disciples often choose the worst part of their master for emulation and praise. They come to that naturally enough. Because the point of attack is the weakest side of a man. In their zeal to defend him they try to bolster up his weaknesses. In that way comes perversion of doctrine.

But Whitman's popularity has carried him beyond the need or limitations of discipleship. The price of popularity, however, is also publicity and reportorial indelicacy concerning the affairs of private life. His reputation is suffering from that now.

I believe in respecting him by study, if not wholly within the bounds of his books, at least always near to them. Therefore I think it more excusable to try to interpret him than to recount the incidents of his personal life. Yet such an interpretation is a kind of biography, but of his soul, his self, rather than of external matters concerning him.

I present him as a personality in the light of his book. That means emphasis upon his ideas and his art. It is the life of a man in his contributions to mankind. Of some men that is the better part of them. It is so of Whitman. He tried to live for others in and through himself.*

---

* Schyberg's Whitman has been published in translation since the writing of this book.

His principal experiment is an attempt to show the development of Whitman's character and artistry through the progressive editions of *Leaves of Grass*. But his judgment that the later revisions and additions did improve the work, instead of sustaining his own, rather tends to support my view that the maturest Whitman, the completed book, is the truer basis for estimating Whitman's thought and art.

As biographer Schyberg is less judicious than Canby. As interpreter of Whitman, my criticism of Allen's Handbook, which borrowed its viewpoint and conclusions mainly from Schyberg, may stand to refute the latter. Allen's literary criticism is more penetrating and informative. Schyberg's comparison with world literatures suffers from misunderstanding of Whitman.

2

IS THE BOOK THE MAN HIMSELF?

✧ ✧ ✧ ✧ ✧ ✧

"This is no book, who touches this touches
a man."

✧ ✧ ✧ ✧ ✧ ✧

A Biographical Note.

HOW MUCH OF WHITMAN'S BOOKS WAS HIMSELF? ONLY
his ideal self was intentionally inscribed there. Deliberately he tried to exclude from his writing much that
we know was in Whitman himself. That effort explains
many of the peculiarities of his character. It explains why
he was so cautious about interpretations of his books and
of himself.

A man who writes his own biography and builds his
own mausoleum cannot be indifferent to fame. It seemed
to be the natural thing for Walt Whitman, a kosmos, to do,
and that he did. Yet as we have remarked he warned
his readers against his biographers.

Although that may cause any biography of him to stand
suspect, nevertheless people want to know about a man
who is worthy to be read or talked about for his ideas
or art. It is reasonable to believe that no book is wholly
unrelated to its author. This brief biographical note may
therefore be an appropriate preface to the following chapters which explore his ideas and his art.

21

However, as we point out, Whitman's writings are not dependent upon his personal characteristics for explanation of their form or content. It is personality in general and most inclusively which he aimed at as the explanatory element of his work.

If the reader is not curious about Whitman's own personality, he can neglect any biography of him. Most of them are misleading. Yet one interested enough in Whitman to thumb over any competent biography of him may glean a few important facts. Facts more significant than those which Cowley mistakenly enumerates as the "three Whitmans existing as separate persons." Whitman combined as does every intelligent mature man or woman many distinct personalities which were not split, separate or divided in him, after he came to himself.

Whitman's familial personality (Cowley's Whitman I), contrary to Cowley, now and again appears in Leaves of Grass, notably in reference to his mother and his defective brother.

His mother was quite a personable woman, not ill mated to the cross-grained nature of her husband. Whitman's adoration was for his mother. He grew up living at home. In his early manhood he remained at home. But he was different from his brothers and sisters. He seemed a lazy pretentious fellow in comparison with them. Two of his brothers amounted to something. Two were mentally defective. Both his sisters got married and lived like folks. One of them was odd. But Walt too was odd.

He took to writing and, early apprenticed to a printer, got into the newspaper business. He had fitful editorial experience for some years. He never remained long at a place. Perhaps there was some instability in him.

But his radical views probably played a more considerable part in his shiftings and short-lived editorial connections. He was a Democrat who hated slavery. In pre-

Civil War days that made him an inconvenient party man, and publishers got skittish of him.

The climax came in his unfortunate journey South to take an editorial position on a New Orleans paper. That relationship was brief. Whether it caused or marked an aberration in the man, he was never afterwards the same. His habits soon changed. Before he had been somewhat of a dandified fellow. Thereafter for a time he followed the occupation and wore the habit of a workman. For a few years he associated closely with his father in the carpenter's or house-building trade.

Undoubtedly, near the beginning of that altered period he suffered some mental disturbance. And his changed style and content of writing evidenced its inspiration in the healing of his mental self. He found himself in the making of a new art and a new way of thinking.

In 1855 he published the first edition of his new type of poems. It got him a temporary recognition from Emerson, who seemed later to withdraw somewhat the heartiness of the first approval. Thoreau acclaimed him. But the poems were not a success.

The Civil War changed his poetic interest. It was another crisis in his life. He was then about forty years old. His brother George, a Union army officer, was wounded. That may have been the occasion for a newly aroused interest, which was in the soldiers rather than in the war. He became a kind of volunteer nurse, went carrying flowers and fruit to the men in the hospitals, wrote letters for them, and did little helpful and solacing acts of kindness to those unfortunate victims of the war. He did that actively for about two years. And then he broke. Whether from emotional strain or his tireless labors is uncertain.

Recovering he got into government service at Washington as a minor clerk. Was fired by a prudish department head who discovered and was shocked by the sexual tenor of Whitman's poems. His friends obtained for him another position in the Department of Justice, where in a sinecure he continued to work undistinguishedly for several years.

There John Burroughs met him and became his outstanding disciple, biographer, and interpreter. His fame was spreading, but he was not a popular poet or writer. Englishmen began to take notice of him and formed a Whitman cult.

And then in his middle 50's he suffered a paralytic stroke. Never again was he a well man, and seemed old and steadily aging after that.

In his youth and middle age he was robust and handsome, tall and well developed. As he grew old the air of unique distinction always in him increased, even to his latest years of feebleness. He was photogenic.

It is generally assumed that the peculiar and special character of his writing reached its zenith in the earlier editions of his work. That is Cowley's assumption about Whitman III, "the real poet." But he continued writing new poems to the very end and making continual revisions of the earlier poems up at least to the time of his partial paralysis. There was a gradual deepening of spiritual thought and insight to his latest years. The year 1881 may be taken as the ripened period of his life. It was after that when Traubel began recording the conversations with him. The Whitman cult was then well established.

A decade after Whitman's death, at the beginning of the 20th century, a new kind of poet developed in America who gave acknowledgment to Whitman as inspiration and leader. His fame was fixed. More recently it has received much additional literary expression, with inevitable debunking, as well as romanticizing.

The biographer may be guided by four turning points in Whitman's life: The library, printing office, and newspaper gave stimulus and provided direction for the youth and education in authorship. Then failure, wandering, relapse, and the resurgence of his spirit discovered the genius of the man, and the outburst of his *Song of Myself* is the evidence of the healing of a spirit that betokened for him a message of deliverance for the downcast and depressed of mankind. Again disappointment, the conflict of emotions that young men feel at the beat of the drums for war, and in himself a deeper revolution against war, were finally resolved in the clear duty of service to the wounded and dying from the battlefields, and that found vent in the most emotional and beautiful of his poems. Later, paralysis, temporary despair, and some permanent disability checked his productivity and in part prevented further great original productions, but deepened his philosophical understanding and enabled him to estimate his own work with profounder insight than has been given to any of his interpreters.

The Mysterious Origin of Leaves of Grass

The origin of Leaves of Grass is hidden in a biographical mist. My own theory is not very substantially supported by biographical data in the nature of confessions from the only authentic source, Whitman himself, who was notoriously unreliable in such matters. I prefer, because it seems to me more verifiable, to resort to psychological interpretation, based on the carpenter-posed portrait and his emotional experiences delined in the earlier poems of *Leaves of Grass*. Every one agrees that between his newspaper editorship and the first publication of *Leaves of Grass* great changes had taken place in him. I conclude he was in that interval a somewhat disordered personality trying to find himself and finally succeeding.

A more complete theory is merely an extension of the one just stated. For *Leaves of Grass* is not the result of a single crisis but of successive crises, at least four. The first one I have referred to. The second came about 1860 as evidenced in the poems then entitled *Calamus,* from which in later editions he deleted some of the most personal ones. Later I will analyze this series, but may now remark that as originally published they express more suffering than any other of his poems. A twofold cause may be assigned, disappointment at the slack reception of his work and distress from the oncoming War. His Civil War experiences ripened him but also produced great perturbations of spirit and physical illness, although again he attained spiritual equilibrium and understanding from giving himself whole-heartedly to the relief of the soldiers on the battlefield and in the hospitals. That experience produced *Drum Taps* and the Lincoln threnody, *When Lilacs Last in the Dooryard Bloom'd.* The fourth great crisis in his life was the paralysis in 1873. That did not end his editorial work on *Leaves of Grass* nor his productiveness, but it did probably affect in some considerable degree that accomplishment of the undertaking he had long projected as indicated in the footnote to the Preface of 1876, beginning "Passage to India—", etc. But out of that fourth crisis he came with sobered sense and greater insight. Remarkably at the very end of his life he gathered up and added to and published the materials which in 1876 he despaired of doing.

The several editions of *Leaves of Grass* underwent considerable changes at his hands, not only from re-editing and revisions, but also from important additions which refute the notion of those who think that Whitman's first great effusion of poetic energy exhausted his genius.

I do not try in the analysis of his thought and my effort to give a systematic interpretation of it to distinguish these levels of his development. They are not so important for my purpose. They belong rather to that refinement of scholarship which is more concerned with details than with the general effect of a work of art. There can be criticism, and justly, of any treatment which supposes that from the start of *Leaves of Grass* Whitman had a clear conception of what it finally became. Indeed, the theory that is at the base of the present interpretation rests on Whitman's view of his work after it had been virtually finished which probably he did not have clearly in mind at the beginning of it. Yet its substance was in the first edition.

Whitman's Character and His Book

Any close scrutiny of Whitman's own character discloses that what he was and what he wrote are not wholly synonymous. And that is not at all strange. Who ever lives altogether up to his ideals? Such a problem introduces the questions of selves, of the contradictory persons borne within every man's character. In *The Autocrat of the Breakfast Table* Oliver Wendell Holmes commented on the many Johns. There are many Whitman's, more than Cowley's three, as many and more than there are different cults of Whitman.

I shall have to decimate many of the reputed Whitmans for the sake of Whitman's masterpiece, in order to make its message unequivocal. I must also point out certain contradictions in the varying personalities of Whitman which give some excuse for the varying and contradictory interpretations of him. In that way we discover what is lasting and valuable in his work and exemplary in his character. There is much in his biographers, critics and adapters, read by them into him, which is not justified by any careful study of his works, and which insight to his character leads us to believe he himself repudiated, although in his conduct he excluded much that he professed in his writings to accept.

He was not an entirely sincere and candid man. Probably the ablest and shrewdest men are not. Until we understand better than wont the contrasts of public and private demands on character we cannot well judge sincerity. It is notably a necessary fact as humorously depicted in the movie drama entitled *Nothing But The Truth,* that reticences and even white lies are not only tolerated but compelled by the conventions of peaceful living. Dr. Richard C. Cabot's rigorous book on *Honesty,* truth telling, should be reflected upon by anyone who accepts his basic premise that a lie is never justified. His definitions show that the statement is made with a quite considerable number of qualifications to the principle.

In the first place, what is a lie? According to Dr. Cabot, only hurtful lies can practically and sensibly be held reprehensible. Else artistic imagination, even poetry itself, would become impossible. We cannot carry on social intercourse peaceably and happily without tact, strategy, polite amenities, which have somewhat of prevarication in them. Even Dr. Cabot gives latitude for campaign lies of politicians and generally for oratorical exaggerations.

What Masters calls Whitman's "whoppers," his deceptions, the frequent absence of candor in him, his tendency to exaggerate, to mislead at times even his closest friends —were never egregious faults in him. Whitman sometimes lied when the truth would have been better. He would have saved embarrassments to his biographers, the authorized and accepted ones, whose reputations have unfortunately suffered because they believed him too implicitly. Had he been more truthful he would have prevented much of the misrepresentation of his thought and work by those not so friendly to him. The falseness of the Whitman "pose" is too easily proven without justifying the misrepresentations of it in Esther Shephard's book. Probably also we would be saved the falsehoods of the romancers which put Whitman in an absurd position, if some at least of their fancies had not Whitman's lies to back them up.

Why do we make so much of this matter? Only because his ideas are important. We hold that they are the greatest interpretation we have of American life and ideals, of democracy, of ethical relations between human beings. That is why we are concerned with the character of the man. Great men are exemplars. They bring to us new modes of conduct. They live for posterity because of some break with tradition for which they are responsible. Tradition at first fights and tries to suppress them as it did to Whitman. Failing in that, tradition falsely pretends to accept them and by interpretation it tries to tone them down or adulterate their thoughts and acts with its poisonous and corrupting debris. And this it is now doing to Whitman.

The Good and Bad of the Whitman Cults

The Whitman cults which brought Whitman to recognition are now detrimental by providing groundwork for the corrupting orthodoxies which are attempting to take Whitman over into themselves.

Should I then be for abolishing the Whitman cults? Not at all. Whitman said he wished no club or sect or school founded and named after him. But I do not object to the Whitman Fellowship. I seek to promote and continue it. It is good for the cultists. It does tend to mitigate the dogmatism of the "hot little prophets". They are far from agreement among themselves. That they can be induced to get along with each other and tolerate their differences is an attainment of social value.

They have value for the interpretation of Whitman. They do indicate tendencies in him. They call to attention facets of the Whitman self, and so wide is their range of interest that all together they make nearly a complete challenge to the more studious interpreters of Whitman. As I set out for myself to investigate from Whitman's own writing whether he was truly represented by any of the conflicting cults, they have led me as I believe to an original contribution and discovery of Whitman as an epochal character and thinker of special moment in the present crisis of the world.

Need for this Analysis of Whitman's Ideas.

The numerous changes which Whitman made in *Leaves of Grass* in the several editions of the work affected the art and expression rather than the matter of his ideas. He expanded rather than altered his aim and purpose. The content increased and gave fuller and clearer expression of the implicit objective at the beginning. His book was a growth which has continued through his influence upon writers who followed him, not only in America, but in England, France, and elsewhere. It might seem difficult to analyze and interpret such a book. But the fact that it expressed a developing trend in modern life which, although we may not be entirely aware of its end, becomes steadily more apparent to us, enables us to understand Whitman better now than perhaps even he could understand and interpret himself.

Later writings on Whitman may show how true this is. There is an increasing appreciation of Whitman. But it is yet far from a full realization of the depth and value of Whitman's thought. Although I have attempted an original study of his ideas, it is apparent that I have been stimulated and aided by recent writers. I had completed my analysis before the publication of Canby's biography and Professor Allen's Handbook. Canby largely confirmed my impressions of Whitman's character.

Allen's chapters on Whitman's ideas and art have not changed materially my conclusions as they stood before reading his very scholarly book. I think Allen can claim support for his opinions differing from mine from much developed in the Whitman cults. His own prejudices, in my judgment mar his conclusions. There is little he has failed to recognize and give some account of. His errors are chargeable, I think, to the Whitman cults, biographers and interpreters. He has done what scholarship is all too apt to do, accepting too unquestioningly the authority of his predecessors. Scholarship and authority characterize his work; independent thinking and original research are wanting. As a critical summary of Whitman lore and propaganda, his book is invaluable. But in the interpretation of Whitman's ideas it bears internal evidence of its fallibility. His typical method is the contrary of original research. First, he assumes a theory, which he exposits authoritatively. From then on he attempts to find confirmation for the theory from Whitman's work.

The assumption to justify Allen's procedure is that Whitman was an ignorant man, though great, and did not know the sources of his own thought. Even if one should admit that, and it has some truth in it, such a method obscures Whitman's originality by trying to fit him into a traditional pattern of thought. It allows too little for Whitman's own special contribution. Furthermore, it attributes to Whitman ideas which are either alien to or contradictory of his thought or which are distinguishable from Whitman's peculiar cast or turn of the thought. Even where Whitman had a similarity of viewpoint or shared ideas common to the general current of thought it is undiscriminating criticism which undertakes to interpret such an original thinker by treating his thought as the same. Allen's analysis is grossly at fault in such respects. But his treatment of Whitman's ideas has therefore served us very well for a test or proof of our own analysis, because it is so often in contravention of our own interpretation.

I will consider Allen's and some other interpretations of Whitman's ideas in order of my presentation of Whitman's religious beliefs, his political views, his economic opinions, and his conceptions of man as an individual, person or self. Allen treats these topics first from a philo sophical and religious viewpoint and secondly as to a socia. philosophy. He describes Whitman's religion as pantheistic, his philosophy as the metaphysical doctrine of the Great Chain of Being, his evolutionism as organicism, his personalism in terms of the Borden P. Bowne school, his social views as Hegelian, his political notions as Jeffersonian and democratic, his economic conceptions as virtually wanting. He sums up: "Walt Whitman's weaknesses as a social thinker are no doubt obvious to any one who has followed this discussion, or who has read the works quoted." This summary of Allen's criticism is too offhand to condemn him by. We will give his criticism more adequate treatment, and I think it will follow very surely that all such interpretations as his miss the elemental purport and extent of Whitman's thinking.

I maintain that Whitman can be understood only if we recognize his preeminence as a pioneer of our latest developments of humanistic philosophy. Not medieval or Christian humanism (Maritain), not any Oriental or Hindu conception of the metaphysical self, not the immanent theistic personalism of the Bowne school, not planetary or cosmic humanism (Reiser, Potter, Bucke), not the transcendental self (Kant, Alcott, Emerson), not historistic determinism (Marx), not irrational romantic humanism (Rousseau), not Freudian humanism; but American democratic humanism. Allen tries to identify Whitman with all of these. So approaching Whitman's thought and with such a method as his, how can he escape the effect of his book, which, despite his assertions to the contrary, denies originality to Whitman's thinking?

A Correct Method of Interpretation.

Whitman's method was literary, not philosophical or systematic and logical. That does not mean that it lacks logical and consistent character. The function of true interpretation of ideas is to discover whatever philosophical content and logic they may possess.

It is very well to compare Whitman's thought with similar expressions or ideas. But we must not confuse his meanings or refuse to accept his definitions of terms when conflicting with the like words and phrases or ideas as used by others. We do not wish to cut ourselves off from the comparative method; we merely insist upon its legitimate use. Let us first try to discover Whitman's thought and then find what parallels, similarities or identities occur in that of others. The careful scholarship of Professor Allen enables us more easily to do that, and that is why we give so much attention to his criticism.

A letter from O'Connor to Burroughs expresses the idea that justifies me here: "To be salutary, criticism must be truthful and severe." But I will avoid expressing my criticism of the Whitman critics in such cutting and scathing language as O'Connor was master of, even had I the power of his pen. But I do propose to be thorough in my criticism of what I regard as loose interpretation which is virtually misinterpretation of Whitman.

What is Best in Whitman?

Opinions vary greatly concerning what is good or best in Whitman's work. There are those who refuse to pass beyond *Song of Myself,* beyond the first edition of *Leaves of Grass.* Others like Bailey think of Whitman as primarily the poet of the Civil War in *Drum-Taps.* Yet others like Masters prefer his later period and speak of the high point of his genius in *Passage to India.* The fact is that Whitman was a developing person throughout his life, and each period yielded something to the whole of *Leaves of Grass* which his executors, though respecting his wishes, correctly deemed not a closed book at his death and therefore appended what are named in the complete edition *Rejected Poems.*

In the first period, which seems to me that of healing from a mental malady, his exultant triumph of the spirit, the feeling of buoyancy in self-discovery and liberation from the inhibitions and fancies of youth, is dominant. But the poignancies of the Civil War produced another rise in him and out of it came the new and wonderful sympathies of his experiences as a war nurse. From that he passed to a spiritualization of his basic philosophy of humanism which he called personalism. That is the period too of his great prose work, *Democratic Vistas.* Afterward came *Passage to India* and what appears to many as a new mysticism but at any rate a deeper understanding and a higher beauty in his poetry. Nor can one pass by as of slight consequence the collections of old age poems entitled *Sands at Seventy, Good-bye My Fancy,* or *Old Age Echoes,* and the prose preface to *November Boughs, A Backward Glance O'er Travel'd Roads.* Those latest writings are indispensable, not because they are Whitman's. but because they contain new grandeurs of the expression of the human spirit.

Was the Man of the Book a Prophet?

Whitman had the pose of a prophet. Much has been written about him as a prophet. His growing popularity will continually raise the question and inquiry about his credentials as a prophet and the contents of his prophecy.

One should always be suspect who claims himself or is claimed by others as a prophet. And experience should teach us even more to suspect those who attempt to interpret the prophet.

When it is recalled that the Republican party has Hamiltonized the democratic Lincoln and the Liberty Leaguers have made a reactionary of the revolutionary

Tom Jefferson, and that orthodox Christianity has taken all the radicalism out of Jesus that remained in the garbled Scripture, then why not expect the content of Walt Whitman to be similarly corrupted? For that is usually the price of popularity to a great man. Therefore it is not in the popular vein to put forth much effort to save the notion that Whitman was a prophet with a momentous prophecy which has value for today when our high-flying world is in a dangerous tailspin. It is less challenging and not disputable to regard him as a great personality. He was a striking and attractive person. The attention he received during his lifetime attests that. Pilgrimages, even of the great, were made to visit him. The foremost literary men of the time took some note of him. Not only Emerson and Thoreau, but also Tennyson. Carpenter and Rossetti made a British cult of him, and many others took notice of him.

A further difficulty for the prophet was that he lived in the Age of Science, as the 19th century boastfully called itself, and that self-conscious period was ashamed to indulge the pretensions of a prophet. That was partly the reason why, if he had prophetic aspirations, they came to naught with his countrymen, even though he humoured their vanities. His eventual fame was better off for that, because the public's rejection or neglect of him made his followers more zealous. Even John Burroughs, notwithstanding his naturalistic tendencies and great sanity, declared: "We must place Whitman, not among the minstrels and edifiers of his age, but among its prophets and saviors."

There was not wanting in Whitman's own time some sad regret at the passing of the prophets. Emerson, himself a kind of oracular person, cultivating the Over-soul in a lofty manner, wished for the fiery enthusiasm and deep conviction of a Mohamet fresh from the desert and unspoiled by civilization. His cultured spirit however could see at most in Whitman but a hybrid of such a prophetic personality. For to the contemporaries of mellifluous Tennyson and Longfellow, if Browning seemed rough, Whitman was uncouth, and not a prophet.

To be a prophet must one not be ahead of his time? It is often said that every man is a product of his environment. If that were so, if no man were creative of something not yet produced in his time, there could be no progress and no prophets. But it is useless to debate the matter with those who believe that progress is an illusion or prophecy dead.

The queerness of Whitman, if a prophet, was that, instead of standing outside the orbit of the world he was in, he tried to be in the real center of things and take his direction from the great permanent currents of time. Whitman did share somewhat the beliefs of many forward-thinking men of his day. For example, evolutionism, but that was not a dominant doctrine then, and Whitman's viewpoints were too progressive for even the most advanced of the great evolutionists.

It is probably the advantage of a prophet not to be immersed too much in the heart of affairs. If Mohamet had not had to settle the disputes of the wives of his harem by resort to revelation, if he had never conducted military campaigns and had left no inspired injunctions concerning war, he would have offered less occasion for ridicule of cavillers and infidels; but then if he had been as detached from everyday life as Buddha, he would not have been the prophet Mohamet.

Burroughs maintained that Whitman was the first in America to give "spiritual and ideal meanings and values" to democracy and our modern world. It may be admitted that without him we would not be nearly so far forward in democracy. Yet without some others, notably Jefferson, Emerson and Lincoln, Whitman would be much less than he is.

Comparisons are invidious. They do not increase the stature of Whitman. They are not in the best spirit of Whitman:

"Whoever degrades another degrades me."

Jefferson and Lincoln also profoundly defined democracy, but they were so engrossed in the affairs of state that they wrote no book of poems or book of anything. Like Benjamin Tucker's *Instead of a Book*, their volume must be a collection of fragments,— of speeches, letters, and state papers that were particularized to some contemporary theme of the day. But Whitman had leisure, he took leisure—such men are heavy borrowers of time—they are parasites upon the activities of other men. Whitman possessed the luxury of time and leisure to be a prophet.

Much barred contemporary recognition of Whitman as a prophet. To the Victorians his advocacy of sex candor was too primitive. To them it was unseemly to write suggestively of homosexualism, indelicately of the sex organs of men and women. They were repelled by what they took to be egotism, bombast, rudeness, self-assertion, defiance of the wholesome customs of mankind, cavilling at everything sacred. Although the most intelligent of them might admit with the analyst of religions that, however disguised, nearly always religion makes appeal to sex feeling, they classed Whitman's expression with the degradation of religious obscenity.

Such outcries against him were quite overwhelming. Stout as his spirit was, resisting Emerson's sage counsel, that it would be better to omit some of his brashest words and expressions, which as a young man he quietly declined, in old age he admitted that in a worldly sense he was a failure for being right.

It was then however that good fortune began to press in upon him. The cult of Whitman was founded, and with it the idolizing mainly of his feet of clay. The Uranians claimed him for their prophet. It is a ticklish point for biographers not so inclined. Their answer is that he preached always the safe and sane regularity of married parentage, and in the light of today's prevalent opinion and practice Whitman was at least a conservative concerning sex freedom.

True, he said anonymously *To a Common Prostitute*: "Not till the sun excludes you do I exclude you." That was only more sweeping than what Jesus said to the woman taken in adultery, of the sinning woman who washed his feet with her tears and dried them with the hairs of her head, and of the polyandrous woman at the well. There was a kind of saintliness in Whitman that kept him undefiled by the world he lived in, and he was generous in according that character to every one else. No kindlier prophet than he ever lived.

Prophets usually rail at other men, especially at those in positions of power. Whitman almost never got down to that level of the prophet. He did not ostentatiously attack the evils of the age. Rather he took the higher role, not like Jesus of dying for the sins of the world, but as a macrocosmos of man he professed to absorb and make part of himself the evil and the good of the world alike. In that he reverses the role of the prophets. He does not denounce or renounce, he accepts—everything. That makes him a puzzling prophet of morality.

By any catalogue of virtues, Whitman in practice, whatever his preaching to the contrary, ranked high. Only in one thing did he lapse noticeably. In a general sense he was a very truthful man. But he shared that very common American trait which our greatest humorist (or patheticist?) , Mark Twain, fluently showed to be very human, and not really bad at all. There is no evidence that Whitman's "whoppers" injured anyone, excepting himself, at the

hands of his malicious detractors. His conscious defense
may be contained in the poem, *All is Truth*:

> "Discovering today there is no lie or form of
> lie, and can be none, but grows as inevit-
> ably upon itself as the truth does upon
> itself,

❖ ❖ ❖ ❖ ❖ ❖

> I feel in myself that I represent falsehoods
> equally with the rest,
> And that the universe does.

❖ ❖ ❖ ❖ ❖ ❖

> Meditating among liars and retreating
> sternly into myself, I see that there are
> really no liars or lies after all."

Undoubtedly he had just title to the sobriquet, "The
Good Grey Poet," which O'Connor bestowed on him.
Such as he are usually enrolled by the expurgators as
wicked men. Whitman appears never to have resented
those attacks, and there were many upon him. Indeed, as
many another, his fame really began when his name appeared on the indices purgationis.

Those who think Whitman a prophet believe him to
be foremost in two ways: That in himself he largely attained the character of man as we wish him to be, and
that also in words of sublime meaning he portrayed the
nature of the ideal man of the future.

The trouble with the conception of prophecy is that
nearly always it is conceived to be the monopoly of religionists and occultists. Was Whitman a mystical occultist? Dr. Bucke did most to develop that interpretation of
Whitman. For those who would like to discover in Whitman an occult fantasy and some unearthly relationship, the

reported method or mode of his poetical composition, in its first stages at least, gives some foundation. To others, as Esther Shephard, it was a pose which tended to prove him a charlatan.

There is possible evidence in his lines that he took seriously the seizure of the poetic frenzy upon him as an irrational or epileptic fantasy:

"The fit is whirling me fast."

". . . the charm of my theme was upon me,
    Till the tissues that held me parted their
        ties upon me."

He seemed conscious in such moods of being somewhat distraught, and to have doubted or be fearing to have doubts of the verity of his visions:

"O my rapt verse, my call, mock me not!"

To such matter of fact persons as scoffed at that he would say:

"What to such as you anyhow such a poet as I?
    Therefore leave my works,
    And go lull yourself with what you can
        understand."

I think rather his mysticism is that, not of the ecstatically maddened person, whether devotee of religion, disordered brain, or some epilepsy, but of the deeply inquiring spirit, intensely absorbed by the mystery of the world about him and seeking, by spontaneous thrust of his mind and emotions into its undisclosed but nearly impinging relationships to him, for vision and understanding of its profound meaning. It was that which gave him a religious bent as well as an attachment to the truths of science.

But upon the evidence to declare Whitman a supernatural occultist is a misinterpretation. Nonetheless, many of the Whitman followers are quite imbued with that

belief. I regard it as one thing for him to describe himself as a kosmos, which he did, and quite another to believe in the metaphysical cosmos.

Probably Whitman still appears to be more of a heretic
than a prophet. His notable heresies concerned religion,
sex and literary art. On account of these his claims upon
popularity was hindered. The offense to conventional
notions about sex probably carried the greatest weight
against him. Emerson protested the sexual passages in his
book. The Massachusetts District Attorney moved against
his Boston publisher and prevented the Seventh Edition
of *Leaves of Grass* to be issued in that city.

His literary heresies brought continual attack upon
him from the high priests of American literature and
frightened even such a radical as Emerson who was at
first enthusiastically inclined toward him. But probably
his religious heresies have stood as much against him.

We are concerned not so much with these heresies that
affected or prevented his acceptance as a prophet as we
are with the essence of his thinking. However, it is necessary to face the problem of his offensiveness to traditional
attitudes in order to arrive at his more profitable themes.
We think he was a major prophet of a new religion, a new
morality, and a new art, of which the essence is the new
humanism. Whitman made a discovery, at least a re-dis-
covery, of the unique worth potential in every human being and made that a significant fact in the universal order
and nature of things.

In the enduring quality of his work is the best evidence of his prophecy or of his personality. Only in that
can it be ascertained if Whitman advanced beyond his
time or to something of worth eternally for the future.
Of course only time after our time can be the final judge
of that. It is enough to know if Whitman's thought and
art are freshly alive today. His future is mainly indicative
from the present. Reputations go up and down and some-

times revive again. The oscillations of fame characterize all the reputations of the great. The permanent enrollment of Whitman's book in the Hall of Fame rests upon the validity of its conception of the human spirit, of the Personality of Man.

"The paths to the house I seek to make,
But leave to those to come the house itself.
Belief I sing, and preparation."

3

PROPHECY OF A NEW RELIGION

❖ ❖ ❖ ❖ ❖ ❖

"I too, following many and follow'd by many,
   inaugurate a religion."

"Divine am I inside and out, and I make holy
   whatever I touch or am touch'd from,
The scent of these arm-pits aroma finer than
   prayer,
This head more than churches, bibles, and
   all the creeds."

❖ ❖ ❖ ❖ ❖ ❖

His Heresy of Churchless Religion.

IF WHITMAN WAS A RELIGIOUS PROPHET HE WAS AS REVO-
lutionary in his conception of religion as in his conception
of sex. A heretic in religion, but a very religious man.
He conceived himself as the announcer of a new religion.
He should be regarded as a pioneer, if not the prophet,
of humanist religion.

He was especially at outs with organized and institutional religion. "Are you not of some coterie? some school
or mere religion?"

Intent upon his own mission he disclaimed any purpose to write "hymns or psalms with an eye to the church
pew, or to express conventional pietism, or the sickly
yearnings of devotees."

He prophecied about that religion: "The old theology
of the East, long in its dotage, begins evidently to die and
disappear."

43

His new religion "is, indeed, too important to the power and perpetuity of the New World to be consigned any longer to the churches, old or new, Catholic or Protestant —Saint this, or Saint that." "Religion, though casually arrested, and, after a fashion, preserved to the churches and creeds, does not depend at all upon them, but is a part of the identified soul, which, when greatest, knows not bibles in the old way, but in new ways—the identified soul, which can really confront religion when it extricates itself entirely from the churches, and not before."

He objected to the new religion being churchiness or biblical and to our American theology being any foreign importation. Yet he was not especially bitter against priests. He was seeking for a religion not of the cloister but one that can endure on "the open road," under the spacious clouds and along the landscape and flowing currents."

Stemming from the Quakers by his ancestry and justified by them with their "inner light" or individual consciences claiming superiority to ecclesiastical dictates, Whitman went much farther than they in affirmation of independent human right to choose its guidance in the spiritual realm. He wrote essays late in his life on Elias Hicks and George Fox, not as a Quaker, but for appeal to such forerunners of his doctrines as a sort of authority for the faith he held.

In the place of churches he put his trust in individual men, in the "dear institution of comrades."

His religious liberalism carried him beyond the most liberal of the churches. He made little exception for the Unitarian clergymen who visited and conversed with him. He doubted if the Ethical Culture movement of his friend Felix Adler could carry much weight against the old ecclesiasticisms.

The morality of the churches seemed to him at best negativisms. They lack spontaneity, the freedom that is essential to morality. They are too much bound to traditional doctrines. They cannot serve a democracy or free men. That is why they are dying.

It is notable that the poet-critic Wilder, with his Christian bias and not modernistic in his viewpoint, nevertheless has to admit that the crucial moral issues have been brought into consciousness today, not by the churches but in literature, in poetry, and especially by the novel. This is a complete answer to Professor Allen's doubt whether solitary religion can progress. If moral reform is taking place beyond the walls of the churches and only belatedly in them, they are not leaders but followers in progress of morality.

We know all too well the truth of that. A friend was telling me lately of urging on a liberal clergyman that he take interest in and preach on such mild reform as co-operativism. But that one replied he had members with as different views as W.P.A. and the wealthy and he could not afford to create dissension among them by introducing economic matters in his addresses.

The Roman Catholic Church is bolder in this respect than the Protestant Christian churches. But its battle against Communism has become more of a jurisdictional fight against the Greek Church which is now almost an institution of the Bolshevik empire. Christianized Bolshevism against fascistically-minded Christianity may become the formation of the new war front.

Formerly there were moral issues involved—revolutionary ethics versus traditional repressive ethics. But with Stalinism revolutionary fervor has waned. Trotsky preached Sorelism—the ethics of violence and fraud against the capitalist order, but that was not consistent with Leninism in power, and in the more conservative capitalist state of Stalin's dictatorship it became treasonous.

Those themes have attained meaning since the prophetic book, *Leaves of Grass,* was closed. Whitman's individualistic religion sounds strange to ears and minds tu-

tored in totalitarism. But can one feel confidence and
security in these new doctrines which bring back to us
the old wars of institutionalized religion? Is there less
truth now in Whitman's belief that true religion is in
man rather than church or state when state religion, Catholic and Communistic, is threatening the peace of the
world? The separation of state and religion was the earlier
battle of liberty. Today is there not need for Whitman's
further reform—the separation of religion from church?

Robert G. Ingersoll delivered the funeral address at
Whitman's tomb. He differed somewhat from Whitman's
views, but, as one who fought a life long battle against
institutional and church religion, it is notable that notwithstanding the great following Ingersoll obtained he
refused to build it into an organization. In that his viewpoint was similar to Whitman's. These men feared the in-
stitutionalization of doctrine, even of their own.

Institutions do not originate ideas. They congeal them.
They are useful in the spread of ideas. They are hampers
upon the creation of new ideas. Creative men are therefore suspicious of institutions. But institutions are themselves creations. Whitman had an inkling of that, in his
conception of the institution of comrades. If the church
be conceived as an instrument for human uses, to be constantly renewed and reinvigorated by the creative geniuses
of mankind, Whitman's objection would be overcome. But
of such a reformation of the church, experience had little
to offer in Whitman's days, and little more in ours.

But even though Whitman might have become recon-
ciled to some kind of democratic and progressive or liberal
church, his total rejection of the ancient and old world
religions and of the churches which carried the traditions
of them made him an arch heretic. But heresy was no longer
a capital offense or penal crime. A heretic was not as readily
extinguished in 19th century America as in the age of
Galileo and Servetus. And so Whitman was enabled to

give new and bolder meanings to conceptions of God and immortality than men had dared before.

Whitman's Theology.

Did Whitman have a theology? Was he a theist, deist, polytheist, pantheist, or atheist? Did he believe with Ingersoll that man made God in his own image?

Certainly one cannot describe him as a theological fundamentalist. In Protestant theology, man as in the biblical story of Job, is on the ashheap in abject humility before God. Whitman's expressions of at least equality of man with God completely oppose fundamentalist beliefs.

In all orthodox Christianity God is perfect and supreme. In Paul's New Testament theology an incorruptible God is put in contrast with corruptible man. Whitman did not admit the supremacy of God. He asks, "Why has it been taught there is only one supreme?" It is disturbing to Matthiessen that Whitman "transferred the supremacy to himself." But Whitman's idea was that there are many supremes. If we understand the democratic doctrine of the equal dignity and worth of all men, we understand Whitman.

And it is also distressing, "terrifying," to Matthiessen that Whitman "proclaimed the individual as his own Messiah." He saw in the face of the dead soldier the face of Christ. He also addressed Christ as "dear brother." Such familiarity is shocking to the orthodox Christian.

Matthiessen says "It was an unfortunate revision that changed 'And I know that the hand of God is the elderhand of my own.'" In what respect was it an unfortunate revision? Surely the revision is more in accordance with Whitman's theistic belief.

> "And I know that the hand of God is the
>   promise of my own,
> And I know that the spirit of God is the
>   brother of my own."

It was not in Whitman's thought or intention to place God first or above man.

Was Whitman a Theist?

Whitman's conception of God quite excludes the notions of theism or monotheism. Although theism is the theology nearest to a commonsense view of the universe, it has inherent difficulties: making God absolutely supreme and good and at the same time permitting evil in the world; a god both immanent in the world and transcending it.

In this theism is distinguished from deism whose God is only transcendent (entirely out of the world) ; and from pantheism whose God is everything, all is God, God being indistinguishable from anything and therefore is nothing at all distinguishable. It would seem that it is easier and more sensible to be either an atheist or agnostic than any kind of a god-believer. But the latter was not Whitman's alternative.

Not a Transcendentalist.

But he was not a theist or deist because he did not believe in the principle of transcendentalism. Some of those who want to deny Whitman any independence of thought try to make him out a Transcendentalist, deriving from the contemporary New England school of Alcott, Emerson and Thoreau. Professor Allen says, Transcendentalism "opened up a new life to him." It may have stimulated his thought. It never convinced him at any time of which there is any record in Whitman's thought. Matthiessen says that Whitman was moving from Transcendentalism back to a kind of materialism. The error of this is a mistake about the meaning of certain passages in *Leaves of Grass*. It fails to take account of Whitman's striving for universality and inclusiveness. He was not a denier or refuter, but an acceptor, of everything. At least, so he affirmed. That affirmation, as will appear, was misleading. Whitman was not a materialist. His naturalism was of quite a different kind. It was humanistic, not theistic.

But in another respect Whitman appeared to have some affinity with theism. For to most theists God is in some sense a person. Personality is a major theme, a fundamental principle, of Whitman's philosophy; but again his is humanistic, not theistic, personalism. For, as we see, he did not admit any super-personality in God. He utterly rejected the transcendental deity.

Was Whitman a Pantheist?

But did not Whitman have belief in the immanent God? Was he a pantheist? Allen thinks Whitman was a pantheist, or more accurately a panpsychist. If he was a panpsychist of course he was not a materialist. But he also describes Whitman as a materialistic pantheist. In the passages he cites from the *Song of Myself* Whitman speaks in the language of dualistic realism, of body and soul, not one more than the other. He as clearly affirms the individual personality and soul as the existence of matter with which the body or corpus is identified. But he is aware of the contradictions. They are incident to the whole that contains multitudes. This is the paradox that "objects gross and the unseen soul are one." But it is a humanistic rather than a pantheistic fact: "You and your soul include all things." It is this soul and not God which is omnipresent in *Crossing the Brooklyn Ferry*. The realistic dualism of body and soul is also the theme of *Starting from Paumanok*:

> "I will make the poems of materials, for I
>   think they are to be the most spiritual
>   poems."

And there too is the suggestion of panpsychism:

> "And I will not make a poem nor the least
>   part of a poem but has reference to the
>   soul,

> Because having look'd at the objects of the
> universe, I find there is no one nor any
> particle of one but has reference to the
> soul."

But the soul is not panpsychic or separate from the body:

> "Behold, the body includes and is the mean-
> ing, the main concern, and includes and is
> the soul."

In the poem, *To Think of Time,* it is even more forcibly put that this human being has meaning, is significant,
beyond thoughts of mortality and immortality:

> "You are not thrown to the winds, you gather
> certainly and safely around yourself,
> Yourself! yourself! yourself, for ever and
> ever!"

> "And I have dreamed that the purpose and
> essence of the known life, the transient,
> Is to form and decide identity for the un-
> known life, the permanent."

Is this conception of identity pantheistic, as Allen thinks?
I do not so interpret it. As we will show in Chapter V
Whitman's conception of Man-God and his soul is entirely
humanistic and not really theological.

Burroughs' Beliefs and Whitman's.

The closeness of friendship between Whitman and John
Burroughs was founded in part upon a similarity of viewpoints. In general one may feel more confidence in Burroughs' representation of Whitman's thought than in others
who had first hand acquaintance. But it would be an error
to assume that they had identity of beliefs. For Burroughs

was influenced first by Emerson. In Burroughs' early acquaintance and fellowship with Whitman they conversed often together, and Burroughs' ideas were considerably changed and remained affected by Whitman's convictions. Late in life Burroughs expressed rather fully his philosophical reflections in his book entitled *Accepting the Universe.* That book is interesting to us because, especially in the last chapter, *The Poet of the Cosmos,* it undertakes to present Whitman as a naturalistic philosopher. We will refer to that special phase of Whitman's philosophy in Chapter IV on *Whitman's Cosmic Man.* At present, however, we are immediately concerned with Whitman's theological views and Burroughs' comments regarding them.

Evidently Burroughs believed that Whitman was a pantheist. But what did Burroughs mean by pantheism? He said most people are unconsciously pantheists. He apparently had in mind the Christian scripture describing God as Him in whom "we live, and move, and have our being". To Burroughs "this is pantheism—all God—cosmotheism."

In his own belief God and Nature are interchangeable terms. They are the same thing. That would appear to mark Burroughs as a pantheist. But I do not find equivalent expression in Whitman and Burroughs quoted none.

Yet there are so many qualifications in Burroughs' exposition of this belief, that one may question whether he was as he believed himself to be a pantheist. The difficulties for theism with its personal God responsible for both the good and the evil in the world he saw. He thought only in pantheism could there be escape for God from responsibility for evil. He identified pantheism with his religion of science. In such a religion God is not a person, the universe and God are amoral and indifferent to man.

A Spinoza was a God-intoxicated man, as he was called. Burroughs was doubtfully such. Nature or God is things as they are. How can one worship or adore or pray to such a God? Burroughs raises these questions. The nearest he can come to a reason for duty, obedience or worship of the Great Blind Impersonal Being is conceiving Nature as Mother we respect her as any thing which bore us.

Taking Nature or God as the All there is no evidence of design or plan in it that he could find. There are different orders within Nature, mechanical, organic, and moral. In mechanical nature the scientific or mathematical laws of chance prevail. In organic nature there are evidences of "the workings of the creative impulse." But Nature is terribly wasteful of life too. Even man partakes of this infirmity and he is a very uncertain creature in his conduct. But it is only in man that the moral nature appears. And science has nothing to do with morality. Morality is therefore not the concern of God.

When man tries to discover plan, design, or purpose in God or Nature he is anthropomorphizing, trying to describe the infinite in terms of the finite. "Man alone has plans and ends."

It is the conception of a personal God that makes atheists of us. It robs God of dignity to think of him in Man's image. It takes away a worshipful respect for him. In this point Whitman would never have said that.

It was Burroughs' purpose "to justify the ways of God to man", to make the Universe acceptable to him, to argue for a worshipful attitude toward that God of Nature. His argument is that if on the whole Nature or God were not beneficient toward man he would not be here and could not survive. The God of Nature has at least given him a chance to fend for himself and endowed him with better instrumentalities through his intellect to get along amid the lavish abundance that Nature spreads before him for the taking. But has Burroughs made out any more reasonable case for the worship of the pantheistic God or as good as might move a slave to gratitude for a careless and indifferent master?

Against the theists Burroughs is clear and convincing: "When we say there is no God, we only mean that there is no being that we can define or conceive of in terms of man. Nothing in the finite can help us in dealing with the infinite. The infinite, the omnipotent, the omnipresent, cannot be a being without sharing the limitations of being, or without being subject to the bounds of time and space. If God is everywhere, he is nowhere; if he is all powerful, his power has no contrary, and hence ceases to exist. One after the other the human and personal attributes we ascribe to him disappear when we try to conceive of him in terms of the infinite. The infinite is equivalent to negation."

Burroughs did not see that some of that argument also refutes pantheism. If God is all, he is nothing, a mere negation. If he is not a person, and is everything, he has no need, as Aristotle proved, to know, feel, or will; he is the same as nothing, or as dead as inert matter.

To prove his thesis of justification of the ways of God to man Burroughs became involved in the unescapable contradictions of such a position. A pantheistic religion can no more remove the objections of the atheist than can a theistic religion. If one can believe in a personal God there is more reason to worship him than a pantheistic God. Burroughs admitted that "the truths of naturalism do not satisfy the moral and religious nature", but even that fact could not remove his prejudice in behalf of a pantheistic religion of science.

The error in his point of view is his conception of science as concerned only with the ways of impersonal Nature and not with the affairs of man. A religion based on such a science is at fault in the same way as the old religion. But Burroughs could not follow through with his logic of impersonal scientificism. His premise was that it is man, not Nature, that has concern for morality. Pure naturalism likewise has nothing to do with morality. And yet inconsistently with such a religion of science, he thought of a scientific religion as one "that moves us to fight vice, crime, war, intemperance, for self-preservation and in brotherly love, and not in obedience to theological dogma or the command of a God; a religion that opens our eyes to the wonder and beauty of the world, and that makes us at home in this world." Burroughs was really a humanist who got mixed up in his terms.

He made the same error as many another freethinker with a naturalistic bias, confusing it with science. Impersonalism is the root of that error. Whitman did not so err. But Burroughs' instinct was better than his reasoning. He perceived most of the elements of the problem. Toward the traditional religions to which he was in revolt he had no tendency to err. He did not see that the so-called new religion of science made much the same mistake as the old. The old passed by this world for the promise of another. But the materialistic religion of science substituted for a personal God an impersonal universe and overlooked the need for man to triumph over that impersonalism. He cannot accept it. He cannot accept the Universe as it is. And if God or gods there be, man must make them over somehow to fit his needs. Nature, passive and impersonal, he must make to obey his will. Burroughs did have some glimpse of this truth which is in conflict with his effort to accept the universe.

Whitman and Hinduism.

The Hindu religions present another type of pantheism. Some of the critics link Whitman with Transcendentalism which is said to be a cross between Hindu pantheism and German Idealism. That description of New England Transcendentalism only proves their bewilderment concerning the actual meaning of the importation of those philosophies and the accommodation of them to American pre-Civil War liberalism and individualistic idealism. But the muddled interpreters have made a cult of it (which we have noted in the Whitman Fellowship) and they go on darkly illuminating American poetry by the reference and analogy of German and East Indian philosophies.

Thus Wilder seeks to explain Conrad Aiken by the Upanishads. That is useful for our present purpose because he attempts to point out two aspects of that Hindu philosophy in contrast with the Christian doctrine of the self. Christianity's emphasis, he says, is upon the immortal self or soul. The Hindu mystics regarded such a conception of personality as an illusion. This mortal self is unreal. It is only the immortal disembodied self that has reality. If that is the distinction between them, Whitman's conception of the self is much nearer to the Christian theistic than to the Hindu pantheistic conception of it.

"The loose term pantheism" which Wilder ascribes to the "new poetry" must be made so much looser in application to Whitman that it loses its significant relation of the typical pantheistic systems. To rid the Whitman tradition of this incubus it may be well to thread the similarities and dissimilarities between the Hindu philosophy and his own.

In the Upanishads the Atman in man is conceived as the same it is in animals, insects, and every other part and parcel of the universe. That and the reincarnation doctrine have close parallels of expression in *Leaves of Grass*. But in the Upanishads man is not thought of as mastering his world, he is escaping it. That man can be master and measure of all things is the Greek spirit of humanism, and in that respect Whitman is a westerner.

In another matter, Hinduism is incompatible with Whitmanism. The caste system is utterly at variance with the equalitarianism of Whitman.

Thoreau quipped that Whitman was a "mixture of the Bhagvat Geeta and the New York Herald." But that is an offhand judgment and not penetrating criticism.

There is in Whitman none of the yogin spirit of purification by isolation from the world and liberation from physical or emotional impulses. Such methods as Allen's of accounting for Whitman by seeking the origins of his ideas outside himself necessarily lead to such confusion as Thoreau's.

There is a better parallel between Whitman's ideas and the Vedantic teaching, but not as Allen maintains in relation to the doctrine of the self. The similarity is in relation to the conception of God. In the early Vedic beliefs God was not conceived as transcendent but the immanent force of the laws of nature and continually undergoing evolutionary change of form. However, Whitman's idea of that evolution conforms rather to modern scientific views. And his idea of the nature of God differs also from the Vedic in which God is never a distinctive person but merged into the undifferentiated whole or All. The Vedic was a pantheistic notion in contrast with Whitman's emphasis upon the individualistic identity of the person.

Whitman and German Idealism.

Nor is the other supposed wing of Transcendentalism, German Idealism, a parent of Whitman's doctrine. Whitman's own assertion and claim to be "the greatest poetical representative of German philosophy" was spoken out of his ignorance of that philosophy. No doubt some ideas of the German philosophers did reassure him in his reaction against the materialism that was so dominant in the radical circles that moved about him. How greatly he misunderstood that philosophy appears from his declaration that "only Hegel is fit for America," because in Hegel "the human soul stands in the center, and all the universe minister to it." But that is not what Hegel taught. It is more like David Hume. For Hegel Universal Reason as God is everything, and a man is only the puny manifestation of that come to consciousness. Whitman's misconception of

Hegel's doctrine as anthropomorphic is important because it is a succinct formulation of the doctrine Whitman himself believed in.

Hegel's Absolute has no place in Whitman's thought. Whitman did not believe in the absolute God, the absolute Church, or the absolute State—the characteristic Hegelian doctrines. Hegel the etatist is not Whitman the democrat. Hegel was encyclopedic in his aspirations. For all his evolutionism Hegel's was a world of fixed status. It was not the fluid world Whitman conceived. But Whitman also aspired to inclusiveness, to universality, and it was this in Hegel which attracted him.

It is this universalism which misleads writers who liken Whitman to Emerson and Hegel. Hegel was a fad and rage of his time who caught the attention of the New England Transcendentalists and they misunderstood what he meant by freedom and reason. Hegel's freedom is obedience to universal laws of Reason which is neither spontaneity nor reasonableness. Emerson's and Whitman's misunderstanding of Hegel should be no special discredit to them when so many English and American professors of philosophy since then and now have been similarly misled by a superficial knowledge of Hegel's philosophy.

It is wholly incorrect to represent Whitman as "transplanting the Absolute Idea's highest realization from Hegel's Prussian state to his own United States," as Nathanson says. Nor did Whitman's statement of the problem of the One and the Many, of democracy and individuality, assume "a characteristic Hegelian form." Hegel's solution was not at all Whitman's. As also Emerson's solution, though democratic in contrast with Hegel's, was not as democratic as Whitman's.

It is the apparently contradictory qualities of "continuity and independence," which Selincourt points to as the essence of the integrity and unity of Whitman's mature lines and illustrates by the paragraph beginning with

"Why is the efflux of the soul?" which also distinguish
Whitman's philosophy from Hegel's. In democracy there
is continuity, in individuality independence, and Whitman would never have sacrificed the latter to the former.
A balance and cooperation of these two principles in true
comradeship was Whitman's solution.

Beach, however, mainly by using the resurrected materials of Whitman's study notes in preparation for his
Leaves of Grass makes out an ingenious argument to identify Whitman's thought with German Idealism. He says:
"Whitman's principle of natural theology is a kind of
18th century deism modified by the idealistic metaphysics
of Emersonian and Hegelian stripe." We have already
shown there is nothing in common between Whitman's
beliefs and deism.

That he was influenced by his study of the German
Idealists cannot be disputed, but his mature philosophy
was not any kind of idealism. He had indeed more kinship
to realism. For, as Beach quotes, he said, Idealism is to be
"ever modified even by its opposite." This is obviously a
criticism of German Idealism. But as we show in this
book Whitman was a scientific humanist rather than a
metaphysical realist.

The spiritism expressed in his notes when reading
the German idealists is not in harmony with his matured
philosophy. As for instance: "The same universal spirit
manifests itself in the individual man, in aggregates, in
concrete nature, and in historic progress." As for history
he said to Traubel it is not automatic: "The free human
spirit has a part to perform in giving direction to history."
Numerous expressions in *Leaves of Grass* show that he gave
a unique significance to the spirit of man as a creative
and effective power by virtue of its own will and desires
which is quite alien to Hegel's and German philosophy
in the general trend.

"Whatever satisfies souls is true."

". . . where I am or you are this present day,
　　there is the center of all days, all races,
And there is the meaning to us of all that
　　has ever come of races and days, or ever
　　will come."

"O but it is not the years—it is I, it is You,
　　We touch all laws and tally all antecedents,
All swings around us, . ."

"Without me what were all? what were God?"

Whitman's is rather the Aristotelian emphasis upon individuality and particularity. It is true that he felt a sense
of the existence of a spirit in all kinds of things akin to
his own or man's spirit. He had a sense of relationship
to all of Nature. But as we will see when we discuss his
ideas of the soul his beliefs were not of the theistic type
resting on a premise of a universal spirit. His philosophy
was pluralistic, not monistic, and that especially distinguished him from the German Idealists.

Was Whitman a Mystic?

According to Allen, Long, Matthiessen, Underhill
and some others Whitman was a mystic. Allen says: "One
of Whitman's weaknesses as a thinker is that logical contradictions did not bother him; he could too readily escape
into mysticism." That is a charge that Whitman was
cloudy in his thinking, but the fault there is rather the
failure of Allen to understand Whitman's thought because he was always trying to identify it with that of some
predecessor of more philosophical repute or with some
known philosophy. He could not really believe that Whitman's thought was original.

It is more noteworthy that Underhill, a prominent proponent of mysticism, claims that "amongst modern men, Walt Whitman possessed in a supreme degree the permanent sense of this glory (of God), the 'Light rare untellable, lighting the very light.' " The quotation is from the *Prayer of Columbus.*

This poem is a favorite with the mystics. Long calls it "an incomparable work of art" "from the point of view of relationships." Some have thought it autobiographical. But the poem evidently meant to Whitman the expression of blind impulse of a man befogged and illusioned by faith in a supernatural God, who confesses he does not know the end and even doubts the vision of his own faith, his belief in the lighting from God. "Am I raving?" Even his actual vision seems a miracle.

But Underhill does not rate Whitman a "pure mystic". And Long, though also claiming Whitman as a mystic, in showing the deficiencies of Whitman as a mystic, really proves he was not a mystic. Whitman's buoyancy and professed exuberance of health and extravertive assertion of acceptance of everything gives an impression of mysticism. But on the other hand, "To him the unseen was not a personality, a being, a life, a living spirit with whom his personality could have dealings." Although he could imagine and write powerfully an imaginary *Prayer of Columbus,* for Whitman to have prayed such a prayer would have been wholly out of character. He was not a praying man.

Another defect Long points out, even as a blemish in Whitman's character. Contrary to the habit and character of the mystic, Whitman "kept on willing things." Long excuses some of Whitman's scapegrace embarrassments, his tendency to lie and exaggerate, his pressing for undue publicity, his egotism, by his disposition to push himself forward instead of the mystic's peaceful and passive acceptance of every situation. I think this correct estimate of Whitman's character, although too disparaging, proves he did not have the temperament of a mystic. He had more poise of character than Long perceived.

Again Long criticizes Whitman because he could not feel and "utterly humanize" "the tie between God and man." Of course the reason is that Whitman did not believe in Long's over-all in-all God. And revealingly Matthiessen shows that "Whitman's mystic abandon was held in check by a similar concrete humanitarianism." The truth is that Whitman was concrete and not mystical in his philosophy of humanism. It embraced men not hypothetical God or the mystical effusion called God.

Wilder attempts to distinguish the theistic and the humanist mystics to the disparagement of the latter. The mystical humanists are too individualistic, which danger has been avoided by the Indian, the Neo-platonic and the Catholic mystics. "Those who are first mystics and then men will always labor under a handicap as regards amplitude and humanity." He does not tell us why. But we believe with Whitman that the Indian effort to escape desire and life and the other-worldliness of Neo-platonists and Catholics who are so pessimistic about human beings and this life are such a handicap that they stand definitely in the way of human progress.

Mukerjee, a scholarly Hindu writer, tries to compromise and find a middle ground between Eastern and Western mysticism which would avoid the errors of each. Western worldliness and gregariousness contaminates its mysticism. The introspective tendencies of the East result in emptiness and "the blankness of the unconscious." In trying to find the path in the jungle and starry mist of the cosmic search Mukerjee states a principle: "True mysticism is an attempt to rise above all relativities, and to reach the supreme expression of personality." Personalism appears to be the one sure guide. But in exploring the theologies we find it difficult to maintain the concept of a cosmic personality that has not identical or specific character. Universality is impersonality.

"God as unconditioned or pure being" is the vague concept at the heart of Mukerjee's definition of mysticism. Whitman's effort to will things, his caution, his humanistic personalism, his concrete humanitarianism, are in conflict with the mystical attitude, and his variance from all the traditional theologies carried him still farther away from the mystic's faith.

But just what is the essence of mysticism? To an interpreter like Underhill its phases are stages in advancement toward an ultimate reality. She sets them forth in order, towit: the awakening of the self, the discipline or purification of the self, the illumination or enlightenment of the self, self-surrender, and finally union of the self with the Unconditioned Absolute. In Underhill the method or way to mysticism remains a mystery. For Mukerjee the method is virtually synonymous with yogism.

Leuba, a scientific psychologist, gives us great insight to mystical phenomena. He has given a great deal of study to the psychology of religion and one of his books treats religious mysticism. He shows that the psychological phenomena are not peculiar to religious mysticism, but are related to other data. The yogin use various means for the inducement of the raptures and ecstacies characteristic of mysticism. Leuba points out that drugs may also produce the same effects. These facts make one suspicious of the mystic's religious interpretation of his illusions and hallucinations.

Leuba relates them to hysterical and neurasthenic states of mind and abnormal sexual impulses. Also to more or less normal dream experiences, poetic fancies, and ecstacies of ordinary normal persons. They do not necessarily belong to or need be associated with religious attitudes.

For the scientist "religious mysticism is a revelation

not of God but of man." In fact the traditional mystical interpretation of these phenomena as supporting "belief in divine personal causation," which Christians and other religionists invoke by prayer and other means to assist, relying on divine aid rather than upon their own powers, is a very mischievous and hurtful dependence. In place of the "mystical method of soul cure," according to Leuba, psychotherapy is today providing something like scientific and manageable methods.

The mystical experience in its purity is really man's sense of the mystery of life and being which always surpasses the range of our actual knowledge. When mysticism exceeds this state of mind and becomes itself an assumption of knowledge it misleads and hinders human effort and progress. It then trenches on the field of absurdity. To Whitman's contemporaries his assertiveness of the ego, of himself as a veritable cosmos, seemed to pair him with the absurdities of the traditional mystics. That leads us next to consideration of the phrase, "cosmic consciousness," which Dr. Bucke invented and applied to Whitman. Was this the form of Whitman's mysticism? Or did Whitman have yet a different cosmic viewpoint?

4

WHITMAN'S COSMIC MAN

❖ ❖ ❖ ❖ ❖ ❖

"Walt Whitman, a kosmos."

"If I worship one thing more than another
 it shall be the spread of my own body, or
 any part of it,
Translucent mould of me it shall be you!"

❖ ❖ ❖ ❖ ❖ ❖

Whitman's Cosmic Philosophy.

ALLEN SAYS: "THE CENTRAL THEME OF SONG OF MYSELF, AND
the basic motive of *Leaves of Grass* as a whole, is cosmic
and human development." Burroughs called him *The
Poet of the Cosmos*—"The world has had but one poet of
the cosmos and that was Whitman"—and said that Whitman's cosmic view was not that of the scientist but of the
poet and philosopher. Rejecting Bucke's interpretation he
summed up Whitman's conception as follows:

"Only one man, so far as I know, has insisted upon
religion, and yet not discounted this world at all, and
that is Whitman. W. saw no better or greater God than
himself, no world more divine than this, no more heaven
or hell than this here and now, and yet he saw it all for
religion's sake. He accepted all, he condemned nothing,
. . . and declared that no man had ever been devout enough.
This is a new religion, a religion of science and of democracy, imbued with human passion."

64

In Burroughs' last (posthumously published) book he said: "We go to Whitman for his attitude toward life and the universe; we go to stimulate and fortify our souls; in short, for his cosmic philosophy incorporated in a man." Although Burroughs may not have comprehended all of Whitman's philosophy or its profoundest meaning, and we think he did not, yet he was nearer to it than Bucke and the cosmotheticians.

The Cosmotheticians.

Fausset, with the misunderstanding characteristic of the cosmotheticians, thought that Whitman confused the cosmic and the individual self and indiscriminately thought them one. But Dr. Bucke regarded just that early period of the *Song of Myself* as the one when Whitman had "cosmic consciousness." Long is in disagreement with Bucke's view that later Whitman either lost the faculty or ceased to repose confidence in it.

Dr. Bucke appears to have derived his notion of cosmic consciousness not from Whitman, but first to have experienced a luminous view which made him aware "of eternal life." From that he went on to ascribing cosmic consciousness to all first-rate geniuses but as in an unusual degree to have been possessed by Whitman in his early poems. In his book entitled *"Cosmic Consciousness"* Bucke quotes passages from *Democratic Vistas* and added his exegesis, in which he departs violently from Whitman's viewpoints.

In the passages quoted, Whitman insisted that the cosmos is important only because of the individual man at the center; that only in the solitariness of the individual can religion be spiritual; that "the consciousness of the soul" is greater than its expressions. Commenting on these passages Bucke says: "We have brought out strongly the consciousness of the cosmos, its life and eternity—and the consciousness of the equal grandeur and eternity of the

individual soul, the one balancing (equal to) the other."
But in that Bucke changed the meaning of the phrase,
"consciousness of the soul."

For in the next sentence he speaks of men being "subjected" by this cosmic consciousness when attained "as
being a preter-human, more or less supernatural faculty,
separating them from other men." But that was not the
case with Whitman. Because of his intense belief in comradeship he could not conceive himself as separated from
other men. Nor with his naturalistic beliefs could he conceive himself as possessed or subjected by any supernatural
power or faculty. On the contrary he maintained that
nature and the cosmos or God are not significant but for
the soul of man. Man gives meaning to the universe.

In the light of Whitman's beliefs and conduct, of which
others were fully informed, Bucke had to admit: "It may
be that Walt Whitman is the first man who having cosmic
consciousness fully developed, has deliberately set himself
against being mastered by it, determining, on the contrary
to subdue it and make it a servant along with simple consciousness, self-consciousness and the rest of the united,
individual self." This is a clever turn away from the em-
barrassment of being refuted by the facts, which he seeks
to accomplish by making Whitman the master of cosmic
consciousness instead of like others being mastered by it.
Whitman makes God and the cosmos his servants.

Bucke nevertheless clings to belief in a separate distinct
faculty of cosmic consciousness. He contends that in the
poem, *Prayer of Columbus,* "The prayer in reality is, of
course, Whitman's own and all the allusions in it are to
his own life, work, fortunes—to himself." If that were
true, one would be compelled to conclude that Whitman
misrepresented his beliefs in everything else he wrote and
to his friends.

Also in the poems, *Now Precedent Songs Farewell* and
To the Sun-set Breeze, Bucke thinks Whitman acknowl-

edged he drew his spirit or soul from Nature. In the first of them, after naming several of his previous poems, he expressly described them as coming, not from Nature, but

> "From fibre heart of mine—from throat and
>   tongue—(My life's hot pulsing blood,
> The personal urge and form for me—...)."

In the poem, *To the Sun-set Breeze,* Whitman reflected that it was in his sensuous experiences of the external world that he had the most spiritual feeling of anything one might call God, and he speculated whether what he experienced there might be an influence identified as a soul. Has everything an individual soul?

> " (Thou hast, O Nature! elements! utterance
>   to my heart beyond the rest—and this of
>   them,)
>
>   ❖ ❖ ❖ ❖ ❖
>
> (For thou art spiritual, godly, most of all
>   known to my sense,)
> Minister to speak to me, here and now, what
>   word has never told, and cannot tell,
> Art thou not universal concrete's distilla-
>   tion?...
>
>   ❖ ❖ ❖ ❖ ❖
>
> Hast thou no soul? Can I not know, identify
>   thee?"

That is strongly agnostic, for "word has never told, and cannot tell." The "Godly" signifies not some supernatural force or transcendent being. It is only Nature that gives "utterance to my heart beyond the rest." If anywhere, the spirit, God, is in Nature. But we will see in discussing evolution and Nature, Whitman's faith and hopes were built on man more than on Nature and God.

Bucke cites other passages from *Democratic Vistas* which he thinks support his conception of cosmic consciousness. What did Whitman mean by this? "The rare, cosmical, artist-mind, lit with the Infinite, alone confronts his manifold and oceanic qualities." This description of the genius is of a man, not of some supernal influence that sets him apart from the average man or the masses. "The last best dependence is to be upon humanity itself, and its own inherent, normal, full-grown qualities without any superstitious support whatever." Indeed, Christ's mission "in the moral-spiritual world" is likened to democratic equality. Although Whitman could say, "Petition, lowly reverent to the voice, the gesture of the god, the Holy Ghost, which others see not, hear not," such recognition of the unique character of the genius, did not for him deny that character in every man. We are just now, some of us, beginning to recognize how universally the potentiality of genius is distributed. Every man is potent with some spark of unique genius. "Taste, intelligence and culture (so-called) have been against the masses, and remain so." Whitman was contending for "a fit scientific estimate and reverent appreciation of the People—of their measureless wealth of latent power and capacity, their vast, artistic contrasts of lights and shades . . ."

Bucke could not overcome the pronounced declarations of Whitman's beliefs so much at variance with his own, and therefore tried to make an out for his theory of cosmic consciousness by assuming that the faculty declined in Whitman with age: "Not that it is to be supposed that he had the cosmic sense continuously, for years, but that it came less and less frequently as age advanced, probably lasted less and less long at a time, and decreased in vividness and intensity." Bucke's conception of cosmic consciousness as a supernatural faculty had nothing in common with Whitman's cosmic man whose consciousness of the cosmos is not preterhuman but something accessible

to the developed consciousness of every man. It is something for mastery and control by man. We will understand
what Whitman could have meant by it when we know
his conceptions of evolution, Nature, and the soul.

Man in Evolution.

The evolutionists made their start in Whitman's time.
Did they influence him? Late in life he said of the *Passage
to India*, "There is more of me, the ultimate essential me,
in that than in any of the poems ... The burden of it is
evolution, .. the unfolding of cosmic purposes." But the
idea was full blown in Whitman's poetry before Darwinism obtained any considerable following.

In the concept "float," Allen remarks, Whitman's evolutionism was expressed several years before the publication
of *Origin of Species*. But, according to Matthiessen (following Catel) , that term signified rather Whitman's habit
of body and spirit, his "limber indolence." Nevertheless
he allows some point to Arvin's assertion that Whitman's
poetry abounds in verbs and participles of motion. He dis-
agrees with Arvin's assumption that floating is less characteristic of the poetry than concepts of "rising" and "strid-
ing on." He admits, that Whitman said: "All the forces
of the universe ... are pulsating, progressive."

Following his usual method Allen accounts for Whitman's evolution by reference to the evolutionism of his
predecessors, Leibnitz, Kant, and Hegel in particular. Such
an interpretation disregards Whitman's originality of
thought or its variance from similar viewpoints. And as
Burroughs pointed out, neither did Whitman's evolutionary ideas follow or carry the same intent as Darwinism:
"Science says man is the ephemeron of an hour, an irri-
descent bubble in a seething, whirling torrent, an accident
in a world of incalculable and clashing forces. Whitman
says he is as inevitable and as immortal as God himself. Indeed, he is quite as egotistical and anthropomorphic,

though in an entirely different way, as were the old bards
and prophets before the advent of science. The whole import of the universe is directed to one man,—to you. His
anthropomorphism is not a projection of himself into
Nature, but an absorption of Nature into himself. The
tables are turned." Darwinian evolutionists were historians,
geneticists. Whitman was prophetic. For him the past
was the prophecy of the future.

Song of Myself, antedating Darwin's publication by four
years, is its own kind of evolutionist poem:

> "My feet strike an apex of the apices of the
>   stairs,
> On every step bunches of ages, and larger
>   bunches between the steps,
> All below duly travel'd, and still I mount
>   and mount.
> Rise after rise bow the phantoms behind me,
> Afar down I see the huge first Nothing, I
>   know I was even there,
> I waited unseen and always, and slept through
>   the lethargic mist,
> And took my time, and took no hurt from
>   the fetid carbon."

> "I find I incorporate gneiss, coal, long-
>   threaded moss, fruits, grains, esculent
>   roots,
> And am stucco'd with quadrupeds and birds
>   all over,
> And have distanced what is behind me for
>   good reasons,
> But call anything back again when I desire
>   it."

In another respect Whitman differed from other evolutionists of his time and before. He did not believe that

man is bound of necessity into the slow and even processes of evolution. He knew that the swifter creative activities of men can go beyond Nature and need not wait for her. But this is the subject of the Soul and the Self, to be considered farther on. Evolutionists of today such as Julian S. Huxley and Hjort have caught up with Whitman and are giving scientific foundations for Whitman's evolutionist philosophy.

The Chain of Being Doctrine.

Allen's special effort is to connect Whitman with the Great Chain of Being doctrine, even though Whitman never used this term "and may not have been consciously aware of the extent to which it (together with pantheism, panpsychism, and the organic principle) formed a background for his thought." True, one who knows nothing of a doctrine may nevertheless be influenced by it unconsciously if it is a prevalent notion dominating the general way of thinking of the time. But one is apt to be misled also in the assumption that an original thinker wears all the habiliments of thought prevalent in his time. Before ascribing such ideas to Whitman I would prefer to know how far he was actually influenced by them.

According to Allen, as in "Whitman's idea of pantheistic evolution," so also "he presents the temporalized Chain of Being, or the whole creation on its journey upward." Following Allen further, Plato's "principle of plentitude" is not specifically Whitman's idea, but the doctrine of fullness "permeates his poetry and thought." "Aristotle rejected plenitude but originated the second principle, continuity," and this idea Allen thinks clearly connects up with Whitman's evolutionism. Also Leibnitzian monadism has possibly a bearing upon Whitman's individualism, as Allen concludes, without recognizing the dualism of soul and body which distinguishes it from the monism of Leibnitz and the German idealists. And "Kant's theory of cosmic evolution was another contribution to the temporalizing of the principle of plentitude." But Whitman could talk of Kantian cosmic evolution "without ever thinking of the Chain of Being."

In the Allen Handbook one can do this kind of butterfly flitting, sipping at the flowers of philosophy, and almost convince himself that Whitman in his largeness was Brahmin, Platonist, Aristotelian, Leibnitzian, Kantian, Hegelian, etc., etc., and be quite unappreciative of the differences between these philosophers and unconscious of the points of Whitman's departure from them. Even though there are analogies which may be legitimately pointed out, yet that is not interpreting Whitman accurately.

Professor Lovejoy whose Harvard lectures brought to attention the Great Chain of Being doctrine, was not responsible for Allen's ascription of the doctrine to Whitman. Wherever the doctrine originated, Lovejoy shows that it came to its foremost expression in the poet Pope's *Essay on Man*:

> "Vast chain of being! which from God began,
> Nature's ethereal, human, angel, man,
>
> ❖ ❖ ❖ ❖ ❖ ❖
>
> From Nature's chain whatever link you
>   strike,
> Tenth, or tenthousandth, breaks the chain alike."

Voltaire was a destructive critic of the doctrine, and Whitman's thought was nearer to Voltaire's than to the theologisms of the 17th and 18th centuries.

Lovejoy made no suggestion that the doctrines of the Chain of Being — plenitude, continuity, or gradation — had any reflection in the doctrines of Darwinian evolution, but that would have been far more excusable than to have noted an analogy of the doctrine to Whitman's conception of evolution. Following Lovejoy's criticism one sees it quite impossible to think of Whitman as being in the line of thought denoted as the Great Chain of Being.

Lovejoy does not leave one in doubt as to his own estimate of the Chain of Being philosophy. He applies the appropriate phrases, omne ignorantium pro mirifico and "the anesthetic revelation" to Pope's reverence for the God who "moves in a mysterious way his wonders to perform" and is subject of taboo, "think not God to scan."

Lovejoy was careful not to over-extend the use of this particular theory of the history of ideas and cautioned against the danger of hasty generalizations and taking the part for the whole and "confusion of ideas"—errors which Allen has unwittingly committed. Otherwise he would not have associated ideas so disparate as Pope's and Whitman's. For the basic notions in the Great Chain of Being doctrine were not merely its ideas of plenitude, continuity and gradation but principally the connection of these ideas with a theistical ground of being, in and through the being of God. And Whitman's conception of God was altogether different from that.

Was Whitman a Naturist?

Nor did Nature any more than God become for Whitman the all in all. But Beach, who points out that nature worship became for many poets of the 18th and 19th centuries a substitute for the Christian religion, includes Whitman among them. "The poetic faith in Nature nowhere appears more full blown than in the poems of Whitman."

As Beach undertakes to provide the text of Whitman to prove his contention that naturism is most prominent in Whitman's beliefs, we are afforded an easier task of criticism of that interpretation which is so contrary to our own. Unfortunately for his thesis he quotes too largely from the notes or rejected early writings of Whitman preceding or in preparation for the *Leaves of Grass* and rests too much on the assumption that German Idealism is a true representation also of Whitman's views. The passages cited by Beach may also enable us to see where Burroughs went astray in supposing that his naturism was also Whitman's for it is not so easy to distinguish Burroughs' and Whitman's viewpoints.

My contention is that to Whitman human nature, which is a higher form of nature and dominant at least in potentiality over other nature, is the really central factor of man's world or universe. Closer reading of Whitman than the critics usually bring to bear on his writings shows conclusively that Whitman was a humanist rather than a naturist.

But Nature was an important concept for Whitman. "Nature, true Nature, and the true idea of Nature, long absent, must, above all, become fully restored, enlarged, and must furnish the pervading atmosphere to poems, and the test of all high literary and esthetic compositions." But he proceeds to distinguish the petty conceptions "of the English poets" and to give his own view of the superior position of man in Nature: "By what we now partially call Nature is intended, at most, only what is entertainable by the physical conscience, the sense of matter, and of good animal health—on these it must be distinctly accumulated, incorporated, that man, comprehending these, has, in towering super-addition, the moral and spiritual consciences, indicating his destination beyond the ostensible, the mortal." Plainly this passage, quoted by Beach, is not merely putting Nature in the place of God, as Beach would have it, but elevates man to the high position in Nature. Burroughs too recognized the superiority of man to the rest of Nature.

Again in *Democratic Vistas* Whitman said: "America needs, and the world needs, a class of bards who will, now and ever, so link and tally the rational physical being of man, with the ensembles of time and space, and with this vast and multiform show, Nature, surrounding him, ever tantalizing him, equally a part, and yet not a part of him, as to essentially harmonize, satisfy, and put at rest." But note the elements of this naturalism. It distinguishes man from Nature, which is "yet not a part of him," at the same time it attempts to "link and tally the rational physical being of man with Nature". It recognizes Nature's stimulus to man, but as we will see because of man's attitude rather than Nature's work. In Whitman humanism is always dominant over naturism.

We cannot agree with Beach that "Whitman's enthusiasm for the Universe . . . was given intellectual support by his belief that the Universe is rational and moral like man." Burroughs disputes any such assumption and so did Whitman. Beach does not quote anything from Whitman to support his assertion. And Whitman said unequivocally in a footnote of the Preface to the 1876 Edition of *Leaves of Grass*: "While the Moral is the purport and last intelligence of Nature, there is absolutely nothing of the moral in the works or laws, or shows of Nature. Those only lead inevitably to it—begin and necessitate it." Apart from man there is little evidence of any intelligence or morality in Nature.

Whitman's humanism did not isolate or separate man from Nature or the Universe. As Beach says: "He insists in his poems that one must never take any person or object separately."

> "All must have reference to the ensemble of
> the world, and the compact truth of the
> world."

This is the poem in which Whitman says "Man or woman is as good as God" and "there is no God any more divine than Yourself," showing clearly that he did not believe that man should be abject or bow himself down before the presence of the Whole as an overwhelming force above him.

But, although Whitman believed in an evolving unity of all things in a universal harmony, he was not a Smutsian Holist. Similar to the above quotation from *Democratic Vistas* he wrote in *Crossing Brooklyn Ferry* of

> "The simple, compact, well-joined scheme,
>   myself disintegrated, every one disinte-
>   grated yet part of the scheme."

The "crowds of men and women" there were to him a symbol of the universe of things, disparate in their separate identities, yet part of the great unity.

> "You furnish your parts toward eternity,
>   Great or small, you furnish your parts
>   toward the soul."

As Burroughs emphasized Nature's lesson to man as tolerance for everything under the sun, good or evil, so does Beach understand Whitman: "The earth is more specifically a symbol of physical nature." As Whitman said:

> "The earth ...
>
> ❖ ❖ ❖ ❖ ❖ ❖
>
> Makes no discriminations, has no conceiv-
>   able failures ... shuts none out."

Of this Beach says: "It is Nature, it is Nature teaching universal acceptance." But Whitman meant rather that man's reflection derives this lesson, and neither he nor Burroughs thought Nature teaches it. So to think they regarded as an unscientific personification of Nature.

The sense of reality Beach thinks was also a lesson

Whitman learned from Nature. "One lesson from affili-
ating a tree ... is that same lesson of inherency, of what
is without the least regard to what the looker on supposes
or sees, or whether he likes or dislikes." This passage
gains something in meaning from Burroughs' comparison
of *Men and Trees.* As he points out, Nature is indifferent
to man. In adjusting Nature to himself or himself to
Nature, he must have a sense of reality, of what is. But
as man he makes laws of economy and of morals not in
Nature which raises indifferent Nature to functions of
usefulness to man.

As Whitman said: "Man, so diminutive, dilates beyond
the sensible universe, competes with, outcopes space and
time, meditating even one great idea. Thus, and thus
only, does a human being, his spirit, ascend above, and
justify, objective Nature, which, probably nothing in itself, is incredibly and divinely serviceable, indispensable,
real, here." Too frequently to be passed by unnoticed
Whitman said of Nature that it is "of no account in itself."

But realism as a particularistic philosophy no more
attached him that did its opposite philosophy, idealism.
Each must be "modified even by its opposite." In humanistic rather than extreme metaphysical senses realism and
idealism complement one another. "We must not say
one word against real materials; but the wise know that
they do not become real till touched by emotions, the
mind."

Read out of context another passage in *Democratic
Vistas* might be taken as proof that Whitman not only
conceived himself as a nature poet but primarily as such.
"Lo! Nature (the only complete, actual poem), existing
calmly in the divine scheme, containing all, content, careless of the criticisms of a day, or these endless and wordy
chatterers." And again in *Specimen Days,* speaking of his
travels in the Rocky Mountains, he said: "I have found
the law of my poems " But as Beach comments, though

contrary to his thesis: "In general, however, his poems are too didactic and human in their interest to admit of very much of this sort of thing." A poem for Whitman was an effort to express the whole. In that sense Nature containing all is the only complete poem. But it is alone the spirit of man which can comprehend and make it something which by itself it fails to be. "Before the fitting man all Nature yields."

It is true that Whitman reads many lessons from Nature. They are reflective, humanistic lessons, out of man's thoughtful experience. There is, for example, the lesson of identity: "The quality of BEING, in the object's self, according to its own central idea and purpose, and of growing therefrom and thereto—not criticism by other standards, and adjustments thereto—is the lesson of Nature." Therefore, every man must be a law unto himself. That is the law of growth.

Thus he reads also the lesson of democracy from Nature: "As the greatest lessons of Nature through the universe are perhaps the lessons of variety and freedom, the same present the greatest lessons also in New World politics and progress." Where materialistic scientists have been wont to read determinism and invariant law, Whitman read Freedom and Diversity. 20th century science tends to agree with him.

Under the impulse of his exuberant humanism, therefore, as Matthiessen points out, Whitman did not as did Wordsworth conceive an opposition between God's country and man's city. "He thought of himself both as the poet of the city and as the poet of the country, differing sharply in this from Wordsworth and Baudelaire." "Wordsworth's particular tendency was to represent people living close to Nature and drinking in its healing power as a restorative to the soulless life of towns. Against any such limitation of range Whitman stood strongly opposed."

Whitman's emphasis was "Be natural! be natural! be natural!" In the chapter entitled *Flight of the Eagle* of Burroughs' *Birds and Poets*, which was an appreciation of Whitman's nature poetry, as Whitman wrote the sentence for Burroughs it read: "Through all that fluid, weird Nature ... he finds human relations, human responsions ... his fields, his rocks, his trees, are not dead material, but living companions. To him all Nature's objectiveness holds a cognizant lurking something, without voice, yet realizing you as much as you realize it." As Burrough's wrote instead: "Like the old poets, he does not dwell upon Nature, ... but upon life and movement and personality. ... everywhere in Nature Whitman finds human relations, human responsions. ... his fields, his rocks, his trees, are not dead material, but living companions." Is not such an expression humanizing Nature?

Yet, says Burroughs in his *Accepting the Universe*, "The Nature that to Wordsworth never betrays us, and to Milton was 'wise and frugal,' is a humanized, man-made Nature. The Nature we know and wrest our living from, and try to drive sharp bargains with, is of quite a different order. It is no more constant than inconstant, no more wise and frugal than foolish and dissipated; it is not human at all, but unhuman." What Burroughs objects to is personifying Nature and attributing to her conduct and character that are not in her but in us. "The beauty, the sublimity, the power of Nature are experiences of the beholder ... Nature is what we make her." Although agreeing in the main with this, we think it is more in the spirit of Whitman to recognize a man-made Nature, a humanized Nature, not as the mistakenly anthropomorphized Nature of his predecessors, but as Nature made serviceable to man's needs.

Whitman's attitude toward Nature was markedly different from that of the Romantics. Burroughs rightly objected to Bliss Perry's comparison of Whitman with Rousseau.

Whitman insisted that instead of "fable and myth," "my book is the first attempt at an expression in poetry of a knowledge of the earth as one of the orbs, and to give wonder and imagination a new and true field—the field opened by scientific discovery."

Edward Dowden also contrasted Wordsworth's and Whitman's nature poetry with much the same distinction made. Wordsworth viewed Nature much as a communion with God. Whitman in the more modern scientific manner conceived man and Nature as not separate but of the same order and system of being. But Whitman anthropomorphizes Nature in a way which would disturb the objective impersonal attitude of the evolutionary scientist of his time and later. Dowden said: "Whitman expresses to me the life and power of the globe itself, and lets me into the secrets of creation. His poems reveal the elemental laws and the great dynamic forces. . . . that are deeds and not thoughts, and have the same indirect personal relation to myself that a man's proper act has to himself." But as Whitman expressed this in his rather clumsy but meaningful way man is not a mere copyist of Nature but discovers the serviceableness of Nature to himself by an act of his own creation. I think Dowden missed the point. As Whitman said this:

"Observing, rapport, and with intuition, the shows and forms presented by Nature, the sensuous luxuriance, the beautiful in living men and women, the actual play of passions, in history and life—and, above all, from those developments either in Nature or human personality in which power (dearest of all to the sense of the artist) transacts itself—out of these, and seizing what is in them, the poet, the esthetic worker in any field, by the divine magic of his genius, projects them, their analogies, by curious removes, indirections, in literature and art. (No useless attempt to repeat the material creation, by daguerreotyping the exact likeness by mortal mental means.) This is the image-making faculty, coping with material creation, and rivalling, almost triumphing over it."

In the variance of Whitman's naturalism from materialistic naturalism it does not become either pantheistic, theistic or mystical naturalism. It is such humanistic naturalism as we have been getting accustomed to from Julian Huxley. Whitman said in the Preface of 1855: "folks expect of the poet to indicate more than the beauty which always attaches to dumb real objects . . . they expect him to indicate the path between reality and their souls." That is what distinguishes him from the mechanistic and materialistic philosophers. But Whitman's is a down to earth philosophy:

> "I swear there is no greatness or power that
>   does not emulate those of the earth,
> There can be no theory of any account unless
>   it corroborate the theory of the earth,

❖ ❖ ❖ ❖ ❖ ❖

> All merges toward the presentation of the un-
>   spoken meaning of the earth,
> Toward him who sings the songs of the body
>   and of the truths of the earth.

❖ ❖ ❖ ❖ ❖ ❖

> But the soul is also real, it too is positive and
>   direct."

Many have remarked the poise in Whitman's character, but whatever defect there may have been in his personal life, and it was in human relations one unusually pure and respectful toward others, in his thinking he tried above all things to strike balance, to discover proportion, to give everything its due, and, as we will soon see, morality in its essence for him was fitness and appropriateness. And so he tried to reckon Nature as it is in its whole order, including human nature. The phrase, cosmic man, embodied his conception of man's supreme function, humanizing or spiritualizing Nature.

Burroughs Wrestles with Contradictions.

Burroughs never became quite settled in the Whitman doctrine. At the end it was not quite so much the carry-over from Emersonianism as a struggle to adjust science and theology, humanism and universalism. Thus he became very conscious of contradictions which Whitman seemed most helpful in removing, but he did not become quite master of the Whitman philosophy. To come to terms with these problems as they appeared to Burroughs, a professed disciple of Whitman, aids in our exposition of Whitman's humanism, to an understanding of Whitman's cosmic man.

First, as we may have surmised, he had difficulty with the idea of "humanizing nature." Probably the best solution he reached was this: "When we seek to interpret Nature . . . we humanize her, which means, of course, that we interpret ourselves. Nature reflects the spirit we bring to her . . . It is our reactions to Nature that give rise to the qualities we ascribe to her. . . . We create the world in which we live. I love Nature, but Nature does not love me." Or, "Nature loves me in my fellow beings." Yet, "She is the primary and everlasting fact; we, as living beings, are the secondary and temporary facts."

It is obvious that there are inherent contradictions in those ideas. He was aware of the fallacy of personalizing Nature, ascribing to Nature human qualities. In that sense he rejected the idea of humanizing Nature. He sees that from any human point of view Nature is amoral, wasteful and uneconomic, and on the whole without plan, design, or order.

Probably he was dismayed by Whitman's solution. It

required more faith than he had to believe that some-how man could triumph and in the end order would suc-ceed chaos. The cosmic man in that sense was too far a reach of the imagination for his practical sense.

He turned to another type of solution, "Accepting the Universe," "to justify the ways of God to man on natural grounds." There was much in Whitman to support this viewpoint, Whitman's perfectionism, which he misunder-stood. Instead a Leibnitzian view took hold of him: "The naturalist sees this as the best possible world, sees that Nature is not an indulgent stepmother, but a strict dis-ciplinarian; that the good and well-being of all is her aim; that suffering and defeat are relative; that God's ways to man are not justified in a day or a week, or in this place or that, but require ages and continents to come to their full fruition." And he did not seem to realize that this also is fallacious personalizing of Nature, and quite in con-tradiction of our human point of view (and he admitted we can have no other), that Nature's ways are haphazard, hit and miss, mere laws of chance.

But he adopts another mode of argument, also appar-ently Whitmanian, that Nature's way at least gives men a chance, an opportunity, to turn the scales of fortune to favor ourselves. That is the freedom and diversity which Whitman derived as a lesson from Nature. But Burroughs went beyond that to adopt the favorite argument of theologians when bothered by reasonable objections to the order or disorder in God's Universe of design, the resort to ignorance, the miracle of ignorance: If we could see everything we would know that everything will in the end turn out right. And Whitman said things like that too. A great deal of Whitman's preaching was for patience, pa-tience to give man time to do better than Nature's slow evolutionary processes. And one cannot deny that Bur-roughs also strongly leaned on that kind of faith in man.

But he had less faith than Whitman, and was therefore more of a mystic because he believed less in willing things. As a naturalist he had to believe that the universe "exists for other ends than our own." Logically it followed if we accept the Universe we must accept its ways and ends rather than our own. The cosmic man in Whitman took a more resolutely human course.

5

MAN-GOD AND HIS SOUL

❖ ❖ ❖ ❖ ❖ ❖

"The mightier God am I,

❖ ❖ ❖ ❖ ❖ ❖

for without me what were all? what were
God?"

❖ ❖ ❖ ❖ ❖ ❖

Whitman's Concept of the Soul.

WHITMAN SAID THAT THE FUNCTION OF POETRY IS "TO IN-
dicate the path between reality and" men's souls. Did his
use of the word "soul" have an affinity or equivalence to
the traditional religious beliefs about the soul?

Allen compares Whitman's meanings with Emerson's
"Oversoul," with the Hindu atman, with Bergson's elan
vital, with the pantheistic doctrine of transmigration of
souls, and concludes that "in some of the old age poems,
such as *Passage to India,* Whitman's imagery of the soul
in flight and his symbolism of immortality come much
nearer orthodox Christian conceptions than in the bolder
pantheism of his earlier works."

This is not interpretation but obfuscation. He can
even quote Whitman and immediately ascribe a different
meaning than that obviously intended and expressed. He
is both self-contradictory and absurd in the statement that
Whitman "conceives God in his own image because God

85

is incarnate in the body." That wholly misrepresents Whitman's ideas about deity. Nor is there any warrant for saying that Whitman believed in the migrations of the soul because he declared, "I am myself waiting my time to be a God." The reality of God for Whitman is in man, not either theism or pantheism or deism or atheism.

Is there excuse for the misinterpretations that Whitman's definitions of the soul were obscure? In an early writing Whitman had said: "I am always conscious of myself as two—as my soul and I." In *Song of Myself* he repeated that idea:

> "I believe in you my soul, the other I am
>   must not abase itself to you,
> And you must not be abased to the other."

What distinguishes my ego and my soul? I think the difference is for Whitman that the ego abides continually with me, while the soul (the imagination of the poet) can wander hither and thither at will and yet remain within the individual self.

By not attending closely to Whitman's own expressions there have been considerable misinterpretations of that duality within the self. Thus Swinburne thought that in Whitman there were two distinct and conflicting men, "the poet and the formalist." It is too extreme to say Whitman was a formalist. He had a conservative side, with respect for tradition and conventions, but that did not make him a split personality. It was an element of his temperamental poise and balance.

O'Connor expressed a view often remarked in criticisms of Whitman's work that the Whitman of the book is "not an individual, but mankind." But that too misinterprets Whitman's meaning. Whitman was eager to be concrete, and avoid abstract meanings. At most the cosmic man is not vague mankind, but, as he expressed it in

Chanting the Square Deific, the living "man, I, the general soul."

Fausset thinks that poem makes a fourfold division of the soul: (1) natural law was symbolized in the elder gods; (2) human devotion or love as represented by Christ and other human gods; (3) Satan, the principle of rebellion or individual will; and (4) the general soul. But the fourth as named by Whitman is the Holy Spirit which includes the other three, God, Saviour, and Satan and pervades all, including man, the individual me, which gives meaning to all the rest. In that poem also has not the individual man the same two elements: (1) "I, the general soul," and (2) "I the most solid"? As we read the poem, not in the gods, nor even in the Holy Spirit, but in man is the square finished and made solid or real.

I do not agree with Allen that this general soul "is nothing but a kind of pantheistic oversoul." Typically Allen quotes and describes as even more pantheistic from *Passage To India:*

"Swiftly I shrivel at the thought of God,
At Nature and its wonders, Time and Space
    and Death,
But that I turning, call to thee O soul, thou
    actual Me,
And lo, thou gently masterest the orbs,
Thou matest Time, smilest content at Death,
And fillest, swellest full the vastnesses of
    Space."

Who is the "I" that shrivels up? Is it not this merely physical man who is but the evolutionist's speck in the Universe, a puppet or victim of natural forces? And who is the "actual Me," that general soul? Is it not the creative masterful man? He who has reason above the apriority, predestination, of Nature and God?

This *Passage to India* is significant in title and theme. India is the land of spiritual thought. But whose is the passage to India? "God's purpose from the first"? It is man at any rate who fulfills it, who does the deeds. Whitman says he makes a new religion, a new worship; though "in God's name," it is for the sake of man's soul; it is a worship of creative humanity, of its captains, voyagers, explorers, engineers, machinists; it is of man evolved, "man's long probation filled.

> "Nature and Man shall be disjoin'd and dif-
> fused no more,
> The true son of God shall absolutely fuse
> them."

It is man who in the fulfillment of his evolutionary progress at last becomes creative and it is we men do a work greater than God's. Though believing in God more than any priest we do not longer dally "with the mystery of God."

But in the verses immediately to follow there seems to enter a mystical immersion of self in God:

> "Bathe me O God in thee, mounting to thee,
> I and my soul to range in range of thee.
> O Thou transcendent ..."

The mystic will read this out of context and declare Whitman a mystic like himself. But straightway Whitman is saying:

> "Athwart the shapeless vastness of space,
> How should I think, how breathe a single
> breath, how speak, if out of myself,
> I could not launch, to those, superior uni-
> verses?"

The voyage does not end with the attainment to God:

"O farther, farther, farther sail!"

In this aspiration of man to the highest beyond God and Nature, the following lines from other poems give additional certainty of Whitman's meaning:

"I only am he who places over you no master, owner, better, God beyond what waits intrinsically in yourself."

"I am myself waiting my time to be a God."

"Nothing, not God, is greater than one'sself is."

"Why has it been taught that there is only one Supreme."

"I asked of my soul whether it would be filled and satisfied when it should become God enfolding all these, . . . and the answer was No, when I reach there, I shall want to go farther still!"

For

"We throb and wait for the God in vain.—I am vast—He seems to console us with a whispering undertone in lack of an answer —and my work is wherever the Universe is —be the soul of man: the soul of man! To that, we do the office of the servants who wake their master at the dawn."

In the convincing light of these expressions how then can we go along with the thinned out meaning of the vaguely insinuated assertions of the mystics, or the moded

orders of traditionalism, or the origins which Professor
Allen would impose on us? Can there be any longer doubt
that by the general soul Whitman meant the potential man
in each and every one of us, in the race of man, from which
there is more to be hoped than from the God of Nature,
the Christ of Love, or the Satan of Rebellion craving freedom within us, or even from the Spirit, the consciousness
of man which is greater than its expressions? Nature, Love,
Freedom and Consciousness are soul, eternal soul, processes.
Man is the swift maker. Not this animal, natural man, but
the spiritual man, the man of the soul. "The heart of man
alone is the one unbalanced and restless thing in the world."

But Whitman would not allow for the separation of
the physical man from the spiritual man. Burroughs mentions "the curious physiological strain that runs through
the poems . . . the glorification of the body and the identifying it with the soul." Whitman said according to Traubel,
"I do not believe in the body as the end, of course, but as
the beginning, or rather, as a necessary item in the combinations of material that go to making of a man. The
body is the other side of the soul." This was said in reply
to the Unitarian minister who expressed preference of the
soul to the body. In *Song of Prudence* he said:

> "Only that person has really learn'd who has
>   learn'd to prefer results,
> Who favors body and soul the same."

To Traubel he remarked: "To have the concrete of the
body first of all—is the original and guaranty of the rest."
Again: "I have great faith in science—real science: the
science that is the science of the soul as well as the science
of the body." And when Traubel tried to get him to equalize the body with the soul, he said: "That is what should
be must be: a powerful loyalty to the body—to the body's
desires, passions, appetites, all of these, well in rein, but
alike, serving the soul, like a faithful steed." In *Song of*

Myself he declared: "I am the poet of the body and I am the poet of the soul." In *Starting from Paumanok*: "The body includes . . . . and is the soul." As Burroughs characterized the purport of Whitman's teaching, it redeemed philosophy and religion from the dogma of evil inherent in the body and that good is peculiarly resident in the soul.

Therefore Whitman's doctrine of the soul is not at all that of those who believe in the soul as impersonal and immortal apart from the physical man. Very early he urged that "Every soul has its own individual quality."

Allen as usual must also misunderstand what Whitman means by the "identified soul." He thinks it means "that at physiological birth each body receives its 'identity,' meaning that a soul is assigned to it, so that each exists through the other," and that this becomes clear if we think of Whitman the pantheist. It is an idea of traditional religion that God makes each human being a gift of his soul at birth. Linking Whitman with Alcott who maintained "that all souls have a personal identity with God and abide in him," Allen says that, although this "sounds a good deal like Christian mysticism," it "can also be interpreted in terms of Whitman's pantheism." Whitman neither said nor meant that. The separation of the soul from the "float" and its identification at birth, which was Whitman's doctrine, can be explained without the aid of any theological concept in terms of biological science.

Whitman's Belief in Immortality.

Whitman did not, like most radicals, scorn consideration of traditional terms. He sought to derive from them intrinsic meanings, because men could hardly have believed so persistently without some reason for their beliefs. However mistaken they carry some idea of fundamental importance to mankind.

In that spirit he said in a footnote to the Preface of the 1876 Centennial Edition of *Leaves of Grass*: "In my opinion, it is no less than this idea of Immortality, above all other ideas, that is to enter into, and vivify, and give crowning religious stamp, to Democracy in the New World." He said further it had been his intention to produce another "Volume, based on those convictions of perpetuity and conservation which, enveloping all precedents, make the unseen Soul govern absolutely at last. . . . to. . . . exhibit the problem and paradox of the same ardent and fully appointed Personality entering the sphere of the resistless gravitation of Spiritual Law, and with cheerful face estimating Death, not at all as the cessation, but as somehow I feel it must be, the entrance upon by far the greatest part of existence, and something that Life is at least as much for, as it is for itself." In *Starting from Paumanok* he had said:

> "How can the real body ever die and be
>   buried?
> Of your real body and any man's or woman's
>   real body,
> Item for item it will elude the hands of the
>   corpse-cleaners and pass to fitting spheres,
> Carrying what has accrued to it from the mo-
>   ment of birth to the moment of death."

In the same section of that poem he said emphatically that the form of the body, the substance and life of a man do not "return in the body and the soul" either "before death or after death." This altogether negates belief in the transmigration of souls. It rejects also the Christian doctrine of resurrection of the body. Nor does it support other doctrines of a substantially fixed immortal soul, whether personal or impersonal. Nor has it anything in common with a materialistic doctrine of conservation of energy or the indestructibility of matter. Those are static doctrines in contrast with Whitman's belief in dynamic continuous change.

In the first place, as the soul is identified and individualized, so too is immortality. "I believe in immortality, and by that I mean identity." In the future of immortality as well as in the past and present no one can acquire or "grow for another—not one."

"The soul is of itself,
All verges to it, all has reference to what
    ensues,
All that a person does, says, thinks, is of con-
    sequence,

❖ ❖ ❖ ❖ ❖ ❖

Not one word or deed . . .

❖ ❖ ❖ ❖ ❖ ❖

But has results beyond death as really as
before death.

❖ ❖ ❖ ❖ ❖ ❖

These inure, have inured, shall inure, to the
    identities from which they sprang, or shall
    spring."

How utterly mistaken then to assume with Allen that Whitman would be in agreement with Alcott in a pantheistic doctrine of "eliminating selfishness by merging the self with the Eternal Self," with Alcott's injunction:

"Depose thyself if thou would'st be
Dressed in fresh suit of Deity."

The very contrary of that doctrine is Whitman's. He would not depose the self. The human self is no more merged in the divine than the life in the plant is merged in the general stream of life.

But immortality is not the peculiar and single possession of man. Everything has it.

> "I swear I think now that every thing without
> exception has an eternal soul!
>
> ❖ ❖ ❖ ❖ ❖ ❖
>
> I swear I think there is nothing but immor-
> tality!
>
> ❖ ❖ ❖ ❖ ❖ ❖
>
> And all preparation is for it—and identity is
> for it—and life and materials are altogether
> for it!"

In this poem, *To think of Time*, it is not pantheism or
Emerson's Oversoul, as Allen thinks, that Whitman meant.
The especially emphatic lines are:

> You are not thrown to the winds, you gather
> certainly and safely around yourself,
> Yourself! yourself! yourself, for ever and
> ever!"

It is the self or individual soul which saves life and
death from meaninglessness.

> "It is not to diffuse you that you were born of
> your mother and father, it is to identify
> you,
> It is not that you should be undecided, but
> that you should be decided,
> Something long preparing and formless is ar-
> rived and form'd in you,
> You are henceforth secure, whatever comes
> or goes."

Identity is specificity, not merger in the Oversoul or Nirvana. Even the idea that "the soul or spirit transmits itself into all matter . . . can live the life of a rock . . . can feel itself the sea . . . feel itself a horse," etc., describes the intuitive power of a man who feels himself into all Nature.

Into the concept of Immortality is carried over also the dualistic conception of the soul. He conceived *Leaves of Grass* as expressing first "the eternal Bodily Character of One's-Self," and secondly "the Kosmic Spirit," "the Eternal Soul of Man, (of all Else too,) the Spiritual, the Religious—which it is to be the greatest office of Scientism, in my opinion, and of future Poetry also, to free from fables, crudities and superstitions, and launch forth in renewed Faith and Scope a hundredfold."

This new religion of Whitman's was not atheism, agnosticism, or skepticism. To the "down-hearted doubters dull and excluded" he gave encouragement and assurance. He assured man of immortality. "Nothing is ever really lost." We are "all surely going somewhere."

But this immortality is not any more wonderful or unique than anything else. It is in fact not a problem: "There is nothing but immortality." For life and death are one whole; one fits to the other; even if I don't know how that may be, I do know that "the past and present indicate that it is good." A *Night on the Prairies* convinced him

> ". . . that life cannot exhibit all to me, as the
>   day cannot,
> I see that I am to wait for what will be ex-
>   hibited by death."

What Whitman preaches is greater faith than men ordinarily have. He observes "how few . . . hold any faith in results." It is not Santayana's mere "animal faith" that Whitman celebrates, although he emulates the dumb beasts who do not "weep for their sins" or whine "about their duty to God."

Nor is this merely the faith or religion of the men of science, for as Burroughs caught from the temper of the time: "Science sees man as the ephemeron of an hour . . . Whitman sees him as inevitable and immortal as God himself." Even the great understanding of Burroughs was too close to contemporaneity to absorb all of Whitman's robust and confident faith in the destiny of man.

I do not know of another who has so thoroughly divested himself of the prejudices of beliefs and traditions, who uses the terms God and immortality with the freedom and realism of Whitman. When Burroughs says that "the idea of identity" of the self "is at the bottom of his unshakeable faith in immortality," his statement is confusing. He gives the impression that Whitman's belief was like the normal belief in immortality based on personal identity, which Hume tried to show unfounded.

Whitman's faith rather rested where Hume contended it only could rest, on beliefs which spring from the depths of experience. And furthermore, immortality for Whitman was not merely a life after death persisting from and like our present life. It may be karma without transmigration of souls. It is rather that continuity of existence which may change its forms, yet even those forms will not be lost.

Whitman's Personalist Religion.

Whitman's conception of personalist religion differs from that of others.

Allen, following the authority of Flewelling, says that Whitman was one of the first and the first in the United States to use the term personalism. Bronson Alcott immediately adopted it and, in the opinion of Allen, "understood Whitman's doctrine if anyone did." Without repeating our previous criticism of the Alcott and Bowne philosophy of metaphysical personalism, we now indicate a further opposition between that viewpoint and Whitman's.

To Alcott, "the antonym of personalism was individualism—a term into which he crowded all human ignorance, strife, misunderstanding, and even reform. All sin and error were due, he came to think, to the effort of individual wills to act as though they were independent of all other wills human and divine." As, according to Long, it was Whitman's disposition for "willing things" that denied him title to be a pure mystic, so too he dissented from Alcott by regarding personality a synonym, not antonym, of individuality. "This idea of perfect individualism it is indeed that deepest tinges and gives character to the idea of the aggregate. For it is mainly or altogether to serve independent separatism that we favor a strong generalization, consolidation." Whitman's insistence "on the identity of the Union at all hazards" is therefore to be understood only in the sense that Lincoln also thought Union essential to individual liberties.

Also passing by Allen's attribution to a Christian origin of Whitman's personalism to give attention to Wilder's more definite statement of the theory that Christianity is the source of the belief in the unique worth of every man: the latter argues the point against the Whitmanian philosophy which is assumed to be the parent of the materialistic impersonalism in the New Poetry. Wilder's error is identification of "autonymous responsible personality" with Christianity. The authoritarianism of both Catholic and Protestant Christianity is antagonistic to individual autonomy, for they do not regard man as capable of self-salvation, but dependent on the grace of God which demands total self-surrender. Such subjection Whitman knew and declared the destruction of personality which requires for its development freedom and independence. It is not Christianity but Whitman who stands in contrast with the impersonalistic pessimism which is so frequent in the New Poetry.

Wilder's plea for a reformation of Christianity to save the world would have effective point if instead of traditional Christianity he could take Whitman's view of the dignity and worth of every individual man.

The Modern Psychoses and Christianity.

When Christianity comes forward with its solutions for all that is wrong with our world today, its wars, its economic maladjustments, our diseased personalities, our loss of faith, we have reason to be skeptical of its value in the crisis, because these very difficulties have become most acute in Christendom. Besides it is Christianity most which we have lost faith in. As long as theologies and eschatologies occupy the first place of attention in the Christian Church it will not do much to solve our present problems.

Psychoanalysis, at first in Freud hostile to religion, is now developing Christianized practitioners, to deal with the psychoses and with modified personality concepts differing from Freud's. Wilder quotes C. G. Jung as one of the modifiers who likens these mental maladies of humans to volcanic outbursts from our unconscious internal selves against which we have no emotional source of protection. This favors the Christian idea that men can't help themselves. But psychoanalist theory often forgets its own practical technique which cures the malady by bringing it up into the clear light of consciousness, of reason, and thus saves for its practitioners the humbuggery of mediation which is the essence of the role of church and priest between God and man. Both prey upon man's sense of his weakness, himself often as great an enemy to himself as are the forces outside himself.

Wilder like, Karen Horney expresses that condition of a sense of helplessness in the afflicted person as one of self-alienation. He suffers from "a sense of unreality." Hallucinations and hysterias follow that state of mind. The impersonal environments in moden life tend to bring about the malady of disassociation in the individual, the split personality. Wilder says: "This main malady or sense of alienation and lostness of contemporary man expresses itself for one thing as a vertigo or what we call a sense of the abyss." But if Christianity ever had healing for such aberrated persons, its power has departed, and Wilder is mistaken in supposing that "Christianity alone" can minister to them now.

For, if self-alienation is the seat of the malady, a religion of self-abasement, self-sacrifice, self-surrender, which is the burden of the preaching of Christianity, is like giving more of a poison to counteract its deadly effects. An overdose does sometimes act in that way. Whitman generally abjured such negativisms. He extolled the self. He deemed the building of a self-reliant, independent personality as not only the best protection against the ills that beset mankind but as also the means by which man attains the greatest achievements of the soul.

Whitman's New Religion of Humanity.

As Allen says: "For a religion of supernaturalism (with reward in a future existence) he would substitute the religion of humanity." But as all the traditional faiths make some claim to humanism today, it becomes necessary to distinguish Whitman's humanism from theirs. Whatever affinity it has with Christianity is only in the humanism of Jesus, to which we have frequently referred as parallel to estimate Whitman's tolerance for sinful persons.

A certain quietude in him also suggests similarity to Hindu spiritualism, but Whitman is not on the side of

passivity or the subduing of the emotional nature of man.
The poem,

> "I sit and look out upon all the sorrows of the
> world, and upon all oppression and shame,
>
> ❖ ❖ ❖ ❖ ❖ ❖
>
> See, hear, and am silent,"

does not mean a Brahminic indifference. His very expression of those sorrows, wrongs, and agonies shows he is
not indifferent.

Although one does not feel the fire of the reformer in
Whitman, his role as a reformer was extraordinarily ample.
He declared the church too laggard for the new religion
to be enshrined in the hearts of men. His is not a religion
to worship God. It has a much larger function to perform.
It is a religion beyond Nature and beyond God. Instead he
advances Man the God to new realms. The true religion
is individual and human.

Whitman is not wrapped in a cloak of mysticism that
thinks it knows but is blind to everything, even to the
ineptness of its own images. He is not an 18th century rationalistic materialist who depersonalized and dehumanized
man. Nor is he a 19th century agnostic evolutionist who
regarded man as a very contemptible being in the vastness
of Nature, nor as did the contemporary theologian vilify
him before God.

Whitman gave the soul of man a new meaning, not borrowed by endowment of its spirit from God, but significant
in itself as an immortal soul of a unique and worth while
individual human being. It is an immortal soul, not by
virtue of a Christian hope in the resurrection of the body
purged of earthly qualities, nor by reason of possessing
platonic fleshless immortality, but for what it is and may
be. The importance of this concept is not only in what
it affirms with clarity of vision but also in the tenacity of

its belief that man, his deeds and thoughts, have permanent value in, through and by himself.

As to traditional beliefs or religion he perceived in them a deeper core of humanism to which he laid hold, not as freethinkers generally eschewing or scoffing at the religious terms of tradition, but using them, surcharging them with truly humanistic meaning. God, Christ, soul, immortality, are for him wholly humanist conceptions.

How can we distinguish true humanism from the pseudo varieties? By the purport. Is man abased before some other entity? Is he subordinated to something else? Is superstition, the placing of God or Nature above man, substituted for faith and belief in man? The true humanist has an abiding and supreme faith in his fellowman above all else.

The religion of humanism may not worship man, but it serves men primarily. It is the contrary of the Westminister Confession of Faith of the Presbyterian Church which is typical of the attitude of orthodox Christianity and which in the Shorter Catechism declares that "The chief end of man is to glorify God and his works." Whitman saw clearly that the chief end of man is to serve himself and his fellowmen.

Whitman and our Contemporary Religions.

The originality of Whitman's ideas about God and man is shown by comparison with the current religious philosophies. I first take the exposition and classification of such ideas by Wieman as basis for my comparison. He classifies beliefs as traditional supernaturalism, the new supernaturalism, theistic naturalism, liberalism, and humanism. To the traditional supernaturalist man is a fallen sinful creature, who hasn't a chance except as he seeks and obtains forgiveness by God. That was the religion of Augustine, Aquinas, and Calvin, and is today that of Professor Machen. The problem of evil is unsolvable by the supernaturalists because their predicament is that God is all-powerful, the creator of everything, and must therefore have made the devil and have allowed men to fall into sin and wickedness.

The new supernaturalism outvies the old by putting God still farther away from man. It finds no place for human reason to make any contact whatsoever with God. Surprisingly it throws out both church and Bible as weak and fallible human things. Human ideals and goals it discards as often opposed to God and also futile or worse. Its representatives are Karl Barth, Emil Brunner, Paul Tillich, and the brothers Reinold and H. Richard Niebuhr.

Theistic naturalism, like supernaturalism, believes that "man exists for God, not God for man," that man can be saved only by humbling himself and surrendering absolutely to God. The essence of this belief is that man must seek outside himself in the reality of Nature for that which will save him. Its representatives are A. N. Whithead, B. E. Meland, John Macmurray, Gregory Vlastos, Charles Hartshorne, and N. H. Wieman, whose authority we are now following. Obedience to God and Nature is the primary tenet of this belief. It is virtually Burroughs' acceptance of the Universe, but Burroughs could not be quite so logical in accepting its implications of the enslavement of man.

Wieman applies the term liberal to a religion which is now rather out of date. It was a reaction against traditional supernaturalism. It believed in the innate goodness of man, but still thought him dependent on God. It placed emphasis upon religious experience and is a kind of liberal mysticism, especially in such representatives as Rufus Jones. They are the descendents of Schleiermacher and include Borden P. Bowne, W. A. Brown, and D. C. Macintosh. Wieman derogatively comments on them as psychological introverts and as "a conglomerate of moral idealism, social entertainment, aesthetic enjoyment of music and other arts, practical guidance in the

conduct of personal life, discussion of economic and political opinions, the magnetic appeal of dominant personalities, all interfused with certain standard ceremonies
and symbols, including use of the Bible, but with nothing
distinctively religious as over against the secular." That
is an unsympathetic estimate by an opponent who prefers
the hard God.

Whitman and Other Humanists.

In the above review of theologies there is little besides the optimism of the liberals that resembles Whitman's beliefs and attitudes. But there remains Wieman's
treatment of humanism. We should keep in mind that
his classification is of historical types, and the humanism
he describes is represented by John Dewey, R. W. Sellars,
A. E. Haydon, and Max Otto. These notable humanists
have come after Whitman, and his originality and power,
I think, gain from comparison with them.

According to Wieman, in this philosophy God passes
into the background or is deemed non-existent. Man is
the only known carrier of ideals. In man's imagination
the Universe takes on meaning. Human nature is the
"supremely worthful reality." But "for Dewey God is
not a figment of the imagination . . . God is the power
which rises up from the universe in the form of striving, climbing, idealistic imagination of man. . . . God
is to be known, then, by scientific inquiry, namely the
science of psychology."

The theistic criticism of the humanists is "that they
are serving a supreme good which they cannot specify
nor put into any final program." Dewey would reply
that the theists are engaged in a self-deceptive assumption of certainty in their belief that the ultimate good
is God.

Turning to another source, Dr. Burrt's *Types of Religious Philosophy* is less theologically biased and gives

more attention to their later developments away from traditionalism. His survey includes Catholic, Protestant Fundamentalist, Modernist, Agnostic, Scientific, Ethical Idealist, and Humanist types. The orthodox Catholic and Protestant religions with their authoritative revelations of church, priests and Bible were repudiated by Whitman and our interest for comparison is with the newer and unorthodox religions.

As for the religion of science, as Burtt describes it, it assumes that man can attain certainty as to his highest good through the power of his own reason and without any supernatural aid. In the cosmic structure there is no concern for human welfare. We have discussed this above in considering Burroughs' cosmic theory and Whitman's variance from scientificism.

Whitman's relation to the agnostics is recognized by Allen as a source of his thought. But Whitman also knew the point of his difference from them. As he said in comparing his beliefs with Ingersoll's: "The Colonel and I are not directly at issue even about God and immortality: I do not say yes where he says no; I say yes where he says nothing." There was too much optimism in Whitman to be temperamentally a skeptic.

As to ethical idealism (which we call ethical humanism) , its assertions of unique worth attaching to every human personality, its faith in the moral freedom of man, and man's social duties—these are tenets quite akin to Whitman's. Felix Adler was a friend and visitor of Whitman during the period of Traubel's recorded conversations with Whitman. Whitman expressed himself about Adler's movement: "I don't see how these Ethical fellows can expect to do much as an opposition to the Church: they may stir the Church up, plague it into reforms, changes, even revolutions—but the Church is bound to continue to be a church imminent, eminent, imperative . . . I am done with the letter of the Church." Excepting for its support of a church, Whitman was in accord with Ethical Humanism.

What Wieman terms liberal religion is a sect of what Burrt describes as modernism. Its emphasis upon the unique leadership of Jesus and "dependence on some cosmic or environmental factor, which we may call God", narrows it too much for Whitman's inclusive religion that draws a larger circle which takes in God and Christ without subservience to them.

What Burtt describes as Humanism is not Whitman's humanism, but that of the Humanist Manifesto of the 1920's. It has too much of socialism in it to overcome Whitman's profound suspicion of the philosophy of en masse. The spirit of sharing and of comradeship sufficed for Whitman, and institutions he held subordinate to purely human ends. "The largeness of Nature and the Nation are monstrosities without a corresponding largeness of the citizen." Nor is the materialistic 19th century evolutionism of the Manifesto accordant with Whitman's humanism. In the Whitman view its rationalism is also excessive. He was more definitely religious than these humanists.

With the increasing popularity of humanism it has become a battle-ground of rival claimants. With Jacques Maritain arguing for Catholicism as the "True Humanism", and President Hutchins for Renaissance or literary humanism, the evolutionary and agnostic humanists cannot have it all their own way.

Another encyclopedic writer, Conger, reviewing *The Ideologies of Religion,* among them occultism, mysticism, supernaturalism, idealism, pragmatism, evolutionism, naturalism, economic nationalism, and humanism, leaves Whitman out of the long list of humanists and places him among the cosmic mystics along with Wordsworth, Thoreau, and John Burroughs.

In Conger's chapter on Humanism are mentioned

such movements and authors and books as the revival of ancient learning in the Italian Renaissance, August Comte's Religion of Humanity, F. S. C. Schiller's pragmatism, English Personal Idealism, Babbitt's and More's "emphasis on man's life" with its appeal to Oriental "intuitive discipline", the Confucian *Analects,* and Unitarian humanism. He says the "positive constructive content" of humanism is "emphasis upon (1) knowledge, (2) nature, (3) man, and (4) social reconstruction", and then proceeds to criticize these premises:

First, humanism is "too rationalistic, positivistic, and withal destructive." Next "it is hard for humanism to unite nature and man in any organic or imposing way." Third, "The humanist emphasis on man and his affairs is" not only "presumptious" but also it "affirms the worth of human existence to such an extent that it strains credulity almost as much as do some of the older faiths which it rejects as superstitions." Furthermore, "humanism has no monopoly on social enthusiasm or ethical consecration." Lastly, "humanism lacks religious power, ... having the form of religion without the content or the power thereof."

Although Conger's criticism may be justified concerning most of the humanisms he has listed, they are hardly applicable to Whitman's humanism. He was not excessively rationalistic. His cosmic view, his social enthusiasm, and his religious power are not weak. His philosophic scheme included man and Nature in an imposing organic conception that compares well with any that can longer hold credulity for modern men. He has been most attacked for the presumptiousness of his claims for the dignity and worth of men; but this is the crux of the controversy. The alternatives are the degrading of man by the traditional religious superstitions and the disparagement of man by pseudo-scientific impersonalism. Whitman had what he called "essential faith in man, above all his errors and wickedness."

A few aditional quotations express the contrast of his attitudes toward the old dogmas, in rejection of authoritarian religion, and his clear faith in religion centered about man.

> "I am the poet of sin,
> For I do not believe in sin."

> "And I say to mankind, Be not curious
>   about God,
> For I who am curious about each am not
>   curious about God."

"The local considerations of sin, disease, deformity, death, etc., ... are to be met by science, boldly accepting, promulging this faith, and planting the seeds of superber laws—of the explication of the physical universe through the spiritual—and clearing the way for a religion, sweet and unimpugnable alike to little child or great savan."

"It remains to bring forward and modify everything else with the idea of that Something a man is (last precious consolation of the drudging poor), standing apart from all else, divine in his own right, and a woman in hers, sole and untouchable by any canons of authority, or any rule derived from precedent, state-safety, the acts of legislatures, or even from what is called religion, modesty, or art."

The Tests of Religion for Whitman's Humanism.

Whitman believed intensely that he brought forward a new religion. To what extent does it measure up to the customary and standard tests of a religion? Here I take Trueblood's *Logic of Belief* for guide.

He states four characteristics of religion: a belief, a cult, a moral practice, and organization. A belief Whitman's religion has clearly; a moral practice too, but too tolerant and flexible for strict religionists. A cult, an organization, he did not wish to have: "The ripeness of Religion is doubtless to be looked for in this field of individuality, and is a result that no organization or church can ever achieve."

The characteristic fruits of religion come nearer to the content of Whitman's creed: Four moods are named by Trueblood: "The mood is akin to poetry", "akin to love", "akin to that of loyalty", "akin to humility". The one word that might sum these up is "reverence". Whitman was preeminent in the first two characteristics. The third was not wanting in him, but was balanced and checked in behalf of the integrity of the individual soul. He was too much of a modern and a democratic individualist to wear the fourth as a habit. He had a deep reverence for the sublimity of Nature and the love of man, but did not cultivate the pose of reverence.

To the different types of logic of religious belief which Trueblood designates as moral, esthetic and religious experience, Whitman was no stranger. The problem of good and evil concerned him greatly, but he had no such approach to it as absolutist moralism. Instead of Herbert Spencer's belief that man must obey Nature, he shared rather Thomas H. Huxley's view "that it is man's high vocation to go against Nature", substituting for it "ethical process", for the ethically "best" instead of the naturally fittest to survive. But he was wary of the religious conscience which whines and prays about its sins and throws overboard its own responsibility onto the large shoulders of God and Nature. He did not believe in good because God is good. As in *Chanting the Square Deific*, he had a place for Satan, the revolter, as well as for the God of stern justice and the Christ of love; none for the satanic scapegoat or the Christ that washes out our sins with sacrificial blood. He seemed to believe in a purgative Nature, at least as compost or manure, death fertilizing life, the wholesome cycle of life and death, given time enough, but that was no more his reliance than upon the "waiting" God. There was no necessity in his moral experience of religion for theological belief in a transcendent being, whether God or Nature. His religious morality found belief and faith in man a sufficient footing.

The esthetic experience of religion played a large part in Whitman's consciousness. A *Night on the Prairies* and other poems in the collection entitled *Whispers of Heavenly Death*, notably *To the Sun-set Breeze*, and many another poem may instance that Whitman's esthetic sense expressed itself in terms of familiar religious themes. The contemplation of Nature especially aroused in him religious thoughts. *Thou Mother with Thy Equal Brood*, a poem of democracy, is veritably the religion of democracy, is the prophecy of a "new, Spiritual World", and it is among the poems which have most appealed to the purely esthetic sense.

The theme of death that sings in so many of his poems, is like an often repeated echo in a stanza of one of his most musical poems, *Out of the Cradle Endlessly Rocking*.

Notwithstanding an intellectual quality, a profound philosophy or religion of humanism, which I have endeavored most to exposit in this book, and which underlies, is the substance of his whole work, what is far more apparent in it is his religiously esthetic sense. His choice of poetry as the principal medium of his expression is an even better evidence that his religious experience was dominantly esthetic. As we have observed he deliberately eschewed the method of logic. The sensuous images of his poetry became nevertheless a logic of symbols which we believe we have successfully translated into the language of philosophy and proved that Whitman's thought was systematic though represented wholly in art.

To those who assume that religion is inextricably joined with notions of God and immortality, which had a special unorthodox significance for Whitman, it may be important that they were a self-conscious expression of his religion. But also it should be remarked with True-blood that "religion is not so much finding God, as re-action to the reality which has found us," but more cor-rectly it may be said, that religion is the reality which we have discovered in and through ourselves, which is the substance of the faith and the sustaining beliefs we have. Religion is the human faith by which we live and work, and it is stronger as it exists without external ob-jects or gods or God or immortality or life beyond this one as the content of its beliefs. Such an intensely sub-jective faith is less likely to be shaken or overthrown by the shattering experiences of life. It is a religion which cannot be lost.

The utter freedom with which Whitman learned to move about in the realm of mythologies and superstitions of the old religions, utilizing them as the poetic symbols of his thought, is a freedom he sought consciously to impart to the readers of his poems. He made those an-cient symbols the furniture of the new temple he reared for the religion of humanity, for man-god and his soul.

6

THE NEW MORALITY

❖ ❖ ❖ ❖ ❖ ❖

"Nothing out of its place is good, nothing
   in its place is bad."

" . . . nor really aught we know,
But know the work, the need goes on and
   shall go on, . . .

❖ ❖ ❖ ❖ ❖ ❖

We know not why or what, yet weave, forever weave."

❖ ❖ ❖ ❖ ❖ ❖

Good and Evil.

THE MOST DIFFICULT, FOR GENERAL COMPREHENSION, OF THE
Whitman themes, is this one on morality. Should we
think of Whitman as a teacher of morals, of morality?
The following chapter on Love and Comradeship is easy
to understand. Those were great themes for Whitman.
He was expansive about them. There is that in all of us
which responds to those sentiments, and anyone can feel
them readily and draw from Whitman the inspiration
he intended. Notwithstanding the considerable contrariety of opinion as to his meaning, especially about sex,
the great central stream of his thought about love and
comradeship flows clear and pure for common understanding.

It is not so simple to describe his thoughts about the fundamental conceptions of good and evil. There are more subtle meanings concerning these opposites which he appears to mingle in a confusing way, almost as if they are indistinguishable.

> "What blurt is this about virtue and about
>   vice?
> Evil propels me and reform of evil propels
>   me, I stand indifferent,
> My gait is no fault-finder's or rejecter's
>   gait."

> "What is called good is perfect, and what
>   is called bad is just as perfect."

> "Good or bad I never question you—I love
>   all—I do not condemn anything,
> I chant and celebrate all that is yours."

If that is not excess of magnanimity in Whitman's effort to encompass all things, what does it mean? Is it indifference to moral claims, disregardful of the hurt and evil in the world, closing one's eyes and ears to the wrongs that are suffered and unwillingness to take one's own responsibility for them? One poem has been so interpreted:

> "I sit and look out upon all the sorrows of
>   the world, and upon all oppression and
>   shame,

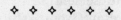

> See, hear, and am silent."

Though a silent observer of evil, he is not oblivious to or unmoved by the wrongs he poignantly describes. He is not like those who know the hurts to human beings

and sit untouched by them. He feels himself sharing in
the guilt:

> "Through me many long dumb voices,
> Voices of the interminable generations of
>   prisoners and slaves,
> Voices of the diseas'd and despairing and of
>   thieves and dwarfs,
>
> ❖ ❖ ❖ ❖ ❖ ❖
>
> And of the rights of them the others are
>   down upon,
> Of the deform'd, trivial, flat, foolish,
>   despised,
>
> ❖ ❖ ❖ ❖ ❖ ❖
>
> Through me forbidden voices,
> Voices of sexes and lusts, voices veil'd and
>   I remove the veil,
> Voices indecent by me clarified and
>   transfigur'd."

> "I see the enslav'd, the overthrown, the hurt,
>   the opprest of the whole earth,
> I feel the measureless shame and humilia-
>   tion of my race, it becomes all mine,
> Mine too the revenges of humanity, the
>   wrongs of ages, baffled feuds and
>   hatreds,
> Utter defeat upon me weighs—all lost—the
>   foe victorious,
> (Yet 'mid the ruins Pride colossal stands
>   unshaken to the last,
> Endurance, resolution to the last.)"

The good and the bad in everyone impressed Whitman:

> "In all people I see myself, none more and
>   not one a barley-corn less,

And the good or bad I say of myself I say
    of them."

To the eminent one he said:

"Who are you? and what are you secretly
    guilty of all your life?"

There is something natural and inborn about this
that does not dismay him:

"Underneath all, Nativity,
I swear I will stand by my own nativity,
    pious or impious so be it."

It is this that led him to accept the evil that is in
persons. He did not exclude anyone. *"To a Common
Prostitute"*, he said:

"Not till the sun excludes you do I exclude
    you."

"I feel I am of them—I belong to those
    convicts and prostitutes myself,
And henceforth I will not deny them—for
    how can I deny myself?"

As in the spirit of Christ he affirmed:

"This is the meal equally set, this the meat
    for natural hunger,
It is for the wicked just the same as the
    righteous, I make appointments with all,
I will not have a single person slighted or
    left away,
The kept-woman, sponger, thief, are hereby
    invited,

> The heavy-lipp'd slave is invited, the
>   venerealee is invited;
> There shall be no difference between them
>   and the rest."

But it is not the evil in such persons that obsessed his vision. He saw the potential good in them:

> "I curious pause, for lo, an outcast form, a
>   poor dead prostitute brought,
> Her corpse they deposit unclaim'd, it lies
>   on the damp brick pavement,
> The divine woman, her body, I see the
>   body, I look on it alone,
> That house once full of passion and beauty,
>   all else I notice not,

> That immortal house more than all the
>   rows of dwellings ever built!

> That little house alone more than them all
>   —poor, desperate house!
> Fair, fearful wreck—tenement of a soul—
>   itself a soul,

> Dead house of love—house of madness and
>   sin, crumbled, crushed."

It is the development, the change, the transformation of such to good that matters. In human relationship they may be transmuted:

> "The gentleman of perfect blood acknowl-
>   edges his perfect blood,

> The insulter, the prostitute, the angry per-
> son, the beggar, see themselves in the
> ways of him, he strangely transmutes them,
> They are not vile any more, they hardly
> know themselves they are so grown."

Such equality makes us interdependent:

> "Whoever degrades another degrades me,
> And whatever is done or said returns at
> last to me."

There is a contagion of good:

> "Divine am I inside and out, and I make
> holy whatever I touch or am touch'd
> from."

He has something that suggests a mystic faith in progress, evolutionary process, in time the great healer and
perfecter:

> "You human forms with the fathomless ever
> —impressive countenances of brutes!
>
> ❖ ❖ ❖ ❖ ❖ ❖
>
> I do not say one word against you, away
> back there where you stand,
> (You will come forward in due time to my
> side)."

But as we have seen that is a belief in man rather
than in Nature apart from man. He puts that test for
those who would assume to teach or be the poets in
America:

> "Have you too the old ever-fresh forbear-
> ance and impartiality?

> Do you hold the like love for those hard-
>   ening to maturity? for the last-born? little
>   and big: and for the errant?"

Therefore he called himself equally the poet of good and evil:

> "The pleasures of heaven are with me and
>   the pains of hell are with me,
> The first I graft and increase upon myself,
>   the latter I translate into a new tongue."

This second line should be kept in mind; it indicates the desirable human attitude toward good and evil. Good and evil are not indifferently the same and are not to be regarded alike.

The self-righteous puritanical or pharisaical person Whitman sought to put away from himself and not to imitate him:

> "Nor will my poems do good only, they will do
>   just as much evil, perhaps more."

> "good and evil—these me."

The purpose and purport of *Leaves of Grass* was

> "Not to exclude or demarcate, or pick out
>   evils from their formidable masses (even
>   to expose them)
> But add, fuse, complete, extend—and cele-
>   brate the immortal and the good."

What is Evil?

Allen says, that "far, then, from actually denying evil, he accepts it as part of reality." But Whitman did say,

> " . . . . . there is in fact no evil,
> (Or if there is I say it is just as important
>   to you, to the land or to me, as any thing
>   else) ."

For Whitman evil is not an entity, it is a condition:

> "Nothing out of its place is good, nothing
> in its place is bad."

> "It is the central urge in every atom,
> (Often unconscious, often evil, downfallen,)
> To return to its divine source and origin,
> however distant,
> Latent the same in subject and in object,
> without one exception."

Evil may be either the condition of unorganized origin of things or their distortion. He reflects upon the nature of compost from which springs beautiful luxuriant growth of living things:

> " . . probably every spear of grass rises out
> of what was once a catching disease.
> Now I am terrified at the Earth, it is that
> calm and patient,
> It grows such sweet things out of such cor-
> ruptions,"

> "What is the part the wicked and the loath-
> some bear within earth's orbic scheme?"

And his reply is:

> "I know now why the earth is gross, tantal-
> izing, wicked, it is for my sake,
> I take you specially to be mine, you terrible,
> rude forms."

> "And the vast all that is call'd Evil I saw
> hastening to merge itself and become lost
> and dead."

which is Whitman's thought, not Hegel's.

Evil also has relation to struggle. In *Chanting the Square Deific,* he represented Satan as that defiant godlike spirit in man which seeks freedom and will not give up. It is the new struggling with the old for place:

> "For what is my life or any man's life but
> a conflict with foes, the old, the incessant
> war?
>
> ❖ ❖ ❖ ❖ ❖ ❖
>
> Ah think not you finally triumph, my real
> self has yet to come forth."

> "Piety and conformity to them that like,
> Peace, obesity, allegiance to them that like,
> I am he who tauntingly compels men,
>   women, nations,
> Crying, Leap from your seats and contend
>   for your lives."

> "For I am the sworn poet of every dauntless
>   rebel the world over,
> And he going with me leaves peace and
>   routine behind him,
> And stakes his life to be lost at any moment."

In life there is "Ever the undiscouraged, resolute, struggling soul of man":

> "Enough that they've survived at all—long
>   life's unflinching ones!
> Forth from their struggles, trials, fights, to
>   have emerged at all—in that alone,
> True conquerors o'er all the rest."

The struggle is not so much overcoming, a conquest, as it is to go on, to emerge. For evil is not a reality, it is a passing condition or status. Disease goes into death, death into compost, compost into the tissues of life, and life becomes identified in the soul. Everything is struggling toward the good, and there is really no evil, no sin.

What is Good?

It is the self-reliant adventurous man who is really good.

> "Me going in for my chances, spending for
> vast returns,

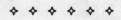

> Not asking the sky to come down to my good
> will,
> Scattering it freely forever."

> "The boy I love, the same becomes a man
> not through derived power, but in his
> own right,
> Wicked rather than virtuous out of con-
> formity or fear."

Good and evil pertain to individual men, to human beings alone, and to nothing else:

> "Nothing is sinful to us outside of ourselves,
> Whatever appears, whatever does not appear,
> we are beautiful or sinful in ourselves
> only."

> "And no man understands any greatness or
> goodness but his own, or the indication
> of his own."

When Whitman said, "only the good is universal," he was not expressing the philosophy of universalism, but rather his belief in the ultimate triumph of good, of good as the surviving thing or goal of conduct:

"In this broad earth of ours,
Amid the measureless grossness and the slag,
Enclosed and safe within its central heart,
Nestles the seed perfection.
By every life a share more or less,
None born but it is born, conceal'd or
    unconceal'd the seed is waiting.

For it (the soul) the real to the ideal tends.
For it the mystic evolution,
Not the right only justified, what we call
    evil also justified."

It was not merely a faith he expressed. It was a philosophic view. Not cosmical, in the sense of pantheistic, or theistic. He did express it as a faith, but also as a rational faith:

"Whither I walk I cannot divine, but I
    know it is good,
The whole universe indicates that it is good,
The past and the present indicate that it
    is good.
How beautiful and perfect are the animals!
How perfect the earth, and the minutest
    thing upon it!
What is called good is perfect, and what is
    called bad is just as perfect."

But, nevertheless,

"The difference between sin and goodness
    is no delusion."

He believed in the perfectability of man: "I believe in the eligibility of the human soul for all perfect things." But perfection is not merely something to come: "There will never be any more perfection than there is now." Although "perfect human life" may be forwarded. So when he says:

> "I praise with electric voice,
> For I do not see one imperfection in the
> universe,
> And I do not see one cause or result
> lamentable at last in the universe",

this is no particular affirmation about the whole, about the universe itself; for,

> "We know not what the use O life, nor
> know the aim, the end, nor really aught
> we know,
> But know the work, the need goes on and
> shall go on, the death envelop'd march
> of peace as well as war goes on,

> We know not why or what, yet weave,
> forever weave."

The work and the need, not cosmic ends or needs, are within our knowledge.

In his expression of the ideal poet and his ideal, he has expressed his conception of the good, of the ethical aim of right relations:

> " . . . the poet is the equable man,
> Not in him but off from him things are
> grotesque, eccentric, fail of their full
> returns,

Nothing out of its place is good, nothing
in its place is bad,
He bestows on every object or quality its
fit proportion, neither more nor less,
He is the arbiter of the diverse, he is the
key,
He is the equalizer of his age and land,
He supplies what wants supplying, he checks
what wants checking,

❖ ❖ ❖ ❖ ❖ ❖

As he see farthest he has the most faith,

❖ ❖ ❖ ❖ ❖ ❖

In the dispute of God and eternity he is
silent,

❖ ❖ ❖ ❖ ❖ ❖

He sees eternity in men and women, he does
not see men and women as dreams or
dots.
For the great Idea, the idea of perfect and
free individuals,
For that, the bard walks in advance, leader
of leaders."

Whitman's Attitudinal Morality.

In such a moral philosopher we should expect attitudes to be treated as having more importance than cardinal virtues. The latter are difficult to make out in
Whitman's scheme of goodness. A few such as love, truth,
wisdom, prudence, justice, freedom, equality, may be denominated. But even they in Whitman's vocabulary signify no absolute ideals but only relative or attitudinal
virtues. Are not all virtues attitudinal? Only to those who
do not believe in absolute virtue. To those who believe
that good is good always and everywhere and bad is bad

without variability, that good and bad are wholly independent of men and regardless of them, only they believe that virtue is a self-existent entity, and bad is a
reality, and not an attitude.

For Whitman conceived good and evil as in some respects interchangeable terms. Evil is translated into good.
If disease is evil, in natural processes it is turned into
good: dead matter becomes earthy compost, the matter in
which life takes root and grows again abundantly. Nature
sweetens foul waste things and makes them useful. The
analogy carries into human life. There too may not crime,
wrongs, sufferings serve our spiritual growth, become at
least a lesson for us? Both evil and the reform of evil thus
propel us forward.

In another respect, as we shall see, without being Nietzschean and glorifying warlike virtues, Whitman does not
disregard them but accounts for them in the processes of
natural growth. Even the evil or wicked man is probably
struggling, though unconsciously, toward a good end; it
is not the old good he is seeking, but new good. What
seemed evil is the beginning of a new good. The Saviours
of mankind have been punished as criminals, Socrates compelled to drink the hemlock, Jesus hung on the cross between the two thieves. Whereas Nietzsche narrowly condemned the virtues of self-sacrifice and humility and peace-
fulness, Whitman saw where they belong, not as absolute
virtues but relative to time and place. Appropriateness is
virtue: everything in its place is good, and the same thing
out of place is bad.

Considering Whitman then as an attitudinal moralist,
we may be prepared for his yet profounder conception of
morality as the making or building of personality. In treating love, comradeship and friendship he is nearest to the
latitudinarian Christian moralists, but other conceptions
show how far apart from them he is. Such subjects as war
and individualism give him often a Nietzschean similarity;

but as we have remarked that is dispelled by his recognition of the Christian virtues which Nietzsche hated. Again, and this is a very frequent attitude in Whitman, there is Aristotelian magnaminity in his expansiveness of temperament. For all his applause of freedom, which some have taken to be mere licentiousness and lawlessness, he makes as much of convention, patriotism, wisdom and justice as would satisfy a regular Confucianist. At heart he was conservative; something in the reformer repelled him, but in his large scheme of morals he could not exclude the reforming moralist. For he too was a rebel and the poet of rebellion: that is not merely the Whitman tradition or pose, it is Whitman—he inspirits revolution in the great cause of human freedom.

The very difficulty of cataloguing Whitman in the ethical systems proves the point we make that he was an attitudinal moralist, and not an absolutist—every absolute moralist must be narrow-minded, which both temperament and convictions would not allow him to be. It was the fanaticism of the moralistic reformer that Whitman disliked; his steadiness and fidelity to a cause Whitman approved. The trouble with the reformer is that he operates so often out of place. He is the evil of inappropriateness.

Epicureanism and hedonism have also an advocate in Whitman. The sexual appetites, pleasures and happiness enlisted him with reforming zeal in their behalf for human good. On the other hand, Whitman's emphasis upon waiting, patience, endurance, and arduous courage denoted the stoical attitude in him.

Strongly tending to be naturalistic, realistic, evolutionary, in his ethics, that was tempered by the fascination German Idealism had for him.

And not less, but rather more precious to Whitman, were the democratic virtues of liberty and equality, with their implicates of personality, freedom of the individual, self-reliance, etc.

Whitman's Synthesis of Ethics.

Whitman's significance therefore as a moralist is his synthesis which avoids what he condemned as coteries and schools of morals and religion. His synthesis finds a place for both Christian and Nietzchean morality, for legalism as well as antinomianism, for Epicureanism and Stoicism, for pleasure as well as for duty, for both naturalism and idealism. His synthetic principle is personal humanism.

We will now show how he dealt with each of these doctrines and found place for each and all of them in the humanistic doctrine which he called personalism. Later chapters may make more explicit and convincing by closer analysis than given here. Keep in mind that Whitman wrote, not as a systematic philosopher, but as a poet, impressionistically and emotionally; yet for all that it is remarkable how accurate and consistent his thought was. He had a clearly formulated ethical point of view.

The Warlike Virtues.

Whereas Nietzsche one-sidedly hailed the virtues of war and strength and condemned those of peace, Whitman saw the contrast of those virtues in a larger aspect. He understood the warlike virtues while abhorring war itself. His reply to Higginson's criticism of him for not enlisting as a soldier in the Civil War where he so valiantly served as a volunteer nurse was, as he stated it to Traubel: "I can never think of myself as firing a gun or drawing a sword on another man." He consistently had the scruples against war of the Quaker faith in which he was reared, together with the Quaker's moral courage. However, the war theme runs first to last through *Leaves of Grass*. In *Drum-Taps* it rises to a threnody. The second poem in *Leaves of Grass* takes measure of the issue.

In that poem, *As I Ponder'd in Silence,* he declares that, as the old bards sang of war, he sings the greater theme

of war with the realization of that theme: " I above all promote perfect soldiers." But it is "a war O soldiers not for
itself alone." The "stern, remorseless, sweet idea" of causes
that urge on war is the theme of his book too. But what he
means to promote are virtues merely incident to war, not
of war itself, even when he speaks in the language of war.

> "My call is the call of battle, I nourish active
>   rebellion,
> He going with me must go well arm'd,
> He going with me goes often with spare diet,
>   poverty, angry enemies, desertions."

The hazards of war not less than its glories are also
incidents of the soldiery course in behalf of peace:

> "O while I live to be the ruler of life, not a
>   slave,
> To meet life as a powerful conqueror,
> No fumes, no ennui, no more complaints or
>   scornful criticisms."

Many years before Nietzsche was heard of, with a profounder conception of the true warrior's role, he declared
"Nothing exterior shall ever take command of me."

> "O struggle against great odds, to meet ene-
>   mies undaunted!
> To be entirely alone with them, to find how
>   much one can stand!
> To look strife, torture, prison, popular odium,
>   face to face!
> To mount the scaffold, to advance to the muz-
>   zles of guns with perfect nonchalance!
> To be indeed a God!"

That is the trial of bravery which may fall to the lot
of every soldier and it is the test of the spirit of the bravest

soldier. And Whitman, the poet, rose to the conception
and appreciation of it. It was a symbol for him of the great
battle,

>". . . the field the world,
>For life and death, for the Body and for the
>   eternal Soul,"

but waged in his

>"book with varying fortune, with flight,
>   advance and retreat, victory deferr'd and
>   wavering."

This is not the one way Superman, imaginative soldier
of Nietzsche, the Napoleonic and invincible soldier, but
the actual soldier, in any life struggle. "The bold, vigorous, joyful, cruel, self-reliant" virtues of Nietzsche's warring supermen do not stand alone in Whitman's more
realistic conception of the soldier; those virtues are inevitably intermingled with their opposites exemplified
and experienced by the same soldier:

>"O to resume the joys of the soldier!
>To feel the presence of a brave commanding
>   officer—to feel his sympathy!
>To behold his calmness—to be warm'd in the
>   rays of his smile!
>To go to battle—to hear the bugles play and
>   the drums beat!
>To hear the crash of artillery—to see the glit-
>   tering bayonets and musket-barrels in the
>   sun!
>To see men fall and die and not complain!
>To taste the savage taste of blood—to be so
>   devilish!
>To gloat over the wounds and deaths of the
>   enemy."

Imagine a pacifist poet writing that! There is something more than mere Quaker in one who can write of war in that way. And there is a realism, a completeness of understanding about war which is missing in Nietzsche though he experienced the actualities of war as a soldier and bore in his body to his tragic death one of the incidents of it. Whitman too felt that his long suffered ills were the result of infectious diseases he encountered and of the arduous labors and fatigues he endured in the ministrations to wounded and dying soldiers, and that without such an experience the deeper emotions of his poetry could not have come forth. "Without those three or four years and the experiences they gave, *Leaves of Grass* would not now be existing."

But in him those experiences became transmuted: he addressed to the soldier a farewell:

> "Adieu dear comrade,
> Your mission is fulfilled—But I, more warlike,
> Myself and this contentious soul of mine,

> To fiercer, weightier battle give expression."

He dedicates himself, all poets, to the "wars to come," not of "that backward world," but of "the future, greater than all the past," to the battlefields and wars "For the great Idea, the idea of perfect and free individuals."

For today he seems realistically prophetical:

> "Are all nations communing? is there going
>   to be but one heart to the globe?
> Is humanity forming en-masse? for lo, tyrants
>   tremble, crowns grow dim,
> The earth, restive, confronts a new era, per-
>   haps a general divine war."

We seem to be going through such a period toward such a goal.

In a wholly different mood from Nietzsche's but of the very essence of Whitman's thinking, out of the destruction and death of wars he saw rising to the gentlest of the virtues, love, the comradeship of soldiers, which could fraternize also with the enemy:

> "Dearest comrades, all is over and long gone,
> But love is not over—and what love, O comrades
> Perfume from battle-fields rising, up from the foetor arising,

> Perfume all—make all wholesome,
> Make these ashes to nourish and blossom,
> O love solve all, fructify all with the last chemistry."

And the love of enemies too:

> "For my enemy is dead, a man divine as myself is dead."

Without the morbidities of weaker spirits, without the illusions of untried soldiers, appraising the virtues of war at their actual value in the larger meanings of destiny, he had also a definite hatred toward the evil of war at the same time he perceived the justifiable reasons for it. And in that very realistic understanding of war he cried with the vehemence of his convictions:

> "Away with themes of war! away with war itself!
> Hence from my shuddering sight to never more return that show of blacken'd, mutilated corpses!

> That hell unpent and raid of blood, fit for
>   wild tigers or for lop-tongued wolves, not
>   reasoning men,
> And in its stead speed industry's campaigns,
> With thy undaunted armies, engineering,
> Thy penants labor, loosen'd to the breeze,
> Thy bugles sounding loud and clear."

Something more than Professor James' "Moral Equivalents of War" in this! The more is, that morality is not the equivalent of war, and that the warlike virtues are not a necessary accompaniment of war but only an incident of it, that the martial virtues are not really martial, but at the same time the consuming wrong that is in war is not to be gotten rid of without arrival at the fundamental justice which is a long time coming. The primitive struggle of war betokens that in men which is winging its way to freedom. Out of the putridity of murderous war Whitman saw rising its opposite, Love, as grass grows in the compost of rotted vegetation.

The Christian Virtues.

So, in Christian virtues, in the Christ, Whitman recognized the complement of the warlike virtues, without the opposition to them which Nietzsche had. Yet he objected to certain tendencies in the morals of Christianity: "To me the negative virtues of the Church are the most menacing, to me the most abhorrent, of all professed virtues." Yet he had a place for them too.

The virtues of self-sacrifice are allied to loyalty to a cause and for country. Martyrdom has its values:

> "I see the clear sunsets of the martyrs,

> ❖ ❖ ❖ ❖ ❖ ❖

> I see those who in any land have died for the
>   good cause,

> The seed is spare, nevertheless the crop shall
>   never run out,
> (Mind you O foreign kings, O priests, the
>   crop shall never run out.) "

> "And lives and works, what are they all at last,
>   except the roads to faith and death?"

Even for the flag, the emblem of democracy, recounting
the struggles around it in war:

> "For the sake of that, my beauty, and that
>   thou might'st dally as now secure up there,
> Many a good man have I seen go under."

Equalized with the other virtues are those of self-
immolation which have been so largely appropriated by
Christianity and other religions, but which Whitman shows
have much wider range of attachment. Nor are they also
only patriotic, they belong to all causes that we have to
fight for:

> "All the brave actions of war and peace,
> All help given to relatives, strangers, the poor,
>   old, sorrowful, young children, widows, the
>   sick, and to shunn'd persons,
> All self-denial that stood steady and aloof on
>   wrecks, and saw others fill the seats of the
>   boats,
> All offering of substance or life for the good
>   old cause, or for a friend's sake, or opin-
>   ion's sake,
> All pains of enthusiasts scoff'd at by their
>   neighbors,
> All the limitless sweet love and precious suf-
>   fering of mothers,
> All honest men baffled in strifes recorded or
>   unrecorded,

These inure, have inured, shall inure, to the
identities from which they sprang, or shall
spring."

Even the philistine virtue of prudence

"Knows that the young man who composedly
peril'd his life and lost it has done exceed-
ingly well for himself without doubt,
That he who never peril'd his life, but retains
it to old age in riches and ease, has probably achiev'd nothing for himself worth
mentioning."

Whitman humanizes Christianity in the divine man as
the suffering God. In *Chanting the Square Deific* he identifies with himself as symbolizing mankind, the suffering
God-man, the Lord Christ, Hermes, Hercules:

"All sorrow, labor, suffering, I, tallying it,
absorb in myself,
Many times have I been rejected, taunted,
put in prison, and crucified, and many
times shall be again,
All the world have I given up for my dear
brothers' and sisters' sake, for the soul's
sake."

The martyrs only partake of the same virtues and sufferings that others have:

"The disdain and calmness of martyrs,
The mother of old, condemn'd for a witch,
burnt with dry wood, her children gazing
on,
The hounded slave that flags in the race,
leans by the fence, blowing, cover'd with
sweat,

> The twinges that sting like needles his legs
> and neck, the murderous buckshot and the
> bullets,
> All these I feel or am.

> Agonies are one of my changes of garments."

And there is nothing that sets this martyred God-man apart from the criminals so far as outward condition appears nor within is he freed from the suffering of them:

> "I am possess'd!
> Embody all presence outlaw'd or suffering,
> See myself in prison shaped like another man,
> And feel the dull unremitted pain,

> Not a youngster is taken for larceny but I
> go up too, and am tried and sentenced."

Whitman's conception of man suffering for man is sublimer than that of the Christian God suffering and doing penance for man, more sublime because presumably the sufferings of such a God could be mitigated by foreknowledge of his mission and destiny.

In another phase of Christian ethic, love, Whitman far exceeded Christian doctrine, although the teaching of Christ also went beyond anything the institution of Christianity has dared. The Christ, whose feet were washed by the woman of the street, who defended the woman taken in adultery, and could respectfully converse with the loose woman at the well, yet probably never spoke with the freedom of acceptance of the common prostitute voiced in Whitman's poem addressed to her. He would hardly have expressed himself in the nearly homosexual emotions that Whitman dared to admit into the poems entitled *Calamus*,

dedicated to "the institution of the dear love of comrades,"
which has a familiar human meaning not echoed in Christian thought. The bodily sexual love of man and woman
is a theme generally averse to Christian sentiment. Not
until Freudianism and not more broadly had another said,
as he:

> "Sex contains all, bodies, souls,
> Meanings, proofs, purities, delicacies, results,
>   promulgations,
> Songs, commands, health, pride, the mater-
>   nal mystery, the seminal milk,
> All hopes, benefactions, bestowals, all the
>   passions, loves, beauties, delights of the
>   earth,
> All the governments, judges, gods, follow'd
>   persons of the earth,
> These are contained in sex as parts of itself
>   and justifications of itself."

No other has expressed so inclusively the many phases
of love: Unrequited love:

> "I loved a certain person ardently and my
>   love was not returned,
> Yet out of that I have written these songs."

The cosmic affinity of Goethe or Platonic love:

> "I perceive one picking me out by secret and
>   divine signs,
> Acknowledging none else, not parent, wife,
>   husband, brother, child, any nearer than
>   I am."

> "Why are there men and women that while
>   they are nigh me the sunlight expands my
>   blood?"

Conjugal love:

"Fast-anchor'd eternal O love! O woman I
love!
O bride! O wife! more resistless than I can
tell, the thought of you!"

Universal love:

"I have look'd for equals and lovers and found
them ready for me in all lands,
I think some divine rapport has equalized
them with me."

Love of neighbors:

"In folks nearest to you finding the sweetest,
strongest, lovingest."

Family love:

"His own parents, . . .
They gave this child more of themselves than
that,
They gave him afterward every day, they became part of him.

❖ ❖ ❖ ❖ ❖ ❖

The family usages, ... the yearning and
swelling heart,
Affection that will not be gainsay'd, . . "

The love of work:

"Ah little recks the laborer,
How near his work is holding him to God.
The loving laborer through time and space."

Self-contained love:

> "I swear I begin to see love with sweeter
>   spasms than that which responds love,
> It is that which contains itself, which never
>   invites and never refuses."

The overwhelming mastery of love and its pervasiveness:

> "Take now the enclosing theme of all, the
>   solvent and the setting,
> Love, that is pulse of all, the sustenance and
>   the pang,
> The heart of man and woman all for love,
> No other theme but love—knitting, enclosing,
>   all-diffusing love."

The most ecstatic Christian apostrophe to love never went to such lengths, but in fact held much that Whitman adored in love as sinful. "The cleanliness of the sexes" was for him a dominant ideal. The Christian inculcation of sex shame and taboo was opposite to his feeling of sex purity:

> "Without shame the man I like knows and
>   avows the deliciousness of his sex,
> Without shame the woman I like knows and
>   avows hers."

In a later chapter the theme of love as Whitman conceived it will be considered again, more analytically and controversially, but what has been cited here on the wide moralities of love should be added there.

The Christian apologist may of course object that his ethic is an expanding one from the seed thoughts of Christ, and if very liberal may include Whitman as carrying on in the spirit of Christ, in which case Christianity would cease to be fettered by tradition. We cannot quarrel with such a liberality. Whitman's free use of Christian symbolism shows he would have welcomed it. But then Whitman would have to be recognized as having liberalized the Christian tradition very greatly.

7

WHITMAN'S SELF-CONTAINED MORALITY

❖ ❖ ❖ ❖ ❖ ❖

"The place where the great city stands is . . .
Where the men and women think lightly of
  the laws,

❖ ❖ ❖ ❖ ❖ ❖

Where children are taught to be laws to themselves, and to depend on themselves."

❖ ❖ ❖ ❖ ❖ ❖

Social Morality.

OUT OF HIS INSTITUTION OF LOVING COMRADES WHITMAN
evolved his glorified average man. That notion might seem
to come under the condemnation Nietzsche heaped upon
democracy as the embodiment of herd morality and mediocrity. But another viewpoint in Whitman's philosophy
redeemed it from such castigation. Whitman placed so
much emphasis upon individual right that he has been
charged with antinomianism. There are many passages
which taken out of context or away from Whitman's own
compilation of his writings would range Whitman as an
anarchist. But as usual he balances up. For those who would
make Whitman out a socialist or a communist, and there
are such, enough can be quoted to justify their doctrinnaire
bias for claiming Whitman as their own.

But Whitman was a Jeffersonian democrat which was

the same thing as a Lincoln republican. In the confused political thinking of today few people know what that means. Liberty Leaguers who falsely profess Jeffersonianism and Hamiltonized Republicans who as falsely profess to be followers of Lincoln muddle us up as badly as do the Bolshevik Communists who call themselves liberals and democrats. Whitman's social morality was not that of the fascist elite nor of the proletarian moralist. The ethics of violence was no part of his intellectual furniture. As Jefferson was an aristocrat but a disbeliever in the claims of a superior class of rulers, so too Whitman believed in the people, in the average man, and held him by right to be law unto himself. That is not herd morality and it is not anarchism. A brief review of his social concepts will prove that and show again the breadth of his viewpoint, of his synthetic thinking.

Whitman's conception of law is a focal point. For all that legalism is fundamentally at variance with morality, imposing a formalistic element in opposition to the claims of individual conscience, setting up social norms of compulsion upon the individual, and by institutions and conventions demanding conformity, enslaving the individual, there is nevertheless a close relationship between law and ethics. The questions of individual right and justice are at the heart of social morality and also are questions of law.

What was Whitman's attitude toward them? He was not equivocal. Whitman's balancing between the different moralities was not mere eclecticism. In his endeavor to be encompassing and inclusive, he did not lose sense of distinctions. He did not become vague and general, which is the vice of impersonalism. He was not a sloganizer. Clichés and deceptive phrases did not characterize a pretense of thinking in him. When we consider his conceptions of law and justice we must recognize that he had a definite social philosophy. To discover the essence of that philosophy we now take up his use of those terms.

A man who is law unto himself has become familiarly a term designating the outlaw. And such a passage as "No law less than ourselves owning, sailing, soldiering, thieving, threatening," gives Whitman the appearance of promoting outlawry. It is as before when we were considering his profession as the poet indifferently of good and evil. Whitman had a profounder conception of law as he had also of what is good.

It seems at least a paradox to speak of a great city as the place where the people think lightly of laws and the children are taught to be a law unto themselves. There are other expressions in which he seems, if not indifferent to law, at any rate antinomian: "Let others promulge the laws, I will make no account of the laws." Quite in the spirit of Nietzsche he applauds a "race henceforth owning no law but the law of itself, race of passion and the storm." He applies the idea to the American nation:

> "Land in the realms of God to be a realm
>   unto thyself,
> Under the rule of God to be a rule unto
>   thyself."

But that is not a negation of law, for immediately he adds:

> "Lo, where arise three peerless stars,
> To be thy natal stars my country, Ensemble,
>   Evolution, Freedom,
> Set in the sky of Law."

Has it never occurred to us that a man, a race or a nation which is a law unto itself is not lawless? If we are to teach our children to be a law unto themselves, we are not thereby making anarchists and lawless brats of them. We are teaching them to be self-law-abiding, self-governed.

We are teaching them to command and rule themselves.
This is the new and better self-operative law:

> "Man properly trained in sanest, highest free-
> dom, may and must become a law, and
> series of laws, unto himself, surrounding
> and providing for, not only his own per-
> sonal control, but all his relations to other
> individuals, and to the State."

This for him bore an analogy to Nature's laws and he
conceived of the administrators of such laws as having "the
grand faces of natural lawyers and judges broad at the
back-top."

> "For justice are the grand natural lawyers,
> and perfect judges—it is in the Soul;
> It is well assorted—they have not studied for
> nothing—the great includes the less;
> They rule on the highest grounds—they over-
> see all eras, states, administrations."

> "The new rule shall rule as the Soul rules,
> and as the love, justice, equality in the
> Soul rule."

> "Remember, government is to subserve in-
> dividuals."

"The ulterior object," "the mission of government," is
to develop, cultivate, and encourage independence, self-
respect, and self-rule. So in a "Thought" he reflects:

> "As if Justice could be anything but the
> same ample law, expounded by natural
> judges and saviors,
> As if it might be this thing or that thing, ac-
> cording to decisions."

It is evident that for Whitman law which is worth the name is not that which is paper law, statute, or the arbitrary or formalistic decisions of judges. It must have the ethical import of justice.

We might too readily conclude that justice is some law of Nature. But that is not what Whitman means by "natural lawyers". To what we have said before about Whitman's naturalism may be added the footnote from the Preface to the 1876 Edition of *Leaves of Grass*: "While the Moral is the purport and last intelligence of all Nature, there is absolutely nothing of the moral in the works, or laws, or shows of Nature. Those only lead inevitably to it—begin and necessitate it." We will comment further on this when discussing the natural virtues.

Individual Morality.

For Whitman the foundation and essence of social morality is individual morality. What distinguishes him from the socialist is his rejection of the social or sociological fallacy that society is superior to men and that they have duties to but not rights against it. Contrary to that doctrine which had flamboyant expression in fascism and is current in most philosophies of socialism and communism, Whitman placed emphasis upon the virtues of self-reliance and self-esteem.

> "Your schemes, politics, fail, lines give way,
>   substances mock and elude me,
> Only the theme I sing, the great and strong-
>   possess'd soul, eludes not,
> One's-self must never give way—that is the
>   final substance—that out of all is sure,
> Out of politics, triumphs, battles, life, what
>   at last finally remains?
> When shows break up what but One's-Self
>   is sure?"

"A man before all—myself, typical, before all."

"Of the lessening year by year of venerableness, and of the dicta of officers, statutes,
pulpits, schools,
Of the rising forever taller and stronger and
broader of the institutions of men and women, and of Self-esteem and Personality."

The social bonds are not formal and external. They
are the living principles which operate in the conscience
and impulses of men:

"Were you looking to be held together by
lawyers?
Or by an agreement on a paper? or by arms?
Nay, nor the world, nor any living thing, will
so cohere."

"To hold men together by paper and seal or
by compulsion is no account,
That only holds men together which aggregates all in a living principle."

The social virtues themselves are but individual virtues. They are:

"The Soul's wealth, which is candor, knowledge, pride, enfolding love."

Justice is in the souls of natural lawyers and perfect
judges; love in "the heart of man and woman," in "the institution of the dear love of comrades" without edifices or
rules or trustees, or any argument. In these are the substance of society, city or nation. And sympathy—

"Whoever walks a furlong without sympathy
walks to his own funeral drest in his own
shroud."

"O the joy of that vast elemental sympathy
    which only the human soul is capable of
    generating and emitting in steady and
    limitless floods."

The social virtues of equality and freedom are also
individual virtues. "Indirectly, but surely, goodness, virtue, law (of the very best), follow freedom." Freedom
is selfhood:

"O the joy of a manly self-hood!
To be servile to none, to defer to none, not to
    any tyrant known or unknown.

To confront with your personality all the
    other personalities of the earth."

The essence of the great city is the freedom and independence of its citizens,

"Where the citizen is always the head and
    ideal, and President, Mayor, Governor and
    what not, are agents for pay."

"I am he who places over you no master,
    owner, better, God, beyond what waits in-
    trinsically in yourself."

"For the great idea, the idea of perfect and
    free individuals,
For that, the bard walks in advance, leader of
    leaders,
The attitude of him cheers up slaves and
    horrifies foreign despots.
Without extinction is Liberty, without retro-
    grade is Equality,

> They live in the feelings of young men and
>   the best women,
> (Not for nothing have the indomitable heads
>   of the earth been always ready to fall for
>   Liberty."

> "The dependence of Liberty shall be lovers,
> The continuance of Equality shall be com-
>   rades.
>
> ❖ ❖ ❖ ❖ ❖ ❖
>
> O lands! with the love of lovers tie you."

In Whitman there is no conflict between freedom and equality:

> "Neither a servant nor a master I,
>
> ❖ ❖ ❖ ❖ ❖ ❖
>
> I will be even with you and you shall be even
>   with me.
>
> ❖ ❖ ❖ ❖ ❖ ❖
>
> If you become degraded, criminal, ill, then I
>   become so for your sake."

He made no exception to the application of the law of equality. Not even the learned, virtuous and benevolent have any priority. Especial emphasis is placed upon the equality of the woman with the man. Indeed, woman is the very source of virtue.

He had a deep sense of personal and social responsibility for bringing forth a sane and healthy race:

> "Bravas to all impulses sending sane children
>   to the next age!
> But damn that which spends itself with no
>   thought of the stain, pains, dismay, feeble-
>   ness, it is bequeathing."

In the love of comrades the virtues of social mutuality shine, and especially trust:

> "Why should I be afraid to trust myself to
> you?"

Companions of the *Open Road* are "trusters of men and women."

The Idealistic Virtues.

The idealistic virtues too are individual virtues, although the polarity of social virtues is also in them. It is in these that absolutist ethics has had most sway. It was probably because of them that Whitman was wary of intellectualism. Nevertheless he valued the idealistic virtues of wisdom, truth, conscience, and duty.

"Perfect sanity shows the master among philosophs." "The wise know that (materials) do not become real (for literature) till touched by emotions, the mind." It is wisdom that is wedded to charity. "Truth includes all." He speaks as if truth is in the constitution of things as well as in man:

> "Great is the quality of truth in man;
> The quality of truth in man supports itself
>   through all changes,
> It is inevitably in the man—he and it are in
>   love, and never leave each other.
>
> The truth in man is no dictum, it is vital
>   as eyesight;
> If there be any Soul, there is truth—if there
>   be man or woman there is truth—if there
>   be physical or moral, there is truth;
> If there be equilibrium or volition, there is
>   truth—if there be things at all upon the
>   earth, there is truth.
> O truth of the earth! I am determin'd to
>   press my way toward you."

Over against the absolutist tone of that passage, consider and try to reconcile its obverse in the poem, *All is Truth*:

> "Discovering today there is no lie or form
>   of lie, and can be none, but grows as in-
>   evitably upon itself as the truth does upon
>   itself,
> Or as any law of the earth or any natural
>   production of the earth does.
> (This is curious and may not be realized
>   immediately, but it must be realized,
> I feel in myself that I represent falsehoods
>   equally with the rest,
> And that the universe does.)

> Meditating among liars and retreating sternly
>   into myself, I see that there are really no
>   liars or lies after all.
> And that there is no flaw or vacuum in the
>   amount of the truth—but that all is truth
>   without exception;
> And henceforth I will go celebrate any thing
>   I see or am,
> And sing and laugh and deny nothing."

Thus when Whitman comes face to face with the absolute virtues he appears to become enigmatical; but as when considering his conception of good and evil, so here as to lies and truth we find the same paradox.

> "Do I contradict myself?
> Very well then I contradict myself,
> (I am large, I contain multitudes.) "

The paradox of truth is that the more the content, the more complex the situation, the less absolute can truth be, unless by generalizing we ignore or disregard the particular differences and contradictions involved. But Whitman also observed that even as to lies the logic of relation also applies. A lie is a product of its situation— it is an effect of a cause, and so has a kind of inevitability, of necessity, about it. Here too the principle of relativity, of appropriateness, applies. The truth is that which is appropriate to the situation; the lie is a lie because it is out of place.

This distinction is made clear in Whitman's discussion of conscience and duty. Although "the simple, unsophisticated conscience" is "the primary moral element," the idea "of intense moral right," yet "in its name and strained construction, the worst fanaticism, wars, persecutions, murders, etc., have . . . in all lands, in the past, been broached, and have come to their devilish fruition." Conscience must have the counterbalance and equal sway of "science, absolute reason, and the general proportionate development of the whole man." The peculiar flaw in abstract absolute idealism he exposed: "Conscience, too, isolated from all else, and from the emotional nature, may but attain the beauty and purity of glacial, snowy ice."

Also Whitman had more faith in natural impulse than for compulsion of duty as a moral drive:

"I give nothing as duties,
What others give as duties I give as living
   impulses,
(Shall I give the heart's action as a duty?)"

His disgust for such a sense of duty he expressed in the notable lines:

"I think I could turn and live with animals,
   they're so placid and self-contained,

❖ ❖ ❖ ❖ ❖

They do not sweat and whine about their
    condition,
They do not lie awake in the dark and weep
    for their sins,
They do not make me sick discussing their
    duty to God."

"Duty," he said to Traubel, "It is a free word—it
is a slave word. The mothers make it a free word—the
preachers make it a slave word."

The Natural Virtues.

Although Whitman said there is nothing moral in
the works, laws, or shows of Nature, yet he thought the
origin of morals is in Nature and Nature makes and leads
to morality. As he defined the relation of morals and Nature more definitely: "Nature is rude and not comprehensible at first." American democracy is likened to the
laws of Nature: "There is no law stronger than she is."
The analogy of Nature as a moral force carries yet farther:

"No politics, song, religion, behavior, or
    what not, is of account, unless it compare
    with the amplitude of the earth,
Unless it face the exactness, vitality, impar-
    tiality, rectitude of the earth."

He likens his own task to that of Nature:

"Let others finish specimens, I never finish
    specimens,
I start them by exhaustless laws as Nature
    does, fresh and modern continually."

Besides its amplitude and diversity he speaks also of
"the coarseness and sensuality of the earth, and the great
charity of the earth, and the equilibrium also." In an

earlier chapter we have considered Whitman's humanist conception of Nature which identifies man with Nature, yet apart from it and superior to it as having gone beyond it to a higher state of natural being rather to aid and perfect Nature than to be in conflict with it.

The fusing and blending of man and Nature seemed to him to have moral import:

> "Nature and Man shall be disjoin'd and dif-
>   fused no more,
> The true son of God shall absolutely fuse
>   them."

"When the full-grown poet came," he took both Nature and the Soul of man "each by the hand";

> "And today and ever so stands, as blender,
>   uniter, tightly holding hands,
> Which he will never release until he recon-
>   ciles the two,
> And wholly and joyously blends them."

In that is the significance of Whitman's conception of natural morality, the attempt to harmonize Nature and the Soul of man. In that sense also he argued in *Democratic Vistas* for "natural standards" in literature.

There was also something Baconian in Whitman's view of Nature. As Bacon proposed by experiment to twist or torture Nature into revelation of her secrets, Whitman thought of the poet as having the function to "link and tally the rational physical being of man, with the ensemble of time and space, and with this vast and multiform show, Nature, surrounding him, ever tantalizing him, equally a part, yet not a part of him, as to essentially harmonize, satisfy, and put at rest. Faith, very old, now scared away by science, must be restored, brought back by the same power that caused her departure." What the

Roman poet Lucretius did must be better done by the modern bard, "who, while remaining fully poet, will absorb whatever science indicates, with spiritualism, and out of them, and out of his own genius, will compose the great poem of death. Then will man indeed confront Nature,... and take his right place, prepared for life, master of fortune and misfortune." His naturalism was thus allied with his stoicism. But he saw the shortcomings of both.

Epicurean Virtue.

For the humanist in Whitman was so strong that he tempered any stoical tendencies in his thought with equal consideration for the Epicurean virtues. Pleasures and happiness are positive goods of immediate worth in Whitman's scheme of life.

> "The efflux of the soul is happiness, here is
>   happiness,
> I think it pervades the open air, waiting at
>   all times,
> Now it flows unto us, we are rightly charged."

But *A Song of Joys* shows that happiness is not merely calm, or tranquillity, or vigorous life. It includes even

> "Joys of the thought of Death ...

> The beautiful touch of Death, soothing and
>   benumbing a few moments, for reasons."

Happiness has a function beyond itself:

> "Whatever forms the average, strong, com-
>   plete, sweet-blooded man or woman, the
>   perfect longeve personality,

> And helps its present life to health and hap-
> piness, and shapes its soul,
> For the eternal life to come."

It is alloyed with its opposite:

> "And of each one the core of life, namely
> happiness, is full of the rotten excrement
> of maggots."

It is nevertheless something worth seeking:

> "Happiness, (which whoever hears me let
> him or her set out in search of this day.)"

But, contrary to most ethical philosophies, happiness
is a strictly individual attainment:

> "He happy in himself, or she happy in her-
> self, is happy,
> But I tell you you cannot be happy by
> others, any more than you can beget or
> conceive a child by others."

And Whitman had no ascetic or mystical conception
of happiness. For him it is instinct with pleasures, sensuality, bodily appetites. He described

> "Walt Whitman, a kosmos, of Manhattan
> the son,
> Turbulent, fleshy, sensual, eating, drinking
> and breeding,"

and declared:

> "I believe in the flesh and the appetites,
> Seeing, hearing, feeling, are miracles, and
> each part and tag of me is a miracle."

I Sing the Body Electric is a vehement protest against ascetic attitudes toward the body, against concealment of the body and defilement of it and the treatment of the sex organs and sensuous love as unworthy, and is a paean of praise of the body and all its parts. A healthy body is a supreme desideratum: "I think all scientists will agree with me, as I agree with the scientists," he said to Traubel, "that a beautiful, competent, sufficing, body is the prime force making towards the virtues in civilization, life, history." In the *Song of the Open Road* he set the test for fit companions:

> "He traveling with me needs the best blood,
>   thews, endurance,
> None may come to the trial till he or she
>   bring courage and health,
> Come not here if you have already spent the
>   best of yourself,
> Only those may come who come in sweet and
>   determin'd bodies,
> No diseas'd person, no rum-drinker or
>   venereal taint is permitted here."

Wholesomeness was an objective for him: "I like to feel that the things I do are wholesome."

Browning never hymned more exultant songs to the joy of living than did Whitman, and Whitman's present, realistic joy of living did not require a supernatural linkage as did Browning's.

> "Joy! joy! in freedom, worship, love! joy in
>   the ecstacy of life!
> Enough to merely be! enough to breathe!
> Joy! joy! all over joy!"

The Confucian Virtues.

There is also a Confucian strain in Whitmanian morality. Whitman was infused with the practical sense which

actuated Confucius. With the difference, however, that
he had less veneration for the old ways and for civilization.
And he gave a somewhat more idealistic turn to the economic virtue of prudence. Nor did the superior man have
all of Whitman's respect, for he saw in the average man a
value to be preserved.

Image-breaker and iconoclast though he was, Whitman
did not discard tradition:

> "For what is the present after all but a
>   growth out of the past?"

The New World is the effort of the Old World ripen-
ing in it. Nevertheless, there is "the lessening year by year
of venerableness." But

> "How many hold despairingly yet to the
>   models departed, caste, myths, obedience,
>   compulsion, and to infidelity,
> How few see the arrived models, the ath-
>   letes, the Western states, or see freedom
>   or spirituality, or hold to any faith in
>   results."

For, "Not traditions, not the outer authorities are the
judges." The tests, the results, "are the judges of outer
authorities and of all traditions."

And civilization may not be all gain. "What is gain
after all to savageness and freedom?" "Provision for a
little healthy rudeness, savage virtue, justification of what
one has in one's self, whatever it is, is demanded."

> "Fear grace, elegance, civilization, delica-
>   tesse,
> Fear the mellow sweet, the sucking of honey-
>   juice,

> Beware the advancing mortal ripening of
> Nature,
> Beware what precedes the decay of the rug-
> gedness of states and men."

America "must sternly promulgate her own new standard, yet old enough, and accepting the old, the perennial
elements, and combining them into groups, unities, appropriate to the modern, the democratic, the west," etc.
"Thus we pronounce not so much against the principle of
culture; we only supervise it, and promulgate along with
it, as deep, perhaps a deeper, principle."

Whitman cannot and does not wish to deny the higher
and superior claims to which Confucius gave such deference. As Confucius conceived the superior man there was
not wanting in Whitman respect, even reverence for him.
But he revolted against mere assumptions of superiority:
"Long enough have the People been listening to poems
in which common humanity, deferential, bends low, hu-
miliated, acknowledging superiors. But America listens
to no such poems. Erect, inflated, and fully selfesteeming
be the chant; and then America will listen with pleased
ears." And then quite in the spirit of Confucius he said:
"That which really balances and conserves the social and
political world is not so much legislation, police, treaties,
and dread of punishment, as the latent intuitional sense,
in humanity, of fairness, manliness, decorum, etc. . . . A
strong mastership of the general inferior self by the superior self, is to be aided, secured, indirectly, but surely,
by the literatus, in his works, shaping, for individual or
aggregate democracy, in a great passionate body, in and
along with which goes a great masterful spirit." His conception of natural and social progress is that of man rising
to "superior realms."

In a democracy the average man becomes important.
Over against this principle of democracy Whitman sets

another, the principle of individuality, personalism. This is different from the superior man of Confucius, but it operates in a similar way; for instead of stressing the excellence of a few or one, it stresses the excellence, the best, in everyone.

In yet another aspect Whitman's ethics was Confucian. Prudence was for him a fundamental concept, but not an all-embracing one: The great city stands

> "Where thrift is in its place, and prudence
>   is in its place."

Although he defines it as "the prudence that suits immortality", this must be taken in his special meaning of immortality as designating what has permanent value:

> "Prudence entirely satisfies the craving and
>   glut of souls,
> Itself only finally satisfies the soul."

> "What is prudence is indivisible,
> Declines to separate one part of life from
>   every part,
> Divides not the righteous from the unright-
>   eous or the living from the dead."

Again, we are dealing with the paradoxical meanings of good and evil, but as concerns prudence it is necessary to take account of everything, in order that everything may have its place and that results may be reckoned. How markedly Confucian!

Aristotelian Ethics.

There is much resemblance between Whitman's ethics and Aristotle's. Whitman's definition of the good as appropriate or fit to its place is a near equivalent to Aristotle's Golden Mean, everything in right proportion.

As magnanimity was most characteristic in Aristotle's list of virtues, there is a similar temper in Whitman to be large, inclusive, and expansive. Aristotle's magnanimous man values himself highly and justly. Whitman's *Song of Myself* and the general tone throughout *Leaves of Grass* exemplifies this virtue. Whitman's expression of it is self-esteem. But the assumption of superiority in relation to other men which is characteristic of Aristotle's magnanimous man is quite alien to Whitman's ideal. They are different in another way: Aristotle's magnanimous man is rather lethargic and self-contemplative. Whitman was and so was his ideal restless, willful and worried by the idea, "Walt, you contain enough, why don't you let it out then?"

Notwithstanding those differences, Whitman's list of the virtues positively suggests Aristotle's rating of them. In his poem entitled *Excelsior* he epitomized the excellent virtues as justice, caution, happiness, magnanimity, pride, courage, truth, benevolence, love, friendship, "a perfect and enamour'd body", ample thoughts, and poetic emotion. A state of well-being notably appears there as ideal, and Whitman had that attitude in common with Aristotle and Confucius, but there was more of the Epicurean in him than in either of them.

The Stoical and Ascetic Virtues.

Although different in spirit from Aristotelianism, Stoicism bridges over the gap between the former and the sterner character of idealistic virtue. High-mindedness also characterized Stoicism. The superior man attitude toward the vicissitudes of fortune was its guiding norm. Whitman's philosophy, despite the dominant note of love in it necessitated a somewhat stoical attitude of man toward his world. The ascetic virtues were to some extent also highly prized by the Stoics, and Whitman did not disregard them or treat them as unnecessary. He felt the necessity for endurance:

> "I see the enslaved, the overthrown, the
>   hurt, the oppresst of the whole earth,
> I feel the measureless shame and humilia-
>   tion of my race, it becomes all mine,
> Mine too the revenges of humanity, the
>   wrongs of ages, baffled feuds and hatreds,
> Utter defeat upon me weighs—all lost—the
>   foe victorious,
> (Yet 'mid the ruins Pride colossal stands
>   unshaken to the last,
> Endurance, resolution to the last.) "

A typical Stoical attitude is that.

The Stoic's indifference to fortune had frequent expression in Whitman's writings. In his specifications for the one "who would talk or sing to America", there are tests that call for stoical virtues of strength of character and impartial attitudes and forbearance:

> "Can you hold your hand against all seduc-
>   tions, follies, whirls, fierce contentions?
>   are you very strong? are you really of the
>   whole People?

> Have you too the old ever-fresh forbearance
>   and impartiality?"

There is of course a fundamental difference between Whitman and the Stoics and all those of aristocratic bearing of the old order. His aristocratic or superior man is not aloof from the masses, holds no contempt for the average man, and is sympathetic with the degraded, diseased, and criminal to the extent that he feels himself in community with them at the same time he does not accept their lot but is hopeful ever for redemption of them from it. This he has in common with Christian asceticism so far as it expressed that attitude which more often it did not do. St. Francis of Assisi inaugurated a new order which at first was shocking to Christian asceticism. But Whitman felt its lesson deeply in his profession of chastity. *Spontaneous Me,* for all its sensuousness, yet extolled chastity:

"Earth of chaste love, ...

❖ ❖ ❖ ❖ ❖ ❖

The continence of vegetables, birds, animals,
The consequent meanness of me should I
    skulk or find myself indecent, while birds
    and animals never once skulk or find
    themselves indecent,
The great chastity of paternity, to match the
    great chastity of maternity."

There is a completeness of loving in Whitman that the morbid half insane nature of St. Francis knew nothing of, as the Stoic too fell far short of Whitman's robust ideal of life.

For Whitman there was a challenge to work and endeavor wanting in the Stoic and ascetic because he was not depressed by their pessimism about this earthly career. Therefore chastity for him is that of the worker, the doer:

"O I see life is not short, but immeasurably
    long,
I henceforth tread the world chaste, temperate, an early riser, a steady grower,
Every hour the semen of centuries, and still
    of centuries.

I must follow up these continual lessons of
    the air, water, earth,
I perceive I have no time to lose."

His courage was similarly inspired: "Not for nothing
does evil play its part among us. Judging from the main
portions of the history of the world, so far, justice is always
in jeopardy, peace walks amid hourly pitfalls, and of slavery, misery, meanness, the craft of tyrants and the credulity
of the populace, in some of their protean forms, no voice
can at any time say, They are not. The clouds break a
little, and the sun shines out—but soon and certain the
lowering darkness falls again, as if to last forever. Yet there
is an immortal courage in every sane soul that cannot,
must not, under any circumstances, capitulate." Therefore, he said:

"I understand the large hearts of heroes,
The courage of present times and all times,

The disdain and calmness of martyrs."
Yet the great city is the place

"Where no monuments exist to heroes but
    in the common words and deeds."

But the strong man had a definite and indispensable
place in his conception of human needs:

"All waits or goes by default till a strong
    being appears;
A strong being is the proof of the race and of
    the ability of the universe,
When he or she appears materials are over-
    aw'd,

The dispute on the soul stops,
The old customs and phrases are confronted,
    turn'd back, or laid away."

This differs from Nietzsche's praise of strength and of
heroes who are Napoleonic, and on the other hand it
avoids Nietzsche's criticism of herd morality and of proletarian mass philosophy without discounting the worth of
great strong men. It does not share any of the extreme
opinion of Carlyle whose great man theory of history also
held democracy in contempt, although recognizing a certain likeness in the critical viewpoint of Carlyle with his
own.

In such similarities of viewpoint which Whitman
shared with every school of thought, while essentially differing from them, appears the inclusiveness of his moral
system that led him to his great synthesis of moral principle. The illustration of it in the case of the stoical philosophy is especially notable because its viewpoint was in some
ways so essential to his general position. In one further
topic, work, we see at once how stoical concepts became
altered in his philosophy, holding their essential quality,
but shedding the narrow and bigoted expression of a class
philosophy which marred the dignity the Stoics and Nietzsche strove to attain. The democratic dignity of work
made the difference in Whitman's philosophy. He did not
share his admiring correspondent Symonds' disbelief "in
the modern gospel of work". He held "it no disgrace to
take a hand" at any useful work:

"I say I bring thee Muse to-day and here,
All occupations, duties broad and close,
Toil, healthy toil and sweat, endless, with-
    out cessation.
The old practical burdens, interests, joys,"

"The hourly routine of your own or any
    man's life, the shop, yard, store or factory,

> These shows all near you by day and night
>   —workman! whoever you are, your daily
>   life!
> In that and them the heft of the heaviest—
>   in that and them far more than you esti-
>   mated, (and far less also,)
> In them the realities for you and me, in them
>   poems for you and me,
> In them, not yourself—you and your soul
>   enclose all things, regardless of estimation,
> In them the development good—in them all
>   themes, hints, possibilities.
> I do not affirm that what you see beyond is
>   futile, I do not advise you to stop,
> I do not say leadings you thought great are
>   not great,
> But I say that none lead to greater than these
>   lead to."

Work provides an explanation of life and destiny when
we lack other knowledge of aim or end:

> "We know not what the use O life, ...
> But know the work, ...
> We know not why or what, yet weave, for-
>   ever weave."

This poem, *Weave in, My Hardy Life,* shows that Whitman had no such mystical cosmic assurance as Bucke attributed to him. Nor had he the faith in the Universe
which sustained the Stoic. But he had faith in the everyday life of man, in his daily work, which was absent from
the Stoic, is not a characteristic of the mystics who generally are escapists, and he had a sense of the worth of work
which is in sharp contrast with the typical ascetic who
regards work as penance for sins and not as a forwarding
instrument of human good.

Whitman's Ethics of Personal Humanism.

It is remarkable how seldom the ethical philosophies have regarded man as the foundation and center of morals. David Hume is a notable exception. Instead of Hume's phrase, "human nature", to Whitman it is in human personality alone that we can discover the synthesis and central principle for the varying norms of human conduct.

Although Whitman found a place for every ethical system, he recognized that no principle is a guide excepting in the place to which it is appropriate. There is no absolute ethical principle which is applicable at all times and in all places. None that can be invariably applied without qualification in every circumstance and to every person. Only by the test of good or value to men, particular individual men, can we ascertain what is good or what is bad. "In the centre of all, and object of all, stands the Human Being, towards whose heroic and spiritual evolution poems and everything directly or indirectly tend, Old World or New." Especially the average man:

> "You average spiritual manhood, purpose
> of all, poised in yourself, giving not taking
> law."

In the Preface to the 1876 Edition, he indicated what is meant by this. It is not the man of great achievements only or so much as average men in practical life "upon and from which position as a central basis or pedestal, while performing (Democracy's) labors, and his duties as citizen, son, husband, father and employed person," whose worth is vital. "In the centre of all, absorbing all, giving, for your purpose, the only meaning and vitality to all, master or mistress of all, stands Yourself." It is the significance of the unique worth of every man that Whitman means.

"How dare you place anything before a man?"

As we observed, when discussing the theisms, Whitman meant that man is the equal or superior of anything in or outside his universe. In the poem, *Grand is the Seen*, he said of comparison with the shows of Nature:

"But grander far the unseen soul of me,

❖ ❖ ❖ ❖ ❖ ❖

. . . . , more lasting thou than they."

In *Chanting the Square Deific*:

" . . . for without me what were all? What were God?"

And he said in the plain prose of *Democratic Vistas*: "The last, best dependence is to be upon humanity itself, and its own inherent, normal, full-grown qualities without any superstitious support whatever." The "essential faith in man, above all his errors and wickedness", was for him fundamental. The poet

" . . . sees eternity in men and women, he does not see men and women as dreams or dots."

Personality has special significance for Whitman's humanism. Without pointing out now the subtleties of his thought about personality, I quote a few passages from *Democratic Vistas* to indicate the moral significance of personality.

"Coming down to what is of the only real importance, Personalities, and examining minutely, we question, we ask, Are there, indeed, *men* here worthy the name?" Personality is the individual superior quality in man, as over against the levelling, average democratic quality. It is "individuality, the pride and centripetal isolation of a

human being in himself — identity — personalism." The
strong men, the creators, models, exemplars, constitute
"the formation of a typical personality of character, eligible to the uses of the high average of men—and not restricted by conditions ineligible to the masses." "The
problem, as it seems to me, presented to the New World,
is, under permanent law and order, and after preserving
cohesion (ensemble-Individuality), at all hazards, to vital-
ize man's free play of special Personalism, recognizing in
it something that calls ever more to be considered, fed, and
adopted as the substratum for the best that belongs to us
(government indeed is for it), including the new esthetics
for the future."

Such personalism is the very essence of religion: "Bibles
may convey, and priests expound, but it is exclusively for
the noiseless operation of one's isolated Self, to enter the
pure ether of veneration, reach the divine levels, and commune with the unutterable." "The identified soul . . . .
can really confront religion when it extricates itself entirely from the churches, and not before."

He thought the formation of such personalities could
be better developed in small communities. In *A Backward
Glance,* written very near the end of his life, he said it had
been his object to imagine himself such a personality and
to put such a person "truly on record" in *Leaves of Grass.*

The creating of these personalities is not confined to
the making of geniuses. Every man's personality is a potential unique worth. It is every man's function to

> " . . . heed himself, unfold himself, (not
> others' formulas heed,) here fill his time."

> "With one man or woman—(no matter
>   which one—I even pick out the lowest,)
> With him or her I now illustrate the whole
>   law;

I say that every right, in politics or what-not,
shall be eligible to that one man or woman, on the same terms as any."

"I say man shall not hold property in man;
I say the least developed person on earth is
just as important and sacred to himself or
herself, as the most developed person is to
himself or herself."

"The youth, the laboring person, the poor
person rivalling all the rest—perhaps out-
doing the rest,

For there is nothing in the whole universe
that can be more effective than a man's or
a woman's daily behavior can be."

This faith in man and in each and every man is what
distinguished most Whitman's concept of morality. As
incident to it is the belief in the unique worth of personality potential in every man.

It was the synthesis of the personalities of all men of
all degrees that Whitman labored for as a moral and artistic unity necessary for the progress and perfection of mankind. Without expanding here what is intended for the
content of this book as a whole, and of which Whitman's
moral philosophy is a summary, we note that he treated as
merely relative to variant human beings what ordinarily
moralists have treated as absolute categories, the so-called
cardinal virtues. In Whitman's thought those must fall
into place; those virtues indifferently good or bad on occasion, become really virtues only in application, fitting to
the time and place, the situation of the particular person
involved. Abstract virtues are like everything else in human affairs—what is one man's food is another man's poi-

son. Thus Whitman among moralists is a modern of the moderns, even to this day. If individualist personalism is the real synthesis that unites the heretofore warring systems of ethics, Whitman was a pioneer of the new morality. His humanistic viewpoint was the broadest, frighteningly broad and inclusive to the Christian who with the example of Christ should not be frightened by it. His healthy human philosophy, which brings the whole man within its compass, high and low, in all his faculties and varying nature, thus allows for every ethical principle, every virtue, its appropriate function in the life of man; but as enlightening and guiding principles, not as enslavements and degradations of the human spirit which have so discredited traditional moralisms.

8

HIS PROPHECY OF LOVE.

❖ ❖ ❖ ❖ ❖ ❖

"Underneath all is the Expression of love
for men and women, (I swear I have seen
enough of mean and impotent modes of
expressing love for men and women,
After this day I take my own modes of expressing love for men and women.)"

❖ ❖ ❖ ❖ ❖ ❖

WHITMAN'S TRINITY, THE THREE GREATNESSES, WERE: "THE
greatness of Love and Democracy, and the greatness of
Religion." He was the prophet of love as he was the prophet of the new religion of humanity. Indeed, love was
the heart of his religion and of his democracy.

His Experience as a Lover.

On the subject of Whitman's experiences in love and
his competency to prophecy concerning it, there have been
considerable controversies. Probably the Whitmanites
have been chiefly responsible for the misunderstandings
on this matter.

Whitman's candor of expression naturally drew to him
many among the millions afflicted by sex disturbances. For
there is no sickness of civilization so prevalent as that relat-
ing to sex. And such persons had a tendency to pry into
the personal secrets of Whitman. He was quite reasonable

169

in the extent of his resistance to them. He found it impossible to explain and so he took to subterfuges to get rid of their inquiries.

Not knowing of any irregularities with the female sex, they suspected him of homosexuality, and evidently to offset such a suspicion he told John Addington Symonds a year or so before his death that he had had six children. There is no credible evidence that he ever had any children.

The New Orleans Woman.

Nor is there a known instance of a love affair with any specific woman. The "New Orleans Creole woman" proved a myth. The "Washington married" woman taxes even more the imaginations of the romancers.

Canby writes skeptically about the New Orleans woman. As to whether a pretty quadroon or a New Orleans aristocrat bore him a child, Canby thinks three months there too short a time for all that to have taken place. Perhaps Canby doesn't know the possibilities of love at first sight.

He may be on solider ground when he assumes that such an affair was hardly within the range of Whitman's sexual nature. For his brother George said he had never known or heard of any woman affair of Walt's. To his family he seemed a womanless man.

However, there is an interesting picture pasted in the notebook of 1859. Holloway thinks it may have been a lover, or Whitman's mother or sister Mary.

The romancers have built much upon the poem, *Once I Pass'd Through a Populous City*, assuming that it is autobiographical, that the city was New Orleans, and that it records his love affair:

"Yet now of all that city I remember only a
    woman I casually met there who detain'd
    me for love of me,

> Day by day and night by night we were to-
> gether—all else has long been forgotten by
> me,
> I remember I say only that woman who pas-
> sionately clung to me,
> Again we wander, we love, we separate
> again,
> Again she holds me by the hand, I must go,
> I see her close beside me with silent lips and
> tremulous."

This is the poem he published in the Edition of 1860
and which remained in all subsequent editions unchanged.
But Holloway in the volume of *Uncollected Poetry and
Prose of Walt Whitman* published another version of the
same poem:

> "But now of all that city I remember only
> a man who wandered with me there, for
> love of me,
> Day by day, and night by night, we were
> together,
> All else has long been forgotten by me—I
> remember
> I say, only one rude and ignorant man who,
> when I departed,
> Long and long held me by the hand, with
> silent lip, sad and tremulous."

Holloway thinks that in the poem as published Whitman "deliberately attempted to mystify the reader."

But what is the way of poets in using their personal
experiences? Do they merely record them? Or do they
also draw heavy drafts upon imagination? Do all of Shakespeare's long roll of stage characters with their great variety
of moral and sentimental attitudes speak continually but
his own inner convictions and thoughts? If not, and the
answer is surely No, then why any more does *Leaves of*

Grass, even when using the personal pronoun I, express an autobiographical incident or intent? Nevertheless, Canby adheres to the autobiographical theory: "The book is both his testimony and himself."

One must recall Whitman's own distinctions of the two parts of himself, his physical conscious self and his roving, imaginative self or soul; body and soul; the I and the You. The ubiquitous I of the roaming soul is more present in *Leaves of Grass* than what any realistic biographer could ever name as the true Whitman. Canby does essay more than that kind of biography, for he calls his "a study of the man, and Whitman the poet, and his symbolic autobiography in the *Leaves of Grass.*" In his chapter on *Children of Adam* he recognizes separation of several personalities of Whitman and insists that Whitman was "neither a 'dirty beast' nor 'the sovereign of the flesh', but a complex erotic type, neither mysterious nor pathological, but requiring the most careful analysis and explanation."

The conclusion of Canby's analysis is that Whitman had heterosexual experience, he deplored prostitution and adultery, and definitely wrote poems with a homosexual implication, but he was intermediate in sex and "was perhaps more autosexual than anything else."

I am convinced that from a purely biographical or autobiographical account of Whitman is not to be deduced the experience or the content of *Leaves of Grass.* As well say that the immured Emily Dickinson had no experience in love. There is much that an introspective person with the aid of vicarious experiences can divine which the most heterosexual person without reflection would never dream. Mere biography is not adequate for analysis of the poetic personality.

Evidence of Whitman's Erotic Experiences.

I do not wish to pass by mere assertion over those biographical data which might indicate that Whitman had passionate erotic experiences that could give realistic foundation for his poems on love. Canby quotes the puzzling entry in the notebook of 1868-1870. In this evidently referring to a woman he had been pursuing he accused himself of a fantasy, "fancying what does not really exist in another, but is all the time in myself alone—utterly deluded & cheated by *myself* & my own weakness"; and after considerable acknowledged "perturbation" he finally resolved to "avoid seeing her, or meeting her, or any talk or explanations — or ANY MEETING WHATEVER, FROM THIS HOUR FORTH, FOR LIFE."

Why try to read into this any other than the obvious meaning, that the struggle was within Whitman's own self, a struggle for self-mastery over a powerful hopeless passion. We may guess that it was unrequited love; perhaps undeclared love. We know really nothing about it.

Anne Gilchrist.

Always a good-looking brute, Whitman was shy of women, and even attractive Anne Gilchrist with her special claims upon him could not possess his person, and she finally settled down to be just a very good friend. But the relationship with that charming and talented woman deserves more than a passing comment because of the light it sheds not only on Whitman's capacity for love and friendship but also because it portrays a certain refinement of his character.

She may have been the first woman of high spirit, nobility and intelligence who appreciated the message which *Leaves of Grass* contained for women. She read the poems first in 1869, wrote *"A Woman's Estimate of Walt Whitman"* published in a Boston journal in 1870, all as an Englishwoman who had not yet seen him or corresponded with him.

He sent to William Rossetti a copy of the 1871 Edition for her, and with passionate suddenness she wrote him a

love letter which he was long in answering. He then ex-
cused himself for the delay:

"My book is my best letter, my response, my truest explanation of all. In it I have put my body & spirit. You
understand this better & fuller & clearer than anyone else.
And I too fully & clearly understand the loving & womanly
letter it has evoked. Enough that there surely exists between us so beautiful & delicate a relation, accepted by
both of us with joy."

The tenderness and tact of his letter is a tribute to his
judgment and feeling, especially in view of his later attitude toward her. For so ardent a woman could not be
gainsaid. She continued to write pressing her suit upon
him and even that she was not too old to present him a
"perfect child". A year passed and he wrote her:
"Dear Friend:

Let me warn you about myself and yourself also. You
must not construct such an unauthorized and imaginary
figure and call it W.W. and so devotedly invest your loving
nature in it. The actual W.W. is a very plain personage
and entirely unworthy of such devotion."

Those who regard Whitman as an irredeemable egoist
must explain the delicacy and humility of that letter. In
the next year he suffered paralysis. She still implored him
to accept her services. And in 1876 she came to America
and brought her daughter Grace who resembled her and
her son Herbert. During the three years she remained
there was close friendship which Whitman greatly enjoyed.
She died in 1885. His poem, *Going Somewhere,* celebrated
that friendship:

> "My science-friend, my noblest woman
>   friend, (Now buried in an English grave
>   —and this is a memory-leaf for her dear
>   sake,)
> Ended our talk — 'The sum . . . . .

Is, that we all are onward, onward, speeding
    slowly, surely bettering,

❖ ❖ ❖ ❖ ❖ ❖

All bound as is befitting each—all surely
    going somewhere.' "

A beautiful tribute to a great woman! Whitman at
least had accepted her splendid companionship.

Burroughs, who probably knew and understood him
as well as any contemporary, said: "Whitman was not a
marrying man." When Anne Gilchrist besought him, "he
had probably already lived out his life of the affections and
emotions, in that particular sphere." Furthermore, he was
a reticent man toward everyone. "He let himself go only
in his poems."

Was Whitman Homosexual?

As for amours with males no one knows them to be
anything but platonic. Canby says, so far there has not
been produced "one scrap of actual homosexuality in
Whitman's life." He may have had homosexual inclina-
tions which he did not indulge. His affectionate letters to
Peter Doyle and other men were most unusual expressions
of love of one man for another. To a modern, especially
to an American, there is something repulsive in such ardent declarations of amativeness between males. In this
respect we are very different from ancient men almost
everywhere.

Puritanism in America has made for prudery in all
human relationships and has tended to repress tender emotions even in the bosom of the family. But it has been
especially marked for inhibitions upon expression of
friendship between men. To kiss and hold hands, as
Whitman advocated, is quite beyond the proprieties for
inter-male Americans. How shocking then in 1856 the
narration in *Song of Myself!*

> "I mind how once we lay such a transparent
>   summer morning,
> How you settled your head athwart my hips
>   and gently turn'd over upon me,
> And parted the shirt from my bosom-bone,
>   and plung'd your tongue to my bare-stript
>   heart,
> And reach'd till you felt my beard, and
>   reach'd till you held my feet."

Canby says this is addressed to the soul and notes that it is followed by the "noble lines" about God as man's brother and comrade. Quite a misunderstanding of Whitman's concept of the soul, showing how much more easily an uncritical reader may translate Whitman's phrases into the usual language of religious superstition. In Whitman's conception the soul is never separated from the body.

To give a spiritual unfleshly interpretation to such passages in *Leaves of Grass* is as absurd as the headnotes to the chapters in the King James version of the Christian Bible which interpolate the Christ and Church motive into the sultry Oriental love *Songs of Solomon*.

Canby quotes Whitman's late disavowal that the *Calamus* poems had a homosexual intent and his declaration that such an inference was "abominable". This revulsion of Whitman to the idea is accepted by Canby as "entirely sincere" and correct, and Canby assumes that the male passion described in that poetry meant nothing more than intense intermale friendship. But "subconsciously he was aware of a dilemma". What dilemma? One within himself? There seems to be something like a confession in the poem, *Here the Frailest Leaves of Me*, in the *Calamus* poems:

> "Here the frailest leaves of me and yet my
>   strongest lasting,

> Here I shape and hide my thoughts, I myself
>   do not expose them,
> And yet they expose me more than all my
>   other poems."

I have rejected the theory that *Leaves of Grass* was or was intended to be autobiographical. But that obviously homosexual sentiments were not intended to be such and were unconsciously or subconsciously expressed is to deny Whitman's purpose to express fully the passion of love in its very inclusive meanings. Even to sublimate that passion without knowledge of its roots in human nature would betray a self-deluded poet. The weaknesses of Whitman on this subject in his senile years appear in his yarn to Symonds and should not be counted against him. Nor should we yield to the unintelligent prejudices prevalent in our society which taboo very common sex practices, driving into prurient secrecy what should be frankly taken into account. Nor by interpretation should we dilute Whitman's exposure of such hypocrisy.

Sex in Whitman's Poems.

Allen calls attention to those who interpret Whitman as belonging to the intermediate sex or a homosexual type, to the homosexual poem of the 1860 Edition omitted from later editions, but he believes that Whitman and D. H. Lawrence "released their erotic impulses in their work, not in their lives."

On the other hand, Canby thinks there are "no truly objective love poems in *Leaves of Grass*." Similarly Long says as to love: "Whitman was in position to utter only generalities." Yet Long distinguishes in Whitman's terms the *Children of Adam* poems as celebrating "amativeness" —woman love—from the *Calamus* poems expressing "adhesiveness"—manly love; and asserts that, although *Chil-*

dren of Adam was intended to be a true picture of man's love of woman, it "is absurd to the point of being fantastic." Selincourt has a different view of the contrast between these poems: "Children of Adam . . . is the praise of sex as distinguished from the praise of love, while Calamus is the praise of love as distinguished from the praise of sex." And also Selincourt is of the opposite opinion as to the specificity and morals of Whitman's conception of sex: "The universal love of which he is the prophet does not reduce itself to a vague benevolence at the core of which we find the worm of comfortable self-deception." When authorities disagree we may hold our own opinion that Whitman was not a novice about love.

Carpenter's Intermediate Sex.

Before searching further for the heart of Whitman's endeavor to enlarge the understanding of human love, we may consider another particular type of love which Whitmanites have attributed to him, notably as represented by Edward Carpenter.

Carpenter was certainly one of the purer spirits who attached themselves to the Whitman viewpoint and sought to carry it forward. To him especially is to be credited the reputation of Whitman as a member of the intermediate sex. What is meant by that? We turn to Carpenter's writings for explanation.

In Carpenter's description of it it is identified with Uranianism and homosexuality. But Carpenter gives a different interpretation of Uranianism than I have suggested above. The term is derived from Uranus, heaven, and means that Uranian or urning love is of a higher order than the ordinary attachments. The Uranian male lover instead of turning to a female has a true romantic friendship with one of his own sex; or if a female Uranian loves only a feminine person. This is the exclusive Uranian type.

He refutes the notion that such persons are necessarily neuropathic, diseased, or degenerate. On the contrary, many of them are robust, healthy, intellectual persons with high moral standards and nothing either abnormal or morbid about them or peculiar in any mental or physical way. Yet they may suffer a great deal from the way they are regarded by the community at large.

However, there is a tendency in the extreme Uranian types to resemble or affect the opposite sex. The male Uranians have feminine ways, manners and tastes, and often the physical characteristics of women—large at the hips, hairless faces, high pitched voices, and graceful carriage. The homogenic female, on the other hand, tends toward mannishness and men's sports and habits. We abbreviate considerably Carpenter's explicit descriptions.

But there are more normal types in which the masculine and feminine characteristics are mingled. In such more normal Uranian men and women are to be found the highest geniuses of mankind in every sphere of action and of mental and artistic achievement, such as Michelangelo, Shakespeare, Alexander the Great, Julius Caesar, etc. One would suppose that he should apply the term intermediate sex to these less extreme Uranians, but he includes both the homosexual and the "more healthy types" in the intermediate sex.

The History of Homosexuality.

In later books with considerable reiteration Carpenter treated more fully of the intermediate sex. He showed correctly that from primitive time homosexuality has been an established and valued institution, especially in religion and military affairs. Readers of Plato's *Lysias* and *Symposium,* of Aristophanes' *Lysistrata,* and Cicero's *De Amicitia* (On Friendship) know that among the ancients love between the sexes was less honored than homosexual love which was deemed more real, more sincere, and more lasting. By them uxoriousness was regarded as a weakness or a vice.

Sublimated, homosexual tendencies are more frequent than most people are willing to recognize. There are certain groups and occupations among us today in which homosexuality is very noticeable, as among hoboes, the celibate priesthood, nuns, Y.M.C.A. and Y.W.C.A., Scout Leaders, and other welfare workers.

In view of such facts it is not so discreditable to Whitman to be regarded as a Uranian, homosexual, or one of intermediate sex.

Was Carpenter True to Whitman?

To Whitman more than to any other person or writer Carpenter may have rightly ascribed, if not the origin of his own convictions, at least the encouragement and assurance of them. Whitman may not have realized to what logical conclusions his principles should have led him. And, although Carpenter went far beyond Whitman's philosophy of love, his spirit remained that of Whitman, and Carpenter may therefore be regarded as a true disciple. But a disciple, in the order of his greatness, is apt to go to lengths which astonish the master and even surprise him to the extent of forcing a repudiation of the disciple's doctrines. I think Whitman would have refused to accept Carpenter's derivations of doctrine from his own. But, as we may learn much concerning the master from his disciples, it is therefore of value to follow Carpenter's directions as indication of the tendencies implicit in Whitman. We have no right, however, nor has anyone the right to call Whitman a Uranian or a homosexual without more evidence than is now available to us.

The Whitman Movement as Interpreting Him.

I maintain in this book, in opposition to the usual interpretations of a man of genius who has greatly influenced thought or social action, that we understand him better by projecting him into movements which have followed because of him, than by attempting to discover him in his predecessors, whatever their likeness to him or the suggestions which their ideas and characters may have made to him. That is why I refuse to accept as explanatory of Whitman such theories as Chain of Being Doctrine and the Organic Concept, or the succession of Romanticism, or pantheism, or mysticism, which I find discordant with his beliefs. I do not object to pointing out the parallels or analogies; these have value. But stressing them as explanations results in missing the unique and original qualities which distinguish the man of genius and which mark him as different from his predecessors. To take account of his likeness to those who have gone before is quite legitimate if that method is used to set in relief his peculiar tenets and unique individuality, what Whitman called his own personality.

The Originality of Carpenter's Ideals.

To see more clearly what was distinctive in Whitman's conception of sex, we consider further Carpenter's conception of the intermediate sex, with the precaution not to attribute to Whitman what is in Carpenter. Carpenter was a great disciple with his own originality, and it would be unjust to find in him nothing beyond Whitman. My purpose is not to present Carpenter's thought primarily, but to use it for the further development of the Whitmanian viewpoint, which is considerably different. But I will seek out especially those ideas of Carpenter which are most in harmony with Whitman's.

Carpenter had more of a naturalist's viewpoint than had Whitman. Carpenter said: "Before the facts of Nature we have to preserve a certain humility and reverence; nor rush in with our preconceived and obstinate assumptions." The intermediate sex of the worker bee which he thought was evolved and "differentiated from the two ordinary bee sexes" suggested to him that "at the present time certain new types of human kind may be emerging, which will have an important part to play in the societies of the future."

Carpenter was a whole-hearted socialist as Whitman was not. Like Benjamin Kidd the hive, the anthill, and the termite colony seemed to Carpenter proper models for human society. Whitman surely could not have gone with the socialists to that conclusion.

Nor was he so humble or reverent before Nature. Man, the creator, held for him more promise than any natural evolution. But Whitman did have respect for "the facts of nature" to a degree that, for example, Hegel had not. It was this new respect for scientific facts which Whitman thought himself the first of poets to take into account. He believed himself to be the first poet of science. But he was also a prophet of science, of humanistic science in contrast with the materialistic viewpoints which were dominant in the new science of his time. Whitman, fighting in the lists against the traditions concerning sex as well as of religion, armored himself with the weapons of a humanistic science fashioned largely by his own skill.

Did Whitman's Social Theory Have a Homosexual Basis?

Whitman has been charged with promoting the idea that "the dear love of comrades" is the basic principle of society, especially of democracy. Carpenter speaks of sex love "as a kind of organic basis for the unity of all creatures" and in "the marriage of men and women, it becomes the very foundation of human society." Whitman would surely have gone as far as that, even though he might have stopped short of the next step in Carpenter's argument "that in its homogenic form . . . it has . . . also a deep significance, and social uses and functions." Perhaps Whitman might have become convinced of the truth of Carpenter's thesis if it had ever been presented to him as we have it in Carpenter's writing; for Carpenter with a wealth of illustration shows how large a part has been played in history and literature by homosexual friendships, and finally cites the case of "Walt Whitman, the enthusiasm of whose poems in comradeship is only parallelled by the devotedness of his labors for his wounded brothers in the American Civil War."

Homosexual License Distinguished.

One must not suppose that Carpenter is arguing for homosexual license. Instead he is condemning the pruriency of those who make "no distinction in their minds between the simplest and most naive expression of feeling and the gravest abuse of human rights and decency; ... who perceive no distinction between a genuine heart attachment and a mere carnal curiosity." What Carpenter approves of is the nobility of homosexual love which is expressed in Plato's *Symposium* and *Phaedrus*. Carpenter impresses the fact that the Greek was not given to licentiousness but "that the ideal of Greek life was a very continent one: the trained male, the athlete, the man tempered and restrained, even chaste, for the sake of bettering his powers."

Carpenter's Argument for Homosexuality.

Carpenter is combatting too narrow a conception of love. In the first place he emphasizes the necessity for everyone to be sustained and inspired by love. "Everyone is conscious that without a close affectional tie of some kind his life is not complete, his powers are crippled, and his energies are inadequately spent." That such ties of affection as homosexual friendships are ruled out he thinks preposterous and hurtful. It narrows love too much to confine it to the family, to spouses, to parents and children, and the children as between themselves. The "comrade union" must also be included. Certainly Whitman believed that also; otherwise many of his poems were thoughtless or the import of them unconscious to himself.

Carpenter seems emphatically to give the first place to the love of comrades. "It is difficult to believe that anything can supply the force and liberty and energies required for social and mental activities of the most necessary kind so well as a comrade union which yet leaves the two lovers free from the responsibilies and impediments of family life." That certainly goes quite beyond the range of Whitman's expressed beliefs. I think he regarded familial love as most important and fundamental and yet contended strongly for the love of comrades too. But his own indisposition to marry is evidence that in his private life he held or at least acted upon convictions like Carpenter's. Indeed, is not every voluntary celibate of a like mind and character as that Carpenter argues for?

Carpenter held a more extreme viewpoint than Whitman, but Whitman perceived the intermediate sex, if only instinctively, in the role of closest homosexual friendships. It was for him an institution, though not necessarily homosexual. To think of it as a new radical form of social attachments functioning like the sexless workers of the beehive, if that idea had ever struck him, would have had his disapproval, and he would probably have withdrawn himself from it as he kept aloof from "free love" and was repelled by Symonds' homosexualism.

Whitman's Special Teaching of Comradeship.

But Carpenter definitely declares Whitman to have been the person chiefly responsible for the new consciousness of the function of comradeship which Carpenter identifies with Uranianism. He says: "Walt Whitman, the inaugurator, it may almost be said, of a new world of democratic ideals and literatures, as—one of our best critics has remarked—the most Greek in spirit and in performance of modern writers, insists continually on this social function of 'intense and loving comradeship, the personal and passionate attachment of man to man.' " He feels that Whitman was quite conscious of the importance of homosexual relationships: "Whitman could not have spoken as he did, with a kind of authority on this subject, if he had not been aware that through the masses of the people this attachment was already alive and working—though doubtless in a somewhat suppressed and unself-conscious form —and if he had not had ample knowledge of the effects and influence in himself and others around him." "A moment's consideration must convince us that such a comradeship may, as Whitman says, have 'deepest relations to general politics.' " But it is not clear that Whitman meant any more by comradeship than deep friendly relationships regardless of sex.

Criticism of the Law against Homosexuality.

Carpenter questions the province of law in punishing homosexual acts: "The homogenic function is a valuable social force, and in some cases a necessary element of noble human character—yet the (English) act of 1885 makes almost any familiarity in such cases the possible basis of a criminal charge." "In so condemning the least familiarity between male persons we think it has gone too far. It has undertaken a censorship over private morals (entirely apart from social results) which is beyond its province."

Carpenter, however, is no extremist. He urges a more tolerant attitude toward "the homogenic attachment" because he believes it to be a valuable social relationship. He recognizes the dangers of abuse. But that is not peculiar to it. "All love, one would say, must have its responsibilities, else it is liable to degenerate, and to dissipate itself in mere sentiment or sensuality." The attitude toward homosexuality of reprobation, and even failure to recognize its social value, causes evil. "The homogenic attachment left unrecognized, usually loses some of its quality and becomes an ephemeral or corrupt thing."

Education of the Sex Emotions.

Therefore, he proposes education of the sex emotions which will give special attention to friendship resting upon homosexual relationships. He charges that by reason of "discountenanced and misunderstood" homosexual relationships "the disease of premature sexuality seems to have gotten possession of our centers of education; erotic practices and habits abound, and (what is perhaps their worst feature) cloud and degrade the boys' conception of what true love or friendship may be. To those who are familiar with large public schools the state of affairs does not need describing." He is of course speaking especially of the great public schools where the English have long trained their upper classes. The indiscriminate attitude which excludes any show of affection puts falsely on a par a kiss and an "act of fellatio" and so results in a boy "smothering and disowning the best part of his nature."

Whitman certainly would have given this proposal wholehearted endorsement. The repressions which pruriency has made distressing to Englishmen have done no less harm to American men. Whitman knew that it is a hindrance to friendship to thwart its emotional expression; therefore he would have comrades kiss and hold hands and caress each other in bodily embrace.

Carpenter's Intermediate Attitude.

Carpenter has taken pains not to be misunderstood. He has framed the issues and he desires to take the path between puritanism and sensuality. "There is no need to be puritanical or to look upon the lapses of boyhood as unpardonable since, indeed, it may be allowed as far as that goes, that a little frivolity is better than hardness and self-righteousness." On the other hand, "Purity (in the sense of continence) is of the first importance to boyhood. . . . To introduce sensual and sexual habits—and one of the worst of these is self-abuse—at an early age, is to arrest growth, both physical and mental." Undoubtedly today some authorities would regard Carpenter as a bit conservative.

But there is practical sense in Carpenter's suggestions: "A boy at puberty wants to know—and ought to know . . . He does not go very deep into things; a small amount of information will probably satisfy him." In him "there is offense, perhaps generally, an actual repugnance at first to anything like sexual practices."

Carpenter shows that primitive peoples and all but modern nations have taken care to give adolescents initiation in sex matters. In comparison the modern school leaves the boy and girl to get misinformation from the "gutter" and by frowning upon sex knowledge leaves their minds open to filthy suggestions and immoral sex practices. It may be countered that schools have progressed since Carpenter wrote. This is true. To Whitman and Carpenter that is largely due. I do not overlook also the influence of Freud, but I cannot praise psychoanalysts for the sensible moderation which distinguishes Carpenter's opinions.

Much more remains to be achieved before the reform is effected which was advocated by Whitman and Carpenter. We can agree with Carpenter as Whitman would have agreed with him without admitting that he has made a case for the existence of a third or intermediate sex.

The Importance of Inversion in Whitman's Work.

Although Havelock Ellis thought that inversion, however important in psychological study of Whitman's own nature, has slight importance for his work or his readers, the biographers generally have not been willing to brush the subject so easily aside. Thus Canby maintains that "one of Whitman's great services was to restore sexuality to literature." But he questions whether Whitman solved his own sex conflict. The question, as Canby poses it, is whether the solution of the Oriental mystic of banishing sex emotion by mystic practices or the frank avowal of sex desire and emotion as Whitman contended, is more successful.

Flaubert's *The Temptation of St. Anthony* is a classic picture of the sex disturbances common to monastic and celibate living. And history provides a striking illustration in the escape of Martin Luther from the monastery and elopement with a nun whom he married as an incident if not the cause of the Protestant Reformation. And there is also the authority of Apostle Paul: "I say therefore to the unmarried and widows, It is good for them if they abide even as I. But if they cannot contain, let them marry; for it is better to marry than to burn."

But marriage was not Whitman's solution. Nor did he take or seek normal sex intercourse for himself. He abhorred the idea of free love. He wrote Dr. Bucke: "Heywood, the Massachusetts free lover, here today, very cordial. I treated him politely but that is all." His oldest friends, Burroughs and Eldridge, rejected Symonds intimations that Whitman's relations with Peter Doyle or other men ever involved any homosexual practices. Whitman was indeed far from the laxity of some of the psychoanalysts who encourage loose sexual relations as cure for hysterical or neurotic cases. His solution seemed to be rather sublimation or more likely indulgence in free sex imagination of the elevated or lofty sort which he termed comradeship, Carpenter's highest type of intermediate sex.

Whitman's Literary Expression of Sex.

The *Children of Adam* poems, which to Long seem "false, unreal, pure romance," to Schyberg were "philosophical rather than personal." But the *Calamus* poems to Long are in point of form "an incomparable work of art" on manly love. Possibly such judgments are suggested by biographical facts rather than deduced wholly from the content of the poems. Allen's Handbook, however, adduces quite a general opinion to the same effect that Whitman's knowledge of actual love is not revealed in his writings, with perhaps one exception. Holloway attempted to classify the several kinds of sex expression in *Leaves of Grass*, which I paraphrase as follows: (1) romantic lyrics expressing normal sex love; (2) philosophic tributes to procreation; (3) physiological emotions accompanying the normal sex act; and (4) the "manly attachment" of homosexual relationship.

If Whitman had some sex experience as he must have had to write what he did with some particularity of description, nevertheless Eldridge and Burroughs were probably right in asserting that it was not the aim or purpose of his writing to give it immediate or primary expression. Universal love was his theme, although he desired to relate that universal love with the very many particular types of it. However, concreteness, content and individuality were always Whitman's aim, and as much in philosophizing love as of any other theme. Mere abstractness was disapproved by him. But, however much he extolled the body, the general soul was always precious to him. That was characteristic of his sublimation of love.

From the first this was uppermost in his thoughts. In an early notebook he said: "Sympathy or love is the law over all laws, because in nothing else but love is the soul conscious of pure happiness, which appears to be the ultimate resting place, the point of all things." He said to

Traubel: "The real capital is love, after all: just love."
"Love is never wrong."

Whitman's Authority on Sex.

His writings are the only credible evidence of his sex
experiences and sex knowledge. They are adequate to
prove his authority, but in no sense are they directly autobiographical.

I think it is sufficient explanation for Whitman's attitude toward his personal love life that he thought it wholly
irrelevant to and tending to detract from the great lesson
he had to teach about love. If we understand the affection
for the human being and all human beings which he
sought to inculcate, we will know all he intended to imply
by the term love. His significance is, as Ellis said, that he
"represents for the first time since Christianity swept
over the world, the reintegration in a sane and whole-
hearted view, of the instincts of the entire man, and
therefore he has a significance we hardly overestimate."

Consequently, it is quite beside the point to argue anything from Whitman's private life. Walt Whitman for
him in his writing and for us is only important as a symbol
of every man. Whether he was a Uranian or homosexual
has no material importance for judging his contribution
to the subject of love. Nor would it matter much if he pretended to more actual experience in love than he had,
either to keep off intruders or to prevent such grave misunderstandings as people are guilty of who mistakenly
believe that one only knows what one has met with face
to face in life. As men we possess the unique ability to live
vicariously in the experience of others and to extend our
experiences much beyond their factual content. Only un-
imaginative people do not know that. Prophets are not
ordinarily men of affairs or men rich in actionable experience. They are for that richer in the experiences of others
whose experiences they employ parasitically as their own.

Accordingly, Whitman, who was never known to be a lover, knew much more about love than do philanderers who indulge the sex passion excessively. There is a poem *Sometimes With One I Love,* from which we have quoted on the morality of love, that shows Whitman knew the compensations and knowledge of love which may grow from unreturned or unrealized or unconsummated love. It is indeed often astonishing how profound are the intuitions of love in quite inexperienced young persons. Only to impossible matter-of-fact people should this require further argument.

Was Whitman's Conception of Love Conservative?

Account must be taken of the conservative view of Whitman on love as well as of his radical conceptions. He sought for a balance between the two, giving both adequate expression. In a footnote to *Democratic Vistas* he gave as reasons for striking a new note in literature for more than one kind of love that "It is to the development, identification, and general prevalence of that fervid companionship (the adhesive love, at least rivalling the amative love hitherto possessing imaginative literature, if not going beyond it), that I look for the counterbalance and offset of our materialistic and vulgar American democracy, and the spiritualisation thereof." These terms "adhesive" and "amative" have been taken to mean respectively homosexual and heterosexual love, but we maintain that Whitman meant by adhesive love the wider circles of friendships including both men and women in contrast with the more restricted relationships of the family which are amative love.

His closest friends were entirely agreed that normal domestic relationships were held by Whitman to be of the most fundamental importance. Harned said, "He was essentially a believer in the family as a unit—and, of course, the individual in the last analysis. His love of his kind was more than a duty, it was a living impulse, and that is the best test as to how far a man is sincere when he espouses the cause of the human race." Although Burroughs wrote: "The home, the fireside, the domestic allurements were not in him;" Eldridge made criticism of this expression: "It seems to me the early poems, especially, are saturated with the love of home and domestic pleasures." The difference between Burroughs' and Eldridge's views of Whitman may have come from thinking of different aspects of the man. Certainly, if Whitman had been a marrying kind of man, he would have shown an amative interest in women. But his love for his mother and his devotion especially to the weaker and dependent members of his family proved his family attachments. Assuredly he was not a destroyer but a supporter of the family. As Eldridge went on to say to Burroughs: "As I knew him, he was, as far as existing institutions are concerned, one of the most conservative of men. He was more passionately attached to the old fashioned family relations than any man I have ever known. This is indicated in many places in *Leaves of Grass*." Had Eldridge written his contemplated book on Whitman we would probably possess a more judicious estimate of Whitman's character than we now have, and it would have shown Whitman in his truer personality as a well-balanced man and having a marked conservative as well as radical side to him.

His Personal and Friendly Relationships.

There was also a never failing purity in his expressions of friendship or comradeship. However, as to women, notwithstanding his determination to declare them on an equality with him, he was not at ease with them. Long expresses this difficulty understandingly: 'There is a difficulty of finding the contrivance to attach men together strongly, and the greater difficulty which has come in modern times with the growing admission of women into friendship."

He observes that Anne Gilchrist's advances frightened Whitman. His disposition was such that "he steers straight for the objective and social, and the entanglement with another's ego frightens him."

Whitman seemed to have admitted that himself. In conversation with Traubel he confessed that Burroughs expressed more of his ideal person than did he himself. "John's prominent features are good nature, good humor, eligibility for friendship; he proposes to include everybody —to accept the commonest character in the tribe; to draw no lines; he is, in fact, for the ensemble. John's world would have no outcasts." Reminded by Traubel of his own profession of inclusiveness, he replied: "True, true, but I am not good natured, no, no, not at all as good and kind as John. I get riled—a fellow like Arnold stirs me up. I accept the world, most of the world—but somehow draw a line somewhere in some of those fellows. John detects in me primarily the lessons of comradeship, the comrade spirit —is drawn to that—sees that as the vitalizing, spinal force." A remarkably self-revealing statement! It showed that Whitman had insight concerning himself. As he grew old probably he came more to himself. His yearning for companionship more than his real capacity was the expression especially of the early poems and did not cease to motivate him to the end of *Leaves of Grass*.

Whitman Versus his Ideal Person.

It is not a single passage that denotes this difference in the reality of himself and the ideal of his poems. His confessions as well as the testimony of his nearest and oldest friends likewise prove it. He got annoyed with his visitors and their adulations of him: "I hate to have people come to me with malice—throw themselves into my arms—insist upon themselves, upon their affection." This was not only his justifiable desire for sincerity of expression; it was also his dislike for effusive professions of friendship for which he was unprepared or which he did not meet with preparedness in himself. It was easier for him to like children, simple, common folk, and old people.

One critic thought Whitman showed lack of comradeship in his abstention from the use of tobacco and having no convivial habits. But I am reminded of an extraordinarily companionable person I knew who had none of such social vices and who once stated his opinion on the matter to me: "Conversation is the brilliant jewel of sociality; the use of tobacco, whether smoking or chewing, interferes with conversation, and alcoholic habits unfit one for the best of it."

The same critic was mistaken in assuming that Whitman had no club habits. In his early newspaper life and later he had fondness for habituation of public haunts. His newspaper career made it professionally necessary. Pfaff's in New York was a bohemian hang-out and he often went there. Canby appears to think he had only a half-hearted interest in such places, and that his notebook references speak of that life as "likeness of me, but never substantially me"; and of the frequenters: "Oft I doubt your reality whether you are real—I suspect all is but a pageant."

Despite his poetic tributes to the ensemble, this aloofness from the crowd was very marked in Whitman. As he stated it to Traubel: "So I please myself I don't care a damn what the public thinks of me." He praised this quality in Thoreau and associated it with his own attitude: "One thing about Thoreau keeps him very near to me . . . his lawlessness—his dissent—his going his own absolute road let hell blaze all it chooses." And the same repugnance came out in his objections to having clubs and societies named after him.

Whitman's Dominant Trait was Wholesomeness.

Notwithstanding the physiological radicalism of his poems which takes up and absorbs the earthiness of Nature

and accepts its filth with the rest, there was undoubtedly
a prejudice in him for the cleanly, healthy, and pure rather
than the gross and unpleasant things of the natural order.
As he said to Traubel: "I like to feel that the things I do
are wholesome." "I think all the scientists would agree
with me, as I agree with them, that a beautiful, competent,
sufficing body is the prime force making towards the virtues in civilization, life, history." Burroughs commenting
on Whitman's tendency to identify himself "with all types
and conditions of men," defended him against any asper-
sion of sexual immorality: "A cleaner, saner, more wholesome man, in words and deed, I have never known."

That was Burroughs' estimation of Whitman the man.
He was not so correct as to the poet Whitman, for he estimated the latter as a naturalist or naturist. He made the
distinction that when we judge moralistically we judge as
the judge judges; but "when we judge as Nature or the
poet judges, we say" as Whitman said *To a Prostitute,*
"Not till the sun excludes you do I exclude you." Burroughs agreed with Whitman that Nature is not moral,
but Whitman did not agree that the Poet is impersonal
and a-moral as Nature. Had the poet the attitude of Nature toward the prostitute he would be indifferent to her,
careless of what happens to her. Not so Whitman, for he,
the poet, said to her:

> "My girl I appoint with you an appoint-
>   ment, and I charge you that you make
>   preparation to be worthy to meet me,
> And I charge that you be patient and perfect
>   till I come."

It was a moral, not a natural judgment Whitman the
poet made of the prostitute. He thought of her as he
thought of the dead prostitute in *The City Dead-house,* as
he thought of all delinquents and maimed persons, as a
potentially beautiful human soul, good and perfect as it

might be made. Whitman accepted her in his poetic ideal-ism not as she was but as a redeemable human being in-herently good.

When we understand *Leaves of Grass* it is not as an autobiographical collection of poems or as a recitation of the realistic things of Nature. Every man's idealisms do denote something of his character, at least his yearnings, but to assume that they are ever quite himself is to over-look the fact that they are ideals because they are not yet attained realities. It is the distinction between I and me, the I as I want to be and the me as I am. Which is the real me? That was always present in Whitman's thought. The two parts of himself: the narrowly confined physical self, and the spirit, the roving general soul, in which the present ego might come to perfection when time and space would permit—a perfection always ideally existent. This theme continued foremost in *Leaves of Grass*.

Love at the Center.

Whitman's great themes interpenetrated. As religion is in everything, so love enters into everything. Love, how-ever, is one subject in which more readily than any other the reader can make his own discoveries from Whitman's many love songs and find echoes awakening to his own experiences of the heart whatever they may be.

For him democracy was also a passion bound up with the "dear love of comrades". Love is at the heart of demo-cracy as it is at the heart of religion. Those who interpret all this to mean a sublimation of sexuality alone and those who object that sublimated Uranianism is an insufficient basis on which to found religion and democracy, have not yet fully comprehended Whitman. His nature and his understanding were not so narrowly canalized. As he at-tempted to include multitudes he tried to encompass Love in all its human attributes, in its failures which denote aspiration, in all its realities of tender attachments, in the joys and sorrows that attend it, and in the great hope of it for mankind. The breadth of his sympathies were a new thing in literature, in morals, in religion, in democracy, and thereby he became rather uniquely the Prophet of Love.

9

PROPHET OF DEMOCRACY.

❖ ❖ ❖ ❖ ❖ ❖

"Where the citizen is always the head and
ideal, and President, Mayor, Governor
and what not, are agents for pay."

❖ ❖ ❖ ❖ ❖ ❖

WHITMAN'S POLITICAL BENT TO DEMOCRACY WAS BASIC. HIS
early training in the newspaper business made him a poli-
tician, if that was not yet earlier in his blood. And he remained politically-minded. He thought it the duty of
every young man to participate in politics. The themes
of immortality and politics, he said, "run through the
volume" of *Leaves of Grass*.

Nature and Kinds of Democracy.

But his conception of democracy was wider than politics. He conceived of three kinds of democracy: political,
economic, and literary.

He said: Political democracy is the only one with which
the world has yet had much experience. "In Lincoln's
formula," it is "the government of the people, by the people, for the people." Whitman did not try to defend the
people or rest his case upon them: They may need tute-
lage for self-government. As Burroughs said: "His is not
the voice of the people so much as it is the voice back of
the people, and gives them sanity and health and perpetuity." He urged, nevertheless, that "The democratic for-

198

mula is the only safe and preservative one for coming times." Democracy en masse is fundamental: it is "the clue to the history of the past." But in democracy there were for him two important opposite principles: the mass and the individual. *Leaves of Grass* begins:

> "One's-self I sing, a simple separate person,
> Yet utter the word Democratic, the word En-
>   Masse."

Gummere, a severe critic, thought this started well, but could Whitman keep the promise of it? He thought Whitman grievously erred by championing individual lawlessness.

But with Lincoln Whitman regarded Union in the United States of America essential. The United States, "divine America," is the continent of democracy. Yet he made no pretense that democracy here is complete. "America is being made but is not made." For "America, too, is a prophecy." He agreed with Felix Adler, "America is not all in all."

Whitman did not conceive America, the United States, or democracy, to be any self-subsisting entity: it is not the State which anarchists so undiscriminatingly oppose, lumping democracies and tyrannical states together. These entities, America, democracy, are only you and me.

"The American compact is altogether with individuals."

That is the only government he could countenance. The big state must be counterbalanced by the big citizen. It is a government of law and not of license. But it is not "to be held together by lawyers", "or by an agreement on a paper," "or by arms". The tie of democracy is love or "loving comradeship." This is essentially a religious ideal. "At the core of democracy, finally, is the religious element." But the religion of humanity, not superstitious religion.

The Elements of Democracy.

But in setting forth the elements of this democracy Whitman's catalogue varies: They are "ensemble, evolution, freedom"; or "freedom, law, and love"; or ensemble, prosperity, and personal expression, respectively, in the three types or stages of democracy, towit, political, economic, and literary democracy; and there is also the element of equality in democracy. All these thread through Whitman's book.

Of them equality and freedom or liberty are especially related to democracy, or more particularly to political democracy, although they are not unrelated to economic and artistic democracy.

Equality and Democracy.

The theme of equality and the unique worth of each and every man is a partial expression of the great message, the inspired prophecy, of Whitman. That is not nearly all of the prophecy. For at the same time that he declares equality, he affirms what rises above it, the greatness of man that incorporates everything, distances it, and then recalls it at desire. This is the large encompassing freedom of man. Contrary to those who assume that equality and freedom are incompatibles, both are necessary to Whitman's conception of democracy.

The conception of equality has usually given a great deal of trouble to those who have sought to maintain it. How did Whitman accomplish harmonization of equality and individual freedom? His contrast of principles, both of which he maintained, gives the answer and the key also to his democratic philosophy. He said:

> "For to democracy, the leveler, the unyield-
> ing principle of the average, is surely
> joined another principle, equally unyield-

ing, closely tracking the first, indispensable to it, opposite, . . . and ever modifying the other, often clashing, paradoxical,
yet neither of the highest avail without
the other. . . . This second principle is
individuality, the pride and centripetal
isolation of a human being in himself—
identity—personalism."

Equality befits the mass, freedom the individual personality. By reviewing each of these concepts in Whitman
we will understand him better as well as gain a new insight concerning the balance or synthesis of democracy
which includes both equality and freedom, both the solid-
ary mass or people and the individual.

But as Myers interprets this idea, "Whitman construct-
ed . . . . a spiritual democracy governed by two principles,
one the unlimited individual, the other the equality of
individuals." That distorts Whitman's conception. ʃWhit-
man had a realistic perception of the limitations that usually afflict individuals.ʃ He believed rather in the infinitely
expanding individual. And Whitman also knew well
enough the limitations upon equality of individuals. He
perceived equality also as a becoming rather than an is.

Whitman's Social Democracy of Equality.

Myers also distinguishes spiritual democracy from social democracy and makes out Whitman's democracy to
be primarily spiritual democracy and only secondarily social democracy. That gives an unreality to Whitman's conception and quite perverts it. Whitman was not a world-
escaping Utopian. He was not prophecying social relationships for some far off age or other continent as yet undis-
covered or telling of some halcyon time in the past. He
had a program of equality for immediate social effectiveness.

His conception of democratic equality is especially an attitude of comrades. "I say democracy infers such loving comradeship, as its most inevitable twin or counterpart, without which it will be incomplete, in vain, and incapable of perpetuating itself." "The continuance of equality shall be comrades."

He gave it extreme emphasis: "I will accept nothing which all cannot have the counterpart of on the same terms." "Neither a servant nor a master I . . . I will be even with you and you shall be even with me."

Democratic equality is like that within the family: "Mother of all, thy every daughter, son, endeared alike, forever equal." The genius of the United States lies not in its leaders or elite, "but always most in the common people." He meant *Leaves of Grass* "to be a poem of average identity." "To sing the song of that law of average identity, and of yourself, consistently with the divine law of the universal is a main intention of those Leaves."

Equality is Recognition of Individual Worth.

But one errs who may think that those are songs of laudation of mediocrity or low grade equality or equalization. Mediocrity which Nietzsche mistakenly understood as democracy and condemned is not meant or praised by Whitman. Whitman's one constant purpose is to elevate the lowly to the height of personality, to the true dignity of man. He recognizes the unique potential worth of every man. To the

> " . . . human forms with the fathomless ever-
>   impressive countenances of brutes", he

says:

> "You will come forward in due time to my
>   side,"

that is, equal with me. Speaking in the voices of the social
outcasts and criminals and for them he declares:

> "Lifted now and always against whoever
>   scorning assumes to rule me,"
> I am "equal with any, real as any."

And to the diseased:

> "But thou shalt face thy fortunes, thy di-
>   seases, and surmount them all,
> Whatever they are to-day and whatever
>   through time they may be,
> They each and all shall lift and pass away
>   and cease from thee."

Whatever your degradation, "do you give in that you
are any less immortal?" This is not the immortality for a
life in another world after death or for some future age.
It is the unique and special value of every human being
here and now.

To the dictators and all the elite he says:

> "Have you thought there could be but a
>   single supreme?
> There can be any number of supremes."

This is like De Tocqueville's description of Americans
of the 1830's: "In America every man is a king."

He claims it to be the mission of the poet to be "the
equalizer of his age and land." It is the poet who "sees
eternity in men and women, he does not see men and
women as dreams or dots." That was his reply to the theologians and scientists of his time who lowered or dispar-
aged the dignity and worth of man.

And when he said that he meant woman too. There was no homosexual disposition in Whitman to depreciate women. He tends even to the other extreme, to make women the special repository of the virtues; at least he insists upon "the perfect equality of the female with the male."

It is in this spirit of equalizing all men upward that he says, I "would fetch you, whoever you are, flush with myself." No passage expresses it all better than this: "I only am he who places over you no master, owner, better, God, beyond what waits intrinsically in yourself." ⟨What you are "intrinsically in yourself" is what is to be brought up to the high level of man's capability, of the ideal for men.⟩

Does Whitman's Equalizing Ignore Distinctions?

There is, however, no glossing over the fact that there are differences in men. Whitman does not deny that. He points them out. He maintains equality in the sense of demanding recognition of the individual worth of each man in respect of those very differences and equal right to such recognition. "That which fills its period and place is equal to any."

But Professor Allen thinks that after Whitman's political and editorial disappointments and with the formulation of his *Leaves of Grass* his conception of equality took on a passive attitude which made no personal or moral distinctions. "The literary role which he assumed in the 1855 edition of *Leaves of Grass* and played consistently throughout all subsequent editions was that of 'the caresser of life' embracing all forms, good and evil alike, with a democracy that made no distinctions between persons or factions." This was a passivity of "almost Brahmin serenity."

The evidence of this, he thinks, appears in several poems. *I sit and Look Out* is one of these. Contrary to Allen's view, that poem does not express a passive attitude.

It certainly contains a moral judgment aroused against the wrongs enumerated there which is not passive acceptance of them.

Allen asks with Myers, Why is Whitman the poet of evil as well as of good? If he was not content to wait the slow evolution of cosmic forces to put all things to rights or equalize the bad with the good? But I ask, Is it consistent to think of Whitman as the great expander, the great equalizer, which he endeavored to be, and also merely a passivist? In what sense, if any, did Whitman accept and equalize good and evil? Did he mean to make a democratic equality between good and evil and not to prefer one to the other? If so, there is nothing to distinguish Whitman from a nihilist. So false a conception of Whitman makes him out the opposite of what he is. His doctrine is neither retirement from the world nor renunciation of it. Identity, and not at all Nothingness, is the substance of his thought.

When in section 19 of *Song of Myself* he sets the meal equally for the wicked and righteous, kept-woman, thief, sponger, slave, venerealee, and declares "There shall be no difference between them", that is not a passive commitment to the idea that they are of equal merit. Not that at all. It is the same idea that is in the conception of equality before the law. It is the democratic assertion that men shall have an equal chance for the goods of life and for spiritual improvement.

And when he says in section 22 of that same poem:

> "I am not the poet of goodness only, I do
>   not decline to be the poet of wickedness
>   also.
>
> ❖ ❖ ❖ ❖ ❖ ❖
>
> I find one side a balance and the antipodal
>   side a balance",

if one has the patience or sincerity to read a little farther in this poem, *Song of Myself*, there is a remarkable affirmance of faith beyond the reaches of science. What does this mean other than regardless of evil appearances or even because of them ("Evil propels me and reform of evil propels me"), Whitman has faith in the good outcome of it all. The trouble with these mysticizers (we have distinguished mystery from mysticism) is that they do not read far enough. They stop with the cinch of a passage here and there that they can read their mystical nonsense into and think fallaciously that is Whitman.

So too in the poem *By Blue Ontario's Shore*, which Myers and Allen cite for the support of their doctrine of passive mysticism which they ascribe to Whitman. What are the countervailing supremes? A mere cancelling out of individuality by the doctrine of equality? On the contrary, "All is for individuals. . . . Produce great Persons, the rest follows." And so far from acceptance of the evil or passivity toward existing conditions, Whitman says:

> "I am he who tauntingly compels men,
>   women, nations,
> Crying, Leap from your seats and contend
>   for your lives!"

And he protests vehemently against "that which spends itself with no thought of the stain, pains, dismay, feebleness, it is bequeathing." And in section 10 of this poem, in which he describes the poet as "the equable man", "the equalizer of his age and land," he reaffirms his faith in "the great Idea, the idea of perfect and free individuals," ending with the paean to Liberty and Equality not at all in a passivist spirit:

> "Without extinction is Liberty, without
>   retrograde is Equality,

They live in the feelings of young men and
    the best women,
(Not for nothing have the indomitable heads
    of the earth been always ready to fall for
    Liberty.) "

If one will read Whitman as a whole, and not in mincing parts, he will be found an unfailing defender of equality in freedom, not sitting passively to accept the wrong as equal with the right, but encouraging action to raise the level of all men to the best that is in them.

Whitman's Conception of Freedom.

For Whitman democracy and equality are nearly synonymous terms, but freedom is a necessary and complementary principle also essential to the existence of democracy. However, liberty or freedom is the more characteristic attribute of individual personality or selfhood which has polar relation to democracy.

Whitman was brought up in a family whose traditions were those of American democracy. They had a leaning to Quakerism, and especially to that of the radical preacher, Elias Hicks. Whitman was early a Democrat of the Jefferson-Jackson variety.

He was opposed to slavery and declared for "freedom to every slave on the face of the earth." Whatever may have been his private opinions, Whitman's gospel treated the negro as an equal and entitled him to liberty and to any thing else as much as Whitman himself:

"The runaway slave came to my house and
    stopt outside,
I . . . went where he sat on a log and led him
    in and assured him, . . .
And gave him a room that entered from my
    own, . . .
I had him sit next me at table, . . . "

I think that wholly refutes Masters and any others to the contrary.

However, Whitman's notions of equality for the negro did not lead him to overlook the necessity of training for civic duties as preparatory to the exercise of political functions. This was the reason why O'Connor fell into a rage with him because Whitman insisted on the negro's unfitness for suffrage. It was said that he had no sympathy for the abolitionists and a poor opinion of the negro. But Whitman's own explanation does him more justice. "Phillips—all of them—all of them—thought slavery the one crying sin of the universe. I didn't—though I, too, thought it a crying sin."

That O'Connor fell out with Whitman over the question discredits O'Connor rather than Whitman. As Burroughs said of O'Connor, he was "a man of extraordinary abilities, but lacking the sanity or moderation of the greatest men." He was a violent partisan, while Whitman dissented "from partisanship whatever its name or form." Whitman's attitude toward the negro was much that of Lincoln's whom Masters and many others, such as the Abolitionists of his time, thought too compromising or indifferent. In fact, none of them were any more steadfast in devotion to the ideal than Lincoln or Whitman, but their impatience made them unfit to deal with a social situation which almost always demands compromise and slow-going methods.

The Importance and Vitality of Freedom.

To Whitman freedom was most fundamental:

"And now, Life, Pride, Patriotism and
    Death,
To you, O FREEDOM, purport of all, ...
I offer all to you."

Liberty is a very strong native impulse and therefore has great persistence and endurance:

> "When Liberty goes out of a place it is not
>   the first to go, nor the second nor the third
>   to go,
> It waits for all the rest to go, it is the last."

But, "Once fully enslaved, no nation, state, city, of this earth, ever afterward resumes its liberty." Evidently, that is the exceptional case.

Faith in Freedom.

His faith is high:

> " . . . O Libertad—turn your undying face,
> To where the future, greater than all the
>   past,
> Is swiftly, surely preparing for you."

He gives courage "to a foiled European Revolutionaire": "Keep on—Liberty is to be subserved whatever occurs." Therefore, "Mind you O foreign kings, O priests, the crop shall never run out" of "those who in any land died for the Good cause."

Whitman's faith in freedom echoed the thought that has been much quoted from Lincoln and which Whitman applied to his conception of freedom: "It is as useless to quarrel with history as with the weather." Asked if history is automatic? he replied: "Not at all: it is free in all its basic dynamics: that is, the free human spirit has a part to perform in giving direction to history." Again he said: "I should feel like warning the moneyed powers in America that threaten to stand in the way: history will deal in a very drastic fashion with opposition like that should it become too stubborn."

These quotations show how wrong is the interpretation of Whitman's thought which merely represents it as reclining upon some blind faith in Providence or some mystical future stance. Whitman's humanism was basic. He believed that men can give direction to history and that evil propels men to assert human rights and they will triumph over wrongs committed, that is, as long as the spark of desire for freedom exists in them.

He expressed the same idea as to science: "The scientific spirit . . . always keeps the way open—always gives life, thought, and affection, the whole man, a chance to try over again after a mistake—after a wrong guess." How different Whitman's conception than that of a deterministic materialist scientificism! Man always has another chance, another guess! Whitman could not believe that science shuts off experiment or freedom of will. That was the very essense of his faith in freedom.

Not long ago on the Invitation to Learning radio program Lyman Bryson felt that a criticism lay against Beard's *Rise of American Civilization* that it gives the impression that history carries on without human intervention, the "drift of history" it was called by another speaker who replied in defence of Beard that his viewpoint is rather that organization is essential to give direction; in organization the common man will have a chance. But this is a blind conception too. What do we see more evidently than that the larger organizational units become the less does the common man have a chance? It was just that against which Whitman made his protest.

An undemocratic unamerican movement has gained considerable vogue of late by preaching the principle of interdependence to replace the doctrine of independence. Professor Harry Overstreet wrote a book promoting this slavish concept. Will Durant has put himself at the head of an organization in the name of a Declaration of Interdependence. Whitman saw clearly the fallacy of such backward thinking.

Freedom is Resistance.

The rule of freedom for local governments is: "Resist much, obey little." For the individual, the race, and the nation that rule is the same. Even our children are to be taught to be a law unto themselves.

To Professor Gummere that seemed utter lawlessness: "He frees the individual from what he calls tyranny; but he sets up no law to which the free individual shall submit. He says that he believes poets to be 'the voice and expression of liberty'; this liberty is license. He declares outright that his aim is to be 'essentially revolutionary'." Again, "Whitman's democracy, in a word, is ochlocracy; he has no ideal social order in mind, but man shall jostle man in a glad turbulent mob."

Not only did Whitman not repudiate law; he recognized and sought the duality and balance of freedom and law, but it must be freedom's law and not the tyrant's law. Such liberty is not license. And if his aim was revolutionary, it was not in any different sense than Jefferson and Lincoln thought of keeping alive the right of revolution. Like Lincoln he was a Union man. And so far from being an ochlocrat, a devotee of the mob, the fundamentals of his doctrine are the offsetting of the mass by the guaranteed right of the individual.

Why did Gummere miss or overlook these expressions which we set forth abundantly in this chapter? I think it was because he followed Bliss Perry's mistake of identifying Whitman with Rousseau, whose influence was hurtful to democracy. Gummere did not fully recognize or even discover the essence of its poison. However, Rousseau is not chargeable with all the sins of Sorelism and Trotskyism or of fascism as some have complained. Gummere revolts against the Rousseau of *Emile* rather than the Rousseau of the *Social Contract*, which are so strikingly in contrast.

In his *Social Contract*, beginning with his famous sentence, "Man is born free, and everywhere he is in chains," Rousseau theorized a new and more enduring chain, the mystic will of the people, which has borne its fruit in our time more demonstrably in the dictationship of the proletariat and the marches of black and brown shirts than in the ideas of *Emile*, the latter best examplified in what is now called Progressive Education. There are two Rousseaus, and neither of them is Whitman, although the spirit of *Emile* comes very close to Whitman.

But Whitman realized, as Gummere did not, the fallacy of Rousseau's conception of the will of the people, and that it must always be checked and held in restraint by constitutional guaranties of the liberty of the individual and for equality between individuals. Gummere, indeed, inclined to the doctrines of the *Social Contract* in his exaltation of the community and his praise of Wordsworth's *Ode to Duty* as a document of democracy.

Freedom is Balanced by Law.

For Whitman as for Jefferson, a strongly centralized government, even in a democracy, is destructive of the rights and liberties of men. For him to be a law unto themselves does not mean the absence of law and government. He says:

> "I see Freedom, completely armed and vic-
> torious and very haughty, with Law on
> one side and Peace on the other,
> A stupendous trio all issuing forth against
> the idea of caste."

Or, as expressed again, it is "Freedom, poised by Toleration, swayed by law."

The Balance Between Individual and Government.

He insists that he is singing of a unity, though contradictory, in Nationality and the "latent right of insurrection." On the one side it is national character or idea to be sought for. But on the other side character "is to stand compact upon that first basis of the supremacy of individuality."

Whitman made a synthesis of en-masse and individual, which was his conception of true democracy. He went to neither extreme, neither to ochlocracy nor to the superman who lords it over the mass, neither the impersonal almighty State nor the lawless individual. He was saved from either of those tenets so destructive to democracy by understanding of the independent individual worth of every man and the necessity for self-reliant individuals under the protection and encouragement of just law and free government.

Self-Reliance.

The principle of being a law unto one's self means self-reliance.

> "You shall not look through my eyes either,
>   nor take things from me,
> You shall listen to all sides and filter them
>   from yourself."

Freedom expresses one's sacred individuality:

> "My final merit I refuse you, I refuse putting
>   from me what I really am,
> Encompass worlds, but never' try to encompass me."

> "I am for those who have never been mastered,

> For men and women whose tempers have
>   never been mastered,
> For those whom laws, theories, conventions,
>   can never master."

Natural Freedom.

He conceives freedom as natural: It is "Nature without check with original energy."

> "I start them by exhaustless laws as Nature
>   does, fresh and modern continually,
> I gave nothing as duties,
> What others give as duties I give as living
>   impulses."

In this period of the rise of totalitarianism, even parading itself as sociology, the slave-minded or socialistic type of authoritarianism is fond of repeating to us that we should prate less of rights and think or insist more upon duties. A sounder social psychology, however, perceives with Whitman that inner living impulses accomplish more and of better quality than does the compulsion of dutifulness. Duty is more allied to restraint; the living impulse is action, buoyancy, faith, growth, and forward looking.

Freedom for All Opinion.

As he demanded freedom for himself, so he enjoined it on others:

"I charge you to leave all free, as I have left all free." He made reference there to freedom from his own doctrines. The passage as a whole has special significance for biography and interpretation of Whitman, and we have referred to it before:

> "I call to the world to distrust the accounts
>   of my friends, but listen to my enemies,
>   as I myself do,

I charge you forever reject those who would
   expound me, for I cannot expound myself,
I charge that there be no theory or school
   founded out of me,
I charge you to leave all free, as I have left
   all free."

Perhaps he spoke more truly than he divined. For the
most part his friendly biographers (I make exception of
Burroughs) have done worse by him than his enemies. And
the schools that have been founded on Whitman have, like
nearly all followers and disciples of great teachers, misrepresented him.

But at any rate he was one prophet and teacher who
did not wish to bind up the minds of the future with his
own doctrines. That was probably because in his effort to
attain fullness and liberty he found the natural way best.

Surely Whitman did not believe he had freed himself
from all doctrine and presented none of his own. He had
a defined and developed philosophy, even a dogma of democracy. But the doctrines of democracy should be different
in this, that they leave minds free to work out the forms
and content of democracy as human experience may en-
lighten us concerning them.

Freedom of Comradeship.

Freedom in comradeship is an element in democracy:

"Affection shall solve the problems of freedom yet."

Freedom is mutuality:

"What gives me to be free to a woman's and
   man's good-will? what gives them to be
   free to mine?"

Freedom and equality in comradeship are mutually re-levant terms: they "live in the feelings of young men and the best women."

"The dependence of Liberty shall be lovers,
The continuance of Equality shall be comrades."

As liberty and equality are definitive of democracy, Whitman's hope for democracy was in them, but his assurance of them he discovered in the extension of human love and comradeship.

Summary of Whitman's Democratic Doctrine.

In an essay entitled "Personalism", later incorporated in *Democratic Vistas,* Whitman summarized his doctrine of democracy:

"As we have shown, the New World, including in it-self, and indeed founded upon, the all-levelling aggregate of democracy, we show it also including the all-variety, all-permitting, all-free theorem of individuality, and erecting therefor a lofty and hitherto unoccupied framework or platform of Personalism, broad enough for all, eligible to every farmer and mechanic—to the female equally with the male—a towering selfhood, not physically perfect only— not satisfied with the mere mind's and learning's stores, but religious, possessing the idea of the Infinite (rudder and compass sure amid this troublous voyage, o'er darkest, wild-est wave, through stormiest wind, of man's or nation's pro-gress) —realizing, above the rest, that known humanity, in deepest sense, is fair adhesion to Itself, for purposes beyond —and that, finally, the theme, great as it is, of the Personal-ity of mortal life is most important with reference to the immortal, the Unknown, the Spiritual, the only perman-ently real, which, as the ocean waits for and receives the rivers, waits for us each and all."

Democracy here is connected with the themes of personality and of religion. As we have seen, for Whitman, the immortal does not pass the bounds of the natural world. Both God and immortality are but attributes of men. In Chapter XI we will see more clearly Whitman's thought, as indicated in this summary just quoted: That democracy and individuality are synthesized in personality and brought to focus in the apex of "towering selfhood"; and that the self is not only body, it is also mind, and in religion reaches to spirit, joining together the mortality and immortality of humanity, unifying Life and Death.

10

ECONOMIC AND SOCIAL DEMOCRACY.

❖ ❖ ❖ ❖ ❖ ❖

"To teach the average man the glory of his daily walk and trade,

❖ ❖ ❖ ❖ ❖ ❖

For every man to see to it that he really do something, for every woman too;

❖ ❖ ❖ ❖ ❖ ❖

And to hold it no disgrace to take a hand at them themselves."

❖ ❖ ❖ ❖ ❖ ❖

To this point we have given attention mainly to Whitman's views on political democracy. He regarded this as having already been largely achieved in America, but it remained to establish economic and artistic democracy. Of the latter he is less definitive about economic democracy.

And yet Whitman was unique and original for giving an economic atmosphere to his writing. Emerson somewhat unconsciously expressed this in sending Whitman's book to Carlyle with the characterization of it as "an auctioneer's inventory of a warehouse." Before Whitman poetry had not been made of the materials of man's every day life. Although Whitman did not specially concern himself with solving economic problems, there is in him unmistakably an economic philosophy. It was that among other things which elicited John Ruskin's approval of him.

218

The Homestead Economy.

With Jefferson and Lincoln, Whitman held the domestic or home economy to be not only the more desirable one, but essential to democracy. This economy is that of "the land in which there are the most homesteads, freeholds." One familiar with this school of thought, which lately has had prominent revival, cannot misunderstand the following:

"The true gravitation hold of liberalism in the United States will be a more universal ownership of property, general homesteads, general comfort—a vast intertwining reticulation of wealth."

These ideas are, of course, Jefferson's. They are clearly expressed in Lincoln's speeches, especially in his President's Message to Congress in December, 1861. Just when so many have been saying that that kind of America has passed away forever, these ideas have been revived in such books as Ralph Borsodi's who has endeavored to prove by his own experiments in living, at Suffern, New York, that it is a more efficient economy and a better mode of living for the average man than that embodied in the capitalist money economy or industrial economy, and that it is a mode of living which any family or small community can practically achieve for itself to its very great economic advantage.

Frank Lloyd Wright, America's greatest engineer-architect, who professes to have been inspired by Whitman and Henry George, has attempted to blue-print this homestead economy as an architect's vision of the new America and has sketched it in his book recently enlarged and republished with the title, *When Democracy Builds*.

Arthur E. Morgan, the engineer-educator of Antioch, has also written in his books, *The Long Road* and *Small Communities Incorporated*, endorsing these ideas as the more socially practical for the preservation of democracy and the making of men. Alvin H. Johnson has also added his authority as an eminent economist; and the late Franz

Oppenheimer, of world renown as a sociological economist, gave the last forty years of his life to the successful demonstration of cooperative home economies in Germany, destroyed however by that infamous wrecker, Hitler, because they were not comportable with his unfree totalitarian socialist economy.

A symposium of writers, whose essays were edited by Herbert Agar and Allen Tate, in the book entitled *Who Owns America,* and in a magazine devoted to the idea under the name of *Free America,* have given it special significance for the South.

A considerable group in the American Catholic Church led by Fathers Husslein and Ligutti have joined it with the cooperative movement. Hillaire Belloc, an Anglican Catholic publicist, wrote about *The Restoration of Property,* in a way which shows that the Whitmanian conception of more general distribution of wealth by small proprietorship is an ideal far from dead in our present day.

Collectivism is indeed not so convincingly the next step in economic organization, as totalitarian communists and monopolistic capitalists too readily assume.

Neither Capitalism nor Proletarianism.

Whitman wished to obviate proletarianism as well as capitalism. It is therefore the business of the poet to "dissolve poverty from its need, and riches from its seat."

"Democracy looks with suspicious, ill-satisfied eye upon the very poor, the ignorant, and on those out of business. She asks for men and women with occupations, well-off, owners of houses and acres, and with cash in bank—and with cravings of literature, too; and must have them, and hastens to make them."

"The great country, the greatest country, is not that which has the most capitalists, monopolists, immense grabbings, vast fortunes, with its sad, sad foil of extreme, degrading, damning poverty . . . Where wealth does not show such contrasts high and low, where all men have enough —modest living—no man is made possessor beyond the sane and beautiful necessities of the simple body and the simple soul."

In other words, poverty and ignorance cannot be tolerated in a democracy, and its function is to end them and create a cultured well-to-do people.

In the light of the evidence of the notable persons who have been inspired by Whitman such as Wright and many besides, it will not do to say with Professor Allen that Whitman "had no program" or merely looked "backward to Jefferson." The democracy of Jefferson and Lincoln may seem backward to such critics and those imbued with megalopolic capitalism and to socialistic and totalitarian-minded persons.

Thurman Arnold's campaign against monopolies proves that "big business" has not yet conquered and enslaved America. For all the compromises that have been made, President Cleveland's diagnosis of the evil remains a standard program of democratic reform. We continue to fight the two communisms he named: First, the communism of special privilege, by which he meant the system of combinations, trusts, and cartels; and second, we oppose the resultant, the product, proletarian communism. Neither should obtain dominance of our America. That was the spirit in Whitman and his protest continues to be alive in thinking Americans.

We can add other notable names of those who have not bowed to Baal and Mammon. Among them John Dewey and the late Justice Louis D. Brandeis. Brandeis' book, *The Curse of Bigness,* recently had documentation of its facts by a lawyer, Morris Ernst, in his very convincing book, *Too Big.* As long as such voices are conscious of the remedy, we may be reasonably impatient at the blindness of presumably educated persons who do not see that Jefferson's and Whitman's economic democracy is forward looking.

To those who are partisans and doctrinnaires of a single-shot economy such as monopolistic capitalism, Marxian communism, Gesellianism, Keynesianism, Georgism, Institutionalism, and such, it may appear that Whitman "had no program." For programming usually means a very narrow and limited conception of human economy. The characteristic principle upon which most of those economists unite is some form of etatism, the economic dominance of the State. Institutionalism is their common voice. They have dehumanized and depersonalized economy. Therefore, they cannot see any forward-looking principle in the social philosophies of Jefferson, Lincoln, and Whitman.

Was Whitman a Socialist Radical?

Traubel himself was a muddle-minded socialist and as an interpreter or reporter of Whitman's social philosophy was one of the worst. But Professor Allen's selection of passages from Traubel is worse still because it is less regardful of Whitman's thought and is designed to show "Walt Whitman's weakness as a social thinker." We complain here as before against the pretense of Allen that his book is a reliable *Walt Whitman Handbook*. It misrepresents Whitman in almost every department of his thinking. Contrary to Allen, Whitman was not at all in doubt that he could not accept the doctrines of anarchists, socialists, and single taxers who were pressing their views upon him.

Whitman was a very tolerant man and allowed his friends very large liberty of self-expression, but there was never any doubt in their minds that he was Jeffersonian in his economic and social viewpoints. So he said to Traubel of an anarchist: "I suppose I am radical his way, but I am not radical his way alone. Socialists, Single Tax men, Communists, rebels of every sort and all sorts, come here."

Though tolerant of them all he was not swayed to accept any of their particularisms. He could take something from each of them, but to be pulled into the camp of any one of them he clearly understood would be a destruction of the free and inclusive economy he believed in. To Traubel's attempt to pin him down and identify him with the fanatical isms he replied: "How much of me is going to be left for myself after all the claims of the radicals are satisfied."

Diffident about criticizing Henry George as of anyone else, he said of him: "It is my impression, however, that he too is the victim of a special twist, bias—not the absolutely direct individuality, the personality, I am looking for—America requires." To single track, one-way minds Whitman must ever remain a puzzle. To them he will be vague, indefinite, uncertain. One of the objects of this book is to deliver Whitman from the radical partisans who would twist him out of his large frame of universalist humanism into some one or other of the narrow fanatical sects.

He remarked to Traubel: "I hate to think any man may not write the best books—any man." That expression identifies his belief with the democratic dogma that there is a unique potential worth in every man, which if it can be brought to expression will be a product of special genius which probably in its particular excellence could not be equally well expressed by any other. It was awkwardly phrased by him as "the average man." It is not so well expressed by the current phrase, "the common man." At least such phrases distinguish the democratic doctrine from the doctrines of the "elite" which fascism embodies, from the proletarian man at the opposite extreme, and from the autocratic dictatorship of the proletariat. American democracy has not agreed to the designation of mediocrity which Nietzsche's doctrines would fasten upon it, although the concepts of average and common man also seem to be a glorification of mediocrity. But the American ideal has tried to level up instead of level down. It has sought to give every man that measure of worth which his efforts can win for himself. Any dead level of ranking or any fixed status or caste it has steadily resisted. Despite his exaltation of the average man, Whitman unequivocally contended for the making of superior men by the processes of democracy.

The Dignity of Labor.

A superior man could for Whitman be a laborer.

"Ah little recks the laborer,
How near his work is holding him to God,
The loving Laborer through space and time."

"Workmen and Workwomen!
Were all educations practical and ornamental
    well display'd out of me, what would it
    amount to?
Were I as the head teacher, charitable pro-
    prietor, wise statesman, what would it
    amount to?
Were I to you as the boss employing and
    paying you, would that satisfy you?

❖ ❖ ❖ ❖ ❖ ❖

I will be even with you and you shall be even
    with me.
If you stand at work in a shop I stand as nigh
    as the nighest in the same shop."

The theme of the poet is

"To teach the average man the glory of his
    daily walk and trade,

❖ ❖ ❖ ❖ ❖ ❖

For every man to see to it that he really do
    something, for every woman too;

that each may be well-rounded in skill and use of the handicrafts,

> "And hold it no disgrace to take a hand at
> them themselves."

Whitman was not one of those who preached to labor that it should be contented with what it gets. He said he was not like the abolitionists who "thought slavery the one crying sin of the universe . . . I see other evils that cry to me in perhaps even a louder voice: the labor evil, now, to speak of only one, which to this day has been growing steadily worse."

Indeed, Whitman believed passionately in free labor: "A great country, in fact, is the country of free labor—of free laborers; negro, white, Chinese, or other." The slavery question, he realized, was much bigger than chattel slavery or negro slavery. He did not make any distinctions between laborers because of color, race, or other condition. "Wage slavery" had meaning for him. As in other matters, he stayed with Lincoln's principles there. Lincoln had said: "No man can be free whose condition for life is fixed as that of a hired laborer."

We may think we have gone much beyond Lincoln's and Whitman's century toward free labor. But how many of us are willing to stand on their radical platform that condemned "wage slavery"? Probably the conservative critics of Whitman would call him a communist today. Yes, the Communists "claim" him too. But how many Communists are protesting against "forced labor" behind the Bolshevik frontier in Europe today now that regime has succeeded Hitler? It was the principle of the thing and not partisanship that moved Whitman.

Wealth versus Men.

His was a humanized economy:

> "What do you think endures?

> Do you think a great city endures?
> Or a teeming manufacturing state? or a pre-
> pared constitution? or the best built steam-
> ships?
>
> ❖ ❖ ❖ ❖ ❖
>
> Or hotels of granite and iron? or any chef-
> d'ouvres of engineering, forts, armaments?
> Away! these are not to be cherished for them-
> selves,
>
> ❖ ❖ ❖ ❖ ❖ ❖
>
> A great city is that which has the greatest
> men and women."

As for himself:

> "I have loved the earth, sun, animals, I have
> despised riches,
> I have . . . devoted my income and labor to
> others."

That was Ruskin's conception too which he termed economic "Value." And almost in the language of Ruskin who called it a disgrace to die rich, Whitman said:

"That he who never perilled his life, but retains it to old age in riches and ease, has probably achieved nothing for himself worth mentioning."

Allen regards such expressions as sentimentalisms: "Sympathy, in fact, is always the key to Whitman's political sensibilities." Sympathy? yes, in the sense that Adam Smith and David Hume, the reflective philosophers, argued for it, and not in the discreditable sense that Professor Allen would have it. They proposed to found a system of ethics upon the principle of sympathy. Whitman translated it to the term comradeship. To the hard, the impersonal, the boasted realists, Whitman's free human economy sounds too Utopian for practical every day use.

But Allen does not overlook that Whitman's "innate conservatism" made him immediately or soon after the expression of such sentiments declare himself impartial between rich and poor: "In the human sense I am on both sides—the side of the rich as well as the side of the poor." But the qualifying phrase, "in the human sense," makes all the difference. It does not qualify what he has said in condemnation of riches. The rich man because he is rich does not forfeit our human consideration, has not lost right to our sympathy. There is indeed an immense difference between despising riches and despising the rich. The first may be, I think is, a virtuous attitude. The second is the very contrary; it is the attitude not only of an illiberal but even of a mean mind; it is a hateful disposition because it hates the man instead of a thing or quality.

However, one should not overlook the footnote to the passage above quoted about "universal ownership of property" which Whitman adds to avoid being misunderstood. To save the universality of his ideas he wishes to include in "these Vistas, a practical, stirring, worldly, money-making, even materialistic character . . . My theory includes riches, and the getting of riches." Further he says: "I perceive clearly that the extreme business energy, and this almost maniacal appetite for wealth prevalent in the United States, are parts of amelioration and progress, indispensably needed to prepare the very results I demand." One can understand these qualifying sentences only by keeping in mind the never-failing insistence of Whitman upon "the aggregate of the nation's middling property owners." He would eliminate the poor and unoccupied persons altogether. This is stated in the paragraph to which this footnote is appended. The average man is an equalitarian norm for Whitman. He desires the aggregate to be wealthy. But this aggregate wealth in a good economy will be so distributed that there will be no extreme poverty. Getting riches in the sense of adding to the possessions of a few at the expense of many did not have Whitman's approval. In fact, he severely condemned such an economy.

The Money-making Economy.

Said Whitman: "Beyond independence . . . money-making . . . is the great fraud upon modern civilization and forethought." Nevertheless, Allen concludes: "On the subject of 'money' Walt Whitman in 1888 even sounded socialistic, though he never got beyond generalities—or we might say ambiguities." Was it socialistic ranting that led Whitman to make the statements quoted by Allen?

"We're heaping up money here in a few hands at a great rate—but our men? What's becoming of our men in the meantime? We can lose all the money and start again —but if we lose the *men*? Well, that would be disaster . . . I should feel like warning the moneyed powers in America that threaten to stand in the way: history will deal in a very drastic fashion with opposition like that should it become too stubborn."

Perhaps, if we believe some of the present day spokesmen for capitalism, history has already dealt out somewhat of that lesson to the moneyed or capitalist class. Recently one of them warned labor that it would suffer from its monopoly of powers as capital has suffered, by legislative restrictions and handicaps, whenever the public becomes annoyed by the tyrannous exercise of excessive power.

Capitalism is being violently attacked all over the world by communist propaganda which is trying to rouse against it the cry that overthrew ancient Athens when the tribute-paying cities cried out against it, "tyrant city." One does not have to be even socialistically minded to entertain such a feeling.

Professor Allen may forget that Whitman lived in the Greenbacker days when money was the main topic of political conversation, and that the Greenbacker principle then derided in 1913 became the basis for the regulation of banks in the Federal Reserve System. Such a bit of historical-mindedness would save some of these critics of Whitman from treating too lightly his very general expressions.

Besides, a professor of literature should know, even if others do not, the difference between the poet's mission and the profession of an economist. Whitman never undertook to be a systematic economist. But nevertheless his instinct, if not his knowledge, saved him from the obliquities which unfortunately hamper the visions of many trained economists. He thought man more important than economic instrumentalities. We might reasonably claim for him that like Ruskin he was a precursor of humanized economics.

Social Democracy.

Burroughs attempted to express the essence of Whitman's social philosophy:

"What he does do, what the up-shot of his teaching shows, is that he identifies himself with the masses, with those universal currents out of which alone the national spirit arises, as opposed to isolated schools and coteries and a privileged few."

I think some correction must be made of that statement which in general is correct. Whitman distinguished the masses and the individual. Democracy is en-Masse. But the freedom of the individual must be preserved. He is not merged or cancelled out by the mass, as the collectivists and totalitarians would have it. Whitman would especially preserve the individual average man. He had as little use for a dictatorship of the proletariat, the dictators who, as Jefferson expressed it, would bridle, saddle and ride the masses, at the dictator's will, as for the dictatorship of the elite for the privileged few. He cared for the dignity and worth of the individual. He had full understanding of the mass, of the mob, which is neither intelligent nor trustworthy as such, and therefore he wished to make democracy safe and intelligent by creating great persons, not a few, but very many. The development of the personality of only a few may be dangerous. In a multitude of great egos democracy will progress and prosper.

Calverton regards Whitman along with Emerson as great relicts of the individualistic 19th century. Collectivism, he thinks, has taken possession of the 20th century, and has left liberalism and individualism behind. Whitman, never an extremist, cannot be charged with the doctrines of laissez faire any more than can Ruskin. Ruskin, especially in *Time and Tide,* preached a kind of aristocratic communism as did Plato in the *Republic* and *Laws.* Neither Plato nor Ruskin ever worshipped the masses. Nor can one accuse the Communist dictators of falling down in worship of the proletariat. Trotsky, who probably never wavered in his communism, expressed contempt for the masses in his booklet, *Their Morals and Ours.*

Whitman, however, had respect for the masses and for the en-masse. But he never became so depersonalized and dehumanized as to feel that the individual should not continue to be the social unit. Great persons, all persons great, was his ever continuing ideal. Trust of the people was his inheritance from Jeffersonianism. That was also Lincolnism, which reaffirmed eloquently the Jeffersonian faith.

Revolt Against the City.

In an essay entitled *Wicked Architecture,* expressing ideas to which Frank Lloyd Wright would subscribe, Whitman scourged the evil of landlordism, which was and is at its worst in New York City.

Whitman was contemporaneous with the extraordinary growth of American cities. In many ways he participated in the urban spirit of that time. He and his family were builders, carpenters. But the revolt against the city had already begun. In his later years the Henry George movement was at its height. Wright has been inspired in his crusade for the reform of the city, for the "disappearing city," by both Whitman and George. But the trend of his ideas follows more closely the philosophy of Whitman than of George.

There may be a difference too in Whitman's view, compared with Wright's, though not much. For one thing Whitman was not alien to the city. He felt deeply its impulses. Burroughs said of him: "Walt, with all his love of the country, was more at home in a city, among many people." Whitman thought city people are more appreciative of the country: "It is the city man, even the big man, the scholar man, who best appreciates objective Nature in her large meanings, growths, evolutions: who enters most naturally, sympathetically, into the play of her phenomena, the divine physical processes."

But the American people have the country in their blood. America has probably not yet developed a truly urban class, unless it be our Jewish population who brought urbanity with them from Europe. Nowhere else in the world has the isolated farmstead been so characteristic of rural life. The American people are nomadic in temperament, always traveling, always going somewhere. The larger number of its people have lived at some time in the country, on the farm.

In Whitman's day the movement was toward the city. It was in the generation after his death that the "back to the country movement" became a national program although intermittently pursued. Probably the reason city men are, if they are, more appreciative of the country is a nostalgia, a yearning for the freedom of the country, for its peaceful atmosphere, its glorious sights and rapturous sounds, to which one becomes more sensitive immediately after escape from the stifling atmosphere, the smog of the city. A John Burroughs or a Thoreau, the nature-men supreme, go to the country and stay in it. For them the country provides a healing for the spirit as well as of the body, which Whitman also experienced.

Whitman's City-Country — Pro and Con.

After his paralysis Whitman found the country wholesome. In *Specimen Days*, his diary, he wrote: "After you have exhausted what there is in business, politics, conviviality, love, and so on—have found that none of these really satisfy, or permanently wear—what remains? Nature remains, to bring out from their torpid recesses, the affinities of a man or woman with the open air, the trees, fields, the changes of seasons—the sun by day and the stars of heaven by night.... Dear, soothing, healthy, restorative hours—after three confining years of paralysis—.." "Shall I tell you, reader, to which I attribute my already much restored health? that I have been almost two years, off and on, without drugs and medicines, and direct in the open air."

After another year or so in the country, he returned to New York and Brooklyn for a visit. He wrote: "After an absence of many years ... again I resume with curiosity the crowds, streets I knew so well, Broadway, the ferries, the West side of the city, democratic Bowery—human appearances and meanings as seen in all these, and along the wharves, and in the perpetual travel of horsecars, or the crowded excursion steamers, or in Wall or Nassau streets by day—in the places of amusement by night—bubbling and whirling and moving like its own environment of waters—endless humanity in all phases—Brooklyn also —taken in for the last three weeks... A brief total of the impressions, the human qualities, of these vast cities, is to me comforting, even heroic, beyond statement. Alertness, generally fine physique, clear eyes that look straight at you, a singular combination of retiscence and self-possession, with good nature and friendliness—a prevailing range of greeting manners, attest an intellect, surely beyond any elsewhere upon earth—and a palpable outcropping of that personal comradeship I look forward to as the subject, strongest hold of this many itemed Union—are not only constantly visible here in these mighty channels of men, but they form the real and averages."

For all our present day pessimism and cynicism—and there were plenty of pessimists and cynics in Whitman's day to whom he was in opposition—his description of the city throng is fairly true, as I believe, to our present day America. He thought it proof that our American democracy is a success. He testified, "I find in this visit to New York, and the daily contact and rapport with its myriad people, on the scale of oceans and tides, the best, most effective medicine my soul has partaken—the greatest physical habitat and surroundings of land and air the globe affords, namely Manhattan Island and Brooklyn, which the future shall join in one city—city of superb democracy, mid superb surroundings."

But back in the country again, he was equally ecstatic about Nature: "O so infinitely beyond anything from art, books, sermons, or from science, old or new. The spirit's hour, religion's hour—the visible suggestion of God in space and time—now once definitely indicated, if never again."

If such ecstatic expressions concerning city and country, in equal mood, were all that Whitman had to give, we could neglect him. The exuberant American has always had a poetic spirit, and Whitman often tiresomely indulged his expansive poeticisms. But these contrasts of sentiment indicate that Whitman tried to be equalitarian about city and country as about everything else.

Frank Lloyd Wright who has an equally exuberant spirit and effusiveness of expressed sentiment has, however, brought it to a particular and abundant expression in creative architecture which not unreasonably may be

claimed as extension of Whitman's personality. Professor
Allen tries to dig in the ruins of decayed and decadent
literatures and philosophies to discover the source of Whitman's ideas. I think it more profitable to explore the ac-
complishments of the Whitmanian spirit which in literature, the arts, religion and science are building a new
and better world about us. In the light of neo-Whitmanism
we shall be more competent to discover Whitman's real
meanings. As Wright has acknowledged Whitman as a
source of his inspiration, in Wright we may recognize the
clarifying fruition of Whitman's ideas for a beautiful America compound of the best in City and Country.

Prudence as Ethico-economic Ideal.

Instead of the word "economy" Whitman uses the
word "prudence" to signify his economic ideal. For him
prudence is an ethical as well as an economic conception,
and as he defines it it is as little acceptable to "vulgar"
economists as were Ruskin's humanized conceptions of
economy. His defining concepts of prudence are such as
these:

> "Charity and personal force are the only in-
> vestments worth anything."

> ". . . all that a male or female does, that is
> vigorous, benevolent, clean, is so much
> profit to him or her."

> "Who has been wise receives interest . . .
> The interest will come round—all will come
> round."

> "Prudence entirely satisfies the craving and
> glut of souls,
> Itself only finally satisfies souls."

To a communistic spirit like Calverton's this sounds
like the boshiest bourgeois, although he is clever enough

not to say that but instead to date it as 19th century individualist liberalism. Calverton throws Emerson into the
same discard. So Communists would break us with the
past of America. Marxism is the only true and infallible
doctrine. Away with the bourgeoisie, especially with the
petty bourgeoisie, for such interfere with the happening of
the prophecies of Marx. According to the Marxian scripture capitalism must build ever more top-lofty structures
in order that overweighting of the capitalist order standing
so unreasonably on its apex may the more heavily and
terribly crash down upon its broad proletarian base. Whitman indeed talked about the average broad-based common
man, and that may have deluded the simple Bolsheviks
of Russia to have given such wide currency to published
editions there. But Calverton is not so misled. He sees
clearly that "Comrade" Whitman is not a proletarian col-
lectivist. He thinks the individualist common man is out
of date and belongs to a different America that is past and
gone. Therefore, he concludes: "Whitman's message is not
for this day."

If the individual man no longer counts; if freedom,
equality and welfare are not measured by results in building the life and personality of the individual man; if men
are but a herd; if the ethics and economy of the beehive,
anthill, and termite colony must supercede free men and
free enterprise—then Whitman is out-of-date. On the other
hand, if monopolistic and totalitarian economy are better
than free enterprise Whitman is out of date. But, as we
believe, Whitman with better understanding saw clearly
the evils that must overwhelm all unfree economies.

Prudence, therefore, in Whitman's sense, is the economy devoted to the building of individual men. However,
it is comparable to Emerson's notion of prudence without
Emerson's characteristic inconsistencies. Emerson says:
"Prudence is the virtue of the senses.... It is content to
seek health of mind by the laws of intellect." And then

adds: Prudence "knows that its own office is subaltern"; that is, it recognizes higher laws. Whitman denies such qualification of prudence:

> "What is prudence is indivisible,
> Declines to separate one part of life from
>   every part."

But it is a pragmatic law rather than a categorical imperative. It is tested by results.

If Whitman's *Song of Prudence* sounds dull and prosaic to us it is because we are not interested in the purport of the poem. If one agrees with critics who make only prose of such thoughts and would save poetry for high sounding sentiments, it is because he does not feel the kinship of the common things we call economic with the best things of human life. In the *Song of Prudence* Whitman declared his economic principles as Ruskin a little later declared them with the ethical and human import uppermost.

"Results" are too earthy for mystical philosophers and romantic poets. Whitman's catalogues and factualism were distressing to his contemporaries whose tastes were for cloudy sentimentalism in poetry and religion. This poem on prudence shows Whitman down to earth more than most of our leading poets at the moment.

Revolutionary changes have taken place since the first editions of *Leaves of Grass* in 1855 and even since Whitman's death in 1892. But he was the pioneering poet of the industrial age. He first gave currency in literature to its terms of every day speech. His "warehouse inventories" gave poetry and literature a new language. What has now become a commonplace of speech makes Whitman readable today as he was not in his own time. And there remains in his writing more inspiration to nobler living in an industrial civilization than one finds elsewhere.

On themes in which the primitives of proletarian literature discover only brutal force and cruel fate and eternal reacting revenge in so far as they are realistic, Whitman with clearer knowledge of the meaning of wrongs sees above all the aspiring struggle of mankind and of all classes for betterment. Where the decadents of literature mouth over the old themes and weakly counsel safety alone on traditional paths, instead Whitman encourages faith in the future. That is why his poetry contains prophecy for advancing civilization. Where others are steeped in gloom because there is so much bad in our world and are therefore ready to give up, Whitman sings, not less aware of the bad, with sane realization that as man has come up through adversity it may even be used by him as means to his further development.

His belief in men is what redeems him from the sordidness and despair of the blackening shroud of industrialism. His belief in men keeps him from seeking escape in the mystical confusions that are the recourse of the traditional religions and philosophies that were born in the ancient world overwhelmed by the dread of Nature's catastrophes and enchained in the enslavement of man by man. Whitman is modern enough to resolve our fears by showing how to prevent enslavement of men by machine or by a Managerial Revolution. He shows that the democratic process upholding the dignity and worth of every individual man can save us from such doom.

He is not ambiguous in his meaning. His spirit accepts but goes beyond any "material prosperity":

"I hail with joy the oceanic, variegated, intense practical energy, the demand for facts, even the business materialism of the current age, our States. But woe to the age or land in which these things, movements, stopping at themselves, do not tend to ideas. As fuel to flame, and flame to the heavens, so much wealth, science, materialism—even this democracy of which we make so much— unerringly feed the highest mind, the soul."

Whitman's International Nationalism.

Whitman's social democracy was not narrowed to the National gauge. He was strongly National, but he was just as ardent for federation of the world.

Allen thinks Whitman's intense nationalism of the first edition of *Leaves of Grass* turned sour with the financial failure of the first three editions of that work, and in consequence by 1868 he had become wholly internationalist. I think there is nothing in Whitman's writings or conversations to support such a thesis. Allen himself quotes Whitman to the contrary: "I had more than my native land in view when I was composing *Leaves of Grass*. I wished to take the first step toward calling into existence a cycle of international poems." And Allen admits that "This latent internationalism was inherent in his thought and literary ambitions from the beginning." It was of a piece with his universalism and his "cosmic consciousness." But typically Allen relates this purpose of Whitman to the Romantic movement.

Whitman was not an internationalist in the sense of a man without a nation, nor was he a believer in one world which would be a super-state. He did not believe in the nonsense which is so common among advocates for the surrender of sovereignty and abandonment of nationalism as necessary means to permanent peace. He was a believer in a federation of the peoples of the world and that is quite consistent with nationalism and the independent sovereignty not only of nations but also of individuals and groups of individuals.

He never disguised or suppressed his belief that the government of the United States is the best in the world, and a model for all others. But he did not think that the United States is perfect or all in all to the exclusion of other nations and peoples.

But his strong convictions were based on principles,

not partisan or nationalistic prejudices. He regarded the
citizen's exercise of the franchise as ı duty and advised
young men to enter politics. Yet he said to the voters: "Dis-
engage yourself from parties." Notwithstanding their
acknowledged usefulness, he thought the independent
voter "most needed" at all times. He was not deceived by
the politicians' pretensions of indispensability: "These
men never get up high enough to see what the problem
really is—never recognize its international obligations—
do not see that it is not political but human."

He did not accept Allen's viewpoint that "In a free
society there is no other practical means of channelling
public opinion and generating social power. Either one
must work through parties and organized groups or forever, like Whitman, let others 'hold the whip hand.' " Is
it not a stupid conception of democracy that it is merely
a political institution and absolutely governed by parties?
That describes the totalitarian governments, formerly of
Italy and Germany, and still of the Bolshevik regime in
Russia and elsewhere. It is not true of the United States.

Our political parties are institutions mainly for the
election of public officials. They react to public opinion
rather than form or channel it. Our democratic agencies
for forming public opinion are, contrary to Ruth Benedict,
far more extensive than political parties. Newspapers,
books, radio, numerous organizations—civic, educational,
religious, business, labor, etc.—are vastly more influential
than political parties. Nor are organized groups a monopolistic power. The people are in and out of groups, constantly shifting in our free society, and not organized
like castes fixedly in groups. That is why with us every
group has a continual struggle for survival. The collec-
tivist philosophy is self-deceiving. Allen's statement is what
Allport calls the sociological or group fallacy. Whitman
wrote for the latter half of the 19th century. But he under-

stood not only democracy but also the movements of any society better than these dogmatic philosophies of collectivism.

Whitman's World-Encircled Humanism.

The principles of the Atlantic Charter, similar to Wilson's Fourteen Points, served so well for wartime propaganda, because they expressed the liberal views of the peoples of the world. But they were betrayed first in the Versailles Treaty and the Covenant of the League of Nations, and now after World War II, which was a product of the purge of those principles, are again being systematically broken in the series of international acts, beginning with the adoption of the United Nations Charter as a compact of power politics, and continuing in the bargaining process of the old diplomacy in treaty-making. From Whitman's writings can be drawn the major proposals that constitute the leading items of the Atlantic Charter.

The Atlantic Charter promised free commerce and free communications. It assured to every people access to the essential raw materials. Whitman advocated a similar policy. He said: "I am for free trade because I am for anything which will break down the barriers between peoples: I want to see the countries all wide open." He conceived free trade in terms of world federation: "I am for free trade—absolute free trade: for the federation of the world."

The free movement of peoples he regarded as also essential to amicable world relations. He thought it also an essential of freedom. He said: "If America is not for freedom I do not see what it is for. We ought to invite the world through an open door—yes, even the criminals, giving to everyone a chance—a new outlook." "America must welcome all—Chinese, Irish, pauper or not, criminal or not, all, without exceptions and become an asylum for all who choose to come." He did not believe in American prosperity at the expense of other nations and other peoples.

His basic principle in politics was "a new cameraderie, fellowship, love." From that one should go to "the farther truer idea of the race family, of international unity, of making one country of all countries."

Of course, to self-styled realists and their feeble imitators this is the veriest nonsense. When Whitman cries: "Away with themes of war! away with war itself!" they believe that goes while the people are war weary. But it is only a truce between wars. Peace is but an interval to prepare and plan for the greater war to come. But to the peace-minded Whitman's prophesies of the end of wars ring true because they are instinctive in the desires of the human heart.

In *Thou Mother with thy Equal Brood* the method of the poet in contrast with that of the political realist may be seen. Nationality is the theme, but it merges into the larger humanism. American democracy is not something to itself alone:

> "Thou holdest not the venture of thyself
>   alone, not of the Western continent alone,
>
> ❖ ❖ ❖ ❖ ❖ ❖
>
> Venerable priestly Asia sails this day with
>   thee,
> And royal feudal Europe sails with thee."

It is not only of the individual, not only of America, that such faith may be justified. One may repeat of the Spain of our time as Whitman in his *Spain, 1873-74:*

> "Lag'd'st thou so long? shall the clouds close
>   again upon thee?
> Ah, but thou hast thyself now appear'd to us
>   —we know thee.

Thou has given us a sure proof, the glimpse
    of thyself,
Thou waitest there as everywhere thy time."

How often indeed the clouds have closed over the struggles of Spain for freedom. But still the people struggle, they rise again and again against their tyrants, and though defeated the spirit of freedom in them is unquenchable, always a menace to their dictators. It is that universally rising spirit of freedom that Whitman apostrophizes.

There is no place in his poems for the self-humiliating, helpless, hopeless fear and despair so profound in the traditional Old World philosophies, which, alas, some of our recent writers and philosophers of America place more confidence in by way of institutional escape than in themselves or in mankind. It is surely not in any circumstance or condition of American life of such deterministic character that they derive their pessimistic philosphy, but from the twists of their own minds, from their own futility and weakness. It was Whitman's faith in the average man, in the individual human being, which saved him from the blackout of social determinism.

11

WHITMAN'S CONCEPTION OF MAN.

❖ ❖ ❖ ❖ ❖ ❖

"And nothing endures but personal qualities."
"I see behind each mask that wonder a kindred soul."

❖ ❖ ❖ ❖ ❖ ❖

OVER AGAINST DEMOCRACY AS A NECESSARY CHECK UPON
it Whitman places the individual. The individual, the
person, the self, have special meanings in Whitman's philosophy, which are fundamental to his thinking, and indeed they constitute the heart of his philosophy, about
which other ideas or notions center.

His Individualism.

Over against equality, the essence of democracy, stands
individuality, which Whitman equally emphasizes: "His
doctrine seems not only to individualize but to universalize." As Burroughs says: "We see united and harmonized
in Whitman two great paramount tendencies of our time
and of the modern world—the altruistic or humanitarian
tendency and the individualistic tendency; or, democracy
and individualism, pride and equality, or rather pride in
equality." Whitman makes a hyphenated or compound
word of this unity, "ensemble-individuality."

"An individual is as superb as a nation when he has
the qualities which make a superb nation." For "the largeness of nature or the nation are monstrous without a cor-

243

responding largeness and generosity of the spirit of the citizen."

In brief, there must be nothing greater than the individual man. The whole is for him. As he said in *Democratic Vistas,* the "wonders of heaven and earth (are) significant only because of man in the centre." And each one is as good as the other.

> "I say the least developed person on earth is just as important and sacred to himself or herself, as the most developed person is to himself or herself."

"Each man to himself," for "no one can acquire for" or "grow for another—not one."

> "Underneath all, individuals,
> I swear nothing is good to me now that ignores individuals,
> The American compact is altogether with individuals,
> The only government is that which makes minute of individuals,
> The whole theory of the universe is directed unerringly to one single individual—
> namely to you."

"All is eligible to all, all is for individuals, all is for you." "How dare you place anything before a man." He said: "I have laid the stress of my poems from beginning to end to bear upon American individuality and assist it not only because that is a great lesson in Nature, amid all her generalizing laws, but as counterpoise to the leveling tendencies of Democracy . . . While the ambitious thought of my song is to help the forming of a great aggregate Nation, it is, perhaps, altogether through the forming of myriads of fully developed and enclosing individuals. Welcome as are equality's and fraternity's doctrines and popular education, a certain liability accompanies them all, as we see." "The new influences, upon the whole, are surely preparing the way for grander individualities than ever. Today and here personal force is behind everything."

That passage has special importance because it shows that Whitman not only emphasized individuality because of the dangers of dehumanism from over-emphasis of equality without equal stress upon individual freedom, but also because it refutes the assumption that for him cameraderie is the single solvent of social problems.

Burroughs summed up Whitman's ideas on individualism as stress upon "self-reliance," that "there is nothing in the universe more divine than the individual soul," and that his work, "taken as a whole, aims to exhibit the modern, democratic, archetypal man, here in America, confronting and subduing our enormous materialism to his own purposes . . . The poet seeks to interpret life from the central point of absolute abysmal man."

"Indeed, he is quite as ecstatical and anthropomorphic, though in an entirely different way, as were the old bards and prophets before the advent of science. The whole import of the universe is directed to one man,—to you. His anthropomorphism is not a projection of himself into Nature, but an absorption of nature into himself." Although as we have shown this is not an entirely accurate statement of Whitman's "scientific humanism," it indicates how completely Whitman deemed individual men to be central in the cosmic scheme of things.

Whitman's personalism.

Whitman uses not only the term individual, but also the terms personality and self to intensify and explain his meaning of the precious value of each and every man.

He does not fear, as state socialists and social democrats fear, the singleness and isolated character of a man. In an essay entitled *Personalism* he expressed this thought:

In contrast to the first principle, democracy, "the second principle is individuality, the pride and centripetal isolation of a human being—in himself,—identity—personalism." The ultimate is the individual. "Even for the treatment of the universal, in politics, metaphysics, or everything, sooner or later we come down to one single, solitary soul."

And modern life demands individuality for the sake of its health and balance: "Singleness and normal simplicity, amid this more and more complex, more artificialized, state of society, how pensively we yearn for them! how we would welcome their return."

Individual, self, identity, person—these often seem synonymous terms. But in many statements Whitman appeared to give first place to personality as the central theme of his poetry.

"Personality . . . has been my general object." "The determined cartoon of personality . . . dominates or rather stands behind all L. of G. like the unseen master & director of the show." And toward the end (1888) in *A Backward Glance* he said:

"*Leaves of Grass* indeed (I cannot too often reiterate) has mainly been the outcropping of my own emotional and other personal nature—an attempt, from first to last, to put a Person, a human being (myself, in the latter half of the Nineteenth Century, in America,) freely, fully and truly on record. I could not find any similar personal record in current literature that satisfied me."

At the birthday dinner in 1891 Whitman said: "I have uttered the *Leaves* for the last thirty-five years as an illustration of, as a radiation from, the personal critter—a fellow, man, individuality, person, American, so to speak . . . individuality, personality, identity, covering our time."

Is the Person Himself or Man?

There is apparent ambiguity in these expressions. For Whitman was a secretive person. His life was not an open book. He was truest to his theme when he spoke of the generalized person. He was not at all the carefree person he wrote about. As Burroughs said: "He was receptive, sympathetic, tender, and met you, not in a positive, aggressive manner, but more or less in a passive or neutral mood." He was a cautious man. His book is forthright and outspoken as he himself was not. He could be one of the best illustrations for the contention that most men disguise themselves, and what they say is partly a pose, partly an escape from themselves, and partly an attempt to balance up and complete their lives. Certainly Whitman greatly exceeded his own actual personality in what he set forth in his writings as the ideal personality.

All-inclusive Persons and Average Men.

He stressed the importance and primacy of the personality. He valued highly the all-inclusive personality like a Goethe or Lincoln. He found a place or role or cause for every personality, good or bad. He recognized the magnetism and drawing power of personality. He also knew that the curbs of equalization have to be placed upon powerful personalities.

He sought for the ideal personality. He perceived that personality is a mask. He observed the duality, the polarity, the diversity of personality,—as general or typical on one side, and identical or specific on the other, thus enabling it to be a medium or mediator between the extremes of democratic mass and individual self. Always he had great faith in the natural issue of personality in the common people, in the average man.

His conception of personality is historically and psychologically true. Review and comparison of latest literature on personality should greatly raise one's estimation of the profundity of Whitman's analysis. His reflections on the subject have not been outmoded or surpassed. To stimulate such study of his work we indicate some of his personalist thought.

Great Persons.

So important did he regard personality that he said: "Produce great persons and the rest follows." "Charity and personal force are the only investments worth anything." For "nothing endures but personal qualities." That is why "all that a person does, sees, thinks, is of consequence."

It is because the greatest personalities embrace so much of our human nature that he was somewhat of a hero worshipper. Especially did he venerate Lincoln, whom he described as "the sweetest, wisest soul of all my days and lands." "He lives, in my opinion, the greatest, best, most characteristic, artistic, moral personality."

In his lecture on the *Death of Lincoln* he said that "four sorts of genius, four mighty and primal minds, will be needed to the complete limning of this man's future portrait—the eyes and brains and finger-touch of Plutarch, and Eschylus and Michel Angelo, assisted by Rabelais."

Goethe was preeminently an inclusive personality and expressed much that Whitman approved. He said to Traubel: "Goethe impressed me as above all to stand for essential literature, art, life—to argue the importance of centering life in self—in perfect persons—perfect you, me: to force the real into the abstract ideal; to make himself, Goethe, the supremest example of personal identity; everything making for it: in us, in any Goethe; every man repeating the same experience."

Burroughs reflects the same idea from Whitman and expounds it: "For a national first class poem, or a great book of the imagination of any sort, the man is everything, because such works finally rest upon primary human qualities and special individual traits. A richly endowed personality is always the main dependence in such cases, or, as Goethe says, 'in the great work a great person is always present as the great factor.' . . . Goethe always looked straight through the work to the man behind it; in art and poetry the personality was everything."

Masters, not so accurately, calls to attention the contrast: "Goethe seemed to look upon personal development as an end in itself; the old teachers looked for collective results." In fact, Goethe and Whitman as well sought for both personal and collective results.

Nor do I believe that either Goethe or Whitman would urge the contrast that Burroughs made: "The creative artist differs from the mere writer or author in this: he sustains a direct personal relation to his subject through emotion, intuition, will. The indirect, impersonal relation which works by reflection, comparison, and analysis is that of the critic and philosopher. The man is an artist when he gives us a concrete and immediate impression of reality: from his hands we get the thing itself; from the critic and author we get ideas about the thing."

Both Goethe and Whitman were inclined to the function of critic. Most of what we are quoting from Whitman in this book is from the realm of ideas rather than things. It is not in the vein of either Goethe or Whitman to draw the distinction so sharply.

Therefore, I can agree only partially with Burroughs' statement that "Whitman's poetry is almost entirely an expression of will and personality, and runs very little to intellectual subtleties and refinements." Whitman undoubtedly tried to give such an impression of his work, and it accords with the traditions of the Whitmanites, but to read Whitman and be unaware of his continual subtleties and refinements is to read him very inattentatively. As we are now pointing out, he defined personality in its different aspects with more clarity than do our contemporary psychologists.

Professing to be the poet of personality, the "chanter of personality," Whitman did not espouse the great man theory of personality. He knew the danger from powerful personalities. "Democracy has been retarded and jeopardized by powerful personalities." The "Power of personality" may be "just or unjust". Therefore it is well for the city "where the populace rise at once against the never-ending audacity of elected persons." He said

> "Of persons arrived at high positions, ceremonies, wealth, scholarships, and the like
> . . . often to me they appear gaunt and naked, . . . often to me they are alive after what custom has served them, but nothing more."

Average Man.

Whitman was specially concerned for the average man. This average man plays a double role: what goes on is in him and for him. He found "the clue to the history of the past" in democracy, in "the average man of today." There is no conflict with the principle of individuality in that conception, for the average man "is the life of one man or one woman today." It signifies rather a universal quality than a mathematical concept. From the "average spiritual manhood" and womanhood, though "may-be unconscious of yourselves," will come the "superber race," "the new culminating man." And whatever is achieved, it is "all for the modern—all for the average man of today."

A Science of Personalism—Humanics.

And so he points further: "In addition to established sciences, we suggest a science as it were of healthy average personalities, on original-universal grounds, the object of which should be to raise up and supply through the states a copious race of superb American men and women, ahead of any yet known."

I think we can say now with more assurance that this new science is not "in addition" to the sciences, but, with Hume, that it is the foundation and center of all the sciences, and we name it Humanics, which includes personalism.

But this new science is not out of tune with Whitman. It probably owes to Whitman its conception. Compare any writer of Whitman's day with the humanists of this generation, and note the relative absence of humanism in Whitman's contemporaries and the similarity of humanist expressions today with Whitman's philosophy!

Subnormal Persons.

Not only great and average persons had Whitman's consideration, but his attitude toward subnormal personalities is also essential for understanding his theory of personality.

As Arvin says, despite all Whitman's reverence for man, "his humanism rested, after all, on no ingenuous illusions." "We must not give too much importance to personalism," said Whitman even when he was speaking of Lincoln. "It is easy to overcharge it—man moves as man, in all the great achievements—men in the concrete mass." However great the man he does not escape his species. There is still somewhat of the common clay in him. He shares the common life of man, the good with the bad.

Surely most of us will not think that one whose sympathies could include all the varieties of mankind in personality has taken personality in too idealistic a sense. There are probably few who do not think Whitman submerged personality in the opposite direction. For he did not exclude the prostitute, the diseased, slaves, or the criminal from the category of humanity. "If you become degraded, criminal, ill, then I become so for your sake."

That idea of atonement differs from the Christian in that we all suffer for any one. Although his ideal is healthy personality, yet sick persons make their contribution also, if it is nothing more than to be rich compost from which flowers and grass may spring.

He speaks of "diagnosing this disease called humanity," saying: "By common consent there is nothing better for man or woman than a perfect and noble life, morally without flaw, happily balanced in activity, physically sound and pure, giving its due proportion, and no more, to the sympathetic, the human emotional element—a life, in all these, unhasting, unresting, untiring to the end. And yet there is another shape of personality, dearer far to the artist-sense, (which like the play of strongest lights and shades,) where the perfect character, the good, the heroic, although never attained, is never lost sight of, but through failures, sorrows, temporary downfalls, is returned to again and again, and while often violated, is passionately adhered to as long as mind, muscles, voice, obey the power we call volition."

In the diseased, the criminal, the imperfect, Whitman saw a constant striving toward perfection.

He described yet another type of literateur, "without the first sign of moral principle, or of the concrete or its heroisms, or the simpler affections of the heart," and asked: "What mean they? The inevitable tendency of poetic culture (of the Nineteenth Century) to morbidity, abnormal beauty—the sickliness of all technical thought or refinement in itself—the abnegation of the perennial and democratic concretes at first hand—what bearings have they on current pathological study?"

There is not only intellectual subtlety in this analysis, but it reveals the source of the malady of "decadent literature," as Whitman clearly saw it. Abnormal beauty, over-refinement, too much attention to technique, are pathological symptoms, an excessive striving for perfection.

His own sense of the healing power of robust health and clean-mindedness made of him a physical and moral physician, receptive to the bad as well as the good of mankind, and put to thorough test his hopefulness and desire for redemption of all mankind.

This was what inspired his ideal of equality: "The least developed person on earth is just as important and sacred to himself or herself as the most developed person is to himself or herself."

The Natural Person.

Whitman had also a faith in nature which made him esteem highly (perhaps too highly) the natural person. In defiance of custom that frowns upon males kissing each other, he spoke of himself and his companion who did so as "two natural and nonchalant persons"; and to "natural persons old and young" he would infuse a custom "to walk hand in hand"; and thus in his *Songs of Parting* he would "announce natural persons to arise."

He attempted to attune himself with Nature, and, says Selincourt, even to accept subjection to the physical world in order to differentiate the spirit or identity of the man. But rather did Whitman conceive man as the conqueror of than the submitter to Nature. He quoted with approval as "An Egotistical Find":

" 'In Nature's grandest shows,' said an old Dutch writer, an ecclesiastic, 'amid the ocean's depth, if so might be, or countless worlds rolling above at night, a man thinks of them, weighs all, not for themselves or the abstract, but with reference to his own personality, and how they affect or color his destinies.' "

His naturalism is not that of an awe for overwhelming Nature, but rather of the natural life that any man may live. He says: "Now I see the secret of the making of the best persons, it is to grow in the open air and to eat and sleep with the earth. Here a great personal deed has room." Travelling on the open road is praised because it demands "the best blood, thews, endurance, . . health. . . No diseased person, no rum-drinker or venereal taint is permitted here." He praises "the West with strong native persons."

Sex Persons.

It is in part naturalness that requires recognition of sex. "All were lacking if sex were lacking."

Selincourt criticises Whitman for not perceiving the individualistic character of the sex relationship. It is true that Whitman regards sexual relationships as much more than an individual matter. "Sex contains all, . .all . . are contained in sex as parts of itself and justifications of itself." But it is because Whitman conceives the individual, (as one socialistically-minded only cannot), as separate, isolated, single; and the sexual relationship is not so purely individual.

And more than that, as Selincourt shows, Whitman distinguished sex from love. But not as Selincourt who thought of sex as individual and love as social. Whitman never made so sharp a dichotomy; he never made an absolute separation between individual and society. Sex also has social significance. He said: "*Leaves of Grass* is avowedly the song of sex and Amativeness, and even animality —. . Difficult as it will be, it has become, in my opinion, imperative to achieve a shifted attitude from superior men and women towards the thought and fact of sexuality, as an element in character, Personality, the emotions, and a theme in literature." This is clearly a recognition of the social importance of sex. But Whitman did not reify or entitize society, as collectivists are wont to do. He neither merged the individual in society nor cancelled any individual out for some other who might be deemed more important and he demanded mutual individual rights in sex as in all other matters. Thus he gave a new dignity to sex in personality. After him and because of him the sex personality was larger, more inclusive, and in all its aspects more respected than it had been before.

Personality and Identity.

For Whitman the function of personality was polar. At one end it was democratic-ensemble—that was his goal for society. At the other end it was individual. The individual side of personality is especially expressed in Whitman's concept of identity. Whitman said that early he saw "that the trunk and centre whence the answer was to radiate, and to which all should return from straying however far a distance, must be an identical body and soul, a personality —which personality, after many considerations and ponderings I deliberately settled should be myself—indeed could not be any other."

Burroughs affirmed Whitman's own interpretation: "Another of the ideas that master Whitman and rule him is the idea of identity,—that you are you and I am I, and that henceforth we are secure whatever comes or goes."

This term identity applies to a nation as well as to a man. As in Whitman's long letter of August, 1856, to Emerson he said: "Of course, we shall have national character, and identity. . . . Such character, strong, limber, just, open-mouthed, American blooded, full of pride, full of ease, of passionate friendliness, is to stand compact upon that first basis of the supremacy of individuality."

Whitman did not personify the nation other than metaphorically and he did not forego the primacy of the individual man. As I have shown elsewhere, only human personality is primary, and only an entity is a person, and that because it has identity or specificity.

The Many-sided Person.

We mistake again if we assume that this individual personality does not allow for multiple persons in one man. Whitman says: "I resist any thing better than my own diversity." "My body no more inevitably united, part to part, and made out of a thousand diverse contributions one identity, any more than my lands are inevitably united and made ONE IDENTITY."

One man, in fact, bears very many personalities or persons. So ran the Latin maxim, on which the lawyer built legal personality, "Unus homo sustinet plurimas personas." Without saying just that in phrases, Whitman says it in effect over and over again. He sings himself, but his imaginative self is composed of the selves of the exhaustless variety of mankind,—from the great, the average, to the degraded.

The Personal Mask.

The mask of personality illustrates the fact of diversity of persons in every man, which he puts on and takes off, constantly changing his personality.

> "As the faces of the masks appear, as I glance
>   at the faces studying the masks,

> I see behind each mask that wonder a kindred soul."

Whitman is aware of the origin of the concept of personality from the wearing of masks in the theatre:

> "Out from behind this bending rough-cut
>   mask,
> These lights and shades, this drama of the
>   whole,

> This common curtain of the face contained
>   in me for me, in you for you, in each for
>   each."

The dramatic personality was always that of the actor behind the mask. The person was that which spoke through the mask. This is the heritage of the theater from the ancient Etruscan stage.

So the question for Whitman was, What is behind the mask? The poem entitled *Eidólons* carries this theme:

> "Thy body permanent,
> The body lurking there within thy body,
> The only purport of the form thou art, the
>   real I myself,
> An image, an eidólon."

The Split Personality.

Shepard tries to make out a case of split personality against Whitman on these grounds, quoting an early writing of the *Calamus*:

> "But that shadow, my likeness, that goes to
>   and fro seeking a livelihood, chattering
>   and chaffering,
> I often find myself standing and looking at it
>   where it flits—
> That likeness of me, but never substantially
>   me."

In the poem as he finally revised it, after the word "flits" there follows:

> "How often I question and doubt whether
>   that is really me;
> But among my lovers and caroling these
>   songs,
> O I never doubt whether that is really me."

What is important is that the split personality, which Whitman probably had had, so far as it was a diseased personality, was healed, and in the *Leaves of Grass* is the record of the healing as a token to others that there is a way for every one to unity of the spirit and personality.

The revised poem, *That Shadow My Likeness,* asserts that Whitman found his real self in his friends and in his poems. Only from a troubled spirit could have come all of Whitman's experiences. Only by a sanctified spirit could his poems have been written. Shepard has not fathomed the Whitman "pose." She errs as do those psychologists who make a chasm between normal and abnormal personality. In the poem entitled *Faces* he observes the mask hiding "some beautiful soul" and says:

> "And I shall look again in a score or two of
> ages,
> And I shall meet the real landlord perfect
> and unharmed, every inch as good as
> myself."

The Ascending Person.

The main lesson that we may gain from Whitman is that "of the rising forever taller and stronger and broader of the intuitions of men and women, and of self-esteem and Personality." *To a Pupil* Whitman says:

> "Is reform needed? Is it through you?
> The greater the reform needed the greater
> the Personality you need to accomplish it.

> ❖ ❖ ❖ ❖ ❖

> Rest not till you rivet and publish yourself of
> your own personality."

Be a personality "to confront with your personality all the other personalities of the earth." One must not

confuse this as have some of the scoffers at it with com-
mercialized popular psychology. It is not "front" that is
signified, but intrinsic human worth, of which Whitman
believes every man is capable.

> "When through these States walk a hundred
>   millions of superb persons,
> When the rest part away for superb persons
>   and contribute to them,
> When breeds of the most perfect mothers
>   denote America,
> Then to me and mine our due fruition."

How could any one ever think Whitman a medio-
critizer? He believed intensely in progressive growth, in
the perfecting of all individuals. He knew the worth also
of exceptional persons as leaven for the raising of all.
He called for recognition of them, even to the parting
away or standing aside of the multitude to give room for
the development of such exceptional worth. He believed
also that there is heredity in worth and we must breed
it above all in and through excellent mothers.

Indeed his conception of personality is not mere magnetism, attractiveness of person. That may be quite an
illusion. He asks of each:

> "Are you the new person drawn toward me?
> To begin with take warning, I am surely far
>   different from what you suppose;
> Do you suppose you will find in me your
>   ideal?
>   ✧ ✧ ✧ ✧ ✧ ✧
> Have you no thought O dreamer that it may
>   be all maya, illusions?"

With that cautiousness about the mask each one of us
presents as a person and the many masks we wear, his in-

sistence was upon that deeper personality, that profounder self, potentially in each of us, in every man, yearning for ascent, and which it is all important should come to full and free expression.

Self.

Back of the person, at its root, is the self. It is closer to the man, more really him, than his person or than his many varied personalities. In Whitman's concept of self may be summarized his philosophy of man.

As Hume spoke of man as the center and foundation of the sciences and of everything in man's world, so is Whitman anthropocentric. "Where I am or you are this present day, there is the centre of all days."

> "You are not thrown to the winds, you gather
>   certainly and safely around yourself,
> Yourself! yourself! yourself, for ever and
>   ever!"

In the center of all, and object of all, stands the human being, towards whose heroic and spiritual evolution poems and everything directly and indirectly tend, old world or new. Burroughs maintains correctly that "his egocentric method of treatment is what characterizes him as an artist." It is the personal self which is so fundamental: "Underneath all to me is myself, to you yourself." In this he both differs from and exceeds Hume, for he insists that man's self is all-inclusive: "You and your soul includes all things." "Grander far the unseen soul of me, comprehending, endowing all those" grand seen things of Nature. Hume had a skeptical thesis to defend which hampered construction of his own conceived science of man. Whitman's religious consciousness removed even the restraints of science upon his creative imagination.

Burroughs said: "His anthropomorphism is not a projection of himself into Nature, but an absorption of Nature into himself." But Whitman said: "These tend inward to me, and I tend outward to them." So far did he go in this tendency as to call himself "Walt Whitman, a kosmos."

Burroughs remarked, "He has been laughed at for calling himself a Cosmos, but evidently he uses the term to indicate this elemental and dynamic character of his work—its escape from nearer, artificial standards." etc. That explanation is not convincing, for Whitman himself declared:

"Man, so diminutive, dilates beyond the sensible universe, competes with, outcopes space and time, meditating even one great idea. Thus, and thus only, does a human being, his spirit, ascend above, and justify, objective Nature, which probably, nothing in itself, is incredibly and divinely serviceable, indispensable, real, here."

> "Whoever you are! motion and reflection are
>   especially for you,
> The divine ship sails the divine sea for you."

Heterodox absurdity to the theologians and scientists alike of Whitman's day, it is the gospel of that distinguished biologist, Julian S. Huxley, who writes today of the Uniqueness of Man.

Whitman's evolutionism was more daring than that of his evolutionist contemporaries:

> "Before I was born out of my mother genera-
>   tions guided me,
> My embryo has never been torpid, nothing
>   could overlay it.

> ❖ ❖ ❖ ❖ ❖ ❖

> All forces have been steadily employ'd to
>   complete and delight me,
> Now on this spot I stand with my robust
>   soul."

And so Huxley affirms that man has not come to a dead end of evolution, and there is no evidence that he will soon do so.

Whitman's evolutionism also signified the moral ascent of the self:

> "They are not evil any more,
> They hardly know themselves they are so grown."

Even religion with its redemptive salvation never before spoke so much for the hope and uplift of men.

Whitman's estimation of the human self is as the supremely great:

> "It is not the earth, it is not America who is so great,
> It is I who am great or to be great, It is You up there, or any one,
> It is to walk rapidly through civilizations, governments, theories,
> Through pageants, shows, to form individuality."

This is the immortal self: "I know I am deathless." For it sums up the past:

> "O but it is not the years—it is I, it is You,
> We touch all laws and tally all antecedents."

"The fitful events . . . are not me, myself." It is "the last keen faculty and entrance price" of old age "to diagnose . . . what it brings from all its past experiences." The real self is of the future, it is yet to be, "my real self has yet to come forth." Whitman conceived it as his mission to delineate this immortal self of past, present and future, "my enclosing purport being to express, above all artificial regulation and aid, the eternal bodily composite, natural character of one's self."

This immortal self is not allied to any supernatural or unworldly spiritual being. However, he uses the resurrection theme of Christianity, as in the beautiful and pathetic poem, *Old Ireland*:

"The Lord is not dead, he is risen again
    young and strong in another country,"

meaning that Old Ireland has come alive again through its emigrants to young America. The self is ever capable of rebirth and somehow survives death. In *Chanting the Square Deific,* in analogy to Christ, he says:

"Young and strong I pass knowing well I am
    destined myself to an early death;
But my charity has no death—my wisdom dies
    not, neither early nor late,
And my sweet love bequeath'd here and else-
    where never dies."

Another theme above exposited — the individuality, identity, unity, diversity, and variety of the person—is closely related to the theme of the self, the other or alter self, or the mass of selves. Whitman speaks of "the vehement struggle so fierce for the unity in one's self." But yet "we are sufficient in the variety of ourselves."

The self is self-contained, for "the soul is of itself."

"Each man to himself and each woman to
    herself, is the word of the past and present,
    and the true word of immortality;

> No one can acquire for another—not one,
> Not one can grow for another—not one."

Yet

> "In all people I see myself, ...
> And the good or bad I say of myself I say
>   of them."

That is "myself, typical, before all." This typical, average man or self is not the same as the mass, for it is said of him:

> "Never was average man, his soul, more
>   energetic, more like a God,
> Lo, how he urges and urges, leaving the
>   masses no rest!"

For "one's-self" is "a simple separate person" in contrast with the democratic "en masse". Therefore, "I too have felt the resistless call of myself." Contrary to those who would merge the individual in the mass, he says:

> "It is not to diffuse you that you were born
>   of your mother and father, it is to identify
>   you,

❖ ❖ ❖ ❖ ❖ ❖

> Something long preparing and formless is
>   arrived and form'd in you,
> You are henceforth secure, whatever comes
>   or goes."

This is Whitman's reply to the dehumanizing tendencies in his time which are echoed in ours, in much of current sociology and literature.

And lastly, there is another type of the self, the free and manly self; he apostrophizes it:

"O the joy of a manly selfhood!
To be servile to none, to defer to none, not
   to any tyrant known or unknown,

❖ ❖ ❖ ❖ ❖ ❖

To meet life as a powerful conqueror,

❖ ❖ ❖ ❖ ❖ ❖

And nothing exterior shall ever take command of me.

❖ ❖ ❖ ❖ ❖ ❖

To be indeed a God!"

"I only am he who places over you no master,
   owner, better, God, beyond what waits intrinsically in yourself."

Thus, the individual, the person, the self, are primary in Whitman's philosophy. Although Whitman opposes the principle of democracy, as en-masse, to these individualistic concepts, it is in the same sense as Jefferson and Lincoln felt the need to guarantee the rights of the individual through the constitutional organization of democracy, as indeed the Constitution of the United States does protect the person, property, and social rights of individual men. Because government is instituted, not primarily for itself, but for men, in order that every man may have opportunity and be encouraged to develop the best that is in him, democracy in America is not Rousseau's tyrannical will of the people in mass, not the arrogance of an almighty state, not an impersonal domineering society, not a blind people under dictatorial leaders.

But Whitman's conception of man went beyond political forms and principles. Rejecting the conception of a soul conferred on man as a gift from above or as something bound even by some universal natural law and dependent on natural forces, he conceived instead that the soul of every man is individual and unique, identified at his birth as separate and distinct, becoming a self, a person.

This individual, personal self has cosmic extent. It has potential power such as Nature does not have in itself. It gives Nature meaning. It gives God and immortality meaning also; without the individual man, the self, the person, they too are nothing.

Those of little faith in man, the "doubters dull", are too willing to accept enslaving concepts. They prefer and even boast an unreasoning faith in God as the all-powerful tyrant over man. Or disbelieving in God, they believe in Nature with deterministic laws that are yet more enslaving of man. Whitman reposed his faith and hope in men.

12

WHITMAN — POET OF DEMOCRACY.

"For you these from me, O Democracy, to
serve you ma femme!
For you, for you I am trilling these songs."

"The prophet and the bard,
Shall yet maintain themselves, in higher
stages yet,
Shall mediate to the Modern, to Democracy,
interpret yet to them,
God and eidólons."

Was Whitman an Artist? The Controversy.

AND NOW WE COME TO THAT SIDE OF WHITMAN'S GENIUS
about which the disputes have been most acrimonious, his
title and rank as an artist. Was he a poet? If so, second
rate, or among the best?

Heretofore we have not considered him as a poet or
artist, but as doctrinaire, teacher, prophet, or philosopher.
We have set forth his ideas and principles which evidently
he believed to be more important than the form of his expression. He regarded form as secondary. Nevertheless, he
struggled to find that form which would adequately express his thought. The form he chose made great difficulty
for acceptance of him by his contemporaries.

It was the matter or content of his message which drew
from Emerson at the first view of it the surprising testimony: "I find it the most extraordinary piece of wit and
wisdom that America has yet contributed. . . . I find incomparable things said incomparably well, as they must be. . . .
I greet you at the beginning of a great career, which yet
must have had a long foreground somewhere, for such a
start . . . the solid sense of the book is a sober certainty. It
has the best merits, namely, of fortifying and encouraging."

Emerson himself was notoriously wanting in formal excellence. But he could appreciate the high quality of Whitman's genius and his prophetic message in the solid, the
substantial part of it. It remains Emerson's notable distinction that he was not only the first but for a long time the
only one of America's eminent literary men to recognize
great merit in Whitman.

Because of the effect of Whitman's work on literature
and thought, Canby suggests, an unprejudiced person can
no longer cavil at the elemental power and literary skill of
Whitman. But despite such praise Canby has sticking
points in his literary gorge which prevent his swallowing
and digesting Whitman whole. Whitman offends his literary taste for refinements. One suspects that if Canby had
been an early contemporary of Whitman he would have
joined in the prevailing aversion. But now he writes with
an effort to understand why Whitman was not nice in the
points of good literary manners.

Canby thinks Whitman's plebeian origin, the tardy
awakening of his esthetic sense and deficient acquaintance
with the best literature in part explains such a discordant
line as

> "Does it meet modern discoveries, calibres,
>   facts, face to face?"

He criticizes Whitman for harsh and raucous sounds
following something he has beautifully said.

Canby does partially reflect upon the parallel between the evolution of the discords in music and Whitman's similar role in poetry. From Beethoven to Stravinsky has been too great a jump for any but modernistic ears. Beethoven knew the value of discords to enhance beauty. He lost popularity as he developed that technique. But that was a beginning which has reached perhaps a climax in a riot of form that marks such a composer as, say, Schoenberg. In literature Whitman expressed a revolt from prettiness which was much more pronounced than that of Beethoven from Haydn and Mozart. It measured a distance at once that may be likened to that from Haydn to Stravinsky.

The violence of Whitman's departure from the traditional forms and mannerisms prevented the easy transition of learning that measures its progress step by step and avoids the errors and perils of rapid change. Therefore, Whitman's experiments are too obviously immatured. But even so, has not the modern temper of the more sophisticated, better learned, and more esthetic taste come to prefer art and literature with less monotonous prettiness than, for example, Poe, Swinburne, or Tennyson wrote?

Democracy of Art.

Besides political and economic democracy, there was a third kind of democracy for Whitman, the democracy of art, of the artist. He thought of the democracy of art mainly in terms of what he regarded the highest art of all, poetry.

His democracy was qualified only by his personalism or humanism. He tested the greatness of art by its humanism. If he had one fundamental theme it was preeminently the dignity of man, free and equal men.

"The true question to ask respecting a book, is, 'Has it helped any human soul?' This is the hint, statement, not only of the great literatus, his book, but of every great artist."

Accepting that viewpoint, we should judge Whitman

as a democratic poet accordingly: First, by his themes, ideals, and the relation of his poetry to himself. Secondly, by the effect of his democratic conceptions upon his art— in what was his inspiration? what was excluded from his art? Lastly, what were the general characteristics of his art, and what distinguished his particular technique? Is there such thing as democratic art? Is it in technique as well as theme? in form as well as content? Was Whitman's theory of democratic art correct? These are questions which may concern us in judging Whitman's artistic achievement.

Whitman's Themes.

As to his themes Burroughs gives a two-fold suggestion: First, that as poet of democracy and egoism he presents them through his own personality. Second, as a cross-section of those major themes, "his working ideas are democracy, equality, personality, nativity, health, sexuality, comradeship, self-esteem, the parity of the poet, the equality of the sexes, etc. Out of these his work radiates."

In a late poem Whitman gave his own resumé:

"My lines in joy and hope continuing on the
    same,
Of ye, O God, Life, Nature, Freedom,
    Poetry;
Of you, my land—. . . .

❖ ❖ ❖ ❖ ❖ ❖

Of me myself—. . . .

❖ ❖ ❖ ❖ ❖ ❖

The undiminished faith—the groups of loving friends."

Gummere's Criticism of Whitman's Democracy.

Gummere, a distinguished professor of poetics a generation ago, attacked what he thought to be Whitman's conception of democracy. Although Gummere had written ex-
tensively and with exceptional scholarly research concerning the beginnings of poetry, yet he was offended at Whitman's free verse. Nevertheless, he had much real admiration for Whitman's writing. But because of his own conception of democracy he was set against Whitman's self-
assumed title as the poet of democracy. He raised the question squarely, "Was Whitman the real poet of the people,
the ultimate expression of true democracy in art?"

Whitman's expressions led Gummere to believe that
Whitman was lawless, licentious, revolutionary, and ochlo-
cratical in his social and political ideas. He identified them
with Rousseauism. All of which we have seen to be a mis-
placed criticism. Whitman was none of those.

But the pith of Gummere's denial of democratic rank
to Whitman the poet is based on the assumption as Montes-
quieu maintained that the essence of democracy is law. If
Whitman's verse could be proven to be artistic, regular,
governed by any definite law or form, then Gummere's objection on this ground would be removed. But then Gummere himself trenches close to the doctrine of Rousseau
when he contends that the democratic ideal is "submission
to the highest social order, to the spirit of the laws, to that
imagined community." For Whitman the ideal was not a
race of submissive men but free men, men who have the
high character to be a law unto themselves. It was, however, as we have shown, freedom under law.

And we will show later, Whitman's technique possessed
form such as Gummere, with his researches in early poetry,
should have been among the first to recognize, but was evidently prevented by his submission to the traditional canons of taste.

272 WALT WHITMAN: THINKER AND ARTIST

The weakness of Gummere's thesis against Whitman shows itself in Gummere's acceptance of Taine as the high representative of democracy in science and in the theory of art. According to Gummere Taine plumped right over to convention as against the creative power of the individual artist, convention rather than genius, as the criterion of art.

Gummere did not seem to realize that Taine's notion was the very essence of Rousseau's idea of the General Will as the origin and substance of the *Social Contract*. That is of course wholly inconsistent and opposed to the method of developing the free mind as set forth in *Emile*, the other side of Rousseau, with which Whitman had much in common.

But Gummere's application to Whitman of the phrase, "voiced at the will of the oversoul by his individual self," is a total misrepresentation of Whitman's thought. The oversoul of the General Will voiced by a dictator as an individual self fits very well the totalitarian doctrines of communism and fascism, but Whitman had nothing in common with such a conception of the role of the individual self.

In reaction against the great man theory of art, the great artist or great poet as originator, Gummere argued for "democratic and communal" orgins of art. But neither the mass production nor the mass consumption theory of art is sound. Historically what is first apparently in evidence is the creative genius followed by communal participation in his work. But actually the community is an imaginative entity and the real participation in a work or product of genius is that of appreciative individuals who become aware of the artistic work. It takes ordinarily quite a while for an original artist's work to gain a public and he gets that public not in mass but one by one and then apparently by groups.

And as for the emotional inspiration of the artist, he is not as Hegel thought a mere interpreter, a mere voice of the Volkgeist. Not as Gummere contends, a mere mouthpiece of the community, into which he was born and from which he cannot be sundered. On the contrary, it is more often the case, as J. B. S. Haldane, though communistically inclined, once maintained, that the great innovator, artist or scientist, is at the beginning so alien to the community he attempts to serve that it often makes a martyr of him and nearly always he has to battle for recognition.

The theory of communal origin of art cannot stand the test of fact. It is a theory which runs well in the blind generalizing eye of a totalitarian philosophy. Lost in the mists and myths of long ago, for Gummere, ruminating in the unhistorical past of art, it carries a kind of specious verity, but in contemporary society one cannot come upon actual discovery of a community producing any significant work of art. And so Gummere has to admit toward the end of his published lectures that in the higher levels of culture it is individual genius that produces poetry "that perfectly expresses the throng".

But even that alteration of the theory is incorrect. It makes the genius merely express the throng, to be its mere mouthpiece, giving it back only what it had before he spoke.

Whitman broke the spell of that superstition upon us. He dissolved what Allport has called the "group fallacy". Because he perceived the reality of the individual self, he beheld the person, the independent man, capable of being a law unto himself. Although that is the principle upon which American democracy was founded, one cannot say that the American community has yet quite grasped the idea. If that is true, what is the truth about the communal origin of the ideal of American democracy? Not only the confused populace, but also many a university professor of philosophy and of political science, not to speak of the ignoramuses about politics in other college faculties, is as muddled up about democracy as was old professor Gummere.

Democracy and Individuality.

Whitman made a synthesis of en masse and individual which was his conception of true democracy. He veered neither to one side nor to the other. He did not fall prey to the idea of superman, the supreme individual who lords it over the mass, any more than he merged the individual in the mass. He was saved from either extreme by recognition of independent individual worth and of the necessity for self-reliant individuals.

Edward Carpenter caught somewhat of the spirit but altered the synthesis. He sought a balance between "individual freedom and savagery" on the one hand and on the other "a complex human humanism" within civilization. Whitman thought the "cure for civilization" (Carpenter's phrase) is rather a proper balance between or synthesis of democracy and the individual. He believed that the United States provided to a considerable degree such a union or synthesis, and was awaiting the poetic expression of it. "It almost seems as if a poetry with cosmic and dynamic features of magnitude and limitlessness suitable to the human soul, were never possible before. It is certain that a poetry of absolute faith and equality for the use of democratic masses never was."

He was clear about both the end and the means to the end: "I have allow'd the stress of my poems from beginning to end to bear upon American individuality and to assist it. . . . While the ambitious thought of my song is to help the forming of a great aggregate Nation, it is, perhaps, altogether through the forming of myriads of fully develop'd and enclosing individuals."

Anthropocentric Nature.

Another synthesis is that of soul and body, or, what is nearly the same, of nature and soul. He says: "I am the poet of the body and the poet of the soul." "When the full-grown poet came" Nature and the soul of man became blended and united.

> "Nature and the Soul expressed — America
>   and freedom expressed — in it the finest
>   art."

Liberty and Art.

Whitman's naturalism was parcel of his belief in the spontaneous, free spirit. He conceived democratic liberty essential to art: "In the make of the great masters the idea of political liberty is indispensable. Liberty takes the adherence of heroes wherever men and women exist . . . but never takes any adherence or welcome from the rest more than from poets. They are the voice and exposition of liberty. . . . Nothing has precedence of it and nothing can warp or degrade it."

> "For the great Idea, the idea of perfect and
>   free individuals,
> For that, the bard walks in advance, leader
>   of leaders,
>
> ✧ ✧ ✧ ✧ ✧ ✧
>
> That, O my brethren, that is the mission of
>   poets."

Personal Reality.

But this liberty is not something abstract. The poem is not something abstract. For the poem is "a personality. It is man himself." As Burroughs says: "A man is an artist when he gives us a great and immediate impression of reality." As Goethe said: "In the great work the great person is always present as the great factor." The personality to Whitman is such a reality. "Leaves of Grass is as direct an emanation from a central personal force as any book in literature," was Burroughs opinion.

Gummere called attention to Whitman's assertion that although third and fourth class poems, and perhaps those of the second class, need not be "actual emanations from the personality and life of the writer", the first class poem must be such. Gummere regards Dante's poetry as a "fusion of personal and communal" quality. In an almost identical sense, in an early rendering of the *Calamus* poems, Whitman said:

> "Comrades! I am the bard of democracy . . .
> But I alone advance among the people en-
>   masse . . .
> I alone of all the bards, may suffuse as with
>   the common people, . . .
> It is I who live in these, and in my poems—
> O they are utterly me."

But to understand this we must keep in mind the two selves as Whitman conceived them as well as the duality of the democratic en-masse and the individual self. There is really a three-fold personality described by him: first, that most immediate self, the individual man of inseparable body and soul; second, the roving self of imagination that penetrates and absorbs everything into itself; and third, that personal self that suffuses itself with the common people, the people en-masse, as if it lives in them.

It was Whitman's purpose that his poems should be "a complete picture of humanity, of society in all its phases, and the world in all its sweep of landscape and oceanic spread" as well as "to express in sharp-cut self-assertion, one's self, and also, or may be, still more, to map out, to throw together for American use, a gigantic embryo or skeleton of personality, fit for the West for native models."

Our post-freudian poets are considerably messed up in their personality concepts if Whitman was correct in his conception of personality. Wilder, trying to interpret them in the light of Jung's psychoanalysis says they are delving for raw materials not in personality but in the area of irrational blind forces. He quotes Jung's assumption that the normal every day personal point of view avails us excepting when we are disturbed or in a panic. In those abnormal states we are the victims of the blind sub-personal and sub-human forces.

A similar point of view was expressed by T. S. Eliot, that poetry is not an expression of personality, but an escape from personality, also an escape from emotion. Edmund Wilson remarks about this that those in the vogue of Eliot have indeed exhibited the lack of both emotion and personality.

Edith Sitwell states the opposite viewpoint when she insists that the great poet, whether traditionalist or experimentalist, individualizes and personalizes by aiding his reader or hearer to understand and know what is below the threshold of our consciousness.

It may well be, as Jung says, that our reasons play us false in a crisis, but is that excuse for the poet being irrational and deserting himself? Or is it not rather his business to keep his wits about him so that he may see something and tell us what he sees in order that we may see it in ourselves or with our own eyes.

These raw materials of the sub-personal and sub-human, however blind or sub-conscious for the human under observation by the great poet, are not unseen by him. What appear to be automatic forces that make mere puppets of men should become in the creative genius of the poet consciously willed forces.

In that respect Eliot is right, the poet is not an emotion

turned loose, out of control. But in what sense does the poet escape from emotion or personality? If he is not using emotions and not dealing with persons or personality, what is his stock in trade? What raw materials does he work with? Is there any literature of an unemotional sort? If so, is it not lifeless? dead? Poetry may be escape from the poignancy of one's own emotions. It is certainly the reflecting upon one's emotions and partially the reliving of them. I do not think it is ever escape from one's own personality. The great poet, as Goethe and Whitman believed, puts his personality into his work.

The poet as seer should be conscious of the subterranean roots of human personality both in himself and in other men. It is his business to bring up out of the depths of man's nature whatever is there. Whitman is a distinguished poet, not only because he was not blind to the irrational forces in man, but also because he had a sublime conception of the art of raising those potential forces so often errant and destructive to a divine expression of man's nobler self. He did not yield to the cynical temptation to depersonalize and dehumanize man. It is the poet's function to inspire, to create personality, not to escape or depress it.

The democracy of art is emphatically humanistic and anthropomorphic:

> "I am the poet of the woman the same as the
>   man."

> "Camerado, this is no book,
> Who touches this touches a man."

Whitman's poems are for "common humanity," "erect, inflated, and fully self-esteeming," not "acknowledging superiors". "His whole work," says Burroughs, "is a radiation of the idea that there is something better than to be an artist or a poet—namely, to be a man."

How Did his Art Express Himself?

Notwithstanding the singing of himself, his poetry is not autobiographical. He strove to keep his actual personality out of his poems:

"As I sit writing here, sick and grown old,
Not my least burden is that dullness of the
    years, querilities,
Ungracious glooms, aches, lethargy, constipa-
    tion, whimpering ennui,
May filter in my daily songs."

He was so loath to impart any biographical data even to his intimate and trusted biographers, because it might limit the ego of *Leaves of Grass* by the limitations of the actual Walt Whitman.

When he described himself, "Walt Whitman, kosmos," did he mean to celebrate his imperfections or the ideality he would wish to be? Certainly the latter. The real Walt Whitman for his poetry is the ideality, not the actuality. So, he said: "The American bards shall be marked by generosity and affection and for encouraging competitors. They shall be kosmos." He thought of himself as incomplete:

"Must we barely arrive at this beginning of
    us?—and yet it is enough, O soul;
O soul, we have positively appeared—that is
    enough."

He conceived himself as the forerunner to the

"Poets to come! orators, singers, musicians to
    come!
Not today is to justify me and answer what I
    am for,

But you, a new breed, native, athletic, con-
tinental, greater than before known,
Arouse! for you must justify me.

I myself but write one or two indicative
words of the future,
I but advance a moment only to wheel and
hurry back in the darkness

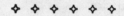

Leaving it to you to prove and define it,
Expecting the main things from you."

"The paths to the house I seek to make,
But leave to those to come the house itself."

Poetry for America in Contrast.

On the ground of making democracy the supreme end
in art he rejected even the greatest of the poets of the past.
Even Shakespeare, because "he stands entirely for the
mighty esthetic sceptres of the past, not for the spiritual
and democratic, the sceptres of the future." "Superb and
inimitable as all is, it is mostly an objective and physiological kind of power and beauty the soul finds in Shakespere
—a style supremely grand of the sort, but in my opinion
stopping short of the grandest sort, at any rate for fulfilling
and satisfying modern and scientific and democratic American purposes."

He conceded that Shakespeare summed up his "whole
age and more", but he objected to "almost lung worship
of Shakespere—the cult worship, the college-chair worship" which exaggerates "the genius of Shakespere".
"Shakespere's sonnets . . . . are often overdone—over-orn-
ate." The Greeks "had some recognition of the common
people—of the dignity of labor—of the honor that resides
in the average life of the race", as Shakespeare had not.

"Past! past! for us, therefore past, that once
so mighty world,

"After the cycles, poems, singers, plays,
Vaunted Ionia's, India's—Homer, Shakespere—

❖ ❖ ❖ ❖ ❖ ❖

(Who knows? the best yet unexpress'd and
  lacking.) "

And yet Canby, perhaps touched with "college-chair"
assiduity, says that one of Whitman's main sources was
Shakespeare. What Shakespeare? the historical dramas and
the oratorical passages. And he says Whitman knew Shakespeare. Whitman was a reader with a wide range through
literature, and he knew the classics. The reason for his
peculiar style was not therefore his ignorance of literature.
Nor on the other hand was it consciously imitative, of either Shakespeare, or of the Bible, or of any other author.
He did not write speeches or verse in the style of Shakespeare.

And he felt that both the spirit and the subject-matter
of Shakespeare were alien to democracy. That, of course,
is an opinion at variance with such as that of Tate who regards Shakespeare as peculiarly a writer of "genuine poetry" because he had no moral, scientific or other purpose,
a great example of "perfect inutility". As if tradition of
the successful manager of Globe Theater and of the practical playwright were mistaken! Did Shakespeare have no
purpose in his flattery of nobility, no bias in making his
villains intellectual persons who were skeptical about as-
trology, his thoughtful and scholarly persons incapable of
firm resolution or effective deeds, his Puritans odious hypo-
crites, his peasants and laborers clowns?

Gummere found fault with Whitman for not subscrib-
ing to the ancient literary formula that tragedy for the individual is genuine realism. In Shakespeare, on the other
hand, the individual comes to tragic end, but the state always survives, "save perhaps" in Timon of Athens. Had

Shakespeare no political philosophy, no religious opinions, no social prejudices? To Whitman Shakespeare was both feudalistic and royalist and therefore inadequate for a democratic age.

Whitman particularizes still further in distinguishing his book as typical of American poetry in contrast with that of others. A Rocky Mountain canyon scene provided a parallel:

> "These reckless heaven-ambitious peaks,
> These gorges, turbulent-clear streams, this
> naked freshness,
> These formless wild arrays, for reasons of
> their own,
> I know thee, savage spirit—we have com-
> muned together,
> Mine too are such wild arrays, for reasons
> of their own."

His poems are not built on the models of traditional art:

> "Was't charged against my chants they had
> forgotten art?
> To fuse within themselves its rules precise
> and delicatesse?
> The lyrist's measured beat, the wrought-out
> temple's grace—column and polished art
> forgot?"

In brief, he insists his kind is "the finest art".

Negation of Traditional Art.

Too much has been made of Whitman's rejections of typical characteristics of poetry, as if he scorned qualities he himself was incapable of. He did not lack style, although he maintained it is not style that makes a great poet. Yet, in Canby's judgment the originality of his style is manifest from the fact that of the innumerable imitations only the parodies are successful, "a sign of distinctive style".

He professed not to seek musical quality, but, according to Selincourt, "among his greatest gifts is his command of the music of words." He abjured prettiness, perfume, ornament, as he distinguished the quality of his poetry from such. The words of true poems "do not seek beauty" but rather beauty follows upon them. He had and did not disdain any of these when his subject was fitting for them.

He feared originality as separating him from the reality of art. Nevertheless, "He or she is greatest who contributes the greatest original practical example." He knew the penalty on imitation: "Poems distilled from poems pass away." Naturalness in place of artificiality was Whitman's aim. That led him from the beaten track.

His Positive Aims.

Aside from the objectives of his great themes correlated with democracy and individuality, Whitman had certain positive aims or characteristics which give uniqueness to his poetry. What were these? For the moment we are speaking not of form or technique but of psychological and moral qualities.

I cannot agree with the apparently contradictory judgment of Selincourt that Whitman's nature was disharmonious with poetry: on one side too crude, on the other too sensitive. Selincourt felt that his need for spontaneity, universality, simplicity and receptiveness could not accord with the necessarily artificial forms of poetry. Burroughs too thought that Whitman's work lacks the charm of the most highly wrought artistry of the poets which it sacrificed for sake of the charm of naturalness.

These were judgments formed before free verse had been widely practiced and before literature had recovered the ancient Hebrew and Greek sense of the greatest poetry.

They did not understand, and there is still general misunderstanding of, Whitman's own practice of poetic art.

What Whitman rated most in poetry was not form or technique, but intellectual and emotional qualities as fitting his great themes: "The greatest poet has less a marked style and is more the channel of thoughts and things without increase or diminution, and is the free channel of himself."

> "The words of true poems are the tufts and
> final applause of science."

> "The great Idea . . . is the mission of poets."

> "And for thy subtler sense subtler refrains
> dread Mother,
> Preludes of intellect tallying these and thee,
> mind-formulas fitted for thee, real and sane
> and large as these and thee,

> ❖ ❖ ❖ ❖ ❖ ❖

> Be thee fact to be justified, blended with
> thought,
> Thought of man justified, blended with God,
> Through thy idea, lo, the immortal reality!"

But such abstract thought is distinguishable from the clear-cut expression that is ideal for science: "I have not been afraid of the charge of obscurity, in either of my two volumes—because human thought, poetry or melody, must leave dim escapes and outlets—must possess a certain fluid, aerial character, akin to space itself, obscure to those of little or no imagination, but indispensable to the highest purposes." This may explain why he wrote *To a Certain Civilian*

> "Why I was not singing erewhile for you to
> follow, to understand—nor am I now;

For I lull nobody, and you will never understand me."

Whitman did not represent cold intellectualism. Everywhere it is deep feeling, passion, and joy of the spirit which
pervades his intellectuality.

His Emotional Quality.

Was Whitman's poetry wanting in emotional quality?
Yvor Winters says so: "He had no capacity for any feeling
save of the cloudiest most general sort." Few would agree
with Winters. Gummere, quoting Meredith that "Poetry
is compounded of 'form and fire' ", added: "Now fire is
something that Whitman can command."
Canby does not agree. He believes that it was Whitman's purpose and search to find a kind of emotional language closer to common speech of Americans than the English models of literature, of an oratorical style; that he
wrote such prose and verse only when he was emotionally
stirred, and then it was in a sort of Biblical style with which
Americans were familiar.
Professor Snyder does not agree with Winters. Indeed,
he classes Whitman with the hypnotic or semi-hypnotic
poets. Notably the poem, *O Captain! My Captain!* is in
that class. Others such as *Out of the Cradle Endlessly Rocking* and *When Lilacs Last in the Dooryard Bloom'd* are
"spell-weaving poems". It might be questioned whether
hypnotic poetry is emotional. It may signify a state of trance
rather than of emotion. However, the poems listed are
surely emotional.
Following Snyder's suggestion, it may be that Whitman's type of poetry does not find an appropriate "esthetic
responsiveness" to induce the hypnotic spell on Winters.
Even some admirers of Whitman, as Selincourt, do not regard these poems as characteristically Whitman and not his
best. Do not such variant opinions indicate different tastes

rather than matter of poetic excellence, which Winters
takes his to be?

Whitman's breadth, his inclusiveness, makes appeal to
widely differing tastes. Some prefer his early poems, some
the late. His oratorical style offends Babette Deutch; it
pleases others. A very catholic taste might accept all of
Whitman's poetry and Whitman's own standards of taste.
For *Leaves of Grass* is his own selection after much re-editing, excisions and rejections.

Thought and Emotional Content.

In theory at least Whitman appeared to give more value
to intellectual quality than to emotion. He said as to his
"own method . . . I have the idea clearly and fully realized
before I attempt to express it. Then I let go." "The first
thing necessary is the thought—the rest may follow if it
chooses—but must not be too much sought after. The two
things being equal I should prefer to have the lilt present
with the idea, but if I got down my thought and the rhythm
was not there I should not work to secure it. I am very
deliberate—I take a good deal of trouble with words: yes,
a good deal, but what I am after is the content not the
music of words. Perhaps the music happens—it does not
harm: I do not go in search of it." "I have never given any
study merely to expression . . . —never fooled with technique more than enough to provide for simply getting
through."

He quoted with approval "Heine when asked of a book
and its writer . . . 'Had he an idea, a point of view, a central thought?' and then, 'has he said what he undertook to
say?' " He criticized Sidney Lanier because his "over-
tuning of the ear, this extreme deference paid to oral nicety,
reduced the majesty, the solid worth, of his rhythms." In
Democratic Vistas he queried and answered: "Adventures?
. . . old histories—miracles—romances? Rather, our own
unquestioned facts."

Matthiessen weighs the matter of emotion and thought in Whitman and concludes that the free-thinking rationalism which he drew from his radical environment was balanced by his intuition firmly implanted in him by Quakerism. Professor Allen inclines to a similar opinion. Observing that nearly every poem has a background of ideas rather than of merely lyrical emotion, he has not expressed himself logically or coherently but by sharing his emotions with the reader. It is the poet rather than the philosopher that he is. That opinion is vitiated partially by Allen's inability to see Whitman the Philosopher.

So too, when Selincourt criticizes Whitman's arrangement of the *Leaves of Grass* because it is made with reference to the thought rather than the "poetic value" of the poems, he goes against Whitman's own judgment that the thought content is more important than any other element. As Pound said: "The only way to enjoy Whitman thoroughly is to concentrate on his fundamental meaning."

"The words of my book nothing, the drift
of it everything."

"My form has strictly grown from my purports and facts, and is the analogy of them."

Was Whitman's Method Logical?

Whitman's form was not that of logic. He said: "Logic does very little for me." He maintained that "It is the very worst sort of logic to try a poem by rules of logic." His method, according to Allen, was cumulative, grammatical and oratorical rather than logical and progressive. So Winters defines the logical method of composition: rationally progressive from detail to detail; and this is applicable to poetic structure. In that respect Whitman's poetry was like Emerson's prose, notably lacking in logical sequence.

But as Winters quotes T. S. Eliot: "There is a logic of imagination as well as a logic of concepts." This should mean that symbols in place of words also have a logic. Symbols represented conceptual words for primitive men and may perform the same function for poetry now. But this is apparently not what Winters means, for he says he is using the word logic figuratively.

But may we not ask for relevancy and consistency in the use of symbols? May we not object to mixed metaphors outside the context of reflective consciousness? In this sense is there not also a logic of symbols? Is there not a truth of reality, truth to life, truth to men, to which the poet is as much bound as the logician? Whitman certainly had regard for such a logic. It was formal logic for which he had little use. What Schiller calls the logic for use or personal logic was quite apt to Whitman's method, and he was at least instinctively conscious of it.

Whitman's Art as Organic Symbolism.

Whitman as a true poet was a symbolist and in a sense his method may be called organic symbolism. But that does not mean all that Professor Allen attempts to elicit from the phrase. For Whitman it was not "the great chain of being doctrine" and it did not identify him with the cosmical theory of life as the fundamental principle of the universe.

In Allen's definitions three inconsistent theories are presented. First, the Organic Principle "means that art is also a product of nature and cosmic processes and grows and develops like an organism." That applied to the artist is supposed by Allen to mean that "his function is to intuit a form which will be as closely as possible analogous to organic growth." The second is plainly contradictory with the first definition. The first makes nature the producer of art; the second makes man, not nature, the maker even though he is declared a copyist or imitator of nature. According to his third statement of "the Organic Principle, it must be shaped from man's inner nature, within, and not from external conventions." The last makes art either a self-evolving thing or derives it from man's inner nature. Yet again, he represents it to be Whitman's belief and exemplification of the organic theory "that form must spring from within, that a poetic experience will find its own natural rhythm in the act of expression." But if the latter was Whitman's view, it is a mechanical, not an organic principle.

The objection to the organic concept is that it is too limited a concept to describe the poet's art. What we must be seeking for is an expression to indicate the unity and coherence of the artist's principle of construction of his work. The organic notion was defined by Coleridge as representing a theory in contrast to the mechanical. Mechanical form would signify the imposition of a predetermined form on the poetic production; while the organic form would signify a natural development of the form from within, on the analogy of a growing thing. It is obviously a very confused conception and not at all apt to describe the work of creation of a poet. The poet is the creator, not tradition, or convention, or Nature. The poem might correctly be said to grow within and out of the artist himself, but it is not an automatic process like the growth of a plant or an animal. It is the product of the artist's creative imagination.

Herbert Read, in whose opinion there have been since the establishment of the industrialist age only two major poets in English—Whitman and Lawrence, may enable us further to criticize the orthodoxy which has been derived from Coleridge's theological and metaphysical dicta about poetry. Read attempts to distinguish organic and abstract form. The organic he thinks is characterized by originality and "vital unity" of structure and content. But for Read art is no longer, as for Coleridge, the product of "Nature,

the prime genial artist, inexhaustible in diverse powers"
and forms, but a "departure from truth to Nature." The
vagueness in Read's definition is the organic concept, "vital
unity" or "natural vitality." Whose vitality? the poet's? of
the work of art? or Nature's? Not Nature's if art is a departure from it. Has a work of art vitality apart from the
artist or as it awakens a vital something in the appreciater
of the art? Does not the organic concept prove inapt either
to describe a work of art, or the process of its creation, or
even its historical evolvement?

Read's definition of abstract form borrows its terms also
from Coleridge and corresponds but similarly varies from
Coleridge's mechanical form. The abstract form is derived
from the organic form as a predetermined structure. What
Read calls organic is more nearly an abstraction from Nature. Abstract form occurs when an artist no longer follows
his own urge, when he is no longer realistic, but imitates
the pattern set by an original artist. Abstract form is therefore not living, vital or organic art, simply because it is
repetitive and not creative.

Had Read emancipated himself from Coleridge he
would have said what he sensed in Whitman. He would
have rid himself from bondage to Coleridge's terms. A
humanistic art is not predetermined by Nature, convention, established organic, abstract, or mechanical form; it
creatively uses anything at hand as the artist's imagination
is able to appropriate it for the expression of his purpose.

Personality in Art.

Read's definitions compel him to take account of the
poet's personality; "Upon the nature of his personality
depends the form of his poetry." From that it would appear
that what he means by organic form is that which comes
out of the poet's personality. He sees that there is conflict
between his viewpoint and Eliot's, which divorces poetry
from personality and emotion.

But he becomes confused again about the concept of character. Taking Goethe's dictum that "A talent is formed in solitude; a character in the stream of the world," he says that what Goethe calls talent he calls personality. But he does not reflect that what Goethe said is untrue. A character gets formed in solitude and a talent gets formed by world contacts as much as vice versa. Nor is a personality formed only in solitude. That is an anarchistic error into which he has fallen.

He errs also in adopting Professor Roback's definition of character as the moralistic "disposition to inhibit instinctive impulses in accordance with a regulative principle." Why should character be only a product of inhibited impulses? Is not positive self-determined action much more productive of character than negativism? It was his understanding of the falsity of that assumption which made Whitman a pioneer of the moral viewpoint which is now almost universally accepted, that we make men and they make themselves, not by withdrawing, not by restraint, not by inhibitions, but by forward impulses intelligently directed.

Read also veers to the Freudian concept of personality as the conscious ego as over against the unconscious id. Freud was considerably self-deceived by his hard categories of superego, ego, and id and by his assumption of the three corresponding entities of conscious, subconscious and unconscious, the latter being incapable of becoming conscious in the ordinary way. One need not go beyond Freud's own analysis to discover that his method contradicts his assumptions. His method brings to consciousness what is categorized as the unconscious. Furthermore, Freudian technique is not the only one for the discovery of the content of the unconscious. That is just the reason for so many special and separate cults of Freudianism. But from such confused concepts Read derives his notions of character and personality in art.

He sets character over against personality as that which an individual selects at the expense or sacrifice of emotions and sentiments of which personality is the common denominator. Character is fixed and unchangeable and not amenable to experience. It is an impersonal ideal. A character is therefore without brains to learn from experience, and a personality is a stream of consciousness yielding to every eddy and current of emotion. Which then would be the greater fools or lunatics—individuals with character or those with personality? Thus to put the poet and the moralist at odds is to dispose of each disastrously. Whitman did not thus put character and personality in opposition to each other and he did not deprive both of the guidance of intelligence.

Had Read not been misled by the confusions and errors of his authorities he could not have accepted without question the absurdity of Keats that "men of genius . . . have not any individuality, any determined character." Attempting to controvert Eliot, he has implicated himself in a worse predicament.

And the worst perhaps is this: A man of character is a man of action; but a poet is only a fluid, restless, unstable personality, open to every wind of emotion and sentiment. Wordsworth and Milton withered when they became men of action. Shakespeare (we know so little about him), was, perhaps, not a minor actor and manager of Globe Theater. And Goethe, well, if we should analyze him more closely would turn out to be "a real poet and a real personality, but a somewhat fictitious character." When Whitman's full-grown poet came he was no such drifting personality. He was at least an inspirer of action. He was a promoter of "brave soldiers." He challenged men to greater deeds, more worthy actions. Read himself has not been content to isolate the poet from action. But he is confused about the theory of personality.

The opposition between Read's and Whitman's theory

of poetry cannot be made more definite than by Read's quotation approvingly from Keats: "Not one word I ever utter can be taken for granted as an opinion growing out of my identical nature—how can it, when I have no nature?" Whitman's contrary view was made explicit by his declaration that his book was a man, himself.

Read maintains that he has shown how the essential nature of poetry depends on the "negative capability" (Keat's phrase) of the personality and how incompatible it is with the "positive capability" of the character. He has quite separated it from the reality of action, has identified it with unstable personality, and divorced it from character.

In an attempted summary of his concepts, however, Read "relates the coherence of the personality to the coherence of thought." But does not that do violence to his definition of personality which is, if organized at all, organized only by thought. For personality in Read's conception of it is the unstable side of the human being. Furthermore, coherence gives form, fixity, as in character, and character is what the poet must eschew.

I think what Read is striving for is something to express the infinite variety of experience and thus to make it available as the fountain and sustenance of the poet's imagination. He thinks it is to be recovered from the psychological depths of our being, and we would have to agree. But what a confusion he is in regarding man's psychological make-up. Over against the unconscious is intelligence. It is like a dog chasing its tail. It is a coherent intelligence at one end; it is a coherent but always moving tail of personality at the other end. I suppose he is striving to be inclusive like Freud by contending that consciousness is not everything.

I quarrel with his phrases rather than his obvious intentions. His misuse of words and ideas hurts more than helps. The emotional or impulsive basis of ourselves is closely related to all that we are. Character is not unrelated to emotion. And character divorced from intelligence, like an uncontrolled and undirected emotion is a wild runaway horse. The poet has been too much identified with pure emotionalism. Read is undoubtedly trying to correct that tendency in poetry.

Whitman's Larger Conception of Art.

The organic analogy was not sufficiently inclusive for Whitman. In the 1876 Preface he said: "Poetic style, when address'd to the Soul, is less definite form, outline, sculpture, and becomes vista, music, half-tints, and even less than half-tints. True, it may be architecture; but again it may be the forest wild-wood, or the best effects thereof, at twilight, the waving oaks and cedars in the wind, and the impalpable odor." It is evident that Whitman deemed poetry an art inclusive of all arts and sciences, all natural things as well as the conventions of men.

In Wilson's discussion of whether verse is a dying technique he concludes much as Whitman that the distinctions between poetry and prose are not very fundamental. His review of the theories of the nature of poetry shows what a variety of particularistic ideas have been held by high authority, which again may justify Whitman's more inclusive analogies to relate all the arts and all kinds of writing in poetry.

Contrary to Whitman's opinion, Read contends that the difference is not form or mode of expression, but of essence. That essence is personality, an organic concept. For Whitman too personality is the essence of poetry, but he did not make it a distinction between poetry and prose.

Wilder calls attention to D. H. Lawrence's distinction that the farmer's life and philosophy is organic, while the city man's is artificial and mechanical. Whitman, as Burroughs thought, had the urban outlook and not the farmer's or country man's.

Hegel thought that the form of a literary work is mechanical and arrived at that conclusion by reference to the mechanical instrument it employs, the printer's art, with its series of symbols. Whitman was a printer by trade, and the impress of his skill is strong in *Leaves of Grass*. But type and printing technique are not poet's brains.

Possibly, the kind of poetry determines which analogy is nearer to the poet's art. Tate distinguished rationalistic metaphysical poetry from symbolist or romantic poetry and related them, the first to beginning at or nearing the dividing or extensive end of the line and the other, the romantic or symbolist, at the intensive end. Whitman can hardly be described in either category. Our analysis of his ideas shows his rationalistic tendency. But, on the other hand, his form and manner indicate a romantic or symbolist tendency. Read suggested the correlation of classical and organic and romanticist with abstract poetry. These distinctions do not help us to classify Whitman.

Matthiessen calls attention to Whitman's recurrent analogies of his poetry with oratory, Italian music, and the sea. Again he remarks Whitman's striving to imitate the "fitful" rising and falling of the sea and thinks that a better phrase to describe his poetry than either organic or architectonic.

Possibly the choice of the title, *Leaves of Grass,* would suggest an organic bias. But as a printer he may also have had in mind the leaves of a book, and then the metaphor would combine both conceptions.

Fausset, criticizing the passage last above quoted, held the opinion that Whitman thought of his work as less a matter of form, outline or sculpture than of vista and music, that Whitman had a split personality which divided mind and heart and lowered his emotional quality, resulting in a metaphysical cosmic vagary. Therefore, he thought that Whitman failed to identify the particular as an expression of the universal. That is partially the viewpoint of a Platonist; an Aristotelian would think the error Fausset's. Is it not the artist's function to universalize the particular? For art gives the particular experience a universal use or currency, the possession of more than the immediate experience. Art makes that experience renewable and repetitive and available to others than the artist who creates the representative work of art.

Is it not unfortunate as diverting from the unique quality of art itself to attempt describing it in physical terms, either mechanical or organic? It has a physical side because of its intimate relation to sense experience. But it transcends sense experience, even emotional experience, in that it is also conceptual. The poet, every artist, particularizes; but the object of his art is to universalize. To make an individual experience the experience of the race. To give immortality to the fleeting moment. Thus to bring the cosmos within the soul of man. To give Nature the meaning which humanizes it, a meaning not in itself. It was such a conception which distinguished Whitman from the vagaries of the metaphysical poets, from the unreality of the symbolists, and separated him from both classic and romantic schools of art. He thought of himself as the poet of science and democracy, a new order of poetry.

Whitman's Art was Experimental and Creative.

To the traditionalist art is not really creative. It is a copy of Nature, or it is convention, or repetitive form. Learning rather than creativity is its characteristic. In Whitman's view Nature does not provide the form, and certainly tradition is not adequate to furnish it. Man is its creator. The new world creates its own forms:

"The Old World has had the poems of myths, fictions, feudalism, conquest, caste, dynastic wars, and splendid exceptional characters and affairs, which have been great; but the New World needs the poems of realities and science and of the democratic average and basic equality, which shall be greater. In the centre of all, stands the Human

Being, towards whose heroic and spiritual evolution poems and everything directly tend, Old World or New."

The human being is the center and object of all art. "I saw, from the time my enterprise and questionings positively shaped themselves ... that the trunk and centre whence the answer was to radiate, and to which all should return from straying however far a distance, must be an identical body and soul, a personality—which personality, after many considerations and ponderings I deliberately settled should be myself—indeed could not be any other." Personal humanism is the great and central theme of Whitman's work. It is this which preeminently distinguishes his aim and purpose.

It was not tradition but traditionalism which Whitman rejected. He was quite aware of the necessary relation of past, present and future. He was quite aware of Kant's notion of the personal point of view, "the last essential reality, giving shape and significance to all the rest." Whitman's expressions often remind one of Croce's theory of history as something viewed from the present:

"It seem'd to me ... the time had come to reflect all themes and things, old and new, in the lights thrown on them by the advent of America and democracy—to chant those themes through the utterance of one, not only the grateful and reverent legatee of the past, but the born child of the new World—to illustrate all through the genesis and ensemble of to-day; and that such illustration and ensemble are the chief demands of America's prospective imaginative literature ... while ... our lands and days ... probably will never have, anything better than they already possess from the bequests of the past, it still remains to be said that there is even towards all those a subjective and contemporary point of view appropriate to ourselves alone, and to our new genius and environments, different from anything hitherto; and that such conception or current or gone-by life and art is for us the only means of their assimilation consistent with the Western World. . . . has not the time arrived when . . . there must imperatively come a re-adjustment of the whole theory and nature of Poetry?"

Whitman was reverent toward the old literature. But as conditions have changed its value must be considered in an evolutionary aspect and not as something now to be copied or imitated. "We require larger measures, in music as in literature, to express the spirit of this age."

And Wilder, a conservative poet-critic, testifies that he has found more ethical enlightenment from the successors of Whitman, the new poetry, than in the poets of the traditional schools. This is the testimony of one who continues to believe that the hope of the world is from traditional Christianity, but not until it has reformed itself to become more up-to-date. Just why has tradition so generally broken down in our time? Is it not because it has failed to make adjustments to the needs of today? That is the weakness of Wilder's thesis: he would give to tradition not only that which it does not have, the up-to-date sense of ethical values, but which by virtue of its inherent tradition of world denial it cannot have.

What is the difference between Whitman and the traditionalist? Is it the difference between experimental and traditional poetry? Sitwell thinks every great poet is both. And evidently Winters would agree. For the errors occur in pseudo-traditionalism and pseudo-experimentalism. The mistake on the traditional side is excessive adherence to traditional forms and failure to use them experimentally, for perception and stimuli. The pseudo-experimentalist error confuses tradition with convention and endeavoring to escape fixed convention he loses the advantage of experimenting with the traditional forms.

T. S. Eliot also appears to mean by traditionalism of the right sort an experimental use. Tradition provides us with many forms and by recombining them we can get new forms.

Gummere contrasts the traditional poem with the narrower product of the genius. The traditional poem is a distillation of time. It is a cumulative communal product, of which the ballad is an example. And he thought not even such masters of the ballad as Burns and Scott would claim that they could quite simulate the traditional poem. Is Gummere's theory of the communal poem convincing? It appears to take advantage of anonymity to erase the identity and contribution of the individual genius who is operative in the group and instead to posit that unprovable character, the group person with group mind and group consciousness who is a fallacy, the "group fallacy." That was the dogma of Rousseau, the General Will of the populace thought of as composing poetry. If ever it did so, it appears now to have lost the gift.

As Winters views traditional poetry it appears also to have the qualities of a person, motivation and feeling. Or, in another aspect, it is a convention which affords the poet a maximum content of meaning and feeling in language with a minimum strain or effort by its provision of form. The objection to such a viewpoint is its excessive claims for tradition. There is, however, the truth in it that no poet of our time worthy of consideration escapes tradition or fails to take advantage of the heritage from it.

But Whitman's viewpoint was rather that of the poet who goes beyond tradition and brings to consciousness new experience which is not contained in any tradition. It is this conception of the artist which distinguishes him from the traditionalist, a viewpoint which has at last found its proponents in critical circles. Whitman felt it necessary to institute a new tradition for democracy, a new form and content fit for its purposes, for the average man, for every man.

13

NEW POETRY AND OLD TECHNIQUES

❖ ❖ ❖ ❖ ❖ ❖

"Rhymes and rhymers pass away, poems dis-
till'd from poems pass away,
The swarms of reflectors and the polite pass,
and leave ashes,
Admirers, importers, obedient persons, make
but the soil of literature."

❖ ❖ ❖ ❖ ❖ ❖

Reappraisal of Whitman's Art.

WHAT A CHANGE HAS TAKEN PLACE IN ACADEMIC CIRCLES
since Triggs was dismissed from Chicago University when
he dared proclaim Whitman a poet of high rank. Professor
Allen's praise of Whitman's skill as an artist is illustrative
of present opinion that is gaining ground in places where
it was formerly denied: "The fact that Whitman so successfully combines thought, rhetoric, syllabic accent, and
stanzaic form in an 'organic' whole is sufficient evidence
of expert craftsmanship and his ability to adapt technique
to his literary purposes."

Whitman's technique is better understood today than
the lofty themes to which he devoted his art. But the low
rating of his art which once prevailed still influences criticism. Even ardent Whitmanites are all too apt to slight
the significance of Whitman's technique in their effort to
redeem him from the vicious attacks of malicious critics.

300

Such concession is a weakness and betrays lack of understanding of Whitman's artistic method, and is very unjust to Whitman's art, though justified somewhat by his own diffidence.

For in *A Backward Glance O'er Travel'd Roads* he admits that abuse had effect upon him despite his philosophic temper to take it as expected. At the end of his work, probably with too much quietude and acceptance, he awaited uncertainly the verdict of history. He had become inured to disappointments. But the method of his art has proved itself, he has been the forerunner of the foremost of America's later poets and the inspiration of more than have imitated him.

It may now be inquired what of that art is to have survival and permanency. At present we speak only preparatory to appraisal of his influence on American poetry and art, as we have already considered his influence on religion, philosophy and science. We have discussed his role as the prophet of personalism and the poet of democracy. Before reviewing his work in comparison with that of contemporary and succeeding poets, the distinguishing characteristics of his technique should be known. But we are still concerned to discover what, if any, effect his aims had upon his poetic art. Does individualistic democracy put a particular stamp upon the nature of poetry?

Purpose and Technique.

The assumption "that his meanings exceeded his mastery, his vision was superior to his technique," rates Whitman lower than he ranked himself and rejects altogether his conceptions of "highest art." He regarded the instrument or art subordinate to its object and theme, but that did not mean that he felt or thought that art is unimportant or that it should lag behind or be inappropriate to its function as conveyer of ideas. He did hold it contemptible to practice art for art's sake, as if it could be divested of or separated from its human ends.

Did, then, Whitman's art fall short of the purpose he had to achieve? Of course it did. But who has succeeded better than he? His estimation of Shakespeare was indicative of his answer. He deemed Shakespeare's art though great not fit for the expression of democratic literature.

In one sense we have to admit that Whitman came far short of complete expression of democratic art; for he did not practice all the arts, not nearly all the literary arts, and did not express every form of poetic art. But in that particular branch of poetic art which he practiced, has any one done it better or as well? Did he have a definite method which served his purpose as well or better than any other he had available or readily at hand, had he mastered the arts already attained and particularly the poetic arts and the essay form he used? The latter is the problem we now consider directly here.

Negation of Techniques.

First considering still his negative attitudes, Whitman sought in free verse to escape the restraints of strict meter and rhyme. He did not, as some suppose, rid himself entirely of them. And yet they seemed to him not fit for his purpose, or to be such a hindrance if bound to them as would defeat his purpose.

> "No dainty rhymes or sentimental love verses
>   for you terrible year,
> Not you as some pale poetling seated at a
>   desk lisping cadenzas piano."

> "Did you ask dulcet rhymes from me?
> Did you seek the civilian's peaceful and
>   languishing rhymes?"

"The conceits of the poets of other lands I'd
    bring thee not,
Nor the compliments that have served their
    turn so long,
Nor rhyme, nor the classics, nor perfume of
    foreign court or indoor library."

Prose for Poetry.

"In my opinion," he said, "the time has arrived to essentially break down the barriers of form between prose and poetry. I say the latter is henceforth to win and maintain its character regardless of rhyme, and the measurement-rules of iambic, spondee, dactyl, etc., and even if rhyme and those measurements continue to furnish the medium for inferior writers and themes, (especially for persiflage and the comic, as there seems henceforward, to the perfect taste, something inevitably comic in rhyme, merely in itself, and anyhow,) the truest and greatest poetry, while subtly and necessarily rhythmic, and distinguishable easily enough,) can never again, in the English language, be expressed in arbitrary and rhyming metre, any more than the greatest eloquence, or the truest power and passion. While admitting that the venerable and heavenly forms of chiming versification have in their time played great and fitting parts ... it is, notwithstanding, certain to me, that the day of such conventional rhyme is ended."

In Whitman's view, then, it would not be a sound criticism, as Deutsch objects, that "occasionally his free cadences are nearer prose than verse." He did think poetry easily distinguishable. But no sharp line should be drawn between poetry and prose. The same thought or sentiment could be expressed in either. The time had passed for slavish adherence to fixed patterns of rhyme and meter in poetry.

Burroughs wrote to Whitman: "Any form is good if it holds good poetry. . . . If a man excels in prose, he is pretty sure to use prose." Whitman wrote in both. Probably most of us would agree that his poetic style is better than his prose style. His prose is too involved, too parenthetical, too long and cumbersome in its sentences, to be easy reading. Yet frequently he wrote the idea first in prose and later restated it in poetry. For example, the 1855 Preface passed into many of his later poems. It was probably easier for him in the first instance to give a prose than a poetic expression to his thought.

Professor Corson spoke to him of "impassioned prose, which I feel will be the poetic form of the future, and of which, I think, your *Leaves of Grass* is the most marked prophecy." Probably Whitman did not disagree with that criticism. Long thinks "Whitman should first be read in his prose works." But I see no point in that. Whitman's transposition of his prose (notably his Prefaces) to poetry, and then leaving that prose out of later editions, is evidence that he preferred the poetry.

De la Mare has attempted to give some light on the question of prose in poetry. He approved Wordsworth's dictum that prose is the language of science. Poetry is for imaginative speech. William Blake made the same distinction. Cardinal Newman excluded scientific prose from literature which is the expression of personal feeling. Coleridge distinguished poetry as having pleasure, not truth, for its immediate objective, to which Wilson objects that that describes also literary prose and is not a proper criterion for demarking prose and poetry.

The history of the distinction between poetry and prose may justify Whitman's contention for assimilating them. Poetry is older than prose. Solon's political ideas were written in verse. Hesiod's *Work and Days,* his *Shepherd's Calendar,* and his *Theogony,* although didactic in subject matter, are versified. According to Pliny, Pherecydes of

Syros, a disciple of Pythagoras, was the inventor of prose writing. Aristotle tried to distinguish the two.

The distinction in English begins as late as about 1550 A.D., but it remained for Milton about 1661 to insist upon a fundamental difference between poetry and prose. Our dictionaries usually distinguish poetry from prose by its metrical structure. Dr. Johnson regarded the verse of Pope as poetry. Not until Coleridge was such didactic poetry questioned. Apropos Coleridge's narrow definition, it may be noted that Shakespeare departed from his blank verse form to express the apostrophe concerning man: "What a piece of work is a man!" That sentiment is emotional literature but not in any recognized poetical form. In his great tragedies and elsewhere Shakespeare felt free to pass from poetry to prose and who can deny that the prose passages are often great literature?

In the light of this history Whitman's experiments should not be regarded as revolutionary innovations, so far as their form approximates prose by lack of rhyme or verse form on the one hand, or their variance from the paragraphing method usual in our modern prose, on the other hand. However, there is form in Whitman's poetry which identifies it and distinguishes it from any customary prose form. Wilson, after discussing the various theories finds it impossible to discover any clear principle for separating prose from poetry, and therefore he would put an end to the controversy whether Pope and Whitman are poets. Certainly the didactic matter of Pope with his heroic couplets, for which Winters argues as a more inclusive and facile technique, lacks the characteristics set up for standard of true poetry by Coleridge, Poe, Arnold, and Housman.

Max Eastman, finding fault with Whitman's mixture of "so much dead stuff" with the poetry in which he had the highest "gift of conveying realizations," attributes that to Whitman's desire to "tally Nature," to express the big round world, the cosmos. And Gummere admitted that Whitman did at times "break down the barrier between impassioned prose and verse" so as to compel "admiration from the most inveterate metrist."

But the conservative temper of Canby clings to the older formula that poetry is imagination lifted to the heights of emotion and that even the best of poets occasionally think and write prosaically in verse. As with that order of traditionalist critics his meaning is obscure. Is imaginative emotional prose poetry? Is oratory poetry? What is peculiar to "poetic emotion"? We are not informed by the oracular authorities.

Whitman, however, made distinction between his prose and his poetry. It was a distinction of form more than of imagination or of emotion. In his work we have the means at hand to observe what was distinctive in his poetry which he did not seek to attain in his prose.

Free Verse.

Whitman has been credited with starting free verse. That significance is not entirely his. That he did give great impetus to that experimentation is unquestionable. But critics who accord to free verse an important place in poetic art are not always willing to acknowledge that Whitman was a great master of it. There is much criticism of his art. Thus Canby remarks that Whitman's "bad reputation for formlessness" is due to "the rambling free verse" in some of his long poems.

But Canby thinks that Whitman compensated in another way for that fault, namely, by a unity of style, and that the free verse writer like the writer of prose especially requires such safeguard. More than one critic seems aware of handicaps under which the writing of free verse labors. It is not a form in which any novice can succeed. The hazards of it are greater, so they say, than with regular verse forms.

For one thing free verse puts a greater burden on the memory, and that is advanced as the reason why Whitman could not memorize, quote or repeat his own poetry. It suffers like prose from less hypnotic effect upon the listener.

On the other hand, free verse has some distinct advantages. As compared with prose, it is freer to employ repetition, measured rhythm, line units, and symmetrical balance of thought and form, which it has somewhat in common with traditional poetry. But its less restrictedness of form enables it to use the resources of both poetry and prose with a widened range of expression not so fully available to either before its advent.

Undoubtedly it was the discovery of the greater facilities of free verse for expression that led Whitman to adopt and develop it to a greater extent than anyone had done before. But did he obviate all its perils? Did it betray him into the vice of commonplace thinking by its easy-going forms? It is urged that the fixed forms of traditional poetry provide a stimulus to invention by the difficulties they impose. The long lists of things to which much objection has been made of Whitman's poems can be argued both ways according to one's feeling. However, if I have succeeded, as I believe, in proving that Whitman among poets was exceptionally profound in philosophic thought, then it may be that free verse was more aid than hindrance to him.

Whitman was not the first to use free verse forms, although his was the triumph of winning definite recognition of it as a mode of poetry, and therefore he has that historical significance. Although before him there was recognized English poetry without rhyme or meter, his innovation in part was that of discarding both. Older poets had occasionally written without one or the other.

Indeed, from long ago meter has been regarded as non-essential to poetry. Aristotle established that point. Wordsworth, Coleridge, Shelley, and Emerson admitted it without putting it in practice. Cowley and Dryden wrote a "formless" ode, irregular in stanzaic form, length of line, and meter, mixing trochaic, iambic and anapestic feet as freely as Whitman did. Although it originated as a misunderstanding of the Pindaric ode, it survived, and not only Dryden's *Alexander's Feast,* but also Coleridge's *Kubla Khan,* Arnold's *Dover Beach,* and Tennyson's *Ode on the Death of the Duke of Wellington* are examples of it.

Prevalent as rhyme is in modern poetry, it was not used in classic Greek, Latin and Hebrew poetry. Hebrew poetry as translated in our English Bible is also rhymeless. It is generally supposed that Whitman drew his principal inspiration from that Bible; we will consider that later. Not only blank verse but other verse forms without rhyme were frequent in Anglo-American literature before Whitman wrote. The choruses in Milton's *Samson Agonistes* and Shelley's *Queen Mab* and Matthew Arnold's unrhymed poems in iambic meter differ from Whitman's verse but show tendencies which preceded him.

One English poet, William Blake, not only wrote free verse before Whitman was born, but also stated the theory of it. He said in explanation of his escape from the bondage of meter and rhyme: "I therefore produced a variety in every line, both of cadences and number of syllables." But Blake was a neglected poet until the Twentieth Century. Whitman borrowed nothing from him.

Among the critics who are unwilling to credit Whitman as the great exemplar and popularizer of free verse is Yvor Winters, who rates Whitman as only a second-class poet. He thinks Hart Crane is a finer poet whose faults are more obvious because he is more definite and precise in use of language. Winters remarks upon Ezra Pound's employment of Whitman's structure, line, and progressive images, but accords to Pound a skill, suavity and beauty declared to be lacking in Whitman. Although such criticism is evidently prejudice, one cannot dispute the formal mastery of Pound's artistry, and Pound's imitation of Whitman's free verse is a tribute to Whitman's originality and craftsmanship. There is little or nothing in common between Whitman and Pound either in spirit or ideas, and these polar differences between them may raise the question whether free verse is distinctively a democratic technique.

Another type of criticism takes Whitman to task because he did not, like most of his predecessors and successors who experimented with free verse, also use other forms or a wider range of style of free verse. Thus comparison is made with Emily Dickinson who disliked Whitman's poetry. But however much she flouted traditional ideas, rhyme and meter characterize her verse and that renders comparison more or less futile. But Whitman did not wholly discard rhyme and meter. It is an exaggeration of Whitman's theories to interpret him as confining New World poetry to the particular forms he adopted for himself.

An attempt is also made to distinguish vers libre from Whitman's free verse, which treats Whitman's style as merely "rhythmical prose," "impassioned prose," "spaced prose," or 'polyphonic prose," and "the Whitmanic chant." Vers libre professed a French origin, but that too imitated Whitman. What mainly distinguishes the later poets of free verse is their larger liberties for intermingling all verse forms.

Wilson, commenting on the post-Whitmanic development of free verse, which has been influenced also by the broken and sprung rhythms of Gerard Manley Hopkins, observes as to the effect of this intermingling of styles some results which are doubtfully an improvement. There is a lessening or neglect of stress or of verse beat, which produces a comic effect even in seriously intended poetry. Sharpness and energy notable in Hopkins and not wanting in Whitman, have disappeared, and instead there is a feeling of demoralization and weariness. He cites the rhythms of MacNeice and Auden to instance his criticism.

One is reminded of Winter's effort to state such tendency as a general law, both moral and metrical: Complexity and emphasis stand to each other in inverse ratio; as one increases the other decreases. He describes traditional poetry as very complex by reason of its endeavor to make a nice adjustment or balance between feeling and motive. Would it not follow then that morality gets lax in our traditional poetry?

We may also recall that Wilder, notwithstanding his leaning toward tradition, remarks that the present advance in moral sensitiveness is not in the traditional religions but at their edges or quite outside of them, and notably in the new poetry and fiction. Rather inconsistently that fact provides him with a text for preaching to the traditionalist poets that they restore the people to the old faiths and the traditional religion to its lost place of moral leadership. But Winters' law gives a reason why there must always be a moral lag in tradition. Tradition carries the burden of complexity. It is straining too much for harmony between the motives it carries over from the past which are no longer relevant to contemporary emotional impulses.

It was mainly his consciousness of the breakdown of tradition and of need for a new and simpler formula of human conduct which led Whitman to his quest for a new mode of literary expression. He returned from traditional religion and literature, not to Rousseau's simplicity of return to Nature, but to science; to humanistic, not physical science only.

Free verse in Whitman's sense admitted of no such excess as it signifies to those who practice it as a license to write in any manner whatsoever. He was severely restrained in his manner and had a definite idea of his objective as well as a style of expression which he deemed fit for the vehicle of his message. It was preciseness of motive linked to feeling which he sought to attain. But neither his motives nor his feelings were traditional. He struck out in new directions. One may be and necessarily is less precise and accurate when exploring new areas of motive and feeling than when following old and well trodden paths of conduct. The proper criticism of Whitman should be whether he mapped out the way sufficiently to enable others following him to find the path? Did he establish a new and better tradition?

In Whitman's free verse is combined the great flexibility and preciseness of prose with the lift and flight of fancy which is the body of poetry. There was a moral order in him at the same time that he escaped the narrowly prescribed modes of conduct which suppress truth and healthful emotions. To what extent, if any, did his writing of free verse enable him to achieve that excellence of a new path of conduct which is handed on to us as the Whitman tradition? It is our problem to discover if Whitman's method of free verse really aided his objectives.

Rhymes.

Although Whitman had declared that henceforth rhyme and meter would be confined or restricted to "light verse" or the inferior realm of "persiflage and the comic", even he did not conform strictly to that prophecy. As pointed out by Allen and others, even in the First Edition of *Leaves of Grass* there were stanzas composed on a rhyme pattern. Such are the first sections in the poems, *Song of the Broad-Axe* and *By Blue Ontario's Shore*. The rhyme scheme is carried throughout a few poems, such as *O Captain! My Captain, Ethiopia Saluting the Colors,* and the song of *The Singer in the Prison*.

In Canby's view Whitman went rhyming whenever he needed it to keep his "sprawling" poem from falling to pieces. Not always end rhymes, but assonances, especially repetitions of the first word in the line. Were there any devices of poetry he did not sometimes use? Possibly Whitman had a better understanding of the use of rhyme than have his traditionalist critics. For as early as the 1855 Preface he said: "The profit of rhyme is that it drops seeds of a sweeter and more luxuriant rhyme, and of uniformity that it conveys itself into its own roots in the ground out of sight." As the remainder of that passage indicates, he knew how to distinguish that utility of rhyme from the common tawdriness and inflexibility of its use, which he eschewed. May it not argue a finer sense in him that he preferred rhyme to be less obvious and mechanical than it had customarily been?

It was an understanding plea that Burroughs made for Whitman's rhyming methods: "Why not allow or even welcome the freedom of half rhymes, or suggestive rhymes?" This is a more correct intimation of Whitman's poetic style than to point to his rhymes as conventional. He broke with the conventions which laid down fixed laws of rhyme, as Shakespeare defied the laws of classic drama with its three invariable unities. As Shakespeare gained in breadth and potency by departing from those conventions, hardly less of a boon was conferred on verse by Whitman who freed it from inflexible forms.

The Stanza.

Metrical stanzas are also not infrequent in *Leaves of Grass*. The variety of them may be seen in the following: *Song of Myself*, section 11, (couplets) ; *Darest Thou Now O Soul* (three lines) ; *Old War Dreams* (three lines and refrain) ; *Gods* (three lines) ; *Ethiopia Saluting the Colors* (three lines) ; *Eidolons* (four lines) ; *Pioneers! O Pioneers!* (four lines) ; song of *The Singer in Prison* (four lines in rhymed couplets) ; the song in section 14 of *When Lilacs Last in the Dooryard Bloom'd* (four lines) ; *Dirge for Two Veterans* (four lines) ; *A Noiseless Patient Spider* (five lines) ; first section of *Song of the Broad-Axe* (six lines in rhymed couplets) ; first section of *By Blue Ontario's Shore* (six lines in rhymed couplets) ; *In Cabin'd Ships at Sea* (eight lines) ; *O Captain! My Captain!* (eight lines, the first four in rhymed couplets, and the last four with second and fourth lines rhymed) ; *For You O Democracy* (five lines and four lines with two line refrain in each, and ending with couplet or parallel verse).

However, one would not expect from Whitman any considerable illustration of traditional stanzaic form. He did not strive to conform to any standard pattern. As Selincourt observes, he frequently used lines of a conventional pattern of meter in stanzas completely free in form, that is, of no recognized or patterned type of stanza.

Meter.

Although Selincourt thinks that Whitman's rejection of meter was due to his inexperience with it, yet he makes admission that Whitman's most powerful poems in meter owe their strength to disregard of established rules. This self-contradictory statement is somewhat comprehensible in the light of Winters' general law which we have discussed above. We found the logic of that law leads to different conclusions than put upon it by Winters. And now we argue from it that the advantage Whitman gained in his free verse by releasing it from fixed metric form was in emphasis and simplicity, at the same time that, contrary to Winters' law, he was enabled to give his poetry a content of thought more profound and complex than contained in the poetry of traditional mould. Whitman's effort to give emphasis to his thought, making the form a mere vehicle of that thought, and his effort to attain simplicity and directness distinguishes his poetry both from his predecessors and his successors who have labored ornament, subtlety, and what Winters calls "pseudo-reference" to the point of obscurity in their thought, if they have any.

As to those who think it a fault in Whitman that he disdained meter, they should be reminded of the opinion of their magisterial authority, Coleridge, who regarded meter as "An artificial arrangement . . . not the peculiar property of poetry." Although Selincourt says that Whitman's inexpertness in poetic technique caused his abandonment of meter, yet he excuses Whitman on the ground of his special needs and objectives for a different art. As the argument goes, Whitman did not appreciate the more subtle forms such as Milton used. Therefore, he had to adopt his forms, forms which his limited ability could use as fit for his purpose. It is an argument of compensation (perhaps unconsciously in Whitman) for his inherent short-comings.

Why not give some attention to Whitman's own version of his reason for abandoning the authoritative principles of rhyme and meter? It surely should not be forgotten that Whitman had long been practicing rhyme and meter before he finally decided for his free verse forms. Granted that he never attained the mastery of a Milton—that is a very great scholarly height, perhaps reserved for Ezra Pound. Whitman admitted, without affecting his doctrine, "that there have been very illustrious poets whose shapes the mantle of such verse has beautifully and appropriately envelopt—and though the mantle has fallen, with perhaps added beauty, on some of our own age—", elsewhere he mentions as such Longfellow, Tennyson, and others—, yet he maintained that the perfect taste and subtlest sense cannot be bound by such rhythmical and metered verse. Was he right? The richness of American poetry in the Twentieth century which consciously proclaimed Whitman as master and guide or without acknowledgment has followed his example, tends to sustain his opinion.

Is Whitman Verse Bound or Free?

Selincourt raises yet another question by his objection to the rhyming and metrical tendency in poems like *When Lilacs Last in the Dooryard Bloom'd*, as lapses from Whitman's own principles. Is not such criticism a misunderstanding of Whitman's principles and purpose? Did Whitman intend that the poets who came after him should wholly abandon rhyme and meter? On the contrary, his own free use of them shows what he meant. To make a scholasticism of Whitman's style or particular method would be a perversion of his principles. In his technique of verse as in his philosophy freedom is the high note.

As he felt free to transpose prose to verse and thus break down the barriers between poetry and prose, no less did he feel free to use meter and rhyme in his poetry. It is crotchety criticism which takes Whitman to task for not abiding with a dogmatic position, which would reject his most traditionally formed poem, *O Captain! My Captain!*, as not characteristically Whitmanian. The very essence of Whitmanism is to choose whatever form or style may fit the mood and the purpose intended. Whitman did not exhaust the possibilities of his method, and the limitations of his practice do not constitute a barrier to any experimental efforts of poets who follow in the Whitmanian tradition. Indeed, they are nearest to Whitman who are guided as to form not by any set of traditions but by seeking that mode of expression which may serve the best to embody the objectives of human good for each and all. For Whitman made the human aim the test of any and all technique.

Canby too thinks that Whitman did not have the skill and ability to pour his thought into the mould of the old verse forms as others had successfully done. Yet he points out that Whitman at 22 was writing for periodicals equivalent to The Atlantic Monthly and The Century in the 1890's, poems which, according to Bliss Perry, were comparable to the average productions of Lowell, Willis, and Whittier at that time, and Canby admits that was success. Why then did Whitman when he was "getting on" abandon the traditional forms and undertake the much more difficult and uncharted task of creating a form and technique peculiarly his own? Why, if he did not think he was achieving a finer art? Were his critical prefaces sincere? The fact is that in spite of the scholastic critics Whitman by general acclaim is now ranked America's foremost writer. At last his own judgment of the superiority of his art has been justified. Only in their wonted tardiness of judgment the critics have not yet caught up to our time. They lag behind the people in whom Whitman like Jefferson confidently believed.

It is something though that the carping critics have been compelled to join the people's chorus and are now trying to find out belatedly what it is in Whitman that has so greatly succeeded. Is it his ideas? Or is it his art? Or is it both? Somewhat more generously than most Canby attributes Whitman's greatness to his humanity which he symbolized in himself. He thinks him not artless though deficient in art, not without ideas though vaguely grasping them as a prophet must.

If our analysis is correct, Whitman's ideas were consistent and remarkably in advance of the most reputed thinkers of his time. We have yet further to explore his art. Although we have criticized the critics, those of Whitman's time who wholly rejected him and those of our time who judge Whitman not by the standards of the new poetry but by the traditional techniques, yet the critics of today have arrived at considerable understanding of Whitman's techniques and everyone now should be able to see him as a great original artist. His techniques are probably more understandable to us than they were to himself. Beside free use of rhyme, meter and stanza, he had other significant techniques that distinguish his verse.

14

WHITMAN'S POETIC TECHNIQUES.

❖　❖　❖　❖　❖　❖

"As Life and Nature are not great with refer-
　　ence to the present only,
But greater still from what is yet to come,
Out of that formula for thee I sing."

"I have not so much emulated the birds that
　　musically sing,
I have abandoned myself to flights, broad
　　circles.

❖　❖　❖　❖　❖　❖

I have felt to soar in freedom and in the full-
　　ness of power, joy, volition."

❖　❖　❖　❖　❖　❖

Rhythm.

WHITMAN DID NOT EXPEND HIMSELF IN NEGATIONS. HIS ART
was not expressed in rejection of rhyme and meter. He had
a definite sense of form. His poetic technique was positive
and clear. He emphasized the importance of rhythm.

　　Did Whitman's rhythmic style distinguish him as did
his free use of rhyme and meter? In the poems, *Thou
Mother with thy Equal Brood,* and *To Soar in Freedom
and in Fullness of Power,* metaphorically he distinguishes

317

his poetry from the music of the song birds and likens it to
the rhythm of the powerful circling flight of the great birds:

> "As a strong bird on pinions free,
> Joyous, the amplest spaces heavenward cleav-
>   ing,
> Such be the thought I'd think of thee
>   America,
> Such the recitative I'd bring for thee."

Of the other similes he used they always predicated
largeness of movement, as the swell and roll of the ocean
wave.

It has been remarked that as the poet of democracy he
did not work much of the speech of the common people
into his poetry. Says Canby, he did not take his rhythms
and idiom from everyday speech as did Robert Frost. But
he did use words of common speech that seemed to his contemporaries inelegant and inappropriate to poetry. And is
it remarkable that his poetic style did not carry the rhythms
of his conversational manner, his letters, or his editorial
prose, as Canby also comments? Canby's conclusion that
his poetic rhythms are those of the English Bible is only
partially true.

In the first place, Whitman's fondness for trochaic movement distinguishes his poetry from the prevalent iambic
movement of the English Bible, English poetry and English
speech. In this respect English differs from classic Latin,
French and Anglo-Saxon verse, in which the trochee pre-
dominated. More than 90 per cent of modern English poetry is iambic. This has come about through organic changes
in our language. Our typical phrase which begins with an
article, preposition, or conjunction, merging into the word
that follows it, gives the rising inflection of the iambic
movement. Another influence has been the dropping of
suffixes and grammatical endings that characterize other

European languages. Other grammatical peculiarities are the placing of the weaker adjective before the emphatic noun and the weaker auxiliary before the stronger verb which tend to iambic stress.

Whitman is unusual therefore in his preference for trochaic and dactyllic rhythm. Why did he thus depart from customary usage? Canby conjectures that it may have been his obstinate desire for novelty, or (and I think this is much more likely) it was because trochaic verse is more emphatic, more in the oratorical style that Whitman fancied. Other advantages may also have weighed with him, for the trochee is a more sprightly and rapid rhythm than the iambic.

Another characteristic of Whitman's verse is a longer line than customary in the poetry that preceded him. At present we consider only the effect of the long line upon rhythm, the general relation of it to Whitman's art being discussed later. A longer line makes the trochee less distinctive unless it is emphasized by phrasing. Whitman was adept in phrasing, not as regular as supposed by Canby, for the patterns are many. Not so often a line of seven stresses balanced about a shifting caesura as to make one think of that as Whitman's style; as often some other number of stresses; and very often three major pauses in the line. And most frequently of all the racing recitative is an impressive feature of Whitman's rhythm.

The complexity of rhythm is comparable to that of speech. Whitman freed himself from fixed patterns of rhyme and meter in order to attain a rhythm more responsive to expression of feeling. But I cannot believe as Selincourt does that in his poetry rhythm and feeling change together. It is demonstrable that even in the most rigid pattern of old verse a considerable range of feeling may be expressed in the same unvaried form. For feeling is evoked by associations which much exceed the quantitative measurements of rhythm. Rhythm therefore cannot aspire to be an immediate and exact expression of feeling. Yet it must be acknowledged that Whitman enhanced rhythm in poetry by freeing it from set patterns.

A given rhythm does not produce the same emotional effects in all persons. For different persons are affected differently by the same rhythm. Thus Snyder shows that Whitman's hypnotic influence which is quite definite is lost on some persons. Just as some people feel more pleasure in listening to the irregular beat of the incoming waves on the ocean beach than to the ticking of a clock, Whitman's irregular rhythm may be more pleasing to those who tire of the sing-song, tick-tick of old-fashioned verse.

Of the four orders of rhythm noted by de la Mare: rising, falling, waved, and level; from Snyder's analysis we may conclude that Whitman's verse is not easily classifiable as any one, for he speaks of the "repetition of a rising and falling pitch pattern." Certainly Whitman's chant is an example of level rhythm, and Snyder's ascription of the hypnotic spell of Whitman is to its wave-like rhythm. Here as elsewhere Whitman presents variety. In another classification de la Mare refers to such varieties of rhythm as "archetectonic, lineal, sectional, periodic, undulent, and numeral," probably all of which may be illustrated in Whitman's verse.

Allen places emphasis upon the parallelism in Whitman's verse which is "both structure and rhythm." He also describes Whitman's reiterative devices as rhythms and includes "thought rhythm" as well as sound or "phonic rhythm", and thus broadens considerably the conception of rhythm. The thought rhythms he connects with the supposed principle of organic rhythms, or as Selincourt terms it, "an identity of substance". But this, Allen points out, is not acceptable to Sculley Bradley, who urges instead that Whitman does have also "identity of pattern" as well as organic rhythm and a unified organic whole. However, what Bradley's analysis of such a poem as *Tears* proves is not identity of pattern but variety in line length, of stresses, including what he calls "hovering stresses", and notably three, more or less, caesuras in a line. Although not quite agreeing with Bradley's theory it leads Allen to say: "Bradley's reading of the lines with hovering stresses also indicates that Whitman had a keener ear for sound and cadence than has been commonly supposed."

To carry out his theory of the organic rhythm, formed from within, Allen instances Whitman's tendency to parenthesis and his careful punctuation. The analogies of ocean wave, operatic chant, and oratorical sweep, which Matthiessen and others use to describe Whitman's rhythm, may argue something else than organicism, even an objective origin of it. But Mary Austin undertakes to give a psychological rendering of the Whitmanian rhythm. With the aid of McDougall and some acquaintance with the songs and dances of the North American Indians she attempts to discover the elemental source in the American environment which Whitman sought and which she thinks Sandburg, Lindsay and Sherwood Anderson have sometimes succeeded in achieving.

As she interprets McDougall's psychology, all rhythm starts in motor impulses. Thus it enters sensory experience and becomes subconsciously stored before it is evoked in consciousness. Therefore mere intellectual appreciations of rhythm are insufficient for the making of a poet or a poem. The poet must first have felt the stress or strain of the movement and mode of poetry in his organism. For example such images as "the roll of thunder or the run of wind in the grass" are not intellectual but sensory experiences. But surely these poetic images have something more of meaning in them than the sensory experience of an organic rhythm. Could the subconscious mind be aware of them before they were consciously conceived? How does the subconscious mind know that the sound is the roll of thunder? Or know that what it hears or sees is the run of the wind in the tall grass? We think there must be a conscious intelligence of these things before they become poetic images.

The objection to such a theory of poetic rhythm is the separation of its origin from intellectual appreciation. Or that a particular form or rhythm is inseparably joined to a particular type or mode of thought. The relationship is different from that. It is not proof of the origin and development of poetry in the subconscious mind that in composing the poet discovers in himself unexpected resources of rhythm that appear to outrun his thought. It is marvellous indeed what any skill attains with an ease that exceeds thought. But in learning of a skill there is a slowness and hesitancy that limps far behind thought at the beginning and only surpasses thought when learned. For how could there be discoveries in ourselves of "treasures of swinging thought" if these had not become a subconscious habit which means that they had been previously thought and so stored away for rediscovery by consciousness?

Miss Austin is right about the eventuality: The true evocation of poetic images in consciousness "is from the autonomic centers of experience." But the experience was not merely autonomic. Nor if intellectual processes have nothing to do with the evocation of the experiences would there be any poets. There is no denying that there is rhythm in Nature and in our experiences. When does it pass into poetic rhythm? Not until it reaches the stage of creative consciousness. The full-grown poet has undoubtedly great resources of subconscious skill stored within himself, but in a given poetic composition he is a highly charged intelligence of immediate consciousness, aware of his task and aware of his aim and with ripe knowledge of the poetic instrumentalities he uses.

Miss Austin idealizes the Amerind poet as the true source of the inherent American rhythm of democracy. As a true poet he aims at affectiveness, not effectiveness; or, as

the ethnologist interprets it, the Amerind poetizes for purposes of sorcery. To her he coordinates his dance steps "by
mimesis", which she relates to Aristotle's principle of "imitation"; but again to the ethnologist this means that the
Amerind symbolizes in his dance the hunter stalking the
deer. To her mystical mind the Amerind has a capacity
and skill of coordination which gathers in his conception
of "Allness" as the Great Spirit.

She thinks that Amerind spirit inspired Whitman but
that his limited intelligence was so "adolescent and gambol-
ing" that he could not respond fully either to the Amerind's coordination in poetry and dance or to his universality of religion. Only such a mystic could probably assume
such a premise for such a conclusion. Whitman did not attempt to imitate the primitive as did Lindsay, nor to express experience in the raw as Sandburg and Anderson have
done. His thought rhythm is of a different kind. It is
philosophic and epical.

If she has correctly stated the rhythmic essentials of
Amerind verse, towit: "internal rhythms, coordinated by
the prevailing motor habit; external rhythms subjectively
coordinated; realization by means of creative mimesis";
then Whitman's verse is at nearly an opposite pole. It is not
markedly mimetic, and it is not coordinated by the prevailing motor habit. His rhythm is not regulated by the heavy
beat of a primitive drum, and his individualistic democracy
does not hark back to the tribal monotony of the Amerind.

Words.

Words had not for Whitman primarily either rhyming
or rhythmical significance, although he did not ignore such
values. Selincourt is probably half mistaken in his opposition to the prosodists who attempt to classify English words
and syllables quantitatively as long and short, and in his
further contention that there is no inherent rhythm in

words. They do have in English a dominant iambic rhythm, and one who, as Whitman, used the trochee so persistently could not fail to take some quantitative measurement of words.

But the meaningfulness of words held his chief interest. For fullness, expressiveness and expansiveness of meaning, not for decoration, he valued them most. Canby absolves him from eccentricity in their use, and acknowledges him a master in the craft of words. He took freedom in their use, not scorning the vernacular, but appropriating any word that served his purpose. For him there was no aristocracy of words, no special poetic language. He did not abstain from neologisms. He adopted French and Spanish words especially with no strict concern about their meaning or spelling. He mixed words indiscriminately together.

Allen contends that he had a rather definite "organic theory of words" which was Emersonian. Leave off the word "organic" and that is true. Canby calls attention to Whitman's essay entitled *An American Primer* which he speaks of as an "important critical contribution" to what has since been called "the science of semantics".

Whitman had almost a worshipful sense of the significance and power of words. He could not have such contempt and scorn for them as the wordy Shakespeare who almost always mentioned them disparagingly. Whitman thought they spring from character: "Words follow character." They are not merely printed symbols. They are not circumscribed by what is spoken. They have meanings beyond themselves. He seeks for the cosmic meanings of words. But again we discern the spirit of freedom which is dominant in Whitman: he is no slave of words:

> "I swear I begin to see little or nothing in
>   audible words,
>   All merges toward the presentation of the
>   unspoken meanings of the earth,

> Toward him who sings the songs of the body
> and of the truths of the earth,
> Toward him who makes the dictionaries of
> words that print cannot touch."

His meticulous attention to words is the exceptional disposition in him to strive for completeness of meaning. Inclusiveness is one of his major aims. It accounts for many of his peculiarities which have caused so much objection to his art.

Parentheses.

This desire, or obsession, of Whitman to include everything also addicted him to the use of parentheses. It is a recurring feature of his technique from first to last and few poems of any length are free from it.

Commas, dashes, parentheses, in such abundance seem queer characteristics for a man of self-assurance. It is no doubt appropriate to interpret them as does Selincourt of the poem, *As I Lay with my Head in your Lap Camerado*, that "Only passion can afford to take gradations, to admit its doubts." Only supreme confidence in one's self dares to be parenthetical.

Various interpretations are made of his intentions concerning them. Allen brings together a number of these, such as Catel's theory that they are a kind of stage direction, or "aside" of the over-all actor, Whitman himself, to the reader. They break monotony and give variety. Often, not always, they indicate a break or change in the rhythm. Matthiessen, who is not too ready to see Whitman's excellences, praises his parentheses as evidencing Whitman's understanding of the need for a check on romantic excesses.

In Whitman's prose the piling up of parenthetical expressions to introduce additional qualifying ideas and to make the thought more exact and inclusive, often confuses the reader more than it aids understanding. In his poetry

326 WALT WHITMAN: THINKER AND ARTIST

Whitman was usually more successful and there the parenthesis frequently gives a dramatic touch in the change of
personality speaking, or a familiar presence of himself, an
interpreter off stage to the piece.

Catalogues.

Whitman's cataloguing, which Emerson described to
Carlyle as "an auctioneer's inventory of a warehouse", is
another example of Whitman's expansiveness which subjected his work to considerable criticism. John Cowper
Powys likened those catalogues to the Biblical lists of kings,
priests and tribes and to Homer's list of the Greek ships,
which would give them a literary status. Long finds fault
with Whitman because he reduced even "God to details".
Allen reads into these an intention pantheistically to unite
himself with the universe. But Whitman differently and
impatiently exclaimed: "Oh God! how tired I get of hearing that said about the 'catalogues'! I resolved at the start
to diagnose, recognize, state, the case of the mechanics,
laborers, artizans, give America—to get into the stream with
them—give them a voice in literature."

Despite criticism he never ceased using them, from *Song
of Myself* to *"The Rounded Catalogue Divine Complete"*
of *Good-Bye My Fancy*. Unquestionably those catalogues
do give increased descriptive power to the poems, and are
notable and unique also in his prose. They were an additional technique to serve his purpose.

Recitatives and Music.

Of a similar sort and important too are his recitatives.
These are one of Whitman's techniques which make his
poetry more nearly allied to music than is traditional English verse.

Whitman often speaks of his poems as chants. He

thought of the chant as peculiarly the mood of his poetry and of himself as in that frame of mind when he composed poetry. Like the chant each line or part divided by caesuras was to be recited in a single breath. He was fond of the Italian opera and in the years of his newspaper editorship he was a regular attendant at performances. The influence upon his poetry of passion for that music is remarkable, it sets him apart from the older poets.

The recitative is especially appropriate to express his aspiration for large movements. As the chant developed from the need to adapt music to a prose text, so in Whitman's effort to remove the separation of poetry from prose it provided an example to illustrate his theory.

Repetition and Music.

Repetition is also a characteristic of musical expression which entered into Whitman's poetry. The poem, *Crossing Brooklyn Ferry*, is a good example of repetition of words, phrases, and themes as Whitman's instrument for obtaining poetic exaltation.

In that poem also is illustrated the trochaic accent which is a notable feature of music. The recitative, frequently broken by three or more caesuras to the line are there, too. Several successive lines beginning with repetition of the same word likewise make the poem typical of his usual style. Selincourt remarks that Whitman was more disposed than other writers to treat words and phrases like notes of music.

But Selincourt's reason for repetition as a technique does not quite strike the point that is true but may suggest it. What distinguishes art from Nature mainly is that Nature never returns to, never reproduces an experience, but art does. The very essence of a work of art is that it enables us to repeat an experience, to live it over again, to feel again the emotions that the original experience called forth.

Lyrical Poetry and Music.

Repetition is especially notable in lyrical poetry. Andrews in a chapter on melody or tone-color emphasizes this characteristic. In the old verse forms of the lyric the refrain line is one of the most frequent devices used. Lyrical poetry is usually defined as the kind of verse which can be set to music. Of Whitman's poems a few are of that typical song form.

But the chant is much more common in *Leaves of Grass* than stanzaic verse. Is Whitman therefore to be classified as less a lyric poet? less songful than the writers of customary old verse? Is he less melodious? less tuneful? because he chanted.

Burroughs was in accordance with the distinction made by the ancient Greeks, at least partially, when he spoke of Whitman's poetry as lyrical, because it is "a personal and individual utterance." The Greeks distinguished the song, melos, as the utterance of a single poet, from the chorus which was chanted. Again it appears that Whitman mixed traditions. He made the chant a medium of individual expression. He broke down the ancient distinction.

Chant or lyric, his poetry sings. Sings in a different way from most of the poetry before, contemporaneous, and after him. Meaning was so important for him that he needed the freer form of the chant. Igor Stravinsky dogmatically declares against regarding as music the song which attempts to give definite expression of meaning. That poetry would then be nearest music which, like Swinburne's gives more attention to sound than to sense. Upon such a criterion also Stravinsky appears to rate down Beethoven's and Wagner's music. If one has some meaning to convey in poetry, he will probably do as Whitman did, even to the sacrifice of song. Should he then resort rather to prose expression?

Whitman's transference of his prose to poetry showed his preference for the latter. He cultivated not only the grand style of the orator and often the beautiful style of poetry, but also in his universalizing tendency he had to include everything. The recitatives, repetitions and catalogues aided him to do this, and as poetry is freer in the use of such devices than is prose, he found poetry the apter expression for his purposes. And his purpose, as he thought, justified him:

"The basis and body and genesis of the Leaves differing from Emerson and many grandest poets and artists was and is that I found and find everything in the *common concrete,* the broadest materials, the flesh, the common passions, the tangible and visible, etc., and in the average, and that I radiate, work from, these outward—or rather hardly wish to leave here but to remain and celebrate all."

De la Mare makes the point that poetry is not merely sensuous sound but also conveys meaning, as does also music to some extent. But the notation of poetry is by words, not notes. The silent reading of poetry has changed its character somewhat. Early poetry was meant only to be heard and audible sound had therefore more significance for it than legible poetry which may be addressed to the mind more than to the ear. Whitman tried his verse by the ear, but he made that test subordinate to the meaning he intended to impart.

Music too had meaning for Whitman, a meaning behind the sounds as he attributed meanings to words beyond themselves.

"Yet strangely even here, meanings unknown
    before,
Subtler than ever, more harmony, as if born
    here, related here,

Not to the city's fresco'd rooms, not to the
    audience of the opera house,
Sounds, echoes, wandering strains,

❖ ❖ ❖ ❖ ❖ ❖

Ray'd in the limpid yellow slanting sun-
    down,
Music, Italian music in Dakota."

As in *Proud Music of the Storm,* it is music for the soul:
"Ah from a little child,
Thou knowest soul how to me all sounds
    became music,
My mother's voice in lullaby or hymn,

❖ ❖ ❖ ❖ ❖ ❖

The rain, the growing corn, the breeze
    among the long-leav'd corn,
The measured sea-surf beating on the sand,
The twittering bird, the hawk's sharp
    scream,

❖ ❖ ❖ ❖ ❖ ❖

The fiddler in the tavern, the glee, the long-
    strung sailor-song,
The lowing cattle, bleating sheep, the crow-
    ing cock at dawn."

But what he heard was more than all of that, more than
the actual sounds of musical notes and musical instruments.
To his soul, to the soul of man, it is

" . . . . a new rhythmus fitted for thee,
Poems bridging the way from Life to Death,
    vaguely wafted in night air, uncaught,
    unwritten,
Which let us go forth in the bold day and
    write."

He had no doubt of the union of poetry and music, and his belief that he wrote songs has been confirmed by composers who have set many of his poems to music.

Parallelism.

Professor Gummere regarded parallelisms as the "social basis of all poetry". Professor Allen ties together all of the special techniques we have described under the general designation of parallelism as the "basic structure" of Whitman's poetry.

Here the question is raised again, How much did Whitman borrow from the English translation of the Bible? Parallelism is typical of ancient Hebrew literature, and that style without its rhythm is reproduced in the English Bible. Is it true that parallelism is characteristic of all poetry, and, if so, is there more of it in Whitman than in other poets? Or, assuming that parallelism is a distinctive mark of Whitman's poetry and also that that Biblical style was familiar to the people and enjoyed by them, why then was appreciation of Whitman so tardy and why did critics attack his style so abusively? It may be that dislike for Whitman's ideas was a more potent cause for rejecting him as poet than anything peculiar to his poetry as such.

These questions may now occupy our attention in the endeavor to ascertain what is unique in Whitman's poetry. Those who try to identify Whitman with older ideas and older techniques are inclined, we think, to make too much of such resemblances as they find. We have maintained that Whitman did not reject tradition outright but used it freely for the purposes of his larger aims. As he was not bound by a particular method of rhyming or meter or rhythm, can we find any other fixity of technique in his style? Is parallelism an exception to his principle of free verse?

What is meant by parallelism, what distinguishes it? Instead of the thought progressively and steadily developing, it doubles back on itself, either for emphasis, or to vary or amplify the thought, before going on. It is something ordinarily like a surging back and forth of the thought. Reiteration or repetition is most characteristic of it, although there are some forms of parallelism of which that is not typical. This repetitive method, which Winters says is the chief method of Whitman, is nearly the opposite of what that critic describes as the progressive method, whether logical, or some other kind of progression, and which in Winters' opinion results in a lax and diffuse style in Whitman's case. Has Winters a prejudice, or is he correct in such criticism?

Dogmatic standards are difficult to maintain realistically in literary criticism, because of the difficulty of categorizing any eminent author by a single style. That is also an objection to classifying Whitman as peculiarly a parallelist. Once we have taken note of the different types of parallelism and of their use by Whitman, we may point out that they are common in other poetry, in Shakespeare for example as well as the Hebrew Bible.

As many as six kinds of parallelism have been distinguished by Hebrew scholars. Of these in the first, called synonymous parallelism, two or more lines express the same fundamental idea in varied form or speech. In antithetical parallelism, the lines express contrasting or contradictory ideas but with similar structure. There is also a synthetic or cumulative or constructive parallelism, in which the thought of the first line is completed or supplemented by the next line or lines. Charles A. Briggs adds a fourth kind, introverted parallelism, which is of so formal a structure that he does not expect to find it in Whitman, for the first and fourth lines and the second and third lines correspond, yet searching may find it as one discovers the unusual regular stanza in Whitman. A fifth, emblematic parallelism, is frequent wherever a simile points a truth. The sixth type shows that progression is not necessarily absent from parallelism; this is climatic or ascending parallelism. Indeed, there is no principle in any of these forms which forbids progression of thought; else there would be no movement forward, but only stagnation, or dull repetition.

Whitman had no knowledge of the Hebrew language, yet his poetry resembles it in style in some respects more than the English version of the Bible. His verse differs from both in accentuation; from the English by greater use of trochee; and from the Hebrew in which the accent falls on the last or next to last syllable, which is impossible to follow regularly in English verse.

A further difference is the frequency of the couplet in the Bible, a two-line unity or distich with anapestic accents. Whitman's couplets do not have such regularity of meter. As Allen remarks the couplet, triplet and quatrain are more frequent in the Bible than in *Leaves of Grass* and less frequent are the long lines of synonymous parallelism and extended catalogues.

Whitman uses rhyme and assonance in about the same degree as they occur in the Hebrew Bible and more than in the English translation. The alphabetical and acrostic poems of the Hebrew are not in the English translation, and Whitman would scorn such formalism.

The resemblance of Whitman's verse to Hebrew poetry is not in the mere fact of his use of parallelism, but that he used it in much the same free way that Hebrew poetry used it, not bound by a set pattern of rhyme, meter, or accent, but, as Briggs points out as to Hebrew poetry, by a general intermingling of the three principal kinds of parallelism.

In another respect Whitman's poetry is similar to the Hebrew. It is in the rhythm of thought as well as of words, which is what is meant by parallelism, and this is what has passed over mainly into the English translation of the Bible.

334   WALT WHITMAN: THINKER AND ARTIST

Now, if we have some inkling of what parallelism is and of the different kinds of it, acknowledging Whitman's ample use of it in free verse form, may it not also be found frequently in the formal poets. For instance, in Shakespeare's *King Lear,* which Edward Dowden, an early admirer of Whitman, declared "the greatest single achievement of the Teutonic, or Northern, genius." In Scene I of Act I, are several examples of parallelism. Thus, when Lear invites his daughters to flatter him: Goneril replies in lines that may be termed at once synonymous, synthetic, and emblematic; Regan, synonymous, antithetic, and emblematic; and Cordelia's speech is antithetical and introverted parallelism.

Not only is parallelism not peculiar to Hebrew poetry, but, as observed by Semitic authorities, it occurred in ancient Acadian, Babylonian, and Assyrian hymns. Furthermore, it is so common in poetry that one may surmise that it is a characteristic phase of any thought. The distinguishing terms to specify the different forms of parallelism signify as much. By the very laws of thought any developed speech or discourse will proceed by noting similarity or likeness (synonymity), or antithesis, and come to some conclusion or synthesis. The other types are but a variation of the fundamental patterns: introversion is antithesis, emblematic is synonymous, and staircase or climactic parallelism is the general chain of reasoning. Formal logic with its variety of terms expresses the same thing.

We must conclude that other characteristics distinguish what is unique and different in Whitman's poetry more than does parallelism. No one style comprehends Whitman's verse. In the combination of elements that characterize his poetry, of which parallelism is a notable one, and not in that single element, is the distinctiveness of his free verse to be discovered.

Lining, Punctuation, and Stanzas.

Another of Whitman's departures from traditional English verse was in his method of lining. Some think by this his poetry was made more prosaic. Others, like E. C. Ross, see in it a farther extreme from prose than traditional poetry.

Each of his lines is a unit of sense. It is that which makes his parallelism stand out distinctively. His lines do not run over choppily as in some recent vers libre.

Trained in the printer's art, his punctuation is an index of his style. The stanza ends ordinarily with a period. There is no period within the stanza. When a question mark or exclamation point ends the stanza it indicates a full stop. The end-stop of each line is usually within the stanza marked by a comma. Semi-colons signify a shift of meaning within the stanza. Commas, question marks, exclamation points, and dashes set off the caesuras.

His stanzas are often of unusual length. In some of his poems there is but one stanza, such as *Our Old Feuillage* with 82 lines, *Respondez* 68 lines, *Apostroph* 65 lines, *From Pent-up Aching Rivers* 57 lines, *Spontaneous Me* 45 lines, and *Scented Herbage of my Breast* 38 lines. In the longer poems there are also such stanzas, as in *Song of Myself*, section 33, 81 lines; *Song of the Broad-Axe*, section 3, 69 lines; and *By Blue Ontario's Shore*, section 6, 41 lines. The catalogued images in those long stanzas unbroken by a single period are not wanting in emotional appeal.

Comparison with Whitman's prose shows clearly how these devices, call them poetic or not, give greater clarity of meaning by caesuric emphasis within the line, by the unit of sense within each line, and by the grouping of lines in a stanza to convey a complete poetic idea.

In Whitman's prose writing there is also careful attention to punctuation. But his paragraphs are not equivalent to stanzas. His paragraphs usually contain more than one sentence. His use of commas there is distinctively different from his verse, and conforms generally to what was customary in his time. His prose sentences are often long and confusingly involved, but correct and apposite to his meaning. Periods, excepting where he uses three like a dash, mark the sentence structure of his prose, in contrast with his poetry in which not the sentence but the stanza's close is indicated by the period.

Oratory.

Another of the affinities of Whitman's verse is with oratory. But it is more in the spirit than as an intrinsic pattern that oratory played its part with him.

He did, in fact, contemplate almost as early, if not simultaneously with the first publication of the *Leaves,* a grand lecturing tour over the United States. It may be that the flop of his first edition discouraged him. And he may have recognized that unsupported by fame he would have slight success as a speaker, for his voice was high pitched, though pleasant, and his slow quiet utterance was not dramatic or forceful. It was his growing reputation late in life which brought remuneration for his lectures.

The enthusiasm, if not the style, of the orator infused his verses. He could feel congenially the seductions to which the orator is prone:

> "O the orator's joys!
> To inflate the chest, to roll the thunder of
>   the voice out from the ribs and throat,
> To make the people rage, weep, hate, desire,
>   with yourself,
> To lead America—to quell America with a
>   great tongue."

The close relationship of oratory and poetry impressed him. He believed that "all great utterance in literature lends itself to the lips." Therefore, the poet aspires to the orator's art.

> "Vocalism, measure, concentration, deter-
> mination, and the divine power to speak
> words;
> Are you full-lung'd and limber-lipp'd from
> long trial? from vigorous practice? from
> physique?
>
> ❖ ❖ ❖ ❖ ❖ ❖
>
> For only at last after many years, . . .
>
> ❖ ❖ ❖ ❖ ❖ ❖
>
> After these and more, it is just possible there
> comes to a man, a woman, the divine power
> to speak words;
> Then toward that man or that woman swiftly
> hasten all—none refuse, all attend."

And oratory is more than public speech, it is the magic art of words and voices. It touches the depths of one's being:

> "O what is it in me that makes me tremble so
> at voices?
> Surely whoever speaks to me in the right
> voice, him or her I shall follow,
> As the water follows the moon, silently, with
> fluid steps, anywhere around the globe.
>
> "All waits for the right voices;
> Where is the practic'd and perfect organ?
> Where is the develop'd soul?
> For I see every word utter'd thence has
> deeper, sweeter, new sounds, impossible
> on less terms.

I see brains and \ lips closed, tympans and
temples unstruck,
Until that comes which has the quality to
strike and unclose,
Until that comes which has the quality to
bring forth what lies slumbering forever
ready in all words."

Whitman Must be Read Entire.

Not any one technique but all together comprise
Whitman's art. Those who go picking out a bit here and
there from his work, saying this poem is artistic and that
is not, are neither in the understanding nor in the spirit
of Whitman. For him his work as he left it was a whole,
incomplete only in the sense that much more is to be done
and added to it rather than to be taken from it by emend-
ment or exclusion.

Whitman did not introduce or produce the ultimate
and only form, the final method of poetry. His example and
his theories did bring into being new forms or the perfecting of the oldest forgotten forms. He called to attention
or into consciousness the method of those forms. In a
sense he produced a new tradition by reviving the oldest
traditions of a primitive world.

He made prose, art, music and oratory more akin to
each other by giving them status in poetry. He expanded
in free verse the popular traditional forms of rhyme, meter
and rhythm, but he put a greater burden on the poet to
use them rightly. It was his principal doctrine that form
should be fitted to the theme. His own practice but partially exemplified and proved the doctrine.

If he had not the capacity to use the traditional forms
with suppleness, he was able to create his own forms and
mould from them an effective poetic style. But to make of
Whitman an exclusive dogma is to do him a great dis-

service by contradicting his basic principle of freedom. Claiming for him more than he was disparages his unusual genius. Yet in the light of his contemporaries and successors the stature of Whitman as poet and prophet grows.

15

AMONG HIS CONTEMPORARIES.

❖ ❖ ❖ ❖ ❖ ❖

"The chief trait of any given poet is always
the spirit he brings to the observation of
Humanity and Nature ... The last value
of artistic expressers, past and present—
Greek aesthetes, Shakespere—or in our
own day Tennyson, Victor Hugo, Carlyle,
Emerson—is certainly involved in such
questions."

❖ ❖ ❖ ❖ ❖ ❖

EMERSON.

EMERSON IS MORE THAN ANOTHER BOOK, AND I DO NOT ESSAY
now to treat of the manifold likenesses and differences between Whitman and Emerson, but only to consider a few of
them. My purpose is to define Whitman, not to measure
Emerson in his greatness, as when Whitman cordially
acknowledged him as "dear Friend and Master". But that
acknowledgement could not do full justice to the Whitman that outgrew the great influence Emerson had upon
him. When Whitman said to Trowbridge he was just
simmering until Emerson brought him to boil, not yet
had Whitman come to mature understanding of himself.

Those who make so much of Whitman's repudiation of
Emerson as ingratitude and a kind of untruthfulness in
Whitman are, probably, incompetent to follow Whitman's

development of an independence of thought which was
original in him and his pioneering expression of the humanistic philosophy recognized in a later day without adequate recognition of him as its author and profoundest
exponent.

I am now reviewing mainly two phases of Emerson's
thinking from which it has been claimed Whitman derived
his inspiration, in order to show that although inspiring
and at least assuring to Whitman, they were not definitive
of him. It is not correct to say that what Emerson preached
Whitman practiced. Whitman's philosophy and practice
were both a distinct advance beyond Emerson's thought
and technique. The charm of Emerson's style, especially
of his sentences, and the prevailing elegance of Emerson's
writing are quite different from the merits of Whitman
as a writer. They are not comparable. Whitman did not
imitate Emerson's technique.

So too in philosophy, it is more the spirit and a tone
than similarity of thought that makes them kindred. Devotion to America they have equally, but Emerson's is
the attitude of a scholar, and Whitman's that of the man
with larger sympathies and nearer to common folk, although they share the democratic dogma.

In religion they are poles apart, notwithstanding both
are liberal and non-traditional; Whitman is wholly humanist as Emerson is not.

Emerson's Poetic Counsels.

If it be assumed that Whitman got his poetic cues
from reading Emerson's Essays, it is presumably from
The Poet that he drew his inspiration, or more certainly
his sanction. In that Essay there are suggestions which
go far toward justifying Whitman's style and manner.

Whitman's preference of thought to form had previously been stated by Emerson: "It is not metres, but a
metre-making argument, that makes a poem." "The

thought is prior to the form." Whitman regarded thought as the primary element and, though not indifferent to form, would not allow it to impede or obstruct the thought. Emerson, although not a formalist, probably regarded form and thought in the aprioristic sense of Plato. When Emerson said "All form is an effect of character," and Whitman said "Words follow character," they may therefore not have meant the same thing.

For Emerson there is a music of the spheres. The poet is one who overhears the melody of things and regards it. That is not merely the sounds of Nature and the rhythms of waves and winds, to which Whitman was also sensitive, but "the soul of the thing is reflected by a melody." From the great round of the Universe "symmetry and truth . . . glide into our spirits." It is by intuition and not intellect that the poet becomes aware of that harmony and melody of the soul or over-soul of things. It is by abandonment of himself to the Nature of things that the poet learns to speak their language. Whitman's mind was too scientific to take all that literally.

Yet Emerson, like Whitman, sensed the weaknesses of mysticism and distinguished the habit and practice of the poet from that of the mystic. Both use symbols. But the poet uses them as a logician uses terms and propositions, only they express for the poet concrete experience in contrast with the abstractions of the logician. But the mystic makes the logical error of mistaking the part for the whole. He is wedded to his symbols as if they are things instead of instruments. The mystic therefore gets lost in a fog of mists and shadows and loses the realistic sense of the sensuous experiences with which he deals.

Emerson with his belief in the Over-Soul and the cosmic Whole had the conception of the largeness of the poet's mission, of the poet as the interpreter of Nature and the Universe by somehow identifying himself with it. But Emerson's universalism made him lose sight of man's function in Nature. He thought of the poet as a reporter, a seer of Nature. In this the poet speaks another language than his own. A great poet is a mirror, a mirror of everything. To function in this way he must renounce himself and simply learn. Thereby he comes into possession intuitively of the secrets of Nature. This abandonment and surrender of himself make the poet like an inebriated man, beside himself and outside of himself, a person possessed by a spirit not his own. He sees things, images them. "Imagination, is a very high sort of seeing, which does not come by study, but by the intellect being where and what it sees, by sharing the path, or circuit of things through forms, and so making them translucid to others." "The poet knows that he speaks adequately, then, only when he speaks somewhat wildly."

One can find a similar idea expressed by Whitman when he speaks of being seized with a fit; but his poetry is no more characterized by such wildness than are Emerson's calm and philosophically tempered essays. And Whitman was not at all convinced, as Emerson apparently was, about the necessity for the poet "resigning himself to the divine *aura* which breathes through forms." But he was as convinced as Emerson that the true inflatus of the poet is not by way of alcoholic stimulation. Emerson with Milton would take water instead. Whitman rather looked and felt within for the urge of the warm, strong clean blood of a vital being.

More in accord with Whitman's mood was Emerson's preaching of the poet's simple tastes and simple living, and use of common things for his material. "Thought makes everything fit for use." "Small and mean things serve as well as great symbols." Near to hand, this America, is the subject for poetry. And when the pure, high-minded Emerson sees that even the obscene "becomes illustrious, spoken in a new connection of thought," what a reminder might Whitman have made to Emerson's attempted persuasion that he omit the sexiest things from the new edition of *Leaves of Grass*. Also when Emerson wrote Carlyle about Whitman's catalogues resembling warehouse inventories, had he forgotten his own saying? "Bare lists of words are found suggestive, to an imaginative and excited mind."

Allen is mistaken in his assumption that Whitman was most indebted to Emerson and Trancendentalism for his theory of words. There is undoubtedly much in common. But to Whitman can hardly be traced Emerson's metaphysical conception of language, words and symbols: "Words and deeds are quite indifferent modes of the divine energy." Substitute "human" for "divine" and that sentence would nearly express Whitman's attitude about the interchangeability of words and deeds. Whitman in his different way could say too: "Words are also actions, and actions are a kind of words." But Emerson goes beyond Whitman toward mystical meaning when he says: "Things admit of being used as symbols, because nature is a symbol, in the whole, and in every part." And of the poet that "It is nature the symbol, nature certifying the supernatural, body overflowed with life, which he worships, with coarse, but sincere rites." Whitman did not believe in the supernatural and he did not worship Nature.

But Whitman could agree that the poet is "the Namer, or Language-maker," that "The poet made all the words, and therefore language is the archives of history and, if we must say it, a sort of tomb of the muses. . . . Language is fossil poetry." As a non-traditionalist Whitman was of course no worshipper of words. He was too much of a realist for that.

Again, Whitman was not so matter of fact as to miss the sense of the imaginative, and in a more creative sense than Emerson's. With Emerson he believed the poet "pursues a beauty, half seen, which flies before him." But not in Emerson's halting conception of something to be discovered in Nature. He would not agree that what the poet pursues he "knows well that it is not his." Even though Emerson says that the image is the poet's own, he means only that it passes into the poet from external Nature or flows into and through him as a universal soul. That is quite the obverse of Whitman's beliefs and meaning.

Emerson's Philosophy.

The persistent effort on the part of the traditionalists to class Whitman as a Transcendentalist because of the influence of Emerson upon him falls afoul of Emerson's own repudiation of Transcendentalism. But it also fails when confronted with the facts of Whitman's wide divergence from the metaphysical philosophy of Emerson.

When Emerson said, "within man is the soul of the whole," he did not mean anything like the humanism which Whitman preached, nothing resembling the philosophy in *Song of Myself* and *Chanting the Square Deific*. There is something of Whitman's philosophy in Emerson's sentence: "All the facts of the animal economy, sex, nutriment, gestation, birth, growth, are symbols of the passage of the world into the soul of man, to suffer there a change, and reappear a new and higher fact." But it is not Whitman, although Burroughs with his Emersonian slant thought so, when Emerson said, Nature "makes a man; and having brought him to ripe age, she will no longer run the risk of losing this wonder at a blow, but she detaches from him a new self, that the kind may be safe from accidents to which the individual is exposed."

Emerson's mystic idea that in the poet's song man gets an immortality that is indifferent to the individual man, impersonal as T. S. Eliot later said,—this is not at all Whitman's view of the matter. For him the individual man came into greater being with the song. Not Nature's way, so careless of the individual, so careful for the race. As a recent anthropologist, Childe, says it, "Man makes himself."

We have seen that Emerson, like the religious votaries generally, would have man renounce himself, resign himself, abandon himself, in order to find himself. That is just the opposite of Whitman whose way to the goal of man is by self-assertion, "I sing myself."

To Emerson, What is a man? "A man is the facade of a temple wherein all wisdom and all good abide. . . . Him we do not respect, but the soul, whose organ he is. . . . All reform, aims, in some one particular, to let the great soul have its way through us; in other words, to engage us to obey." "There is no bar or wall in the soul where man, the effect, ceases, and God, the cause, begins." Emerson believed that great superstition. Whitman did not. Said Whitman: "The mightier God am I. . . . For without me what were all? what were God?" Emerson's Over-Soul is wholly alien and not any kindred to Whitman's soul. The Over-Soul is not the human soul. "That Unity, that Over-Soul, within which every man's particular being is contained and made one with all other," is quite another entity from that identified human soul, inseparable from the body, which Whitman celebrates in *Leaves of Grass*.

Emerson was not a consistent philosopher. He believed that God is impersonal. Yet he could say: "Ineffable is the union of man and God in every act of the soul. The simplest person, who in his integrity worships God, becomes God; yet forever and ever the influx of this better and universal self is new and unsearchable. Ever it inspires awe and astonishment. How dear, how soothing to man, arises the idea of God, peopling the lonely place, effacing the scars of our mistakes and disappointments! When we have broken the god of tradition, and ceased from our god of rhetoric, then may God fire the heart with his presence."

As one reads on, Emerson's "rhetoric" appears more unctious than his reason. It gives him no difficulties, as after conversing with Whitman and only partially under-

standing Whitman Burroughs had difficulties, about wor-
shipping an impersonal God. Burroughs tried to accept
the Universe and justify the ways of God to man, yet could
not write of the poet as did Emerson: "He is sure that his
welfare is dear to the heart of being." Burroughs was convinced that the Universe is indifferent to the individual
man's welfare. Burroughs could go no farther than to argue,
Man is here, he has come to what he is, and therefore the
Universe must be favorable to him rather than otherwise.

That sort of undiscriminating acceptance of everything which Burroughs erroneously thought characteristic
of Whitman, may have been nearer to Emerson's viewpoint: "There is no fact in nature which does not carry
the whole sense of nature; and the distinctions which we
make in events, and in affairs, of low and high, honest and
base, disappear when nature is used as a symbol." Emerson
conceived the poet as one "who re-attaches things to nature
and the Whole—re-attaching even artificial things, and vio-
lations of nature, to nature, by a deeper insight,—disposes
very easily of the most disagreeable facts." Rather than
merging all or attaching all things to Nature, Whitman
drew lessons from Nature, notable lessons of freedom and
diversity, but also of tolerance, opportunity, another
chance for the individual.

Whitman, as the cosmic poet, felt in the sense of the
astronomer's wonderment the vastness, the infinity of the
Universe, but he felt it with the exhiliration of one who
comprehends somewhat of it, and not in the sense that
Emerson conceived of it by which man loses himself as
an insignificant being absorbed into the universal realm
of an immensely vast Universe.

Whitman owed inspiration to Emerson's influence, but
the Emerson philosophy did not detain him; he went beyond it to the humanism which allows dignity and unique
worth for himself to the individual man.

BROWNING.

Life, Love, and Immortality.

Many have remarked upon certain similarities between Whitman and Browning. But neither was very appreciative of the other. Professor Corson could not convince Whitman that Browning was "his man". Browning spoke harshly of Whitman to Buchanan. The dissimilarities are as striking as the similarities. Both had difficulties with the public because of their style of writing, though not the same. Both shocked the public by their radical ideas. But Browning treated traditions and conventions with more respect than did Whitman. The uniqueness and originality of Whitman is made more distinct by comparison with Browning and by noting the differences in them in the particulars in which they resembled each other.

Probably they were nearest alike in a healthy robustness of nature and optimistic temperament. But they experienced and expressed themselves in a different way. One feels the athletic character in Browning which is vivid and strong, as in verse IX of *Saul*:

> "Oh, the wild joys of living! the leaping from
>   rock up to rock,
> The strong rending of boughs from the fir-
>   tree, the cool silver shock
> Of the plunge in a pool's living water, the
>   hunt of the bear,
> And the sultriness showing the lion is
>   crouched in his lair,

> How good is man's life, the mere living! how
>   fit to employ
> All the heart and the soul and the senses for
>   ever in joy!"

This physical optimism in Browning was temperamental but also metaphysical and theological. Whitman's optimism was likewise temperamental, but with more realistic rationality than Browning's. In Whitman too optimism was a studied purpose, an intention, which he sought to retain despite his physical disposition. In *Sands at Seventy* Whitman expressed apprehension that his old age ills would filter into his daily songs.

Browning's attitude was different but as resolute in his faith:

> "I have lived, seen God's hand thro' a lifetime, and all was for best."

Although Whitman believed in an ultimate best, he was too realistic to see all for the best. For Whitman good is a triumph, in the course of evolution, not just a present achievement. And it is man's triumph, not God's all-seen primordial plan.

For Whitman life signifies the "struggling soul of man; ... Ever the soul dissatisfied, curious, unconvinced at last." Quite in contrast with Browning's protestation of certainties. Whitman regarded the wrangling of theologies and philosophies as subdued by "the calming thought of all," towit, "the round earth's silent vital laws." For him the mystery of the Universe has a "mystic human meaning," not pantheism. It was rather something that occurred to Whitman in the presence of Nature, not necessarily inherent in Nature, even though the Sea seemed to speak to him

> "The tale of cosmic elemental passion,
> Thou tellest to a kindred soul."

In Whitman the soul is enmeshed inextricably with the body. So to Browning, "nor soul helps flesh more, now, than flesh helps soul!" But for Browning that is only "now."

But even now the hazard of the struggle with eternal consequence goes on in the man who is being striven for by both God and devil:

> "No, when the fight begins within himself,
> A man's worth something, God stoops o'er
>   his head,
> Satan looks up between his feet—both tug—
> He's left himself, i' the middle: the soul
>   wakes
> And grows."

Man's worth is not in himself but as subject for the conquest of the warring potentates of Good and Evil.

For Browning, "The best is yet to be," but not as heralding man's achievements. It is God's work, supreme and sublime, which matters. "Trust God" and leave it to Him, is the message of *Rabbi Ben Ezra*. It is immortality that of necessity makes up this world's incomplete, even if man is "a God though in the germ." Man is moulded by God as the potter's wheel shapes the vessel of clay.

> "On earth the broken arcs; in the heaven, a
>   perfect round."

And it is only the divine aristocracy of genius that has a look in on the ultimate perfection:

> "But God has a few of us whom he whispers
>   in the ear;
> The rest may reason and welcome; t'is we
>   musicians know."

God's favored few, the musicians, the poets!

Browning was a special pleader, the advocate of a dogmatic cause. He had a Christian faith, which, though liberally entertained and not too rigidly maintained, he kept faithful to. His fundamental tenets of leaving all to God, utter trust and confidence in God, and an implicit belief in a future life as absolutely necessary to give our present life meaning, are the continuous theme of his poems, although in a few of the later ones he began to show or at least to consider some doubts. Perhaps he spoke those doubts only to refute them.

In *La Saisiaz* occur the most dubious expressions. The sudden death of a woman friend was the occasion of the poem, but it was stimulated by the discussion of a symposium in the *Nineteenth Century* magazine on *The Soul and Future Life,* which greatly interested him. Characteristically he took the attitude of a contributor to the symposium; that was cognate with his dramatic instinct, and so he engaged, as he said, in the "fence play" of the debate. Philosophically or theologically there is no original thought in this or any other poem of Browning's. He has however re-expressed old ideas with originality, force, and dramatic intensity. An unusual personal note, which after his early poems he had ceased to use, was revived in *La Saisiaz,* and there in contrast also with his earlier poems, he states the pessimism at which he had arrived through experience:

> "I must say—or choke in silence—'Howsoever
>   came my fate,
> Sorrow did and joy did nowise—life well
>   weighed—preponderate.' "

As Browning became more pessimistic with age, not so Whitman. Whitman was more realistic, philosophically profounder, less restrained by preconceived beliefs or by any traditional cult. He was not afraid to venture, not afraid to doubt. Whitman demanded more evidence and relied more on reason and knowledge than did Browning. Browning insisted that his beliefs, his faith, the instincts of his heart, were sufficient grounds for his tenets of immortality and of the perfection of deity and Heaven.

352 WALT WHITMAN: THINKER AND ARTIST

In contrast with Browning Whitman believed in man, believed in man independently of any force or power outside him. Although not a professionally trained philosopher he studied the philosophies more attentively than did Browning and was influenced especially by the German idealists, the Transcendentalists, and the skeptical rationalists of France and America. But he never entered the lists of philosophic debate. He confined himself to a poet's expression. Yet he made an advanced philosophic contribution to personalistic humanism.

Triggs, who sought to find likenesses between Browning and Whitman, found a notably common quality in them which he called esoteric, by which he meant expression of the soul, or personality. He distinguished formal, objective, or impersonal art by the name exoteric. But neither soul nor personality meant the same thing to them. Browning attached the term soul to his beliefs in God and immortality. For Whitman it is the vital and psychic principle without theological or eschatological dependence. For him, furthermore, immortality carried none of the baggage of traditional religion.

Although both strongly emphasized personality and individuality, Whitman gave these terms more specific and more humanistic meaning. Browning would not say as did Whitman:

> "The whole theory of the universe is directed
> unerringly to one single individual—
> namely to You."

> "I have but one central figure, the general
> human personality typified in myself."

It is not the implied egotism in the statement which would have offended Browning, for he was more egotistical than Whitman. Browning objected to the idea of man as the center of the universe, even of the universe of man, which he could not conceive of as existing. It is all God's universe and not man's universe.

> "Man—as befits the made, the inferior thing—
> Purposed, since made, to grow, not make
>   in turn,
> Yet forced to try and make, else fail to
>   grow—
> Formed to rise, reach at, if not grasp and gain
> The good beyond him—which attempt is
>   growth—
> Repeats God's process in man's due degree,
> Attaining man's proportionate result—
> Creates, no, but resuscitates, perhaps."

As Orr correctly said, Browning's "faith in personality is naturally abstruse on the metaphysical side, but it is always picturesque on the dramatic."

Browning's poetry of love had also a theological aspect, but the sentiment sprang from his temperament and from his bodily robustness and health. He gave it a Christian interpretation and in this respect Whitman had little in common with Browning. For Whitman love found its principal expression in comradeship. The love of woman meant more to the personal experience of Browning. Triggs thought love the principle of unity in Browning's poems.

Browning's great love was for Elizabeth Barrett, and her early death left him with a Beatrice in Heaven which he never ceased to worship. Yet in old age he wrote some significant love poems which seemed to have a terrestrial inspiration. But Browning early cautioned against regarding his poems as autobiographical. As he himself remarked, dramatic poetry, consisting of "so many utterances of so many imaginary persons," if successful, cannot be merely personal expressions. Indeed, in one poem, *Fifine at the Fair,* Browning took the freedom of a dramatist to express at length the feelings and philosophy of a libertine. However, the poem incorporated so much of the ideas accredited as Browning's own that it caused consternation to his admirers at the time of its publication.

In *Fifine,* nevertheless, we may be coming closer to understanding of the most unorthodox part of Browning's philosophy, a synthesis of good and evil, and in that again there is a surprising resemblance to Whitman with the usual difference also discoverable. In section XXIX of that poem is expressed the idea of the perfectibility of things and especially that of the perfection of every human being in his or her place which may be nearly paralleled in Whitman's poetry of the *Leaves of Grass.*

> "No creature made so mean
> But that, someway, it boasts, could we in-
> vestigate,
> Its supreme worth: fulfills by ordinance of
> fate,
> Its momentary task, gets glory all its own,
> Tastes triumph in the world, pre-eminent,
> alone,
> Where is the single grain of sand, 'mid mil-
> lions heaped
> Confusedly on the beach, but, did we know,
> has leaped
> Or would leap, would we wait, I' the century,
> some once,
> To the very throne of things?

> As firm in my belief, quick sense perceives
> the same
> Self-vindicating flash illustrate every man

> And woman of our mass, and prove, through-
>   out the plan,
> No detail but, in place allotted it, was prime
> And perfect."

The argument continues that the imperfect, which is
the individual (and no two individuals are alike), with
the artist's aid is joined to others and by refinement

> "Art, working with a will, discards the super-
>   flux,
> Contributes to defect, toils on till,—fiat lux—
> There's the restored, the prime, the indi-
>   vidual type!"

And this comes by guess

> "In the eternal progress,—love's law, which
>   I avow
> And thus would formulate: each soul lives,
>   longs and works
> For itself, by itself, because a lodestar lurks,
> An other than itself, . . .

❖ ❖ ❖ ❖ ❖ ❖

> This constitutes the soul discernible by soul."

Thus arises the true from the false, the good from evil.
Each thing seems fitted to its particular element, the fish
in water, the land animal to air, and each would drown or
suffocate in the other environment. What is good for one
is evil for the other and vice versa.

Where then is absolute good? The truth of truth is,
that "I am I." There is an individual test of good:

> "Since there can be for each, one Best, no
>   more, such Best,

For body and mind of him, abolishes the rest
O' the simply Good and Better."

Does that mean that only individual truth or good is absolute? and that only for himself? For, in the larger sense,

"Yourself are, after all, as false as what sur-
    rounds;
And why not be content?"

But in *Fifine* as in *Abt Vogler* "the philosophy of the imperfect" is expressed and approved for the total plan which is the perfect.

This philosophy might enable that Don Juan to love together at once Fifine in the flesh and Elvire in the spirit; but it turns out badly, for returning from the love of the flesh he finds that the object of his love of the spirit has vanished. Even if it be assumed, for excuse of Browning, that he wrote this poem as a confession of sin for having attempted to marry again and as repentance for forgetting the sacred memory of his dead wife, yet it must be acknowledged that *Fifine at the Fair* has a daringness of conception in the casuistry of love which one cannot parallel in the experimental thoughts of Whitman concerning the divine passion.

The theme that good is non-existent but for evil, that even lust is the sire of virtue, appears to be the meaning of the verses in *The Statue and the Bust*:

" . . . . Oh, a crime will do
As well, I reply, to serve for a test,
As a virtue golden through and through,
Sufficient to vindicate itself
And prove its worth at a moment's view!

❖ ❖ ❖ ❖ ❖ ❖

The true has no value beyond the sham.

❖ ❖ ❖ ❖ ❖

If you choose to play!—is my principle,
Let a man contend to the uttermost
For his life's set prize, be it what it will!"

Surely he is saying that the lust unfulfilled is no better than the deed. To do is better than not to do, even though the deed is a crime. I do not find such boldness or reckless-ness in Whitman's speech. But how the pious do draw in-spiration from Browning's Christianity, while they have been wont to berate Whitman's lustfulness!

TENNYSON

Style, Sentiment, and Seriousness.

Tennyson, whom Whitman called "the boss", reigned triumphantly during most of the latter half of the Nine-teenth century. He was then the prime favorite of Queen Victoria who made him first the Poet Laureate and then a Baron of the realm. But in the quarter century before that first honor befell him his going was not easy. Acclaimed by "The Apostles" of Cambridge, that but moved the deadly ridicule of another potentate (of the *Quarterly*), Lockhart, the son-in-law of Sir Walter Scott. For all his dignity or be-cause of it Tennyson was a self-made object for pointed levity.

Like Pope he early lisped in numbers, notwithstanding the great Coleridge thought his meter bad, unscanable, and advised him to take a year out and confine himself to well tried examples before attempting to experiment. That is traditionalism always!

From Spenser and Shakespeare to Tennyson and after we can trace the length of a style. Hume condemned Shake-speare for having perpetrated the model. More probably it was Spenser's *The Faerie Queene* that gave it vogue. Its characteristics are mythical and legendary fancies, ornateness, sentimentality, prettiness, surfeiting sweetness, and such became the orthodox taste and test for poetry. Tennyson was not its worst practitioner.

Whitman was a severe critic of that poetic art. He had much to say about Shakespeare and Tennyson whom he linked together. Although Canby thinks that Whitman had a sense of inferiority and a feeling of humility when he contemplated the great artistry of Tennyson, Whitman's own expressions hardly bear that out. For Whitman described Tennyson as "the bard of ennui and of the aristocracy and their combination into love." He put Shakespeare in the same category. "The old stock love of playwrights and romancers" he regarded as an "unnatural and shocking passion for some girl or woman, that wrenches it from its manhood, emasculated and impotent, without strength to hold the rest of the objects and goods of life in their proper positions. It seeks nature for sickly uses. It goes screaming and weeping after the facts of the universe, in their calm beauty and equanimity, to note the occurrence of itself, and to sound the news, in connection with the charms of the neck, hair, or complexion of a particular female." He considered all such poetry to be the product of the unhealthy and foolish chivalry of feudal times. Therefore he thought of Tennyson along with Shakespeare as belonging "essentially to the buried past".

Nor is Professor Thaler convincing or consistent in his thesis that Whitman later retracted those criticisms. The passages he quotes show that from first to last Whitman held much the same viewpoint toward his contemporary and Shakespeare. Thaler's theory has to fall back on the unsupported assumption of Whitman's inherent "contradictoriness". Apparently he chooses to overlook *A Thought on Shakespere*:

"Superb and inimitable as all is, it is mostly an objective and physiological kind of power and beauty the soul finds in Shakespere — a style supremely grand of the sort, but in my opinion stopping short of the grandest sort, at any rate for fulfilling and satisfying modern and scientific and democratic American purposes."

At the same time, in *Sands at Seventy,* Whitman paid tribute to the poets of tradition:

> "To get the final lilt of songs,
> To penetrate the inmost lore of poets—to
>   know the mighty ones,
> Job, Homer, Eschylus, Dante, Shakespere,
>   Tennyson, Emerson."

Nevertheless he sought for a higher art than theirs:

> "Had I the choice to tally greatest bards,

> Or Shakespere's woe-entangled Hamlet,
>   Lear, Othello—Tennyson's fair ladies,
> Metre or wit the best, or choice conceit to
>   wield in perfect rhyme, delight of singers;"

in Nature he perceived something beyond their expression, something in the great American scene superior to their garden-like refinement. He did not regard such elegances as the essence of the highest poetic art.

However, "Tennyson's sweet sad rhyme" received no such harsh treatment from Whitman as it had from Tennyson's contemporaries before he reached the laureate honors. Besides Lockhart there was Lytton Bulwer who wrote a satirical poem that pilloried Tennyson's "purified prettiness of phrase" and ridiculed his poetry as feminine and childish:

> "Let Schoolmiss Alfred vent her chaste
>   delight
> In darling little rooms so warm and bright."

The reference is to Tennyson's early puerile poem, *The Darling Room,* which Lockhart too had lampooned and which is now left out of complete editions of Tennyson. And they also omit Tennyson's infuriated reply in verse, in which he characterized his critic as Shakespeare's cynical for which he immediately repented and penned his after-thought to the *London Punch.*

The picture of Tennyson during those trying early years of awaiting fame is not as beautiful as the legend of him. Indeed there was in Tennyson a streak of vulgarity which oddly contrasted with the ultra-refinement of his poetry. Carlyle described him as one who smoked "infinite tobacco". From that, too much liquor, and irregular meals were attributed his ill health and hypochondriac temperament. The story is told of the visit from Longfellow when Tennyson shocked that good gentleman with salacious conversation for which he later apologized that just then he had descended from his celestial heights of poetic purity and had to light on the dungpile for balance. But this was the earthy agrarian taint in him which was also characteristic of our notable American saint, Abraham Lincoln. Whitman, about whom there is no legend of purity, was distinctively a clean mouthed man and not even profane as Traubel misrepresented him to be.

The exceptional period of gloom in Tennyson's life was the "ten years of silence" after the death of Arthur Hallam and it is relevant here to note the significance of that famous friendship which played so large a part in Tennyson's life and was the inspiration of the poem renowned as his best, *In Memoriam.* To Tennyson's contemporaries that poem was disturbing because of its evident homosexuality. The unusual friendship between Tennyson and Hallam was self-consciously homosexual. Hallam regarded himself a Uranian. In sending to Leigh Hunt a copy of the *Poems by Two Brothers* (Alfred and Charles Tennyson), he described them as addressed to "the elect church of Urania, which we know to be small and in tribulation". Therefore, one suspects the beginnings of Whitman's popularity in England as due to the coterie of Uranians.

Tennyson's liberality on sexual questions was a point of criticism in clerical circles and especially concerning that pathetic poem about a triangle, *Enoch Arden,* and the condemnation of the morality of that poem led Queen Victoria herself to question him about it, and he very adroitly quieted her misgivings by pointing out the child, "not his", and leading her to the tombstone and final resting place of that self-effacing hero.

It was probably on this side of his character that Tennyson from the beginning and all his life through was so "thin-skinned", as he admitted himself to be and even took a kind of pride in that quality, although loathing the gossip and scandal which he feared as the incident of his fame, to which he referred in the verse:

> "The tiny trumpeting gnat can break our
>   dream
> When sweetest: and the vermin voices here
> May buzz so loud—we scorn them but they
>   sting."

Aloof and distant as he was to all but intimate friends, he frequently expressed admiration for Whitman and gave him the signal and unusual honor of an invitation in the early 70's to come to England and stay at Tennyson's as a guest. Later Tennyson wrote to Whitman occasionally, addressing him as "Dear Old Man". Tennyson even expressed admiration for Whitman's poetry, and that was a very unusual thing for him to do, at least in the case of contemporaries. Thus he spoke approval of Swinburne because when visited by that young man Swinburne made no mention of his poetry and did not ask him to read any of it.

It is likely that some of the toning down of Whitman's

criticism of Tennyson as recorded by Traubel was due
more to the flattery to which Whitman was susceptible and
for which he felt indebted to Tennyson, than any change
of opinion or because of humility or feeling of superiority
in Tennyson's genius or art.

In fact on occasion he repeated to Traubel his dislike
for the laureate's tendency to be a "ladies' man" and to be
"the great expression of modern ennui—the blue devils that
afflict modern civilization. It is the background of every
poem—every one of them." Again he said: "He reflects the
upper crust of his time, its pale cast of thought—even its
ennui. . . . Tennyson is the imitation of Shakespere, though
a refined, educated, travelled, modern English dandy." And
much the same viewpoint is expressed in *A Word About
Tennyson,* published in 1888.

On the other hand, in that same essay Whitman acknowledged a moral worth in Tennyson, though somewhat
qualifiedly: "His moral line is local and conventional, but
it is vital and genuine. . . . He shows how one can be a
royal laureate, quite elegant and 'aristocratic', and a little
queer and affected, and at the same time perfectly manly
and natural." Whitman could also tolerate Tennyson's
"non-democracy" as natural to him. And despite Tennyson's gloom he found in him "faith. It is not a note of triumph, but it is there."

He thought "Tennyson in England and Emerson in
America . . . the best recent examples" of "original writers."
He insisted that the people who think of "Tennyson and
Swinburne as masters of poetic form should not forget that
both of them have in later years taken all sorts of liberties
with the code."

Notwithstanding Whitman's apparent approval of Tennyson's belief in immortality, again it is qualified for himself as "not formulating anything" but in Mrs. Gilchrist's
phrase as "going somewhere", even "though we may little
comprehend its meanings—its inmost suggestions."

The hearty and robust faith abundantly expressed by Browning is not to be found in Tennyson's poetry. As Whitman observed, "the original 'Locksley Hall' . . . was essentially morbid, heart-broken, finding fault with everything", and he thought it was cynically repeated in *Locksley Hall Sixty Years After;* although the following were not among the lines he quoted as "most striking":

> "Evolution ever climbing after some ideal
>   good,
> And Reversion ever dragging Evolution in
>   the mud."

Whitman tried to keep the querilities of his old age out of his poems. Tennyson as he grew older took his inner state of mind to be a true picture of the world, a world from which he kept himself so carefully away that he knew very little about it. That had been a fault with him from college days, in which he was encouraged and sustained by "The Apostles" of Cambridge. He and they, notwithstanding their inadequate equipment, believed they had a world mission to perform and that they were born to set that world aright. They were a very snobbish lot of little aristocrats.

But Tennyson did have towering qualities and even a discernment of causes and movements which he expressed so nobly as to merit the praise he won from Whitman and to be entitled to more respect than our sophisticated time is willing to accord him. For Tennyson as for Whitman it was prophetic vision, insight and foresight, which enabled them to interpret their time as one of transition and to believe that the future might hold for mankind a hope of peace and goodwill among men.

Tennyson saw as did Whitman the need for maintaining the dignity and worth of the individual human being as security to society itself. For, as he said: "The whole of

Society is at present too like a jelly; when it is touched it shakes from base to summit. As yet the unity is of weakness rather than of strength. . . . Our aim therefore ought to be not to merge the individual in the community, but to strengthen the social life of the community, and foster the individual."

Even more is our jelly-like "One World" in a state of feeble quiver than in Tennyson's time, and the need for the remedy he perceived is greater now but probably less understood. Our society has become less secure as it has become more unified. For in that process we have made the individual more dependent and less self-reliant. The very essence of totalitarianism, the terrible scourge of this Twentieth century, is its doctrine that the individual is swallowed up and merged in Society.

Had Tennyson never tried to build his work to the measure of a world plan he would be a far less significant poet. The adverse critics of his didactic poetry are mistaken. It was not this which Whitman deplored. He valued highly the character of the man as it appeared in great verse of admitted beauty, not rejecting those qualities in the making of the New World, but believing that the challenge of Democracy calls for going beyond them in both thought and art.

16

HOPKINS—THE UNKNOWN RIVAL.

❖ ❖ ❖ ❖ ❖ ❖

"In all people I see myself."

"I have looked for equals and lovers and I
find them ready for me in all lands,
I think some divine report has equalized
them with me."

❖ ❖ ❖ ❖ ❖ ❖

GERARD MANLEY HOPKINS

TRADITIONALISTS TELL US THAT ANOTHER CONTEMPORARY
was the greatest poet of all. No doubt those who name Hopkins for that preeminence may be motivated largely by partisan interests. But the influence of Hopkins today is so
great that he cannot be ignored. Moreover, it is important
from our point of view to take the measure of a poet of
Whitman's time who might be a rival. And in the case of
Hopkins there is a special reason for comparison.

Herbert Read who can hardly be denominated a religious partisan of Hopkins once made comparison to Hopkins' credit rather than Whitman's. He may later have altered that opinion. But then he contended that when the
history of the 1920s of English poetry is finally written it
will find Hopkins' rank exceeded by no other for that period. He spoke of Whitman as a "blind emotional force"
and denied him the distinction of emancipating poetry

from formalism of diction, rhythm and meter. That revolution, he said, was begun by Wordsworth and completed by Pound. At least he recognized emotional force in Whitman which such as Winters deny. And probably Read overlooked Pound's Cantos when he said Whitman had made no intelligent contribution to the technical development of verse. The best of critics may be short-sighted and mistaken.

Hopkins was a scholar as well as practitioner of poetic art. He knew the literatures of the world and studied their techniques intensively. He experimented with his innovations to the extreme. Therefore, Edith Sitwell thought he should not be taken as a model, because he had carried his experiments to so complete a state of development that nothing remained to be done to perfect his style. It has been frequently remarked of both Hopkins and Whitman that neither has had successful imitators.

But as we have shown that in ancient, notably Hebrew, poetry there was some likeness to Whitman's verse, so in Anglo-Saxon poetry there was at least the root of Hopkins' verse. Besides what often seems an excessive use of assonance and alliteration, Hopkins was more original in his revival of Anglo-Saxon rhythm which had long been out of use in English poetry. Hopkins named his variety "sprung rhythm". It differs from the usual English meter by permitting an irregularity of syllables from one to four in a line. The regularity is in the number of accents rather than a pattern-like iambic, trochee, anapest, etc. The latter Hopkins distinguished as "common rhythm".

As unlike as Whitman and Hopkins appear to be, one of Hopkins' poems led Robert Bridges, then Poet Laureate of England, to ask if Hopkins had read Whitman. Hopkins replied that the poem was not written in imitation of Whitman, but that he was aware, scandalous as it might be, that no other living man was so much like himself as Whitman.

The poem questioned is the one entitled *The Leaden*

Glow and the Golden Echo. What may have suggested the comparison to Bridges is partly the length of the lines which vary considerably, from seven to thirty-three syllables. Also there is notable repetition and cataloguing in the poem, also characteristics of Whitman's verse. But there are striking differences in feeling tone and sound which distinguish this and other poems of Hopkins from Whitman's. The nervous excitability which is continuous in Hopkins' style is at the farthest extreme from the ponderous roll likened to the ocean wave in Whitman's poetry. We have to look elsewhere for that community of character which Hopkins felt for Whitman.

I do not find any close parallel of the two until near the end of Hopkins' career. That final likeness was so striking and so different from the middle or early period of the notable development of Hopkins' genius that I defer consideration of it until we have taken view of the poetic achievement which in Hopkins' extreme admirers' opinions is regarded as his best. For one typical poem we may take *The Windhover* which has received the most extravagant praise. Some think it the height of artistic achievement. It is a sonnet in a form original with Hopkins, and an enthusiastic critic ranks it above the best of Donne's and Shakespeare's sonnets. Hopkins himself once thought it the best thing he had written, but that conviction may have been expressed in the exuberance of his discovery of the new form and his delight in the sheer technique of it.

His dedication of that poem "To Christ our Lord" has moved the piety of the Catholic commentators who perceive mystic meaning in it dear to the hearts of the faithful. On the face of the poem it is no more than an impressionistic description of the flight of a falcon. In itself it is not easy to understand and for nearly all readers would require a commentary and for a few words a special dictionary. But at that it is not the most difficult of Hopkins' poems.

That award might go to the one entitled *Tom Garland,*

even with Hopkins' interpretation and explanation of it to Bridges. Father Pick discovers in it statements of Catholic doctrine. But for the author it seemed rather to have significance as pointing out grave social injustices. However, Hopkins had to admit that his muse had come to have excessively private meanings, and set himself to correct that, and indeed came far toward accomplishing a communicable message. It cannot be said that he was indifferent at any time to being understood. He thought his poems were to be tested by the ear, were to be heard rather than read. However, very few of them may be understood immediately on a first reading or hearing.

Unmistakingly they do convey an effect which he aimed at, of an explosive character, and which he attained by technical means. In considerable part his technique made the difficulty for either hearer or reader. Intense compression of phrasing, ellipsis by omission of articles, connectives and relative pronouns, giving weight to nouns by piling up modifying phrases in the manner of the German language, the substitution of one part of speech for another, inversions—with such devices there was almost no limit to his poetic license.

Undoubtedly such freedoms greatly expand the use of language. They give infinite variety to verse, greatly exceeding that customary in prose. Evidently he got pleasure from such variety, and so does the reader. It may be a fair criticism that the variations come too thick and too fast for comprehension short of analysis that deprives us of much pleasure which properly we expect from a literary work.

Among the licenses and irregularities employed consciously by Hopkins were reversed feet and counterpoint rhythm, by which he meant that monosyllables, iambics, trochees, anapests, dactyls, and paeons interchange within the line in common or running rhythm more than is the usual practice in English poetry. But although allowing for such interchanges, Hopkins nevertheless thought it better in common rhythm generally to preserve and keep the form chosen, either of rising or of falling rhythm.

Hopkins' emphasis upon hearing to test his poetry is illustrated by his conception of the relation of counterpoint and sprung rhythm. He thought them inconsistent, and that sprung rhythm makes counterpoint superfluous, for it gives the desired variety mentally supplied as when in music one attends to the melody rather than the accompaniment.

Indeed Hopkins was striving to link poetry and music. Some adverse critics of Whitman have charged that he lacked the musical ear with which Hopkins was gifted. But the music of Hopkins also requires a guide. For Hopkins was as idiosyncratic a musician as he was a poet. He neither read music nor played an instrument. Yet he essayed to establish a musical notation of his own. His confidence in his own compositions, notwithstanding the adverse criticisms of trained musicians, was not lessened, and this was characteristic of the man.

Like Poe and Swinburne, sound with him often appears to triumph over sense. This is one of the sources of obscurity complained of in his poetry. But he believed that once his meaning was discovered it exploded into the mind of the reader. He labored for abrupt effects, though in a very involved way. However, we are told that Hopkins' poetry stands in contrast with Swinburne's, because language comes first for Swinburne for its own sake, while Hopkins makes it a servant of thought. But we are stunned by the paradox, expressed by Daiches, that the devices of his technique often render his thought unintelligible.

The paradoxes, if paradoxes they are, are numerous. He appeals from the eye of the reader to the ear of the hearer, from sense or understanding to sound to give meaning to his verse. He preaches against bad rhymes, yet few or none of repute forced far-fetched rhymes more than he. He has only been exceeded by his imitators in the splitting of a word at the end of a line to make a rhyme, thus carrying over an awkward syllable to begin the next line. Alliteration and assonance become such a passion with him as to mar most of his work and become offensive to taste.

In fact the greatest paradox of all is the union of something akin to the most obvious insanity with a conscious mastery of form and extremely subtle organization of logical thought. On the side of insanity his writing is an almost perfect illustration of hebephrenia, with its characteristic neologisms, verbigeration and stereotype. On the side of sanity he was a diligent student of prosody and an exceptional scholar in technical knowledge of poetry. Whitman did not so excel.

Hopkins' knowledge and skill of construction is especially displayed in his sonnets, a form of verse of which he was particularly fond, a type of verse which is ranked at the very height of excellence in poetic art, and to which he gave a new and original turn of expression. His poetry was written predominantly in sonnet form. Excluding *The Deutschland* nearly seven-ninths of his poems are sonnets.

He preferred the Italian to the Shakespearean sonnet. He remarked that the Italian sonnet is longer in the line than the English sonnet; and besides having more syllables, the Italian syllable is longer. He criticized the English sonnet as being too short, and he attempted to achieve the effect of the Italian sonnet by his use of sprung rhythm and "outriding feet" in his sonnets. And so he made the English sonnet more flexible and capable of more expression than it had before.

As Whitman saved poetry from the bondage of rhyme and meter, Hopkins saved the traditional forms of poetry from becoming static and unprogressive.

The Priest and the Poet.

The conflict between the priest and the poet in Hopkins cannot be gainsaid. It had both moral and tempermental aspects. When he wrote to Bridges that it was not pleasant to make confession of his like-mindedness with Whitman, he told nearly all of the story. But it was a gross exaggeration when he professed to have in himself a worse Hyde than the Hyde of Stevenson's Jekyll-Hyde. That was but the habit of a Christian to expatiate upon his sins.

In Hopkins' case there was an early tendency to melancholy which increased as he grew older. It was probably this more than anything else which led him to enter the Catholic Church and take orders as a Jesuit, for the duties of which he was by nature quite unfitted. He was a very earnest and sincere person and his sense of duty and obligation was so extreme that it intensified his inherent sufferings. The severe regimen of the Jesuit discipline caused him both mental and physical distress which his determination to accept and endure as penance for his actual weaknesses and imaginary sinfulness again and again brought about nervous prostration and such physical ills as diarrhoea and vomiting.

Hopkins had a fine intellect and the delicate sensitiveness of an artistic nature, and in consequence the militaristic rigors imposed by the Jesuit order's method which coarser natures thrived upon produced in him only unbearable torture that even his strong will could not surmount. His efforts only caused him humiliation. All these in the psychological atmosphere of the Church counted for the attribution to him of saintliness. But from any other viewpoint they evidence the sad mistake in the judgments of those who advised him. His retiring nature seemed fitted for the seclusion of the Church, but surely in some other order of a milder sort he could have found an environment that would have better served and developed his peculiar talents.

The manual duties of his novitiate were very burdensome to him notwithstanding his brave endurance of them. But it was hardly better or even worse when he preached and taught. His sermons were labored with the over-wrought care he bestowed on his poetry. To the common-sense auditors they often sounded ludicrous, as when he likened the Church to a milk cow; and when preaching on the text: "And Jesus said, Make the men sit down"; he re-iterated the idea so many times that students and fathers roared in laughter.

As a teacher he was not more successful. It was no de-fect of scholarship that attended his failure. Jowett, the authority on Greek at Oxford, recommended him as the most brilliant of that University's prize-winning students. It was not lack of interest or endeavor. He overworked himself in his desire to be accurate and just toward his pu-pils. In fractionated markings on examination papers he became so bewildered, panicky and exhausted that he was unable to add the figures.

In all these distresses of his priestly career it may be a debatable question whether the Jesuits made or hampered the poet inherently in him. He confessed that he conceived his taking orders as conflicting with his interest in poetry. He burned what he had written before he became a Jesuit, resolved to write no more, and for seven years abandoned the writing of poetry. But in the winter of 1875 at the re-quest of his rector he wrote a poem entitled *The Wreck of the Deutschland* in commemoration of the five Franciscan nuns who were drowned. In that he used a "new rhythm" which had long been haunting his ear, as he said. He did not publish that poem because his superiors disapproved.

Although that poem released his poetic powers, he for-bade Dixon to publish any of his poems because he deemed it an act of insubordination or double-dealing with his su-periors to do so without their consent. In 1881 he wrote Dixon that literary activity was incompatible with his pres-ent duties. He was then fearful that the composition of his poems had been a waste of time and had given rise in him to vain-glorious thoughts. He could not think of asking his superiors for permission to publish.

He was especially influenced in that attitude by the Jesuit treatment of literature as only a means to an end, as he said. Catholic writers have been quick to refute the imputation that Christianity, the Church, or the Jesuits were responsible for Hopkins' feeling in that matter. As we have suggested, it is probable that the more potent cause was his own melancholy which took him into the Church, hoping thereby for relief in the supposed consolations of religion. That did not dispel his inner conflicts, but on the contrary, as his letters furnish such abundant evidence, they were increased by the burdens and trials of his noviate, his teaching, and his priesthood in the service of the Church. And it is just as clear that he conceived a conflict between his esthetic sense and the ascetic vows that bound him.

To the humanist of Whitman's way of thinking such ascetic hindrances to art are both very absurd and hurtful. But from that conclusion, to which I agree, it does not follow that had Hopkins been a humanist he would have attained greater artistic excellence any more than one can say that because he was a Jesuit he was a great poet. One Catholic writer has tried to prove that his poetic and priestly attainments were inseparable. That would mean that one not an adherent of Hopkins' religion could not learn from or adopt his poetic technique. That assumption is quite disproven by the vogue he has had with and his imitation by the Communist poets. And despite his asceticism there was a humanistic strain in the man which is certainly not alien to Whitmanian humanism. Others have pointed out both qualities in him.

As to Communism, there is that famous passage in his letter to Bridges, in which he expressed belief in the future of Communism, and that such revolution would soon and justly come. He declared himself a kind of Communist. But his type was Ruskinite rather than Bolshevik. There is in fact a socialistic, or even Communistic, vein in recent Catholic thought which is obscured because the words "socialism" and "communism" are reprobated by the orthodoxy of Roman Catholicism. The writings of A. J. Penty and others indicate Catholic consciousness of the fact. On the other hand, Whitman was not a socialist or communist of any variety, but of the American radical school which is typified by Jefferson and Lincoln.

The Later Hopkins.

Especially as Hopkins came toward the end of his life he had more in common with Whitman's humanistic attitudes. That was what both had in common with Ruskin. It was a sentiment and a theory with Ruskin; it was a Christlike attitude in Hopkins; it was more actual, more intimate and more direct in Whitman. The Christ-man akin to Hopkins and to all men was a tremendously impressive idea to Hopkins as it was to Whitman. In one of his latest poems, *That Nature is a Heraclitean Fire and of the Comfort of the Resurrection,* he said unequivocally, What Christ is and was I am. That idea was also expressed by Whitman in the poem, *A Sight in Camp in the Daybreak Gray and Dim,* as he looked at the face of the dead soldier:

> "Young man I think I know you—I think this
>   face is the face of the Christ himself,
> Dead and divine and brother of all, and here
>   again he lies."

And in Whitman's *Chanting the Square Deific* the second stanza carries the parallel to the life of Christ as often repeated in the lives of men. Whitman's conception of Christ "with bent head, brooding love and peace, like a dove" (*Democratic Vistas*) is so like the lines in Hopkins' sonnet, *God's Grandeur,* that it may have suggested the latter. Possibly these are chance resemblances. But there are other frequent passages which show the likeness of their thought and philosophy of humanism.

In the sonnet, *Felix Randal the Farrier,* the ministrations of the priest to the dying man are like those of the war nurse in Whitman's *Drum-Taps.* Whitman's doctrine of the inseparability of body and soul finds an echo in Hopkins' sonnet, *The Caged Skylark.* In the poem *Ribblesdale* there is the same notion of the subordination of Nature to man, of the need of man's just tongue and hand to interpret and mould Nature, which is so fundamental in Whitman's philosophy of humanism. In a letter to Bridges Hopkins identified Nature with himself, quite Whitmanesque.

Hopkins seemed to have as definite a conviction about the supremacy of the individual self as had Whitman. In an untitled sonnet, beginning as "Kingfishers catch fire," he is emphatic as Whitman's *Song of Myself* that every being declares itself as its mission. In his exegesis of the poem he interpreted it, "Christ being me and me being Christ."

He closes that sonnet with repetition of the idea that Christ is revealed in the faces of men. His proclamation of the divinity of man much exceeds any humanization one expects from a Christian priest. In the sonnet entitled *To What serves Mortal Beauty* there is the daring declaration that the law of Love commands the worship of men's selves. And in sonnet 39 is the more daring suggestion that Christ in bliss emulates the deeds of men who do what they can as what he would do were he flesh again.

This Hopkins was a strange Christian and a stranger priest. There was a great deal of the heretic in him. It is not strange then that he thought Whitman more like himself than any other living man. He did not follow the Jesuits who based their theology on Thomas Aquinas, but early in his studies he came upon Duns Scotus, whose emphasis upon the individuality of the particular man most impressed him. In the sonnet *Duns Scotus's Oxford* he wrote of that medieval scholar as the one who gave him serenity of spirit. His loyalty to Scotus got him frequently into difficulties with his Jesuit superiors. To Patmore, Hopkins sharply criticized the schools that misunderstood, misquoted, and in that way undertook to refute Duns Scotus.

In the last, the closing cycle of Hopkins' life, his poems took on an unwonted clarity of meaning. It was as if the clouds of religious conformism were being chased away; and, although his mood was the least happy of his life, for the conflict had become excruciatingly painful, yet he faced his doubts and despairs with courage and sometimes with vehement desparate resistance, and he was more candid about his delusions than ever before and did not attempt, as he had been in the habit of doing, to deny the existence of his doubts and uncertainties of faith.

In contrast with Whitman whose humanistic faith grew and took into the human sphere the circumference of the Universe, the religious faith of Hopkins failed at times and he expressed himself occasionally in terms of profoundest skepticism. That is an easier mood to understand than the robust faith that Whitman proclaimed and it makes Hopkins more akin than Whitman to the prevalent doubtings which appear so characteristic of our contemporary poets.

The later poems of Hopkins show how his melancholy moods varied with a general tone of free-thinking skepticism. It is not true that, as Father Pick says, "Hopkins' spiritual aridity was poetic aridity." His aridity, both poetic and spiritual, was from his fear that he was going dry. He felt the thirst of death in him. He had felt that drought in his Oxford days, when he turned to the Church for succor, and now as he was fast sinking in health and spirit he cried out to the "lord of life, send my roots rain."

But it is in the sonnet named by Bridges *Carrion Com-*

fort, which is a synonym for Despair, that his most terrible anguish of spirit is expressed. Resolved not to yield to despair, like Job he questions God for casting him down rudely under foot, for breaking and bruising him, for the toil and terror of his existence since he "kissed the rod", that he a "wretch lay wrestling with (my God!) my God." Father Pick makes out of that poem a joyful submission to the divine will with self-surrender.

In fact he did not surrender, he did not abandon his self-will, but glorified it as the Christ, the human deed. It was paradoxical but necessary that Bridges, the free-thinker and non-church humanitarian, should have been the one friend who could be trusted with his poems, the rescuer of them from oblivion, and their publisher. The Church authorities did not dare to publish even *The Wreck of the Deutschland.* The intimacy of Hopkins with deity, the humanization of Christ, were too much for the Thomist fathers.

In that series of poems of the last years he fought his lonely way through despair to the transfiguration of Christ in himself. In Ireland where he was quite immured in the Church he was most lonely. Sonnet No. 44 portrays that distress. His misery is more poignantly expressed in Sonnet No. 45 and is bitterly charged to God's decree. In sonnet No. 41 even more explicitly are the doctrines of the Church found wanting: the Comforter is not comforting and Mother Mary is no relief. Sonnet No. 47, which Father Pick reads as "the priest's complete resignation", evidently meant for its author that neither prayer nor patience availed to assuage his suffering.

Hopkins clearly felt he was fighting the battle alone and that he had to rely on his own strength. In the first quatrain of *Carrion Comfort* that is positively spoken. He will not let despair overcome his will to be. He can hope, wish and do something.

In another poem, of the last year of his life, already

referred to, *That Nature is a Heraclitean Fire*, is also forcibly expressed that affirmation of the human self which overcomes despair in his sudden revelation by insight that man is Christ and that even this poor Jack-self is "immortal diamond". This conclusion is not what Father Pick assumes, that the destiny of man is in Christ, but that the willing, striving man *is* the resurrection of Christ. As in sonnet No. 39, the Christ, looking down on man who is doing all that he can do, cries it is a "Christ-done deed" of "God-made-flesh", and if he were to come again he would do the same.

Hopkins came at last, almost too late, to Whitman's answer to the enigma of human destiny, not as clearly or convincingly as Whitman. His involved style of inversions and tumbled speech more fitted for music than sense in the crabbed forms of sonnets which even his poetic license could not make free, forbade wholly clear expression. And then too the confines of his religion and the obligations to it he had taken on in the severity of Jesuit discipline would not permit the gleam of light in his late discovery of that truth in him from the first to have any full expression as it approximated in Whitman. But the likeness of himself to his great contemporary he recognized.

It is notable that of the great wrestlers with Fate of the Nineteenth Century whom we have discussed, those with Christian hope—Tennyson, Browning, and Hopkins—came to the end with doubts and perplexities about their religion, and that Whitman with only human hope, with only faith in man, maintained an optimistic spirit despite his consciousness of the misfit of things in the realm of Nature, in God's Universe. Whitman could believe that in the large view of the Future it would end well. Browning's early exclamation, "God's in his Heaven, all's well with the world," sank low with his declining years. Tennyson and Hopkins were always in the gloom of melancholy, and their last days were worse than the first. Whitman more than they felt the scourge of disease gathering its forces of destruction within him but only hoped that his verse be kept from reflecting the ills of his body.

In that hope did Whitman admit that the spirit may escape the body? Rather he believed it may retain to the end bright whatever of spirit shines within. The flicker out at the end leaves a cooling gray-white ash hardly less pure than the flame of light and a breath of air may lift it to dissolve in the atmosphere. That ethereal quality seemed to Whitman no less an attribute of body than of spirit or soul. In death and in life alike therefore he beheld an immortal body.

One misrepresents Hopkins who thinks him wholly given over to a religion of pure faith or simple belief in the tenets of Christian religion. Before those last "terrible sonnets" he may have written or intended to write for the pious purpose or subject to piety. But what shall we call any poet's work?

In the reading public's mind it will probably always be within the range of his mediocrity, before he attains maturity. In case of all the poets we have been reviewing and comparing here the public and for the most part the critics have preferred the work of the immature poet. The latest poems of Hopkins less praised are his best. Sensing a new faith, in himself, and a "new form" to express it, his vision was clearing. He no longer strove according to some external model of Church doctrine or pious art. There may be at the end reflections backward to the old dogmas as there was in the beginning with *The Wreck of the Deutschland* some foreshadowing of his latest moods. He throws aside the pretense, the efforts to believe in spite of his reason, and speaks directly out of his heart in his last poems. But from the first he was searching for the truth within himself, although like every novitiate he was drawn to an external source for the discovery and verification of the truth within.

His Humanist Concepts.

It is remarkable that the concept which remained with him as a central viewpoint was recognized and formulated by him at Oxford before he sought to take orders. It was the concept of "inscape," a word which he coined. Inscape was his conscious aim in poetry. It is like but has a larger meaning than intuition. The word "landscape" suggested it. But his function as a poet he conceived as not merely descriptive of an external object, nor, as the pietists would have it, "God in the object," but the object in man, although he feared in the period of his novitiate to accept and acknowledge his real aim.

One should be cautious about the interpretations which stress the religious significance of Hopkins' meanings. In a letter to Dixon he called inscape the soul of art and pertinent for the describing of Whistler's genius. To Patmore he wrote of it as the distinctive individual quality of style imparted to the representation of the object by the artist. It is what appears in the artist's work when he is intuitive, that is, when he puts himself into the object or, more aptly, when he brings the object into his own creative consciousness.

Distinctiveness and individuality, even to the degree of oddness or queerness, are what he emphasized in the letters to Patmore and Bridges, as the quality of inscape. It is a stage in the development of personality. It goes beyond the merely potential self. Other terms he used for analysis of inscape also stressed personality.

One of these terms was "pitch," to describe the process of inscape. Pitch is the beginning of inscape. "Doing" is the verb to express it. The next step in the process is indicated by one of Hopkins' German-like coined words, "doing-be." For this he might have used the word "act" but for its ambiguity as deed done as well as being done. Hopkins wanted a word to imply both action and existence. When there is a series or chain of "doing-be's" we are approaching but have not yet attained self or personality. Personality is an addition or overlaying of nature or inscape. Inscape thus appears to be the incarnation or reification of the active act or doing-be. Then the true self or personality comes into being.

"Instress" was another term denoting the effect of inscape, self or personality felt by one beholding it. It completes the process of the development and production of a work of art.

There is nothing necessarily religious in these meanings. Hopkins' own earlier attitude was undoubtedly to endeavor to give religious significance to all his activities, although he was sensible even about that. Furthermore, during his novitiate he adopted the Jesuit disregard for literature, and therefore piety should not be too much emphasized in interpretation of his work. Until the late poems it should be treated as a temporary or transitional idiosyncracy and not a permanent or necessary feature of his work.

Accordingly for those who have nothing in common with Hopkins' professed religion of Catholicism or Christianity Inscape may nevertheless be a concept of value. Notwithstanding its subtlety and strangeness it has merit for appreciation of the worth and dignity of man, man's genius, appearing in a work of art, and may therefore become a common possession as heritage from his thought. The concept of self or of personality was for him as for Whitman the most important content of poetry. From this we can understand the community of feeling (would he have called it "instress of feeling"?) he had with Whitman.

As to the relative influence of Whitman and Hopkins on their successors, Hopkins has probably given a new vogue to the traditional forms of poetry by his innovations. They are free verse of a different kind than Whitman's. One may cite the authority of Professor Daiches who maintains that in respect of "details of arrangement and structure" Whitman's influence has been the greater. It would be contrary to fact to deny Hopkins a large share with Whitman in forming the style of contemporary poetry. In thought Whitman was both more original, profounder, and more inclusive. That from a source so different in origin and environment as Hopkins' there should come so nearly approximation to Whitman's thought and philosophy of humanism is a most significantly affirmative fact. Their differences of poetic art, both contributing greatly to more freedom of expression, when their thought content is fully understood, should have important consequences in advancing humanistic philosophy. Their humanism may give new life to religion which now in both belief and practice is ebbing low toward threatening death. After review of another significant contemporary, a look at Whitman's successors may confirm our opinion that what Whitman so largely pioneered has not been superseded by later styles of art nor outmoded by new fashions of thought.

17

DICKINSON AND WHITMAN.

Strangers but akin.

❖ ❖ ❖ ❖ ❖

"... I wonder if other men ever have the
like, out of the like feelings?

❖ ❖ ❖ ❖ ❖

Does he harbor his friendship silent and endless?"

IT IS HARD TO BELIEVE THAT EMILY DICKINSON WAS A CON-
temporary of Whitman. She was born a decade later and
died a half decade earlier. She knew of him reputedly and
not personally. Her closest literary friend, Thomas Wentworth Higginson, was contemptuous and inimical toward
Whitman. Whitman knew nothing of her. In fact, excepting for intimate friends, she was unknown until after her
death, about when Whitman died already famous.

Whitman lived in the current and stream of his time;
she lived apart from it, but not above or below it. Her
rebellion was aloofness. Her intenseness was narrowly personal, not throbbing for or with anything human she perceived in her environment. This impersonality toward
what was outside her some have taken to be evidence of
an instinct within her for universality. She expressed poignantly and veraciously her own experiences and they became
for her the absolute. And exquisitely she translated those

experiences in phrases which falsified them for others because she lacked the philosophic learning to accord them with the range of accurate speech to express such emotions in the universal language. As she lived outside the circle, or rather in an enclosed cell, of her environment, monadically sealed away from her contemporaries, she did not possess the interest or the historical knowledge to acquaint her with the language of inherited and traditional wisdom. The little she knew of it rather repelled her. She made no attempt to be universal or inclusive in Whitman's understanding of such an effort.

She did range extraordinarily about the realm of her own experiences. Continually she practiced self-analysis. Because she shut herself in upon herself she was the more competent in that. One cannot say that invariably she made an accurate analysis of her own emotions. One would not expect her to render that of others, for she did not explore the hearts of others except as she saw them revealed in herself. Even her descriptions of spiritual experiences are very vague as if she were striving to attain a mystical envelopment of experience.

But one can easily overstress the differences between her and Whitman, and the disparagement of either to the gain of the other is the loss of both. Wholly separate from or unconscious of each other they had so much in common that their differences are often more matters of degree than of kind. Like Whitman Emily was philosophical rather than metaphysical. Her philosophical tendency is shown in the division or classification of her poems (though made by Higginson) under the several titles, "Life, Love, Nature, Time and Eternity," and "The Single Hound" or identity. Her conceptions of these themes made her nearer to Whitman than to either Emerson or Thoreau. It is remarkable that with a different environment and a different approach there should be so much similarity in their viewpoints.

In contrast with Whitman she had a distinguished family. Her grandfather, father and brother were leading lawyers of Amherst, and officials of the local college and church. Especially her father was a man of affairs, in politics (a term in Congress) , and prominent in promoting the business of the community. Again in contrast with Whitman's her family was orthodox. Although she was regretfully unable to get religion, to give herself to God, in her schooldays, it was not until she was in her thirties that she definitely realized her separateness from orthodoxy.

Whitman's education was had in the printing room and the library. Hers was beyond the usual scholastic training of upper class women of her time. She lived in an academic environment, but professed to have learned little from it. Benjamin Franklin Newton, a law student in her father's office, and as a young lawyer and Unitarian, did influence her considerably and encouraged her to be a poet.

Whitman's bachelorhood is matched by Emily's spinsterhood. As there is no reliable evidence of Whitman's love for a particular woman, there is little evidence that Emily Dickinson ever had a specific lover. Besides Newton one other man did move her very greatly. He was a Presbyterian preacher at Philadelphia, the Reverend Charles Wadsworth, whom she met in 1854 when her father was Congressman. There was probably no closer relation between them than he was briefly her spiritual adviser. Notwithstanding he was happily married an intermittent correspondence went on between them, broken off during the 60's and resumed in the 70's. She had been writing to several clergymen, among them the Reverend Edward Hale, requesting instruction, but besides Wadsworth mainly attracted the Reverend Thomas Wentworth Higginson who was quite impressed by her and did seriously attempt to guide her literary endeavors. But it is only the ardently inventive imagination of Emily Dickinson, the poet, which can invest these masculine encounters with the romance of tender sentiments. The nearest attachment which might have approached love-making may have been Newton's, but he went away and shortly afterward was married. Was there more between them than platonic friendship? Nobody knows.

It is remarkable that Higginson, a Unitarian minister, and later a successful writer, also a feminist who took no stock in women, nevertheless counselled her to abandon meter and rhyme and try the Whitman style of writing. She replied she had not read Whitman but had heard his book was disgraceful. Heretics are often shy of each' other, and by that time quite conscious of her own wayward thinking she may have preferred to go her own way without diversion by another spirit whom she may have intuitively deemed too powerful an attraction and felt safer in following the lead of her own developing genius to new untried paths. Therefore she gave as little heed to this advice as to Higginson's other more conventional recommendations. Her originality, despite her professions of modest discipleship and solicited aid, was steadfastly adhered to.

In another respect she was the very opposite of Whitman. His blatant publicity seeking was most contrary to her nature. To her publication almost as much as fame seeking was repulsive. Only three of her poems were published in her lifetime, and she fell out with sister-in-law Sue because of violating her wishes by sending one of these to a publisher. She accepted the apparent verdict of her literary friends that she was unpopular.

Indeed her poems do appear to be herself and therefore to violate the accepted canon that intimate personal feeling has no place in literature, which T. S. Eliot has now expressed as the impersonalism of poetry. Despite Whitman's large "I" he never exposed his ego to the public gaze in such intimate way as Emily almost invariably exhibited hers. If in fact she was so self-revealing and not merely given to fictitious self-dramatization, then might one the better understand her reluctance about publishing herself. She had contempt for the human deep-voiced frog bellowing to the bog his name.

Again, her style of poetry is nearly the very opposite of Whitman's. His was expansive, verbose, long-lined, adjectival, lengthily explanatory, heavily weighted with parenthetical expression, resonant and grand, ponderous and slow in movement; and hers the antithesis of all that. The dogmas of Pound and Eliot and the erratic heresies of others of the recent American school are but the scholastic rendition of what Emily consciously practiced and developed as her unique style. Not only did she institute in her verse free rhyming or no rhymes and took ungrammatical liberties, but condensation, compactness, conciseness, which Eliot thinks the essence of poetic expression, contribute principally to the nervous energy, rapidity, and sharp-cut features which distinguish her poetry. At the same time the prevalence of common meter or hymn style and iambic quatrain in which customarily she wrote give some basis for her popularity with the traditionalists who persistently set her up as authority against Whitmanism. But Whitman would have welcomed her as proof of his tenets that verse must break away from the fettered style of the jinglers and prettifiers. Therefore she shares with Hopkins and Whitman the role of teacher to present day poets.

Comparison of three poems of each may illustrate their differences of style and method. First, the locomotive poems: Comparing Emily's "I like to see it leap the miles" with Walt's *To a Locomotive in Winter,* the latter is longer, has a greater number of images, is more accurate and definite in description, is more philosophical and conscious of the historical relation of the great machine, is more impressive as to the general significance of a locomotive, and is expressed in the characteristic Whitman style we have designated above. On the other hand Emily's poem

has the spirit attributed to childish wonderment, although
not as simply understandable as poems for children—there
are big words, literary allusions, and quaint expressions
beyond a child's comprehension. It is the poem of an
adult with something left of childish simplicity, and with
the characteristic Dickinson style so much affected now by
imitative poets—with compression and ellipsis removing it
yet farther from the range of the child's mind. Although
Walt invokes the locomotive to serve his muse and utilizes
its physical substance as symbols to substantiate his theory
of verse, particularly as favoring images of grandeur rather
than mere melodious tunefulness, almost everyone would
regard Emily's verses as more intimately and directly personal notwithstanding her theory that poetry is oblique
and indirect expression.

Again, illustrating both theory and content, Whitman
maintains the music is in the hearer and not in the instrument which is merely excitive. Whitman's expression
of the thought (in the second stanza of section 4 of "A
Song for Occupations") might be read as rhythmical prose.
It is explicit and names instruments of music to empha-
size the point. Similarly Dickinson: The song of the oriole
is in the hearer's ear; it is within, not without; contrary to
the skeptic, it is in one's self. Dickinson's instance is that
of a music-maker and raises a doubt. Does this confusion
signify what is characteristic of poetry? Do the rhyming
and meter serve to hide the inconclusiveness of the thought
and none the less leave us satisfied? If so, it argues that
poetry is illusionment, make-believe, and fulfills its functions as such. Another passage would seem to affirm that
as Dickinson's conception, maintaining that melody is in-
definable; and yet another that the discordant drums are
demanded by the delicate musical ear. It is the spirit of
the poet who does not want to be bound too much by the
laws of poetic form while yet acknowledging them. How
much of that attitude is temperament and how much art?

In Dickinson one feels that temperament, in Whitman's case rather a theory of art, produced the effect.

We take yet another comparison made to Whitman's discredit. Wells extols Dickinson's poem, "When I was small, a woman died," as exceeding in truthfulness any of Whitman's war poems and he accuses Whitman of yielding to the contemporary war hysteria. Her poem starts with the familiar swing and stanza form of the ballad, and the third stanza begins likewise, but excepting the second and fourth lines of the third stanza it is unrhymed and irregular in meter. It differs also from the ballad in its personal note and complex involvements of meaning. Nevertheless, the telling power of the poem is indisputable, and that although the narrator is hesitant about passing judgment on the facts or event to record any express feeling of her own. Incompletion, a fragmentary thought, an unthought-out event, is the impression one receives from it. As for Whitman's many war poems compared with this meager one of Dickinson who lived through the Civil War barely touched by it so far as her poems indicate, and the charge that Whitman had no intelligent understanding of that War, if that opinion is not the mere prejudice of the critic, it must denote a critical taste which prefers the bareness and immediacy of primitive literature to the fluent expression of modern writers.

Dickinson did indeed have somewhat of that tendency in her thinking, for in self-criticism she suspected the fluent passage as false. But in her own writing sophistication is all over the page. Her psychological nuances are of the most subtle sort. She is an analyst of the heart as only the most modern can be. Simplicity and naivete were an appearance but not a fact in her.

Dickinson will fairly qualify for Read's definition of a metaphysical poet. Many of her poems are built around a designated concept which is then illustrated or expanded by poetic imagery. But she was not a metaphysical poet in the popular sense any more than was Whitman. Both were philosophical and reflective rather than speculative and in thought as well as temperament. Emily was even more skeptical than Walt. Both rested profoundly on faith in being and the human order and not upon dogmatic beliefs. Whitman has been criticized because he organized *Leaves of Grass* on a rational plan. As Higginson concluded, Dickinson's poems fitted into a conceptual classification. And as we will now see, her thinking about those fundamental concepts was a near approach to Whitman's more radical and more positively defined philosophy.

What did life mean to her? Not the fullness, abundance, expansiveness, and joyfulness it meant to Whitman. She was not so optimistic. One can imagine that poem satirizing a preacher of "breadth" to caricature a Whitmanite. And one may find affirmations of asceticism threading her verse. She declared she can endure much grief better than a little joy. And suffering is the discipline that gives triumph to the spirit. She knew the numbing which follows intense pain, but also that it is token of death. Death seemed to her a country from which no traveller to it returns; there was no inspiration of hope in it; it is changeless, but she could feel the divinity of the brave dead as shame to the living. The breadth of Whitman that embraced death as the root place of life and possibly its fulfillment, was beyond her comprehension. Rather for her was death an evil to be met stoically. More for her than for Whitman life is power and gain, a great adventure, and danger intensifies life.

But on the whole it is a humanistic philosophy that Dickinson believed in. She learned that God and Nature do not supercede man. If God and Nature are not one in her thought there is a close relationship. She probably distinguished that God from the God of Christian theology whom she disliked. She interpreted the story of Jacob wrestling with the Angel of the Lord as having "worsted God."

Certainly man could rival God as creator. God is a distinct person, indifferent to human fate and, as depicted by the Bible, a tyrannical and unjust God. God at best is "not far off from furthest good man." Recurring to the biblical God, his Son Jesus is the one beloved as Priscilla preferred John Alden to Miles Standish. As for God's guidance it is not by a friendly hand but in a thorny path. She felt differently about Jesus who preferred the lost, who gave some hope after death. Yet she was doubtful if Jesus' love for man was equal to that of one's love for a particular person. And she interpreted Christ's coming as preferring earth to heaven and humanity to divinity.

Nature like God seemed to her regardless of man, a stranger to him, mysterious, unnoble, unfriendly or not helpful. About God and Nature she was agnostic, though not disputing in some way her identity with them. Closer to her and more akin were the bee, the hummingbird, the oriole, the robin, the flowers, and even the green snake in the garden, than loveliest Nature great like God. And these may have seemed to her superior to man's artistry.

Almost as completely as Whitman she thought divinity is only Me. It is the divine in man that places him above Nature. The grown-up person comes to realize that it is not Paradise or kings but men who are to be propitiated. And man grows within and achieves himself. In God or Nature is not the spontaneity of creation but in a man. We are absurd when we pray to Heaven; man is his own place, ourselves is reality, existence. Great as is the sun that rules the earth and sky, man is busier with his own business.

The meaning is clear, Man's power is within, not outside himself. Explicitly the best in the soul is embodied in the flesh. It is by the struggle within, she thought, we win. The soul's adventure is its own identity in the body. It is remarkable that independently thinking Dickinson and Whitman arrived at the same humanist conclusions so different from other contemporaries. But he was earlier and more definite in that idea.

Also for her as for him immortality was a frequent theme, with a similar conclusion. She was very skeptical about an after life, but not yielding to the notion that this world is the end of all. However, immortality is not something in after time, a hereafter, it is now. We experience it here and meet it here every day. Danger especially discloses it to us. Instinctively we know this immortality. Or, in a different mood, I am the term between the eternity of the past and the immortality of the future, and death is an incident of that continuity.

Such a round of being, pointing in the identity of the particular living being, also characterized Whitman's belief. This is not the orthodox belief of either religionists or philosophers. It is the humanist conception of immortality, not in terms of drifting bodiless spirit, but rather a scientific conception of continuity and relatedness. It is not the Great Chain of Being doctrine, nor the soul given to the body at birth by God. It emphasizes rather the individual separate identity, and, though related to the whole of Nature, it is this separate activating man who is for himself mainly the creative force. For it is man and not the outside show which concerns us. When we rise above fate, then we are really men.

But these ideas were expressed obliquely, by slant, and not openly and frankly even to the Unitarian clergymen she wrote to, not for instruction but for confirmation of her silent convictions. Housed with a stern puritanical father, not understood by her set of friends when in her schooldays she could not bring her heart to accept God, finding a secret solace in framing her thoughts in the disguise of poetic symbols, gradually she withdrew more and more into the solitude of her own house and garden and found more acceptable as token of human contacts she really desired the companionship of a large dog and the unspeaking creatures of earth and sky about whom she philosophized as though they had the feelings and consciousness of men. In such moods developed the genius of her art and her thought.

To those few whom she sought out and to whom she communicated her rarest treasures, she seemed, as to Higginson only a "cracked" and "eccentric poetess," and her strange spell of dramatic speech with its hidden meanings disturbed and "unnerved" them. A strange little aristocrat, robed in white, plain and commonplace enough in her face and figure, she belonged to an eerie world excepting for the fewer still who are privileged to commune with genius and to recognize it as the supremely sane. One man of her generation might have shared her thoughts. He could have hardly understood her speech, and he was too shy of women to have met her soul, and she had a bad report of him. What barriers of custom and rumor exclude even the great from the sacred converse and intimacies of the noblest human spirits!

But in the degree of her physical aloofness from the world she became the better acquainted with the secret chambers of the human heart. Before Freud she had discovered by the subtler and surer means of personal experience what he uncovered by observation and experiment and she carried farther in her own consciousness to the summation both of theory and practice. She knew how her knowledge and discovery of the lower depths of the soul would frighten the people on the street and that therefore it was well, safer for herself and for the populace, to keep locked within herself the secrets of her inner life. She knew that by "subjugating consciousness" or self-abdication we do not conquer ourselves. Wiser than Freud she knew that consciousness of our captivity is liberty. And if one could achieve that suppression of self, then he would be dead. Indeed he becomes superman who perceives the giant of conflict within himself and reckons with it. It is self-reliance that creates the God in man. Faith in ourselves is the sustaining power. It is the union of heart and mind, of emotion and intelligence, that makes an integrated self, and they must both be open to the great outside world at the same time they are self-contained and also able to shut the world out so as not to be the sport of the elements, God or Nature. Our human house must have doors. Our lonesomeness is largely vain because we do not know what we want. Nevertheless, longing with extraordinary constancy may provide us at long length with the necessary vision. But it must not be loaded down with too much pain, for at last that stupefies and we let go and die. For peace of life we must work even when there is no reward and although the only stimulus is to get through with the job. We can overcome the tedium of life with imagination, by living in the realm of possibility, and by doing with a will what we can within the range of possibility. In this indirect way we get at the wisdom of life. Denied it, our wills are thwarted, our intelligence blanked, our heaven of hope dies out, and wisdom is lost on us. In other words, a certain degree of success must attend our efforts, although by hazards of life those fewer who win have won. It is they who know that defeat is nothing but defeat. We come slowly by what we get in reality. And success is most alluring and highly prized by those who have not experienced the struggle to attain it.

Thus this woman threaded the mazes of illusion and reality and became at home with herself more successfully than known by those about her. They knew she was a good cook. They did not know she was a great poet. And still less did they know that she had entered and taken possession of the house of wisdom.

And how did this lonely spinster, living apparently outside the house of love, acquire acquaintance with its intimacies and accommodate herself to its departure from her external life? Did she have compensating resources within herself? Or did she somehow sublimate her passions and go beyond to higher stages of the spirit?

Here again there is a parallel between herself and Whitman. From out of the despair and sickness of the spirit she gained health, wholesomeness and vision. She healed her own spirit and made it whole again. And more, like him too, she left a record and pattern of her triumph for solace and example unto others. Only that is the actual achievement of genius.

Her coying confidences she entrusted to cryptic verse, partly to Unitarian clergymen happily married, and perhaps shyly withheld from a youth (unfavored by her father) who may have awakened her passions, went away, married, and shortly died, but just before death willed to her his haunting spirit; and that she cherished, dwelt with it as an unwed wife, and had intercourse with it until she had explored all the recesses of love in her nature. The revelation of those experiences were too tender for publication, but as she grew familiar with them they passed into memory and at last into verse when the flush of girlhood was gone and she was then a full-grown and deeply experienced woman.

The mystery of Emily's love affairs is almost as much a mystery as Whitman's, although her poems appear more autobiographical. Yet are they? She wrote to Higginson that when in her poems she used the personal pronoun "I" she did not mean herself, but "a supposed person." And such was Whitman's "I", a potential "I", may be, but not the actual or historical Whitman. And her loves too, were they not just as imaginary, and none the less true experience? She had felt what she wrote with that fine discernment which lives much beyond physical experiences. An intuitive person, an introspective person, an introvertive person, is in one way an exceptionally understanding person. Such persons have difficulty enough in their social relationships because they read the depths of their own minds and souls, because personal knowledge is more intimate than ever possible concerning another person, and they often mistake the transjection of themselves as that other person. But in this respect Emily was shrewder than most and made no attempt in fact or in verse to interpret the universe under the misapprehension that it was herself. The excellent poise or balance she established in herself is what raises her revelations so far above the meanings of mysticism as well as separating them wholly from psychotic states.

It does not matter then, (or how absurd it is to go as nearly every biography of her does, fumbling in the gossipy rumors,) whether she had a romantic affection for the young Humphrey who died so pathetically, or Reverend Gould who in Amherst days was the idol of the girls, or with adulterous thoughts about Major Hunt, the husband of her bosom friend, or Reverend Wadsworth also securely bonded in marriage! What a little temptress she was as a pretended confidant of pastors, especially of the Unitarians! What woman has never had a flurry of the heart and regrets for what she failed to cultivate, sighs for what might have been! But in Emily such sentiments and such reflections found a deeper nature and the genius to analyze and embody them in a deathless art. Whitman did not rival her penetration, although he became more significantly prophet of the ideas of better relations between lovers and friends.

Looking back on her experiences in love she thought of the beginning as a precious treasure untreasured by a simple school girl. And if the poems be autobiographical, its tell-tale beginning was an unpracticed schoolgirl's letter, written with a heaving breast. An affair, which had gone no farther in real experience and without other real loves to supplement and continue it, must go on in romantic dreaming, and hers did so—much more in the suspirations of famished love, consuming itself in imaginations, until at last with nothing more to feed upon, it expired for want of nourishment. That may be the history of the affair.

Of her poems on love, those of absence are most numerous. Poems of enjoyment and fulfillment are few and indistinct—they have the atmosphere of distance. There are more about love lost. It was a nun's life of secret passion within. It was a life that was the grave of love, the place where it was buried. Though love is life and immortality, the alpha and omega of which the rest of the "living world is but a shade," yet for her it was a sacrificial life, a Calvary. That life of love was like a little brook that would dry up in the heat of the noon, or it was like an arctic flower that would stray into a summer climate, and so travel between pain and paradise. Love is thus a seat of contradictories, as far apart as earth and heaven, life and death.

And this over against the other recurring thought that in love two are one. She felt herself a ghostly bride. Thus married she declared herself wife, a finished state of comfort, a woman grown, looking back on girlhood's longings as pain, or as mere playthings of life, dropped for the "honorable work" of woman and of wife. And in that fulfillment of passion contradictories enter again. It is an Eden that to unacquainted lips is a delirium, and those wild, wild nights!

In the aftermath is regret that one did not drink more deeply of the cup that had touched the lip. Or yet more bitter consciousness of poverty of soul when she realizes that she is a mere idolator of dead love. But there are even greater hazards in forgetting or learning to forget, for that may spell death.

But in the greater wisdom of experience and knowledge one learns that the tie back to those specters of regret or idolatry is living in the past. Escape, too, whether backward or forward, is not living, of which the essence is adventure and carrying us on to divinity.

Friendship is akin to love, but there one finds antagonism between one's friends. And friends, the best, are physically the unacquainted ones, private to ourselves, persons we have met who don't know us. Indeed, those who come to us late because their friends have died or since they neglected us are as good as enemies. These are reflections of a woman of warm friendly impulse who had shut herself in the more to appreciate and treasure true friendship. Whitman, with a manner of universal hospitality, yet in his intense reservations, as recorded in the conversations with Traubel, was not less aloof than self-immured Emily. He did not let his closest friends break through his guard of personal immunity.

The longing for human sincerity, true recognition of herself, was a poignant desire of her heart, and she expressed it eloquently in many poems. She knew so well that nothing else is of such priceless value as this, the appreciation of a person's intrinsic worth. Nevertheless, it is not the worth achieved—that is unworthy. Personal worth is beyond estimation—it always runs ahead—it is in the potential, as yet unrealized. Therefore, it is futile to defend a friend against attack. And that accounts for Emily's rash assertion, in a sense of helplessness in such a situation, that destruction of the human race would enable us to glorify it. We could then see men as a noble experiment.

But, aside from these disturbances in friendship and in our own human nature, it is "good to be alive," and especially alive in consciousness of being one in and with another. That was a unity, however, that seems, if we believe the poems of "The Infinite Aurora", to have been more real in anticipation. Even so, she thought that maidenhood with its seal of longing and chastity taught her more than wifehood could. But she doubted the fairness or justice of such slow long drought of engagement that sealed virginity. How factual and commonplace becomes the married state, nothing left to imagination, compared to the pleasures of fantasy that continue to be built on hope, painful though they be. Such experiences were spiritualized infinitely and interpreted (not without some bitterness) in terms of mortality and immortality. They mingled profoundly with unbelief in the Christian doctrines. Death is the only release for our sick selves. We are sustained by our spirits rather than by some far off event. There is consolation to have been known, to have been recognized though forgotten, for there could not be forgetting without prior recollection. Nevertheless there are complaints against the infidelity of forgetting.

Surely she had tasted that sorrow, perhaps in the haunting spirit of the dead who had married another. A "dull lad" the father may have deemed him and charged her to forget, and did she then disobey secretly? Did he think he was the one hurt most? Her silence he mistook, but then she herself by later confession knew too late what she dismissed from her life for the sake of obedience. All this appears to be autobiographical.

It meant to her a continuous dying in living. That was why life and death were equally intimate terms to her. But faith did not overcome skepticism about another life or another world where lovers might reunite. Immortality is something else. It is the partaking of another. Again it is impressed upon us that divinity is a human quality and immortality is here and now in the living. Man is both deity and eternity. Love is longer than life and defies the grave; it is the resurrection. In quantity it is beyond both heaven and hell.

For being is eternity, immortality. Death is the "white exploit," and in the poems collected under that title death is viewed from this side of the great divide, because death achieved there is no communication from the other side. In these poems there is stark realism intensified by the imagination and made vivid by narrative. She observed the quiet when death comes, as if the dying ones are grateful for it. When death has arrived it is a "silver reticence," a "solid calm."

But from observation, nevertheless, she would save tears for the living that are wasted on the dead. Like Whitman there seemed to her inseparability of body and soul. Dickinson conceived it as flying but wafting the flesh and electrically vitalizing it so that "the body is a soul," and as such it glows on until dissolved in death.

Death shuts us out with "lids of steel," but the grave is a mysterious ample container of one we love. Yet she would prefer the place of the living to the city of the dead.

She quotes scripture and the ambiguities of Jesus about death. It was Jesus who said, "God is the God of the living and not of the dead." His assurance, taken to be of immortality, that some there would not taste of death, can that comport with the idea that the dead cannot be immortal? The immortality of the departed is in retrospect a delight. What they are in the hereafter is a doubt, a gambling chance, for they are beyond our observation. Again with resort to scripture, Paradise is for the very few. For the many, you and me, it is not preferred.

It annoyed her that praise is heaped on the dead who cannot glow since it was earned here, not in the hereafter. If Heaven is such a fine place, if death is achievement, who would not be eager about it? Heaven or Hell, nobody knows anything about it, the country or the direction, beyond the gateway of death. If either is there beyond, if true, we'll know quick enough. The only certainty of Paradise we know is the certainty of death. Here in this mortality is immortality, in contrast to Reverend Channing's "A Poet's Hope." And so "The White Exploit" closes not on the serene affirmation Editor Bingham presumes. Who but an orthodox or fundamentalist Christian clergyman thinks the Psalmist believed in the Christian Heaven and the Resurrection? Emily's subtleties are too much for simple believers.

Her immortality is of the kind the poets make who light lamps that burn with "vital light" after the poets are dead. The theme of relation of body and soul is also matched as relation of mind and heart. The mind is a parasite dependent on the heart. The expansiveness of the mind like Whitman's roving soul is token of immortality. Apparently she did accept the poet's superstition that the word is a spiritual inflatus to be found by searching. And also the idea of William James and the intuitionists about reason closing the doors to inspiration. And she did not become emancipated from the further notion that Nature itself is poetry. She believed in the mystery of the poet's soul. And this led to the further assumption that fluency betrays an arid mind, notwithstanding the contrary belief that the poet's work begins with oiling the wheel. Beauty is the infinity of our incorporeity, in which idea the poetic wings get grounded again.

So too, truth is stable and her own support, her own supernal structure. The idea is a powerful thing, and a remark may set it explosively off. Nevertheless, like Whitman too, she believed in slanting the truth, though telling it whole. We cannot bear to be told direct. The Victorian repression had a hold on these daringest spirits.

The poet's craft and creativeness seemed to her only a necessary beginning, an obligation even though it is surpassed in the loftier vision. But inspiration, though an upper something, is not an inflatus from God, as the medievalists taught.

But the inspiration of the poet is not fed on fame. For fame is cheap, to be had by begging. It is a profanation of poetry. It is given usually when the poet is dead. It is therefore a vain request, "a futile diadem."

Her disdain for fame was probably born of mixed emotions and experiences. In the first place, her poems were intimate experiences of her own heart of which she was sensitively conscious. She lived in the repressed puritan atmosphere of New England, of which her father was a high priest, and her devotion and obedience to him were suppressive. The Unitarian clergymen were mystified and even frightened by something adventuresome they felt in her. The respectability in which she lived left her no other expression than the secret outpourings of her poetic soul. Obliqueness therefore became second nature to her and she mistook it for art and believed that the truth must be told in a veiled fashion.

But for all this awryness the truth was precious to her. And she became aware of its source in life, in man. The humblest human heart is greater than anything else. Nature is magnified by our deeds.

What are the great truths? We live in hope and it assuages suffering. Too much assurance or certainty displaces hope and produces less good work. Compensations or rewards therefore are not the greatest stimuli. When we see the end we slacken, and that is a very solemn fact. The creative soul must have freedom and spontaneity. The soul is more fragile and mortal than the green things of Nature. Play makes the soul's work easy. Pain retards it. The soul is always trying to identify itself, although this is an evidence of something ailing it. Our dreams give a deceptive and temporary sense of enrichment.

Only half wisdom runs through the section of "Bolts of Melody" entitled "That Campaign Inscrutable." Silence is apostrophized. Loneliness, shame, patience, grief, joy, bliss—are topics sometimes written upon more fluently than profound.

The skeptic and unbeliever show up in these themes. Prayer often repeated to a disappointing God is disillusioning; "thou shalt not" would be kinder. Skepticism is a cautionary measure against fearful happiness. But happiness is a powerful stimulus. Even decay goes on by stages; we are eased off by degrees to the end. Doubt aids us to get our footing; delusion makes living possible. There was not just one Calvary but may be as many as there are persons. Faithfulness to the end unto the "Crown of Life" is spurned as unfit for the fit, emphasizing again the irreverance for orthodoxy in Emily's religion. But she justified her unbelief: One doesn't get satisfaction from believing what one doesn't believe.

Yet this short life of ours has magical extent. It means more to such as the atheist. There's much or little in our power. There's an economy in happiness that keeps us sane. Notwithstanding Adam's fall from Eden anyone who wills can dwell there. It is only necessary to balance up between sorrow and delight. The trouble is our human nature craves what is beyond its perspective or prospective. We shun simplicity.

Our memories should be silent lest they silence us. But escaping them we escape from the mind of man. True memory keeps its root or origin, and attempt to suppress it is futile, a psychoanalytic observation.

But these observations do not put a blight on man's endeavors. What he undertakes he will achieve when encouragement balances with obstacle. We must be reminded that the best things are not the obvious. The best is what is not yet realized. Heaven here is better than Heaven that may be. Strength is strengthened by the faith of others in it. We do not know how many opportunities or visitations of opportunity escape us. Work, not chance, is luck.

In the final section of "Bolts of Melody," "An Ablative Estate," love is impersonally observed—her latest reflections after the emotion was past or dead. To have it is pain, without it is woe. The lover must not beg for love, for then he will be rejected. Love is always indiscreet. But do these impersonal observations evidence greater wisdom because the emotion has departed? T. S. Eliot's formula does not work well even when the gifted poets exercise it.

Furthermore, as she knew, reason acquaints us with the fact that calculated experiment is not very useful in life. It is an afterthought. Surprise somewhat tempered gives life and endeavor a stimulus.

"Circumference" is probably the most favored big word in "Bolts of Melody." Circumference, she declared, had become the business of her life. She called it the "bride of awe." Does it indicate in her the same outreaching characteristic as Whitman's desire for expansiveness and inclusiveness? Faith is of the same quality. It is always renewable or mendable when torn. Even "utmost is relative," but yet we are always striving toward it.

Life is a balance of things. Suspense is sister to wonder. Bliss and woe, though seldom found side by side, are equals. Happiness yields to anguish. Crushed things give sweetest tears.

We are so constituted that we would rather play with men than associate with God. The particular thing is news and more interesting to us than the cosmic or universal. To stint we must have known plenty.

The soul is likewise limited. It can go to sleep and the utmost it can do is try to comprise tomorrow. Yet the soul is indestructible and cannot be taken from itself. It possesses itself by silence. Consciousness is its essence. Yet we secretly dread to look consciousness squarely in the face.

"An Ablative Estate" ends on the note that belief in God and Heaven have gone out, but it is better to have had that belief than none at all. Emily like Walt, though a disbeliever in orthodoxies, never lacked faith, the essential belief in men.

Between the fullness of birth and the emptiness of death is the "tenderer experiment toward men," but apparently she thought we are indecisive about all these events, unless the adjective "tenderer" indicated her own bias. Our indecision may come from the fact, strangely expressed, that on all sides of us, everywhere we go, "we are molested equally by immortality," and that makes "a bland uncertainty." The idea may be that in the immensity of

WALT WHITMAN: THINKER AND ARTIST   405

existence we get confused by life and human experiment.
She asked, "Is immortality a bane that men are so op-
pressed?" It is with her always the human that can give
comfort. Even in dying, she would trust in a friend, not
Jesus, as comforter.

Early she came to the conclusion regarding God that
the world had a predominant place in her affections. Taggard thinks that without knowing it Emily was looking
for God in people and she wouldn't let them give her anything but God because she was treating them like God, so
she was deceiving herself by thinking she was searching
for the opposite of God. No, she was not mixed up as much
as that. She did indeed identify God with paternal tyranny.
Contrary to Taggard, it was the reputed "gravity of God"
that repelled her. The "beloved teacher," the tutor, was not
any traditional God, though he taught her immortality,
himself died. She never got as far as Whitman who identified man with all the gods—Jove, Christ, Satan, and the
Holy Spirit. God to her remained the biblical God or ap-
paling Nature, and never man, even when as in the case of
her father and some other dominating men they bore the
image of God or God the image of them.

Taggard charges Whitman with indiscriminateness, accepting everything on equivalent terms as if no differences
exist; and contrasts Dickinson as the aristocratic chooser
with discriminating taste. But Whitman's "I embrace all,"
is shown by the conversations with Traubel to have been
not at all his real character. He was critical and discriminating, as much as she. Her penetration was more acute
but her philosophic understanding and wisdom were less
than his.

Taggard paints Emily a little Puritan in her outward
demeanor, but within, in her escape from that appalling
decorous environment, living at least in fancy a dissolute
life, revelling in thoughts of drunkenness, gluttony, lar-
ceny, vagabondage, and witchcraft, and experiencing in

other moods, as a rebel from her protected and prosperous upper-class life, imprisonment, blindness, beggary, torture on the rack, and martyrdom. That is quite contrary to the autobiographical record of the poems and letters. She did indeed say to Higginson that his letter had no effect of intoxication upon her because she "had tasted rum before." In other words, her head was not turned by the recognition that she was a poet. But even a stodgy Unitarian preacher, the excess of puritan morality, could not have misunderstood the metaphor. Now a poet has a license to live multiple lives she has never experienced, and Emily's imagination was adequate. But the effect of her poetry is not licentiousness. In fact the morality of it goes all the other way. For those who want to exaggerate the puckish spirit in Emily that sometimes drove her staid father from the table, our lengthy citation of only some of her abundant moralisms may be distasteful. But, as we regard them, they are sensible and not puritanical.

Slowly as the Twentieth century has been discovering the geniuses of Dickinson and Whitman, we may lose sense of the present forwardness and contemporeity of their thinking because it is phrased in the language of opposition to the orthodoxies which in their day wore the badges of high culture but have now status principally among the lower literate. Because those traditional beliefs are lodged firmly in the minds of the masses who are steadily rising in power, they are not as passé as our sophisticates assume, and the mode of attack upon them taken by Whitman and Dickinson has value, especially as against the neo-medievalism taught in our universities as well as in the churches of the land.

It is principally because of that cultural lag that the biographies of Dickinson, as of Hopkins even more, but less of Whitman, have been more obscuring than interpretative of the particular role in life and literature so greatly achieved by her genius. As much as the wrong that is being done to the memory, thought and art of Whitman, even greater is the distortion of her work, alas, to some considerable extent by those who have done the most to obtain recognition of her. But in history what great pioneer of progress has not been a victim in some degree of both the ministrations and misrepresentations of those who professed to advocate him! We must expect that, but not accede to it. We must make clear that Dickinson's denouement and influence on the poets and literature of today is a mighty reinforcement of the principles Whitman fought for and more distinctively pioneered.

18

HAS THE FULL-GROWN POET COME?

✧ ✧ ✧ ✧ ✧ ✧

"When the full-grown poet came,
Out spake pleased Nature . . . , saying, *He is
    mine;*
But out spake too the Soul of man, proud,
    jealous, and unreconciled, *Nay, he is mine
    alone.*"

"The proof of a poet shall be sternly deferr'd
    till his country absorbs him as affection-
    ately as he has absorb'd it."

✧ ✧ ✧ ✧ ✧ ✧

Whitman's Successors.

SUCCESSORS ALWAYS APPEAR AT DISADVANTAGE IN COMPARISON
with the great of the past. That reflection should counsel
caution against quick judgments. But often in the light of
experience those deemed great among contemporaries
dwarf into mediocrities in a later time.

As Whitman and Hopkins had fewer votaries of their
own time than now, this chapter becomes perilous, even
though I do not essay the task or function of determining
who among our contemporaries may be entitled to the lau-
rel of greatness. Rather I choose a few among those who
acknowledge themselves indebted to Whitman or who nevertheless show marks of his influence in their work. I am

not selecting only those who are avowed Whitmanites, such
as Masters, Sandburg and Crane, but also two who profess
and defend traditionalism, Pound and Eliot, all of whom
have written at least partially under the inspiration of
Whitman.

These are all Americans. I have not taken any of the
English poets for comparison, because that would have ex-
tended this work more than my present purpose allows.
But also for another reason: Eliot and Pound have expatri-
ated themselves and have adopted and been adopted by the
British and may therefore be somewhat representative of
Whitman's influence abroad.

This selection is not assumed to be an exhaustive study
of the effect of Whitman's art or thought on present day
literature. It is intended rather to aid in discovering something in Whitman by observing certain trends of his influence. At the same time as before in the case of his contemporaries it is necessary to distinguish differences from
Whitman in these moderns. They do not always represent
viewpoints which are Whitmanesque. They would hardly
merit attention were they merely copycats of Whitman. Although I am disposed to think none of them has attained
the excellence of Whitman's thoughts, they may have surpassed his attainments as an artist. Or at any rate taken
together they represent advances of artistic skill, and that
too in comparison with all past literature.

But a plea should also be made for our contemporaries
that they have contributed great value in thinking as well
as artistic excellence. We can better judge Whitman because of them. If none has attained his breadth of understanding, his encompassing sympathies, all together or col-
lectively they surpass him.

But to measure the superiority of our time to the best
of the past as typified by Whitman again would require
much more study and space than can be allotted here. We
believe we are correct in ascribing to Whitman the genius

of summing up the best thinking of his time and advancing upon it, in so far as the roles of a poet are apt for the purpose. We do not know where to find a similar genius of our time. At least we do not think Whitman has yet received his due of public recognition.

Nor has any successor appeared to rate in public favor with Whitman. We have the expectant faith of Whitman that he may appear. He may already be among us unknown and unsung. We make no attempt now to acclaim any such. In our opinion none of those named here is worthy to have the mantel of Whitman fall upon him.

Edgar Lee Masters.

Among the first of the florescing poets in the wake of Whitman was Masters. A poet of mark, he is further significant for this study as author of a biography of Whitman and of his own autobiography in which he makes caustic remarks about his contemporary in the style of Whitman, Carl Sandburg.

Masters' biography of Whitman is not eminently critical or judicious and is marred by the prejudices which are characteristic of his work. At the same time he correctly calls attention to some of the principal weaknesses in Whitman. For example he speaks of Whitman's admiration of Scott but excuses it as a youthful romanticism atoned for by Whitman's reverence for the Bible, Shakespeare and Homer. But as Traubel's records of conversations show Whitman never tempered his early sentiments about Scott. And yet it was Scott more than any other who wrote glamorously about knights and ladies, most condemned as subject matter by Whitman. And it was Shakespeare he criticized for that errancy. Whitman's weakness for Scott was the grandiloquence of that writer reflected as the prevalent note of Whitman's verse in its notable oratorical style.

Masters absolves Whitman from a mother fixation and an Oedipus complex by contending that Whitman had for

WALT WHITMAN: THINKER AND ARTIST   411

his father both genuine admiration and respect. Surely he did not even in secret harbor enmity toward his father, for they worked together building houses when Walt could have escaped that occupation.

Slovenliness and disorderliness are characteristics Masters attributed to Whitman. That is surely not true of Whitman's mental habits and it is not even correct about his physical habits. The piles of accumulated papers, clippings, notes, and other literary materials Whitman had in the room about him at Camden, of which Traubel gave considerable indication, is not proof. The same thing can be said of Lincoln from similar evidence. The clerkly mind and the polished flat top desk of the typical business executive with a corps of secretaries may appear to signify orderliness but rarely does a genius with breadth of achievement work in such a manner or in such an environment. Whitman had a powerful mind and he was meticulous about details, such as punctuation, paragraphing, and the format of his work. He was physically a clean man. Masters' exaggerations as in these matters are markedly present throughout his biography.

Masters also characterizes Whitman's editorial writings as slovenly and worthless. But, contrary to Masters' conclusion, it was not Whitman's incapacity as a writer, it was his opinions which brought about the crisis in his newspaper work. He was a Democrat but not the kind acceptable to the Brooklyn Eagle and the New Orleans Crescent. This the Southern bias of Masters is loath to acknowledge.

What Masters calls Whitman's "harmless mendacity", or more accurately "whoppers", is not an unjust criticism, but in his case it was a vice which "leaned to virtue's side".

Masters is quite right when he says that without Jeffersonianism Whitman's democracy is inconceivable. By liberal quotations he shows that Whitman largely borrowed his political and social and economic philosophy from Jefferson.

Also, by selection and quotation from the Preface of 1888, *A Backward Glance O'er Travell'd Roads,* Masters attempts to refute criticisms like Santayana's that Whitman cut himself off from tradition. But the quotations rather stress Whitman's disavowal of purely literary aims "in respect to pictorial talent, dramatic situations, and especially in verbal melody and all the conventional technique of poetry." Instead Whitman insisted that "poems of realities and science and of the democratic average and basic equality" are greater, and the latter is the kind of poetry he thought he had produced.

Another point in Masters' quotation from Whitman: America demands of poetry that "it should nourish with joy and pride completion of man in himself." That is a very important declaration of Whitman's humanic philosophy. It is found in Volume IX of the Complete Works in *Notes on the Meaning and Intention of Leaves of Grass.* However, probably Masters did not perceive the humanistic significance of this passage. It is fundamental for Whitman's own interpretation of his poetic aim.

Chapter Seven of this biography, on the Civil War side of Lincoln, is perhaps the best account of that era in Whitman's life. The critical comment is better than most of the book. It silences some of the myth about relations between Whitman and Lincoln. It shows the gradualness of Whitman's absorption in the acts of mercy on the battlefields and hospitals. This chapter fails to point out Whitman's abhorrence of war, which was one of the effects of his Quaker uprearing, but later Masters comments that Whitman's war experiences did not diminish his hatred of war; probably they increased it.

In this chapter too Masters is silent about his own dislike for Lincoln. But he regards *O Captain! My Captain!* as Whitman's best poem in formal verse and rhyme. It has technical blemishes but these are compensated for by the emotional depths and sweet sorrow of its lyrical harmony.

He notes that according to Traubel Whitman first thought that he liked better his original less lyrical but more descriptive poem, *My Captain,* which is published in Traubel's second volume but not in *Leaves of Grass.*

Masters' treatment of the personal sex problem of Whitman is considerate and generally acceptable in the light of the evidence. It is not as critical of Carpenter's uranianism as Whitman would have been. It emphasizes masculine love more than Whitman did. It credits Whitman with less knowledge and experience in the love of women than he probably had and accepts too readily, though not wholly, the assumption that the *Leaves of Grass* is devoid of love for women. Without evidence apparently he assumes that Whitman was deserted by the mother of his unacknowledged child. Anne Gilchrist's love for Whitman is inadequately dealt with. He is mistaken in the assumption that Whitman did not write her into a poem. *"Going Somewhere"* is unmistakably written of Anne Gilchrist.

And if he means as he seems to say that Whitman never sang tribute to a woman, he overlooks lines he himself quotes:

> "Fast anchor'd O love, O woman I love,
> O bride, O wife, more resistless than I can
> tell, the thought of you!"

And he quotes too from Whitman's notes: "Put in a poem the sentiment of women (mothers) as preceding all the rest." And Whitman many times performed that task which he had set for himself. There is probably not a function of women which is not celebrated in his poetry. Above all Whitman recognized her right of equality with men.

In the estimation of Whitman's poems Masters agrees with Whitman that *Passage to India* is his best, the height of his art. But he thinks two succeeding poets have excelled Whitman as an artist. If one prefers traditional methods and regards rhyme and meter as essential to the best poetry, that determines the matter against Whitman. But if artistry is saying the important thing effectively and with emotional appeal, which of the American poets are or is superior to Whitman?

Masters pays considerable tribute to Whitman; yet, in view of his own low estimate of the America of today, he must think Whitman's philosophy of America impractical and untrue. But there is much in the art of Whitman that has missed Masters' comprehension and there is even more of Whitman's philosophy which is beyond his understanding. Masters has written about some of the poets of America. Can he name one who has written with the profundity of thought, with the sweep of understanding and sympathy, with the buoyancy and reasonableness of spirit, of Whitman?

It was Whitman's judgment that his American contemporaries were poets rather of English stock than of the breed that America demanded for its poets. Masters says contradictory things. He says Browning and Tennyson lacked either the national or the world vision Whitman had. Yet he thinks Whitman did not do for America what they and lesser poets did for England. Masters' own critical vision is not clear.

Vachel Lindsay.

In Masters' biography of Vachel Lindsay, he proclaims that poet as one of those or the one to supersede Whitman. In Masters' autobiography he calls Lindsay "America's greatest lyric poet." Whitman had been dead more than twenty years when Lindsay published his poem, *General Booth*. Prettiness and affected refinements had continued to be the popular style for poetry in America. Although not pressing the indebtedness of Lindsay to Whitman, Masters discerns some community of spirit between them. But there were great differences too.

Masters admits that Lindsay's moralizations were of a lower order than Whitman's preachments of comradeship. He agrees with Masefield that Lindsay sang of freedom and America as lustily as did Whitman but with more refinement and of a different America. He ranks Lindsay's *Old, Old, Old, Old Andrew Jackson,* as equal to or better than anything of Whitman's. He practiced what Whitman wrote about. He lived for a considerable part of his career a tramp on the open road. He lived among the people whom Whitman celebrated. He was a Jeffersonian like Whitman. Only in his feeling of the largeness of America could he be called a spiritual son of Whitman or one of the poets of America to follow Whitman's lead. These are some of Masters' judgments of comparison.

On the other hand, Lindsay differed from Whitman in preaching a "gospel of beauty". But something in his poetry was akin to jazz. It was syncopated dance rhythm, though lyrical poetry. He was a singer nearer to tradition than Whitman. Much in him was contrary to Whitman's creed. He had race prejudices which Whitman had not. He had a semi-orthodox religious strain in him. The tragedy of his career,—a late marriage, developing paranoia, and suicide,—gives a terrible climax to the mad spirit that possesses much of his poetry. Masters' own balance sheet, more than favorable to Lindsay, does not convince one that Lindsay was Whitman's supercessor.

Masters Self-estimated.

The other poet to supercede Whitman, as we infer from Masters' hints, is no other than himself. He has written an autobiography in which he has made an estimate of himself as a poet and as a man. He describes himself as a split personality or many persons. Every complex man is that, and it should be a good qualification for a poet, if only Masters would not assume that means a sort of Jekyll and Hyde, for he gives himself a histrionic pose of good and

evil nature. An inner selfish person belying his outward
professions of democratic self-effacing character, as he represents himself, is probably a self-deception.

His own conviction that he possesses a dualism of nature, a conflict of the within and the without, betrays lack
of the unity of being, the self-possession, of a Whitman, a
quality, however, which Whitman arrived at only when he
found himself as expressed in *Leaves of Grass.* There was
undoubtedly a better side in Masters than that which so
frequently went awhoring.

Some of the conflict in him seemed to be expressed in
the opposition of city and country. In his autobiography
he thinks of Chicago, if not paradise, at least escape from
hell. Spoon River is down-state, anywhere in the Middle
West territory of Chicago. It was, as Babette Deutsch remarks, his early experiences in the country, reflected upon
in the larger light of his interpretive experiences as a Chicago lawyer, that gave the subject matter of the poems upon
which his fame rests.

It is the downside, the pessimism of Masters, that is
mainly expressed in his poetry. When he was objective,
humanly descriptive, as often in *Spoon River,* it was not
far from great art, and was deservedly popular. In his own
judgment he has written nothing better than are in that
collection.

But neither the spirit nor the style of Whitman is in
them. Seldom have they the grand swing and resonance of
the Whitman long line. They are often rough. Their
rhythm is short, sharp and choppy, like the contemporary
band music that had vogue a generation ago.

Master's Adoption of Santayana's Views.

It is notable that Masters took the cue for his principal
points of criticism of Whitman from Santayana's chapter
entitled *The Poetry of Barbarism* and did not question the

validity of the premises of that high priest of authority: as, towit, "that the earliest poets are the most ideal, and that primitive ages furnish the most heroic characters and have the clearest vision of a perfect life", with Homer as the great example. "Nowhere else can we find so noble a rendering of human nature, so spontaneous a delight in life, so uncompromising a dedication to beauty, and such a gift of seeing beauty in everything. Homer, the first of poets, was also the best and most poetical."

Homer, it is granted, was the supreme barbarian poet. But who thinks the barbarian code an ideal model for human conduct? Did Santayana? Was it a defect of understanding, taste or morals that led Santayana to characterize Browning and Whitman as poets of barbarism? He charged against them the founding of a cult of irrationality, with "rebellion against discipline, and with pandering to passions." He called Whitman superficial. He said: "This abundance of detail without organization, this wealth of perception without intelligence and of imagination without taste, makes the singularity of Whitman's genius." Probably the true source of such misjudgments was an incipient revulsion of Santayana to the American environment which led him to become an expatriate in England; but finally not happier there he retired to a religious place of seclusion in Italy.

What Masters particularly seized upon in Santayana's essay was the passage: "In Whitman's works, in which this new literature is foreshadowed, there is accordingly not a single character nor a single story. His only hero is Myself, a 'single separate person', endowed with the primary impulses, with health; and with sensitiveness to the elementary aspects of Nature." Masters remarks that Whitman's wide reading of novels did not teach him to write fiction.

Of an opposite disposition Masters wrote novels in verse and thumbnail sketches of characters in profusion. For the most part they express his autobiographical note that there is nothing in life but those elemental aspects of passion and irrationality of which Santayana mistakenly accused Whitman. When from the grave or elsewhere Masters' characters say something else, as in the *Ann Rutledge* poem, they seem, if not out of character, out of place in the volume.

Criticism of Masters.

One must not suppose that Masters made no trial of polite verse, no attempt to write in traditional forms. Indeed, he boasts that he had mastered the classic forms as represented by the great poets whom he had studied assiduously, but he adopted his form of free verse for the sake of more musical rhythm and greater emotional scope.

His want of the finest skill is more apparent in the older forms than in his free verse. For example his ballads would be better if, as in one of the best, *Cassius Graccus Johnson*, he had ended three stanzas earlier. But likewise his delightful free verse poem, *Cricket in the Kitchen*, is marred by the last two stanzas. Probably these faults in taste and judgment are more obvious in his later published verse.

But, aside from what is most offending in Masters,—his prejudices, his predilection for the seamy side of life, his misjudgment of men and women, the darker side of his own nature,—one nevertheless discerns in him some influence from the spirit of Whitman which he acknowledges had been his youthful inspiration. His misunderstanding of Whitman may be partly explanatory of his failure to rid himself of nostalgia for Victorianism. That is evidenced not only by his poems in the traditional patterns but also in the *Spoon River Anthology*, as in *Ann Rutledge* and the virtuous episodes. The portrayal of his erotic adventures in which he impugns the motives and characters of his enamoratae exhibits the same prurient tendency in him. The puritan and the libertine were in conflict in his dualistic character. That was characteristic of the Victorian conscience. Masters never attained Whitman's reverence for all human beings.

Sandburg and Masters.

The qualities of Whitman, in both style and convictions, were closer to the heart and mind of Sandburg. Yet what repels Masters in Sandburg's poetry also distinguishes Sandburg from Whitman and is much of what is above criticized in Masters. Masters praises the beautiful imagery and rough tenderness in some of Sandburg's poems, but thinks most of them are more shockingly and rudely realistic than Whitman's. They lack the Homeric dignity of Whitman. They apostrophize a lower order of man and Nature than Whitman celebrates.

Masters refutes the assumption that Sandburg was an imitator of himself. At the time of the *Chicago Poems* Sandburg had written only one "character picture". There was no resemblance between their themes, their words, their images, their forms, or the music of their poetry.

Dissimilar as are the Chicago or Illinois poets among themselves, the influence of Whitman upon them is unmistakable. It encouraged their creative freedom, and gave much of their direction, especially their religion of democracy, though later Masters became bitterly critical of American democracy. They seized upon Whitman's political and social democracy more readily than of other elements in him because that was also part of the milieu in which they lived. Whitman was not the only or even the greatest prophet of American democracy. He drew from the great sources, Jefferson and Lincoln and others. Whitman's humanism, the sense of the dignity and worth of the individual man, was also in the American tradition. In this Emerson was the inspirer of Whitman and was even more available to these poets. But Whitman had pioneered the mode of expression with more forthrightness and with less obscurity than did Emerson.

One thing these successors have not realized, and Masters might have obtained the hint of it from Santayana whose genius recognized it but failed to see it described Whitman. Masters might have read from Santayana's essay instead of the detracting criticism of Whitman that principle which Whitman most of modern poets has exemplified, namely, that "where poetry rises from its elementary and detached expressions in rhythm, euphemism, characterization, and story telling, and comes to consciousness of its highest function, that of portraying the ideals of experience and destiny, then the poet becomes aware that he is essentially a prophet." But Santayana, overrating Homer the barbarian and Dante the medievalist, was unable to perceive that Whitman realized his specification of the prophetic poet.

Masters cannot rid himself of votarial dependence upon tradition and places his measure of poetic art on the plane of story telling and fails of the higher art expressing the ideals of experience and destiny. Lindsay was so much of the tramp that he had to travel with light baggage and could not carry any profound philosophy or intelligent conception of the world, but nevertheless was a true poet of such emotions as one not attached to the deeper and more settled experiences of life could entertain. Sandburg with less of learning than Masters, and not having the lyrical gifts of Lindsay, has a spirit of the breadth of human relationships more like that of Whitman but with much less penetration.

Sandburg is a reporter and editor above the level of newspaperese. But in the work which is the greatest source of his renown, not his poetry, but his biography of Lincoln, —the most readable of all the biographies of Lincoln, not the most interpretive,—he has achieved a triumph of editing and has comprehended Lincoln the story-teller as no one else has done, but falls far short of understanding Lin-

coln the logician, statesman and ethical genius. The superficial quality of the Lincoln biography is less a characteristic of Sandburg's poems, but they too do not penetrate
much below the surfaces of things.

What entered the soul and understanding of Whitman
is still beyond the experiences of the Twentieth Century
interpreters of the American scene about Springfield and
Chicago. Yet they are valuable to us. As minor poets they
have enriched the American tradition. Especially Sandburg, less an artist than either Lindsay or Masters, has surpassed them as reporter of the contemporary Middle West
America and he has felt more than his rivals of that school
the wisdom of American democracy. *The People, Yes* is
great reporting, but like his *Lincoln* not quite fathoming
America, because Sandburg is not possessed of a philosophy
equivalent to that Whitman and Lincoln had.

In homeliness and homespun quality Sandburg is distinctive. He is a modern and his want of veneration for the
old and dignified and his appetite for up-to-dateness is expressed in his quotation from an early American versifier:

> "T'is vain for present fame to wish,
> Where persons first must be forgotten;
> For poets are like stinking fish,
> They never shine until they're rotten."

He is a plain, simple man, with the soil in him, and he
has that kinship with the things that grow from the soil and
are affected by weather which enables him to write with
directness about them. That means, of course, that he is
much more than a mere child of Nature. He is an artistic
master of natural speech. He is a person of very human
sympathies. Whitman would have liked Carl Sandburg. He
would have acknowledged him a true American poet.
Whitman would probably have been astonished by such an

American but very curious about him and glad to know that America has produced such a son from a foreign humble stem!

Hart Crane and Whitman.

It is preeminently Hart Crane who has been designated by some recent critics as the neo-Whitman or better than Whitman. When Crane was drunk, it is reported he declared himself Whitman, Baudelaire, Jesus Christ, etc., but never Hart Crane. In his sober and intelligent moods probably with some reason he contended that he knew Whitman's intent and purposes better than did Tate, Winters, et al. of the company of his own ardent admirers.

Unquestionably Whitman stood to him not only as ideal and model but also as epochal person in the career of America. Of the six outlined and projected divisions of Crane's masterpiece, *The Bridge,* number III was to present Whitman in a Washington hospital discoursing with a dying soldier on themes of death, disunity, and immorality. In the unfinished poem so flattering were the tributes to Whitman that Tate criticized them as sentimental defects. In the poem entitled *Cape Hatteras* he intended to write an ode to Whitman, and Horton regards those references to Whitman as almost the only sincere and worthy portions of it.

Crane's feeling for Whitman was intense, and he defended Whitman zealously. Replying to Tate's criticism of his sentimentality about Whitman, he admitted the truth of the accusation, but charged that such detractors seem not to have read *Democratic Vistas* and Whitman's condemnation of materialism and industrialism and to be ignorant of Whitman's generous and liberal viewpoints.

This was both a defense for himself, for his sentimental moods, and for that in Whitman which he responded to and called "positive universal tendencies". This is the mysticism, the cosmic consciousness, which Crane like so many others misinterpreted in Whitman's thought.

As Crane was composing *The Bridge* he wrote Munson that it made him more aware of Whitman's influence upon him. His most distinctive tribute to Whitman is contained in the section of *The Bridge* entitled *Cape Hatteras*. Horton criticizes that poem severely as merely simulation of sincerity excepting for the portions describing Nature and those on Whitman. As to Whitman the poem is rhapsodical, spiritistic and nondescript. Little enough is it pertinent to Whitman.

Interestingly, those who have praised Crane most have spoken slightingly of Whitman. Thus Winters, who treats Crane as a decadent, related to Whitman in theme, rates Crane the better poet. He contends that the irrationalism which is obvious in Crane, was in Whitman, but he sees it in Crane because he is precise in use of language and not so vague and indefinite as Whitman.

Winters' criticism of Whitman as deficient in emotional power we have shown to be counterbalanced by the opposite opinion of other severe critics of Whitman. As for anti-rationalist doctrines our chapters on the religion and philosophy of Whitman show clearly either want of understanding of Whitman's ideas or prejudiced opposition to Whitman's thinking by Winters. We will have more to say of these matters and of logically precise expression as gifts of Whitman and Crane in comparison.

Waldo Frank, who wrote the Introduction to the *Collected Poems,* describes Whitman and Crane as poets of possibility in contrast with Robert Frost, the poet of probability, the realist, a scribe of realization. This is evidently intended to think the worse of that element in Crane which made him akin to Whitman. But we think Frank has not grasped the meaning of Whitman and errs, as we will show, in treating him with Crane as belonging to the "old order", to the old tradition.

Crane suffered greatly from the prickings of these critics at his Whitmanism, and in his replies to them indicated somewhat of his unlikeness to Whitman. In form, as Winters points out, he did not at all follow Whitman. He did not want them to think he was aping Whitman's style or being uncritical about it. In form and style his relationship was to Poe and the French poets inspired by Poe, Baudelaire and Rimbaud, and their Anglo-American successors, and not to Whitman.

And he is also doubtfully a successor of Whitman in theme, notwithstanding his own professions of Whitmanian faith. There is the bawdiness of Baudelaire in him. But neither the prophecy nor the expression of the nobility of love that characterizes *Leaves of Grass*. And it is a very superficial and erroneous conception of Whitman that may claim community with him in Crane's homosexuality and debauchery of which there is no evidence in Whitman's conduct. However, that notion and the Uranian gospel about Whitman may account in part for Crane's emotional attachment to Whitman and it probably provided an alibi for Crane's weaknesses in those respects both to his own mind and that of his shallow associates of similar intent. Of such attitudes as "love a burnt match skating in a urinal", "Magdalene, . . . the burlesque of our lust—and faith", there is no parallel in Whitman's verse. This has filtered through French literature into ours, not that the French are more salacious than Anglo-Americans, but as in nearly everything they have been more artistic and brilliantly alluring.

Horton excuses Crane's social vices of homosexuality and keeping company with prostitutes as compensation for his failures of friendship. There are expressions in his poems about the bitterness of hurts from friends (last two lines of *To the Cloud Juggler*) ; the venality and consciencelessness of friends (ending lines of *Key West*) , as well as of loneliness. Not a little of misanthropy was in him too (as concludes the fourth stanza of *Cape Hatteras* and in the fourth stanza of *Passage*.). *The River* (in the fate of Dan Midland) and *Reliquary* express the pessimism that runs as an undercurrent everywhere, frequently rising to the surface of the poems.

The theme of Americanism especially has been pointed to as Whitman's inspiration to Crane. Horton thought he was the first to repeat the sentiment after Whitman. But that is quite to overlook the clearer expression in both Lindsay and Sandburg. Crane's recognition of Whitman's primacy as the democratic poet has the merit of unhesitating acknowledgment. He could understand Whitman's Americanism better than Whitman's art.

However, Crane thought of Whitman as a revolutionary genius. To the contrary, Frank classifies both Whitman and Crane in the old tradition. The distinctiveness of Crane is that he imports the speech or terms of industrialism in the old forms. Frank thinks of Whitman as belonging to agrarian culture. To illustrate he contrasts Frost and Whitman. Frost describes farm folk, but they are the bleached out remnants on the bleak hills of industrialized New England. Whitman could still have a "vision", but Frost sees the reality. Crane is also visionary; he can have dreams that really belong to the old order and not to the realistic, soulless, materialistic present.

Why is not Frost also antique, even though his "persons" are hard as granite or steel? For he is not a materialist and he cherishes the old religion and the ancient philosophy from Plato to Fichte. On the other hand, Whitman, though not Crane, is not merely at the turning point of philosophy to its modern expressions; Whitman was pioneer of the new humanism. He was not Hegelian, not a worshipper of the state; nor was he Marxian, no blind follower of a proletarian dictatorship. He knew the resulting evils of both nationalism and industrialism. He had a vision above the sink of proletarianism. Does that make him now old-fashioned and a traditionalist?

Whitman, Frank forgets or doesn't know, was the first
to turn into the symbols of poetry, as Frost has sparsely
done, and with more variety of expression than Crane's,
the instruments of our industrialized world. There is a
great deal more than the old agrarian order in Whitman's
Song of the Broad-Axe, Song of the Exposition, and *A Song
for Occupations.* The Machine Age had already come, and
Whitman was conscious of it. In *To a Locomotive in Winter* he expressed it:

> "Type of the modern—emblem of motion
>   and power—pulse of the continent,
> For once come serve the Muse and merge in
>   verse, even as here I see thee."

The locomotive in this verse he took as symbol of the
departure of his chants from the traditional themes:

> "No sweetness debonair of tearful harp or
>   glib piano thine."

Although for Crane the Brooklyn Bridge had succeeded
Crossing Brooklyn Ferry, and in place of the locomotive the
nasal whine of the airplane was bringing about a new universe, nevertheless he correctly perceived, with better insight than the critics who praised him to the disadvantage
of Whitman, that the connection of the best that might be
of this new order is with Whitman. Whitman was more
than prophet, first spokesman, first realization in poetry of
the new order; to those who can understand he pointed the
way for men to be master of the machine and to realize human personality.

Likening Whitman's ethereal quality to something more
than the flight of the heaven-ascending birds is Crane's conception of Whitman as the cosmic poet. Wilder interprets
Crane as a mystic and a pantheist. To Winters and Frank
such cosmic mindedness as Crane professed lacked clarity

of vision. Winters says that Crane did not have the needful "check of a comprehensive philosophy". Frank too says
he was wanting in "a unitary principle or theme", but
thinks he had the mystic's substitute, and that critical judgment will accord him that "great human value". Crane,
probably moved by these criticisms of his friends and knowing his own limitations, shied away from the pretense of
possessing a philosophy and took the tack that poetry really
doesn't mix with philosophy or theology. He observed that
poets like Dante and Milton can outlast the theologies they
believed in and represented.

The poetry of Whitman has not yet had to endure the
test of such divorcement. Or rather few have recognized
that one may, as Burroughs indeed contended, go to Whitman for a philosophy. One would hardly go to Crane for
a philosophy. For Frank's assumption that Crane's genius
is the revelation of an intuition "of organic unity between
his self, the objective world, and the cosmos" seems doubtful, since the life of the man was lived irregularly and un-
quietly and ended in suicidal disaster. If that is a philosophy it is Don Juan's, driven by the perilous unrest of internal passion.

Undoubtedly there was genius in Crane. More completely than Eliot who thinks of poetic genius as re-combin-
ing or reweaving the threads of tradition, Crane did that in
The Bridge: romanticism, symbolic poetry, stream of consciousness poetry, metaphysical poetry, common rhythm,
sprung rhythm,—he worked with much skill in both traditional and free verse forms. Deutsch therefore calls him
an eclectic and comparing him to the brilliant and scholarly Eliot says the latter lacks the power of Crane to transmit the spiritual universe of the poet.

But although admitting Crane's genius I have to agree
with Winters that it is incomplete poetry. Abounding in
many finely descriptive lines, much of it is the poetry of a
youth with habits formed in adolescence—he began writing

content and guaranty of truth not in concepts? Bergson thought so. As he maintained correctly immediate perception has contact with the external world which the concept does not have so directly. But he attacked the scientific concept as unreal because of its analytical method which parcels experience into fragments of time and space. The effort of the consciousness to be timeless and spaceless is one of the characteristics of the mystical method, which therefore claims to be one of the ways of knowing. But conceptual thinking, contrary to Bergson, is not only analytical, it is also synthetic. And as the Gestalt Psychology has taken so much pains to prove, even perception takes in whole situations usually without minute estimates of the actual character of the individual particulars in the situation. The particulars are estimated by their relation to the whole. Science or exact knowledge is not our usual perceptual or conceptual way of thinking. It is more accurate. But is it of a different order of thinking? That is not demonstrable.

Crane's way of thinking about the metaphor and his use of it brought criticism and he undertook to defend himself. Thus when Miss Monroe asked him how a portent could be wound in a shell, his reply was a protest against being confined to simple experiences or analogies. That of course would throw out Bergson's direct intuitions. It argues for the right of the poet's imagination to put together what is wholly dissociated in immediate perception. In the poet's emotional experience he may join together images which would seldom or never occur to matter-of-fact people. Therefore, Crane contended that the poet's experience is a legitimate exception to the rule against mixed metaphors.

Such an argument however, if allowable, would make poetry to a considerable extent the private expression of the poet, and Crane contrarily recognized the necessity for making clear to the reader his meaning and admitted he may have failed to acquaint the public with the context of his symbols. That is the nub of the matter. If the author does not indicate the connection between the objects of perception which otherwise are totally unrelated in experience, he is writing solely for his own understanding. His writing then becomes nonsense verse so far as others are concerned. It does not illuminate experience for the reader and therefore he is not justified in publishing his poems.

Whitman believed that the public has the right to call upon the poet to indicate "the path between reality and their souls". We maintain that he did exceptionally achieve that end. It is a hard test for the poet. But obscurity due to inadequate expression is an entirely different thing from that which is the defect of the reader's understanding. A new emotion, a new idea, is always in difficulty with those who can only tolerate what is familiar to them. Tradition is always on the side of such ignorance and is ever ready to blame the really creative writer for the obscurity which is not in his but the reader's mind.

To the ignorant, philosophy or theology or science is obscure, and the aversion to such in poetry is a prejudice in favor of commonplace thought. But Crane thought he discovered another reason for separating poetry from philosophy and science. He contended that the poet has not merely a different method but also a totally different kind of experience.

It is true that we do not judge the merit of Homer, Sophocles or Euripides by the same pattern as we judge Flato and Aristotle; nor Dante by the model of Aquinas; Shakespeare by Bacon; Milton by Hobbes or Locke; Burns by Hume; Goethe by Kant; Wordsworth and Shelley by Bentham and Mill; Browning and Tennyson by Herbert Spencer and Darwin; Hopkins by Cardinal Newman; Crane and Eliot by John Dewey and Bertrand Russell. But Whitman stands in a class by himself; his work can endure philosophical and theological inquiry concerning his meaning. Yet he too adopted, not the manner and the logic of

19

WHITMAN AND THE EX-PATRIATES.

❖ ❖ ❖ ❖ ❖ ❖

"Nature and the Soul expressed—America
and freedom expressed—in it the finest
art."

❖ ❖ ❖ ❖ ❖ ❖

The Case of T. S. Eliot.

AN EXPATRIATED AMERICAN, A GRADUATE OF HARVARD UNI-
versity and an instructor of philosophy there, who like
George Santayana could no longer endure his native land;
reared a liberal in a democratic family, he turned Anglo-
royalist; a grandson of a Unitarian preacher, he became a
convert to Anglo-Catholicism; in brief, reacting from New
England Emersonianism to religious and political traditionalism—that stock picture of T. S. Eliot is the antithesis
of Whitmanism. Such revolt of a native against the American scene and everything in it, if true, is a phenomenon
that at least needs explanation in a work presenting Whitman as the essence of the true American faith. Is Whitmanism pragmatically a failure because it does not hold to loyalty such of its intelligent sons?

Of course there are and always have been in America
its Tories, Anglophiles, and men of every European creed.
As at present from Communist to Roman Catholic we have
insistent minorities that would substitute or superimpose
their dogmas in the place of the philosophy of Jefferson,

Lincoln and Whitman which is recognized as the typical American philosophy by all except those who continue to repeat that what America lacks today is a philosophy, by which they mean that the American philosophy is not harmonious with the imported doctrines which are always struggling to advance themselves against it.

The arresting phenomenon is a case like Eliot's. It may seem natural and logical that he should expatriate himself. It would be an honest response to the American too frequently disposed to say to the disdained ones, "If you don't like this country why don't you go back where you belong." As Americans of the right were saying to Henry Wallace at the moment, "If you want to be a Commie why don't you go to Russia." However, the Bolsheviks long ago made it clear that they don't want the American breed of radical there. And as Santayana found when he tried to adopt England, our reactionaries are very unhappy abroad. America must take account of its own and make greater effort to assimilate the spirits among us who seem so alien when in fact they are a product of the American environment.

For that reason Eliot as a man, even if reactionary and traditionalist, is a necessary person to come to terms with if we are fully to understand ourselves and properly to place Whitman not only in the total scheme of America but also in the world. Catholicism which Eliot professed to adopt in its English variety of High Church or Anglo-Catholicism has a vital significance in American life. Protestantism has more numerous adherents and is more widely spread, but it too is almost as much an importation in America as Catholicism. And what we call the distinctive American creed, excepting as an influence which has greatly altered the transplanted European dogmas of Protestantism and Catholicism, is also a minority though born of American life. What is there in the older European traditions to attract a good mind like Eliot's?

Probably we underrate the traditionalists. There is the

poem about men making cities. Eliot's joinder of body
and spirit in canto IX suggests Whitman's doctrine of
their inseparability and that neither must deny the other.
Traditional theology, not art, may prefer Eliot's expression of these ideas.

But neither Eliot the poet nor Eliot the critic rated
form above content. Indeed one can quote him here as
opposed to that dead formalism which to us means traditionalism. And also Pound, whose *Cantos* Matthiessen
calls formless, spoke slightingly of form as needful for
those whose matter would otherwise be dull and as immoral pandering to public taste. He thought Eliot had a
merit above that. However, I take canto V of Eliot's *Burnt
Norton* to mean that form and content are co-existent and
neither precedes the other. But Eliot's conception of the
function of form is profounder than that. In canto IX of
the *Choruses* one can assume an Aristotelian sense that
essential matter is chaotic until it has form. It is this
Eliot means when he denies that art is emotion. But art expresses emotion by an "objective correlative" which can re-
evoke the original raw emotion. That is what man does in
all his creations. He does not transmit just what he has felt
or thought, but the symbol of that feeling or thought in
such way that himself or others may be stimulated thereby
to relive or repeat the experience as if the original stimulus
were present.

For Eliot, no more than Whitman, was a formalist. That
becomes clear as one penetrates what he meant by the relation of emotion, intellect, thought and reason to poetry.
Eliot's emphasis upon creative meaning as the object of the
artist's endeavor as he expresses new feelings and new aspects of things is different from the scientist's endeavor only
as the symbol of art differs from the abstract conceptions of
thought. In a phrase the poetic expression seemed to him

to be "contemplative emotion" in which the emotion is represented and suggested by poetic symbol.

The form is not an end in itself, for then it would be dead, but it is an object which stimulates or evokes thought and emotion. If Eliot did not quite say this, it is implicit in what he did say.

The Free Verse Technique of Pound and Eliot.

The dicta of Pound, to which Eliot especially in his earlier poetry conformed, set forth three technical principles as basic: concreteness, economy of speech, and recurring musical rhythm. The first and third of these are substantially equivalent to joinder of content and form, sense and technique. These denote the similarity of Pound's *Cantos* to Whitman's long lined verse, but, one must add, without the eloquence, high style, or music we are accustomed to find in Whitman, and, notwithstanding the erudition of Pound, he lacks Whitman's profundity of thought.

In several respects Pound's and Eliot's writing of verse departs far from Whitman's style, and one of these is the second of their techniques which is also called "compression". According to Eliot it is the application of this principle which most distinguishes poetry from prose. He thought Whitman "a great prose writer" and, perhaps, because Whitman's prose is so notably expansive and provides a good illustration to fit Eliot's theory.

Pound related that he and Eliot had agreed to abjure "the dilution of vers libre" as exemplified by the "general floppiness" of Edgar Lee Masters, and the result was expressed in Eliot's second volume of poems, not the first, and in Pound's own *H. S. Mauberley,* and that there was "divergence later" from that technique. Examining these poems of Eliot and Pound we find them quite similar in style: most of them rhymed quatrains, colloquial and flippant in manner and bitter, satirizing the vulgar Philistines, revel-

rotic? Apparently that is what she means, for she speaks of primitive realities and lost memories. Indeed much of *The Waste Land, The Hollow Men,* and *Ash Wednesday* seems the rich rubbish of the subconscious state of an exceptionally literate mind.

Yet more astonishing are Cleanth Brooks' 37 pages of closely printed commentary on Eliot's 22 pages of poem and 8 pages of notes explaining the mostly literary allusions of *The Waste Land,* which Brooks thinks though consciously written as a poem had an unconscious origin. And Matthiessen who dislikes so much the somnambulism of Whitman takes no offense at it in Eliot.

A similar explanation of Eliot's obscurities is given by Deutsch. She attributes them in part to a troubled mind in a disordered civilization, which to Eliot is "nonsense," but even more often, she thinks, they are due to Eliot's symbolisms and musical shorthand.

If the function of an artist is to interpret emotion, to create symbols which may reproduce the original emotion, these poems hardly fulfill that standard or ideal. They are too much the raw stuff awaiting the hand of the artist to pattern them into conscious experience. Eliot's sympathetic critics admit they had conscious meaning for him which he failed to communicate. Eliot himself has intimated that such criticism is appropriate. In a lecture on Joyce's *Ulysses* he commented upon the gain of emotional intensity at the expense of clarity. But clarity has significance for emotions as well as for thought and it is a prime excellence of art. However valuable may be the stream of consciousness method to the psychoanalyst, its presence in a novel or poem or other form of literature is merely providing the matter of a confused subconscious self brought up into memory. Much more is required to give it meaning.

Whitman antedated recognition of the Freudian technique. But in the Calamus poems and elsewhere he surely had the sense of it, as in *Recorders Ages Hence*:

> "Come, I will take you down underneath this
> impassive exterior,"

and in *Are You the New Person Drawn Toward Me*:

> "Do you see no farther than this facade, this
> smooth and tolerant manner of me?"

And Whitman is distinctively interpreter of that inner self. It Eliot a comparable analyst? He exhibits his skill in "The Cocktail Party", but not to the satisfaction of a psychoanalyst.

He is classified as a symbolist, and one of the most skillful of them. And symbolism has interpretive utility. Matthiessen treats the symbol as if its function were to give the illusion of reality, of imparting the feeling of a greater than itself. That comes near to description of a bastard art. It is true that an art is not an end in itself. Nor is it merely representative. A true art will express a realizable ideal. It will use symbols not for the purpose of creating an illusion of reality but to indicate how the ideal may be realized. Otherwise it is false art or what Eliot condemned as dead art.

In his essay, *The Use of Poetry*, Eliot makes clear his own comprehension of what he calls illegitimate obscurity. The reader has no right to complain of what resides in his own defect of understanding, of novelty, of what is inherently difficult in the subject matter, but it is a fault of the author when he leaves out what is necessary to the understanding of the poem. For then compression has gone beyond the bounds of legitimacy. When it is necessary to supply meaning by extensive notes or commentary the poem itself is incomplete.

to Eliot's doctrines of tradition and orthodoxy we may attend to now. For he relates the "process of depersonalization" to the "sense of tradition".

He desired to give art such an objective basis as science is assumed to have, and he mistakenly supposed science to have attained objectivity by being impersonal. Therefore, Eliot proposed to depersonalize art. He undertook to demonstrate this proposition in two ways. First, by the hypothesis of traditionalism, he would relate the poet's work to all that had been written before him. Thus, the poet's personality would be merged in the great communal achievement we call tradition.

But, to criticize that hypothesis, why confine it to past achievements? Why not include all the possibilities of poetry, of the future as well as of the past? Such expansion of the concept, though logical enough, probably seemed too unrealistic to Eliot. Whitman did think of his own poetry in that larger relation. Instead of taking the path of orthodoxy and tradition, he distinguished his goal of democratic poetry from the feudalistic poetry of Shakespeare and others and from the poetry of prettiness of his contemporaries, and thought of the poets to come after him as achieving his aim.

But the weakness of Eliot's thesis is more obvious in the other aspect of his theory that poetry is impersonal. What is the relation of the poem to the poet himself? Is that relation impersonal? Not to Whitman. He said, "I sing of myself", but it was a very inclusive self, not merely autobiographical, and yet not impersonal.

To illustrate his point Eliot compared what goes on in the poetic process to the chemical process. Thus platinum is used in the manufacture of sulphuric acid and as an anode for electrolysis because it remains unattacked and undecomposed under all the conditions in the chemical reaction of the other elements brought in contact with it. So Whitman expressed the hope in the poem *As I Sit Writing Here* that the aches and ennui of his old age would not filter into his poems. On the other hand, Edmund Wilson expressed annoyance at the "personal vein" in Eliot who described himself as an "aged eagle" at forty years of age. But what a dry and uninteresting thing poetry would be if the joys and sorrows of the poets had never been expressed in their poems, if their own feelings and emotions and thoughts had been left out! If this were what Eliot meant by objectivity in art, it would class out Tennyson's *In Memoriam*, Whitman's *Out of the Cradle Endlessly Rocking, When Lilacs Last in the Dooryard Bloom'd,* and indeed the expressed intent of Whitman's poems. And in fact not only that first stanza of *Ash Wednesday* to which Wilson referred, but also the poems that mention "Mr. Eliot" and the "I" of the *Notes on "The Waste Land"* upon that criterion should not have been written.

But Eliot was trying to describe by inexpert use of the word "impersonal" something which is a very important characteristic of art. The artistic product is not a mere replica of the original thought or emotion of the artist. He believed we experience differently in the enjoyment of an art than any experience outside of art. In only one respect is that true: It is probably impossible to experience twice or again just the same emotion or the same thought, whether artistically or otherwise reproduced. But by means of an art we can come more nearly to reproducing a previous experience than by mere recollection or memory or by trying to put ourselves in the original situation. Nature changes her face so continuously that natural situations do not repeat themselves. Memories are notoriously inaccurate.

What then is it about art which is different from Nature? It is this: Art is an artificial means, an invention of man, by which he undertakes to evoke repetitive ideas and feelings. Art therefore differs from Nature, not so much in the effect and not by producing a different experience than the natural one, but rather is art different as being a

ing for new human emotions to express appears to contradict his idea that art is a different kind of emotion. If he means that art is not human emotion or does not evoke human emotion, then poetry is not only depersonalized art but also dehumanized art.

He seems to have been frightened by the idea of the hazards taken by a self-reliant man. He cites the awful example of D. H. Lawrence who started in life without a tradition or institutional guidance and with only an inner light. But Eliot has not pointed out in what way tradition or orthodoxy is the sure and safe guide that can be substituted for the inner light of reason, understanding, or other human faculty. We are led to believe that he means it is the total or all of the poetry that has ever been written. Would that be any sure guide? Or would it not rather be a greater confusion because of the conflicting ideals within the total poetic tradition? Has not that total tradition even greater difficulties for the aspiring poet than Eliot finds in the vagaries of a poet's own personality? Although Eliot disclaims a theological intent in his conception of tradition, nevertheless his epithets of "unregenerate", "irresponsible", "self-deceived", "self-conceited", "impure", "prejudiced" as descriptive of personality when free indicate that his theory of impersonal poetry is rooted in the doctrine of original sin and the fall of man.

Humanist and Religious Poetry.

What Eliot was probably groping toward with a true instinct, but greatly hindered by prejudices and fears that made him believe in traditionalism, was the conception of the poet as the humanist would conceive him. This can be demonstrated by many passages in his critical essays quite contradictory of his impersonal and traditionalist dogmas we have discussed. However in two essays he has specifically argued about the relations of humanism and religion. In the first one he thought humanism dependent upon supernatural religion. Ethical humanism cannot stand alone. But in *Second Thoughts about Humanism,* published later, he conceded that there are at least a few individuals for whom pure humanism is sufficient and he thought them a valuable type.

Do Eliot's poems reflect his true religious beliefs? If so, they indicate that he has been gradually changing his viewpoints. Before he declared himself an Anglo-Catholic his poetry could be pronounced rather skeptical of church and religion, and later than that he passed beyond the ecclesiastical pale of religion. *The Hippopotamus* is unmistakably a satire on the Church. *Mr. Eliot's Sunday Morning Service* conveys no more reverent mood.

However much Mr. Eliot may protest against the interpretation of *The Waste Land, Ash Wednesday,* and *The Hollow Men* as the disillusionment of the author and urge that it is rather the poet's conception of disillusioned men, at least *The Hollow Men* makes mockery of the Gospel message of the Kingdom of Heaven. And the dry bones in *Ash Wednesday* are surely mockery of the virtues of the Virgin Lady, and the poem ends without hope in the uncertain balance between "teach us to care and not to care."

In the *Ariel Poems,* which follow *Ash Wednesday,* the Magi, speaking long after of their journey and of the Birth at the tavern, thought that Birth was like Death, — had merely upset things, disturbing the old order, which gave them no ease and so made "another death" welcome.

Another of the witnesses of the Birth of Christ, old Simeon, unlike the Gospel story, got no joy of it and was tired of life.

With *Marina* a change creeps in; there is a hope of the Resurrection, for the life beyond. And in the *Choruses from "The Rock"* there is not only more of the spirit, thought and style of Whitman but also the utterance of a sincere religious faith. In his essay, *After Strange Gods,* Eliot said that most religious poetry is bad because of its

20

HIGH POINTS IN WHITMAN'S PHILOSOPHY.

❖ ❖ ❖ ❖ ❖ ❖

"I here personify and call my themes, to
make them pass before ye."

"Know you, solely to drop in the earth the
germs of a greater religion,
The following chants each for its kind I sing.
My comrade;
For you to share with me two greatnesses,
and a third one rising inclusive and more
resplendent,
The greatness of Love and Democracy, and
the greatness of Religion."

❖ ❖ ❖ ❖ ❖ ❖

The Great Tradition.

WE HAVE BEEN DISCUSSING TRADITION. WHITMAN GREW OUT
of and helped to make the great American tradition. In the
literary aspects of it his name is inseparably joined to the
names of Emerson and Thoreau. In many respects he differed from them. We have distinguished his philosophy
from that of Emerson. Both of them plotted the ground of
liberalism before him.

Thoreau was the geographer of Concord who made it
the microcosm of the Universe. Emerson always went rang-
ing into the Universe at the same time he emphasized the

American doctrine of the importance of the individual. Thoreau was a kind of Diogenes with a lantern peering among men for a real general principle, but not finding it he had to be continually putting back to the wilderness for restoration of self-contentment. Emerson, with full consciousness of the mystic's aberrations, was, as Bertrand Russell has said of John Dewey, intoxicated by Hegel's vision of a Universe. Whitman conceived man as not less than a microcosm, and, if we could take literally some of his expressions, he was a pure humanist: Man is the whole Universe.

I do not think Whitman always knew his own mind. For instance, he erred about the affinity of his thought with Hegel's. I believe we can see his directions and indirections (some biographers stress the latter) better than could he. But he did perceive man's destiny better than did either Emerson or Thoreau. I would not forego any of them. They were equally great expressions of America at a time of crisis, the pre-Civil War period. To Emerson is due the first literary awakening of America to itself. To Thoreau the forthrightness of conviction willing to stand alone for principle, for righteousness, for humanity of man to man. Emerson said we must become Americans and cease our pupilage to Europe. *The American Scholar* was his declaration of the independence of American thought, it was the proclamation of the American philosophy of life. That was especially the point at which he gave inspiration to Whitman.

Thoreau was more radical. He was an extreme individualist, a leftish expression of the American doctrine of freedom. His *Civil Disobedience* was the individual's demand that government shall never be permitted to violate individual conscience, or, if government should do so, then it is the right of individual to defy government.

Whitman was one coming after the pioneering thought of Emerson to envision American democracy and the ex-

is man who has created and personified God, Christ, Satan, and the Holy Spirit of Life. Man has made them all, and but for him they have no conscious existence. It is that creative, expansive man who is expressed in *Chanting the Square Deific*. The least accordant with man's being is the relentless, inexorable, unforgiving God, as the almighty gods all are. But that God of stern justice, "executing righteous judgement", must submit to "the mightier God am I", the gentle, merciful Christ-man. Christ, the suffering god, is but the infinite host of suffering men; personified also as the laboring Hercules; also god Hermes, the messenger of sorrow, the conductor of the dead to Hades. Whitman's Satan is even more august, lofty and proud than Milton's Satan. This Satanic spirit of man defends the despised criminal, slave, and outcast, and is unconquerable, "Lifted now and always against whoever scorning assumes to rule me," and demanding equality "with any, real as any." The moral implicates of these delineations of the godhead, "including God, Saviour and Satan," show the exceptional breadth of sympathetic understanding in Whitman's humanism.

The God of Justice is not all of morality—it has its place. The mercy of Christ, which Nietzsche's morals ruled out, was for Whitman the undying moral force of love. Satan, the spirit of evil, is transformed by Whitman's conception to be a moral force also, struggling against all that degrades man, even making a virtue of human craft and cunning to survive. Satan is thereby creative, uttering "words, in new lands duly appearing" as well as in the "old ones". And what a conception of moral beauty and holiness is expressed for human life or all life, *Santa Spirita* not only "leaping easily above hell," but also transcending Paradise! Life is not merely pantheistic being, but transcendent as well as immanent in the Universe, and especially identical with the roving "general soul" of man.

The images of this poem are so many as to become con-using to the systematic and logical mind that would further restrict itself in religious and moral cults. They are not confined to the narrow range of the theisms, theosophies or theologies. Nor do they lose themselves in the vagueness and indefiniteness of the mysticisms. Whitman's religious philosophy has as little use for the escapism of Nirvana as for the other-worldliness of the Christian Heaven. What is unique in his religion is that it is man-centered—it is wholly humanist.

Likewise his morality, his ethics, is no straight-laced puritanism, no Nietzschean code of aristocracy; it is not better than man at his worst still struggling for survival—it therefore includes promethean ethics. It is not a morality quenching desire in the yearning for peace and tranquility —it has nothing in common with the morals of the religions of despair. It does not exclude perfection, the dream of man at his best,—but the cosmic man, Walt Whitman, is no superman, for he is all that man is—all that human sympathy can embrace. If these beliefs are not logical and systematic, they can be defended as at least real as well as ideal. Whitman's effort to be inclusive, to recognize and give a place to everything, to be the poet of evil as well as of good, did not make him immoral or amoral, but gave his morality, his ethics, a larger, a universal content.

Love Life.

Whitman ran amuck of the Philistines, the Anthony Comstocks, and therefore became confused with the free lovers, the homosexuals and the sex perverts, and all this because his generous ethics was not understood. Whitman's bad reputation rests mainly on his early poems in *Children of Adam* and *Calamus* collections, and the grievances of even defenders, excepting Haniel Long, are especially against the latter. But as in other phases of Whitman's work both sides of the controversy have mistaken or missed his

meaning. Whitman is the universal man and nothing human was alien to him, the bad with the good must have
some meaning or it would not be, it would not exist. It was
not any prudishness that made him aloof to Ezra Heywood,
the free lover, or tell the Uranian whopper that involved
him in a worse predicament to ward off the pertinacious inquiries of John Addington Symonds who endeavored to
fasten on him a homosexual bent; those evasions were
caused by his resolute desire for wholesome all-embracing
sex relations rather than to be addicted to or identified with
any one sex expression.

The introductory poem of *Children of Adam* signifies
his intention to be all-sided in his "curious" interest concerning sex, "amorous, mature, all beautiful to me, all won-
drous,". In the next poem he expressed determination "to
make illustrious, even if I stand alone among men, . . .
singing the phallus, singing the song of procreation." He
celebrated the trembling passion of the sex act, "what the
divine husband knows," and the "children prepared for":
this is glorification of "the work of fatherhood", of which
sex passion is an indispensable part.

In *I Sing the Body Electric* he made clear his moral purpose toward the loved ones to "discorrupt them, and charge
them full with the charge of the soul." He inveighed against
"those who corrupt their own bodies" by concealment, the
pruriency of clothes. He glorified the body: "To be sur-
rounded by beautiful, curious, breathing, laughing flesh is
enough, . . . I do not ask any more delight." Of the attractiveness of "the female form", he said:

> "Be not ashamed women, your privilege en-
> closes the rest, and is the exit of the rest,
> You are the gates of the body, and you are the
> gates of the soul."

> "If any thing is sacred the human body is
> sacred."

And the mere naming of the parts of the body is a paean in praise of it.

He did not hesitate to say:

"Sex contains all, bodies, souls,
Meanings, proofs, purities, delicacies, results,
  promulgations,
Songs, commands, health, pride, the maternal
  mystery, the seminal milk,
All hopes, benefactions, bestowals, all the
  passions, loves, beauties, delights of the
  earth,
All the governments, judges, gods, follow'd
  persons of the earth,
These are contain'd in sex as parts of itself
  and justifications of itself."

The extravagances of Freud do not exceed Whitman, but are false because they sum up everything as contained in infantilism and are too little informed about the adult man and woman. Yet, as the Freudians know the hysterics of those who fear love, Whitman was before them in recognition of

"The consequent meanness of me should I
  skulk or find myself indecent, while birds
  and animals never once skulk or find themselves indecent."

The apostrophe to

"One hour to madness and joy!

❖ ❖ ❖ ❖ ❖

To drive free! to love free! to dash reckless
  and dangerous!

❖ ❖ ❖ ❖ ❖

To be lost if it must be so!"

is an abandon allowable, may be, to poetic license. But it is a purpose already defined, including the low not less than the noble:

> "O you shunn'd persons, I at least do not
>   shun you,
> I come forthwith in your midst, I will be your
>   poet,
> I will be more to you than to any of the rest."

This is in the spirit of a New Testament extravagance, in the parables of the Lost Sheep, the Lost Coin, and the preference for publicans and sinners over the elect and favored members of society. Orthodox Christians have beclouded the social breadth of those episodes in the life of Jesus, and it has remained for writers like Whitman to have restored the spirit of Jesus to modern literature.

Calamus, which is objectionable to many because of its songs of "manly attachment", of loving comrades, is still alien to American literature because of the custom here to eschew very intimate male friendships and, indeed, one must go to ancient literature, for instance Plato's *Symposium,* to find a near parallel, but there Whitman's and the modern affection for woman was absent. Whitman's singularity, his unique contribution to love life, was not stress upon any one phase of it but his endeavor to speak the whole language of love.

Loneliness and Death.

In that effort to understand he conceived the mingling of love and death:

> "I am not sure but the high soul of lovers
>   welcomes death most."

> "Give me your tone therefore O death, that
>   I may accord with it,

> Give me yourself, for I see that you belong
> to me now, above all, and are folded in-
> separably together, you love and death
> are."

This poem, *Scented Herbage of my Breast,* seems to be
linked closer with death than with life:

> "O I think it is not for life I am chanting
> here my chant of lovers, I think it must be
> for death."

For in life we are indifferent to life or death. Life appears to be impermanent, in death love may become everlasting. The appeal of the lover is then to Death:

> "That behind the mask of materials you pa-
> tiently wait, no matter how long,
> That you will one day perhaps take control
> of all,
> That you will perhaps dissipate this entire
> show of appearance,
> That may-be you are what it is all for, but it
> does not last so very long,
> But you will last very long."

Calamus was published in the year of crisis, the saddest
of his years if judged from his own feelings, as well as the
year of crisis for the Nation. *Hours Continuing Long, Sore
and Heavy-Hearted,* is the most despairing of the problem
poems written by Whitman, and rejected because of Whitman's desire to be always inspiring. He retained his most
significant poem on death because it expressed the same
kind of hopefulness which is the substance of the hope for
immortality, but it avoids here as elsewhere identity of expression with either a popular or the usual type of philosophical belief in a future life. Rather he gives here sub-

stance of reality, "the real reality," to death more than to
life. Yet, for all the intense sorrow and loneliness of the
Calamus poems they end with apostrophe to the fullness of
life in the concrete, compact and visible, but in comradeship
with the unseen, roving, general soul of man.

More than already indicated the *Calamus* collection is
rich in the Whitman themes. *Whoever you are Holding
Me Now in Hand* is a poem suggestive of the jealous lover,
but sublimated to express the peculiar affection of those
readers of *Leaves of Grass* who are stoutest and most steadfast of soul, who alone can penetrate the meaning of his
book; and he urges any others to "release me . . . and depart
on your way". It is a poem of reaction from disappointment he met with in the failure of the public to receive his
earlier publication of the poems. How discouraging to his
poetic energy became this jealousy was expressed in the rejected *Calamus* poem, *Long I thought That Knowledge*:

> "For I can be your singer of songs no longer
> —One who loves me is jealous of me, and
>   withdraws me from all but love,
>
> ❖ ❖ ❖ ❖ ❖ ❖
>
> I am indifferent to my own songs."

Comradeship and Democracy.

The *Calamus* poems are abundant in the other Whitman themes. *For you O Democracy* may be justification for
Selincourt and others who identify "the love of comrades"
as Whitman's idea of the foundation of democracy, which
so easily becomes a misinterpretation of Whitman's meaning.

> "Plucking something for tokens, tossing to-
>   ward whoever is near me,
>
> ❖ ❖ ❖ ❖ ❖ ❖
>
> And this, O this shall henceforth be the token
>   of comrades, this calamus-root shall,

Interchange it youths with each other! let
    none render it back."

The calamus-root may be intended for a phallic symbol
of comradeship.

Conflict and Separateness.

In the *Calamus* poems the symbols of the body have a
unity of a different kind than unites those in the poems of
the *Children of Adam*. In the latter lusty, expansive love
is the central theme. In the *Calamus* collection one feels
rather the tensity of love, friendship, that desires to hold
the lover or friend apart, to hug him closely to one's self as
an exclusive possession. Breathing is a life symbol elsewhere; here it issues in "ill-supprest sighs", "beating and
pounding" pulses, "in husky pantings through clinch'd
teeth," morbid signs, in the struggling to hold a friend; yet:

"Not in any or all of them O adhesiveness!
    O pulse of my life!
Need I that you exist and show yourself any
    more than in these songs."

Here he was evidently conscious of the conflict, of some
inappropriateness for the *Leaves of Grass* of the untoward
feelings that creep in destructively to comradeship, but cannot be eliminated without losing the reality of a full and
inclusive account of the role of friendship which has its
negative as well as its positive side.

In the *Calamus* poems the negative side is only less than
dominant. This comes to complete realization in the poem,
Of The Terrible Doubt of Appearance, the fear of delusion,

"That may-be reliance and hope are but spec-
    ulations after all,
That may-be identity beyond the grave is a
    beautiful fable only."

But he resolves such doubts in the consciousness that

> "To me these and the like of these are curi-
> ously answer'd by my lovers, my dear
> friends.
>
> ❖ ❖ ❖ ❖ ❖ ❖
>
> I cannot answer the question of appearances
> or that of identity beyond the grave,
> But I walk or sit indifferent, I am satisfied,
> He ahold of my hand has completely satis-
> fied me."

What probably upset the tender-minded most in the *Calamus* poems is that one entitled *The Base of all Metaphysics*. This was a later addition, not among those first published, and therefore subsequent in spirit and thought, but essential to the completion of Whitman's philosophy. After enumerating the ancient and modern metaphysical systems, both divine and secular, Christian and pagan, he concluded humanistically that underneath them all he saw:

> "The dear love of man for his comrade, the
> attraction of friend to friend,
> Of the well-married husband and wife, of
> children and parents,
> Of city for city and land for land."

Happiness Achieved by Frailties Overcome.

The *Calamus* poems began in morbid thoughts which became altered and changed from the bitterness and suspicion and jealousy of one love to the large and overflowing comradeship of many friends and lovers. In the original poem of *Roots and Leaves Themselves Alone,* he acknowledged the alteration in himself from discontent to happiness:

> "For I must change the strain—these are not
> to be pensive leaves, but leaves of joy."

And this contrast of moods is also expressed in the poem, *When I Heard at the Close of Day,* in the anticipation of happiness at the coming of a friend and the realization of happiness with the friend close by, laying beside him,

> "And his arm lay lightly around my breast—
> and that night I was happy."

It was in the recovery from the crisis that he wrote self-consciously the lines:

> "Here the frailest leaves of me and yet my
>   strongest lasting,
> Here I shade and hide my thoughts, I myself
>   do not expose them,
> And yet they expose me more than all my
>   other poems."

This is a confession of the autobiographical character of the *Calamus* poems which departed from his purpose because of their expression of his intensely personal sorrow. *Here the Frailest Leaves of Me* was placed next before the last of the original *Calamus* poems, which indicates his reflective judgment upon their intrinsic nature.

Sublimated Passion.

The homosexual urge in friendship does not alone distinguish the *Calamus* poems—it is discoverable elsewhere in *Leaves of Grass,* intermingled with expressions of the wider, all-inclusive varieties of love expression,—but it is particularly expressed in the poem, *Earth, My Likeness,* in which he made the confession:

> "I dare not tell it in words, not even in these
>   songs."

He believed the "germs" of it are "latent in all men."
It need not be an actual affair or relationship of mutuality:

> "I loved a certain person ardently, and my
>   love was not return'd,
> Yet out of that I have written these songs."

Perhaps that poem is autobiographical too. It might
be argued that the sublimation of homosexual love without
its practice was what Whitman recognized as the source of
his own concrete passion for comradeship. Probably he set
forth that conception in the poem:

> "Fast-anchor'd eternal O love! O woman I
>   love!
> O bride! O wife! more relentless than I can
>   tell, the thought of you!
> Then separate, as disembodied or another
>   born,
> Ethereal, the last athletic reality, my consola-
>   tion,
> I ascend, I float in the regions of your love
>   O man,
> O sharer of my roving life."

The Roving Self.

A wife, he had none in actuality, but it was the thought,
the imagination of having one, which was infused in the
ascent to that universal life which he conceived as his "roving life", identical, I think, with "the general soul", which
he thought of as his other self, the roving self, or his sublimated self in complete comradeship with all men and all
women. And yet in these *Calamus* poems the more fre-

quent emphasis is upon the particularized individual personal lover. As in the poem, *Among the Multitude,*

> "I perceive one picking me out by secret and
>   divine signs,
>
>
>
> . . . .—that one knows me."

Nearer than "parent, wife, husband, brother, child," is the really understanding person who is my true comrade. He identified that person especially as one, and all those, "realizing my poems, seeking me". There is a kind of union in this that rises above the individuality of the immediate bodily self; it is the roving general self that makes the union, and that is also "really me", as in the poem, *That Shadow my Likeness.*

Thus, the *Calamus* poems end with the conception, which pervades many of them, of the two aspects of self. It was later expressed by Whitman as Personality. But the cosmic Walt Whitman was not impersonal like Emerson's Over-Soul. Personality is merely a phase of man's being. Humanity is a wider concept than personality.

Whitman's Intuition of Man.

What really distinguished Whitman from his contemporaries and his successors was his clearer perception or intuition of man's being. He did not get lost in the mysticism of religion which forgets its human origin and nature. The reality of God is man. It is not man who is the manifestation of God, but God is the manifestation, it is the reflection, of man's consciousness of his higher being.

Beliefs in immortality Whitman treated skeptically but not without seeking for a more realistic conception of human destiny than in the bourne or haven of some other

imaginary world. Death he saw, not as a gateway to a
Paradise unrelated to man's world, but somehow in the
order of things as a part of the cycle of man's existence,
and perhaps a fulfillment of it.

Individualization and Democracy.

The harrowing experiences of friendship described in
the *Calamus* poems, undoubtedly long known to him before that most poignant crisis, so individualized human relationships for Whitman that he could never be allured by
the impersonal configuration of the "beloved community"
of a mystical Royce, or to Hegel's state as the embodiment
of cosmic universal Reason, and he was much less attracted
by the narrower Marxian insignia of constricted proletarian communism. For Whitman comradeship was intensely personal at the same time that it prefigured all social
institutions. Comradeship is the cement of society. It is
not Royce's or G. Stanley Hall's Christ as the head or mystical symbol that is the bond of society. It is not Hegel's
Volkgeist that is embodied in the State. It is not Karl
Marx's mass. Whitman did express himself in the dichtomy
of individual and mass. He described democracy as en
masse, and he seemed to conceive America, land and nation, in a somewhat mystical fashion. Democracy is the
average man, the common man. Democracy in the institutional sense, as officialdom or majorities, had no sacredness
or superiority in Whitman's eyes. As strongly as Thoreau
he thought it the right and duty of the individual person
to stand out against it whenever it threatens his freedom.

Nor did Whitman suffer or even entertain the delusion
that so pervades present day thinking and acting, the excessive nationalism and societism, which so disastrously dis-
turbs the peace of the world and threatens to enslave all
mankind, a disease of thought and conduct which is not
confined to the totalitarian systems of Europe and Asia,
but also characterizes certain sociologically-minded persons

among the learned as well as those obsessed with institutionalism, organizationalism, monopolism, ecclesiasticism, and such disorders of society—cults utterly opposed to humanism.

The Poetic Symbol.

Some have thought Whitman platitudinarian and vague. They have misunderstood his aim and his method and the inevitable difficulties for a philosophic poet. We can hardly think or talk without generalizations, and science and philosophy abound in them. Concrete particular images are less communicable to understanding. But the poet more than any other speaker uses concrete images to convey general ideas; he uses the particular as symbol of general meaning, and thus gives the appearance, the impression of actual reality, immediate sensuous reality. Whitman labored to enlarge the language of poetry, which he chose as the vehicle of his thought.

Whereas other poets had been content with the stock paraphernalia of the poet, of which we have already given considerable examples from the viewpoint of Whitman in his effort to surpass them, now we attempt in a few sentences to sum up the unique difference of his symbolism.

In the first place, he took himself as symbol: I, Walt Whitman, I sing of myself. Secondly, he conceived the two selves, one symbolized by the body, and the other the roving spirit, or that personality which may take on the almost infinite variety of forms, not only of human characters, but transfigured in the endless situations and experiences that man may have. The abundance of those images were the occasion for Whitman's extraordinary catalogues of things and persons, which in their human perspective are more significant and sublime than Homer's catalogue of the ships, a much praised passage.

In Whitman's poetic art, not less than in the content of his philosophic and social thought, he tried to make apparent the human reality. Although his thought is not beyond the range of systematization—we have shown that it can be treated somewhat systematically as humanism or humanist philosophy—he chose rather the vocation of the poet, the image-maker, to express that thought, probably because of his intense desire for concrete rather than abstract meaning, as the livelier representation of human reality. The humanist in him clothed the philosopher in the garb and speech, in the personality, of the poet.

INDEX

INDEX

A

Abolitionists, 225.

Abstractions, 3, 290.

Accent, 300, 318, 320f, 323f, 327, 333, 366.

Action, 292, 344.

Adler, Felix, 44, 104, 199.

Agar, Herbert, 220.

Agrarian, 425f.

Alcott, Bronson A., 14, 91, 95.

Allen, Gay Wilson, 18, 20, 30ff, 48, 55, 59, 69, 71, 85, 87, 90f, 96f, 99, 117, 177, 189, 204, 221, 222, 226ff, 238f, 287ff, 300, 311, 320f, 324, 325, 326, 331, 344.

Allport, Floyd H., 239, 273.

Altruism, 243.

America, 141, 156, 199, 218, 231, 235, 238, 255, 262, 273, 280, 297, 301, 318, 336, 414, 417, 421f, 425, 434f, 470.

Amerind, 321ff.

Anarchists, 15, 141, 222, 291.

Andrews, C. E., 321ff.

Anthropomorphism 70, 79, 80, 82, 260.

Appropriateness, 81, 111, 118, 123f, 149, 157, 164, 168.

Aristotle, 59, 71, 125, 157f, 295, 305, 307, 431, 438.

Arnold, Matthew, 193, 305, 308.

Arnold, Thurmond, 221.

Art, Artist, 3, 80, 109, 260, 267ff, 288, 290ff, 294, 297, 300f, 315f, 327, 329, 338, 352, 359, 380, 382, 409, 413f, 420, 424, 432, 434, 443, 445ff, 447f, 471.

Arvin, Newton, 69, 251.

Ascetic, 153, 158ff, 163, 373.

B

Atheist, 48, 53, 95, 403, 452.

Atlantic Charter, 240f.

Attitudes, 117, 122ff.

Austin, Mary, 321ff.

Average, 139f, 159f, 164f, 200, 223, 229, 242, 247, 250, 264, 296, 329, 470.

Bacon, Francis, 151.

Ballad, 299, 389, 418.

Baudelaire, 78, 424.

Beach, Joseph, 58, 73f.

Beard, Charles A., 210.

Beliefs, 96, 109, 116, 121, 404, 451.

Being, 78.

Belloc, Hilaire, 220.

Benedict, Ruth, 239.

Beauty, 252f, 283, 344, 401, 415.

Bergson, Henri, 85, 429f.

Bible, 166, 176, 281, 285, 318, 326, 331, 332, 333.

Biographies, 6f, 16f, 18f, 20, 21, 279, 407.

Blake, William, 304, 308.

Body, 90f, 153ff, 172, 349, 375, 379, 400, 460f, 471.

Bolsheviks, 15, 45, 140, 225, 235, 374, 485.

Book, 19, 128, 172, 269, 286, 287, 293.

Borsodi, Ralph, 219.

Bowery, 232.

Bradley, Scully, 320f.

Brandeis, Louis D., 221.

Bridges, Robert, 366ff, 371, 373, 375, 376.

Briggs, Charles A., 332ff.

Browning, Robert, 36, 348ff, 378, 414, 417, 431.

Buchanan, Robert, 348.
Bucke, Dr. Richard M., 12f, 18, 39, 63, 64ff, 163, 188.
Burns, Robert, 299, 428.
Burroughs, John, 6, 11, 24, 33, 35, 50ff, 64ff, 74, 77ff, 90, 96, 175, 188, 192f, 198, 215, 231, 243, 247, 248, 255, 260f, 270, 275f, 283, 304, 312, 327, 345, 347, 427, 456.
Burtt, E. A., 103ff.

C

Cabot, Dr. Richard C., 28.
Caesura, 319, 321, 327.
Cadence, 303.
Calverton, V. F., 230, 234f.
Canby, Henry Seidel, 5, 15, 18, 20, 30, 170, 172f, 175, 177, 188, 174, 268, 281, 283, 285, 306, 311, 315f, 318f, 324.
Capitalism, 220ff.
Carpenter, Edward, 10, 35, 178ff, 274, 413.
Carlyle, Thomas, 162, 326, 344, 360.
Castes, 239.
Catalogues, 226, 326, 329, 344, 367, 471.
Catel, Jean, 69, 325.
Celibate, 184.
Chain of Being Doctrine, 32, 71ff, 181, 288.
Chant, 321, 326, 328.
Character, 60f, 81, 197, 222, 291, 293f, 296, 324, 342, 348, 361, 411, 416, 418, 419.
Charity, 234.
Chastity, 160.
Childe, V. Gordon, 345.
Christ, 35, 38, 47, 87, 99, 108f, 114, 124, 133, 134, 138, 168, 367, 374, 377, 391, 457f.
Christianity, 35, 45, 55, 63, 73, 92, 97ff, 124, 131ff, 168, 190, 252, 298, 350, 353, 357, 371, 373, 375, 379, 381, 399ff, 457ff, 462.
Church, 43ff, 104f, 450ff, 471.

City, 78, 139, 145, 230ff.
Civilization, 164, 274, 362, 442.
Civil War, 22, 25, 34, 126, 183, 389, 412.
Citizen, 244.
Cleveland, Grover, 221.
Coleridge, Samuel Taylor, 289f, 305, 308, 314, 357, 429.
Comic, 303, 309, 311.
Common Man, 223, 276, 470.
Communal, 272f, 299, 446.
Communism, 14f, 46, 139, 143, 220, 225, 230, 235, 373f, 434, 470.
Communities, 219, 470.
Compost, 118, 119f, 153.
Comrades, 15, 66, 130, 139, 147, 182f, 192f, 201, 215, 235, 241, 245, 276, 415, 456, 462f, 464f, 467, 470.
Conflict, 119, 465.
Conformity, 119f, 140, 375.
Confucius, 106, 125, 154ff.
Conger, George P., 105ff.
Content, 281, 299, 313, 438f, 471.
Corson, Hiram, 304, 348.
Cosmic Consciousness, 12, 65f, 95, 163, 238, 423.
Cosmic Man, 12, 64ff, 84, 245, 261, 266, 279, 347, 427, 459f, 469.
Cosmos, 64, 261, 404, 427.
Cosmotheticians, 12f, 17f, 65f.
Country, 78.
Cowley, Malcolm, 8, 10, 22, 24, 27.
Crane, Hart, 308, 422, 441.
Creativity, 46, 166, 182, 296ff, 322, 344, 380, 402, 429, 438.
Creed, 456.
Criminals, 124, 134, 146, 160, 252.
Critics, 300, 312, 316, 379, 428, 436, 441.
Cults, 4f, 6f, 28, 417, 456f.
Culture, 68, 156.
Custom, 253.

D

Daiches, David, 369, 381.
Dante, A., 420, 427, 431, 444.

Friendship, 183, 186, 192, 383, 398, 424, 465, 467, 470.
Frost, Robert, 318, 423, 425.
Future, 280.

G

Generalizations, 471.
Geneticism, 70.
Genius, 166, 180f, 223, 248f, 272, 299, 339, 395.
George, Henry, 219, 222f.
German Idealism, 56, 71, 73, 125.
Gilchrist, Anne, 173ff, 193, 413.
God, 47ff, 50f, 63, 64, 67, 75, 80, 83, 85f, 101ff, 109f, 123, 127, 165, 176, 217, 233, 265f, 326, 346, 350f, 377, 390f, 402, 404f, 452, 457ff, 469.
Goethe, J. W. von, 135, 247ff, 276, 278, 291, 292, 451.
Good, 111ff, 244, 355ff.
Government, 142, 166, 211, 213, 244, 265, 455.
Greeks, 280, 283, 308, 328.
Guilt, 113f.
Gummere, F. B., 199, 211ff, 271ff, 276, 285, 299, 305, 331.

H

Happiness, 152f, 403.
Harned, Thomas, 191.
Health, 153, 253.
Heaven, 64.
Hebrew, 283, 308, 332, 333f, 366.
Hegel, G. W. F., 14, 56f, 69, 118, 273, 294f, 425, 455, 470.
Heine, Heinrich, 286.
Hell, 64.
Heresy, 41, 46, 386.
Heroes, 161, 275, 417.
Hesiod, 304.
Hicks, Elias, 207.
Higginson, T. W., 126, 383f.
Hinduism, 54ff, 85.
History, 58, 70, 162, 199, 209ff, 250, 297, 301, 344.

Holism, 76.
Holy Spirit, 87, 458.
Holloway, Emory, 170f, 189.
Homer, 326, 359, 410, 419, 431, 471.
Homosexuality, 134, 170, 175f, 360, 424, 459f, 467f.
Homesteads, 219.
Hope, 402, 450, 463.
Hopkins, Gerard Manley, 309, 365ff, 428, 431, 437, 441.
Horney, Karen, 99.
Horton, Phillip, 424.
Housman, A. E., 305.
Humanics, 250f.
Humanism, 6, 15f, 22, 52, 62, 78, 81ff, 99ff, 101, 103f, 105ff, 150, 152, 164, 165, 167f, 250f, 269, 274, 296f, 315f, 340f, 345, 347, 352, 373, 375, 376, 380ff, 390, 412, 420, 425, 429, 450ff, 455f, 469.
Human Nature, 74f, 103.
Hume, David, 56, 96, 164, 251, 357.
Humility, 108, 124.
Huxley, Julian S., 5, 12, 71, 81, 261f.
Huxley, Thomas H., 12, 108, 432.
Hypnotic, 285, 307, 320.

I

I, Me, 87, 165, 172, 196, 257, 386, 395, 471.
Idealism, 56ff, 77, 104, 121, 196, 251, 443.
Ideas, 30ff, 45, 237, 286, 304, 309, 325, 348, 431f.
Identity, 56, 67, 78, 83, 95, 166, 201f, 205, 254, 264, 346, 392, 402, 465.
Illusions, 251, 259, 388, 394.
Imagination, 284, 288, 289, 293, 297, 343, 344f, 394, 429, 432, 471.
Imitation, 288, 323, 444.
Immortality, 69, 91ff, 110, 157, 198, 217, 262f, 266, 345, 348, 350, 379, 392, 399ff, 404, 463, 465f, 469.
Impulses, 150, 291, 293, 310.

INDEX

Inclusiveness, 48, 404f, 459.

Independence, 120, 142, 145, 210f, 227, 455.

Indirection, 388, 455.

Individuality, 15, 56, 58, 87, 97, 120, 123, 139f, 143ff, 153, 157, 164ff, 167, 199, 201ff, 213, 223, 235, 243ff, 264, 274, 345, 352, 355, 363, 375, 419, 444f, 449, 455, 470.

Industrialism, 422, 425f, 428.

Ingersoll, Robert G., 46, 104.

Inspiration, 343, 401.

Institutions, 45, 144, 242, 450, 471.

Intellect, 284f, 321, 343.

Internationalism, 238ff.

Intuition, 395, 420.

Invention, 345, 448.

J

James, William, 401.

Jefferson, Thomas, 17, 35, 36, 131, 139, 207, 212, 219, 221, 265, 374, 411, 419, 434.

Johnson, Alvin H., 219.

Johnson, Samuel, 305.

Jung, C. G., 98, 277.

Justice, 142f, 144, 161.

K

Kant, Immanuel, 14, 69, 71, 297.

Karma, 96.

Keats, John, 293, 428.

Kissing, 253.

Knowledge, 430.

L

Labor, 224f, 226, 280.

Law, 78, 139ff, 144, 185, 205, 211ff, 271.

Lanier, Sidney, 286.

Lawrence, D. H., 178, 294, 450.

Leibnitz, G. W., 69, 71, 83.

Leuba, James H., 62f.

Liberalism, 102f, 330, 454.

Lies, 27f, 60f, 148f, 411.

Lincoln, Abraham, 6, 17, 34, 36, 142, 198, 208, 219, 221, 247f, 265, 360, 374, 411, 412, 419, 420f, 434.

Life, 144, 160, 163f, 250, 265, 288, 317, 330, 348, 404, 452, 458, 463, 469.

Lindsay, Vachel, 321, 323, 414f, 420, 425.

Line, 319, 327, 335, 366f, 370, 440.

Logic, 109f, 287f, 313, 342, 429, 431f, 441, 459.

Long, Haniel, 60, 65, 97, 177, 189, 192, 304, 326, 459.

Love, 131, 139ff, 158, 160, 188, 191, 196f, 254, 348, 353f, 356, 394ff, 403, 424, 454, 459ff.

Lovejoy, A. O., 72f.

Loyalty, 108, 434.

Lucretius, 151.

Lyric, 327f, 414, 420.

M

Magnanimity, 112, 125, 158.

Man, 2, 12, 16, 52, 63, 69f, 74f, 77, 83, 86, 87, 106f, 116, 123, 133, 134f, 151, 158, 165f, 182, 200, 217, 227, 237, 244, 260f, 265, 269, 297, 340, 345, 346, 352, 380, 391f, 404, 405, 412, 437, 455f, 469.

Man-God, 85ff, 265, 284, 346, 394, 405.

Maritain, Jacques, 105.

Marriage, 9, 182, 188.

Martyrdom, 131.

Marxism, 222, 235, 425, 470.

Mask, 256f.

Masses, 68, 159, 166, 199, 213, 227, 230, 251, 264, 272, 470.

Masters, Edgar Lee, 13f, 28, 33, 208, 410ff, 440.

Materialism, 48f, 78, 81, 92, 237, 422.

Matthiessen, F. O., 47f, 61, 69, 78, 287, 295, 321, 325, 437f, 441ff, 448.

McDougall, William, 109, 321.

LEAVES OF GRASS

A

Adieu to a Soldier, 129.
Ah, Poverties, Wincings, and Sulky Retreats, 262f.
America, 200.
Apostroph, 335.
Among the Multitude, 135, 469.
Are You the New Person Drawn Toward Me? 259, 443.
Ashes of Soldiers, 130.
As I Lay with My Head in Your Lap Camerado, 325.
As I Ponder'd in Silence, 126ff.
As I Sit Writing Here, 446.

B

Base of All Metaphysics, The, 466.
Behold this Swarthy Face, 253.
By Blue Ontario's Shore, 111, 114, 116, 118, 119, 120, 122f, 129, 144, 146, 155f, 159, 164, 165, 199, 206, 300, 311, 313, 335, 352.

C

Calamus, 26, 134, 177, 189, 251, 450ff.
Calming Thought of All, The, 435.
Carol Closing Sixty-nine, A, 270.
Chanting the Square Deific, 59, 85, 87, 108, 119, 133, 147, 165, 169, 263, 374, 457ff.
Children of Adam, 172, 177, 189, 459ff.
City Dead-House, The, 115, 195.
City of Ships, 112.
Crossing Brooklyn Ferry, 49, 76, 327.

D

Darest Thou Now O Soul, 312.
Debris, 153, 167, 404.
Dirge for Two Veterans, 312.
Drum Taps, 26, 33, 126, 375.

E

Earth, My Likeness, 467.
Eidolons, 257, 267, 312.
Eighteen Sixty-one, 302.
Ethiopia Saluting the Colors, 311, 312.

F

Faces, 258.
Fast-Anchor'd O Love, 136, 413, 468.
For You O Democracy, 313, 464.
From Noon to Starry Night, 113, 144, 154, 159.
From Pent-up Aching Rivers, 335.

G

Gods, 312.
"Going Somewhere", 174, 413.
Good-Bye My Fancy, 34.
Grand is the Seen, 260.
Great Are the Myths, 142, 144, 146.

H

Had I the Choice, 359.
Here the Frailest Leaves of Me, 176f, 466.
Hours Continuing Long, Sore and Heavy-Hearted, 463.
How Solemn as One by One, 256.

PROSE